Parallel Processing Systems

Parallel processing systems

Edited by

DAVID J.EVANS

Professor of Computing, University of Technology, Loughborough

CAMBRIDGE UNIVERSITY PRESS

Cambridge

London   New York   New Rochelle

Melbourne   Sydney

Published by the Press Syndicate of the University of Cambridge
The Pitt Building, Trumpington Street, Cambridge CB2 1RP
32 East 57th Street, New York, NY 10022, USA
296 Beaconsfield Parade, Middle Park, Melbourne 3206, Australia

© Cambridge University Press 1982

First published 1982

Printed in Great Britain at the University Press, Cambridge

Library of Congress catalogue card number: 81-38445

British Library cataloguing in publication data
Parallel processing systems
1. Parallel processing (Electronic computers)
2. Electronic digital computers
I. Evans, David J.
001.64   QA76.6
ISBN 0 521 24366 1

CONTENTS

PREFACE

This publication is based on an Advanced Course on Parallel Processing Systems given at the University of Technology, Loughborough, from 15 September to 26 September, 1980. The course was sponsored by the Science Research Council under the auspices of the Informatics Training Group of the EEC Scientific and Technical Research Committee (CREST). The course lecturers provided a carefully arranged integrated programme of lectures, which were supplemented by specially invited contributions.

CONTRIBUTORS

Course director
D. J. Evans, Department of Computer Studies, University of Technology, Loughborough, Leicestershire LE11 3TU, UK

Professor J.-L. Baer, Department of Computer Science, University of Washington, Seattle, Washington 98195, USA

Dr R. H. Barlow, Department of Computer Studies, University of Technology, Loughborough, Leicestershire LE11 3TU, UK

Professor P. H. Enslow Jr and Timothy G. Saponas, School of Information and Computer Science, Georgia Institute of Technology, Atlanta, Georgia 30332, USA

Professor D. J. Evans, Department of Computer Studies, University of Technology, Loughborough, Leicestershire LE11 3TU, UK

Professor Dr M. Feilmeier, Institut für Rechentechnik, Technische Universität Braunschweig, Pockelsstrasse 14, 3300 Braunschweig, West Germany

Professor C. Girault, Université Pierre et Marie Curie, U.E.R. 50, Institut de Programmation, Tour 55-65, 4 Place Jussieu, 75230 Paris Cedex 05, France

Professor Dr W. Händler, Institut für Mathematische Maschinen und Datenverarbeitung (Informatik), Friedrich-Alexander-Universität Erlangen-Nürnberg, Martensstrasse 3, 8520 Erlangen, West Germany

Dr M. Hatzopoulos, Unit of Applied Mathematics II, University of Athens, Panepistemiopolis, Athens 621, Greece

Professor D. J. Kuck, Department of Computer Science, 222 Digital Computer Laboratory, University of Illinois at Urbana-Champaign, Urbana, Illinois 61801, USA

Professor H. T. Kung, Department of Computer Science, Carnegie-Mellon University, Pittsburg, Pennsylvania 15213, USA

Dr I. A. Newman, Department of Computer Studies, University of Technology, Loughborough, Leicestershire LE11 3TU, UK

Professor D. Parkinson, DAP Support Unit, Computer Centre, Queen Mary College, University of London, Mile End Road, London E1 4NS, UK

Dr G. Roucairol, Université Pierre et Marie Curie, U.E.R. 50, Institut de Programmation, Tour 55-65, 4 Place Jussieu, 75230 Paris Cedex 05, France

Mr A. J. Slade, Department of Computing, Science Laboratories, University of Durham, South Road, Durham DH1 3LE, UK

Professor J.-C. Syre, ONERA-CERT, Complexe Aérospatial de Lespinet, 2 Avenue Edouard Belin, BP No. 4025, 31055 Toulouse, France

Dr P. Treleaven, Computing Laboratory, University of Newcastle upon Tyne, Claremont Tower, Claremont Road, Newcastle upon Tyne NE1 7RU, UK

Dr S. A. Williams, Department of Computer Science, The University of Reading, Whiteknights Park, Reading, Berkshire RG6 2AX, UK

Dr M. C. Woodward, Department of Computer Studies, University of Technology, Loughborough, Leicestershire LE11 3TU, UK

INTRODUCTION

D. J. EVANS

In the last few years dramatic improvements in circuit device and computer architecture technologies together with new concepts in system organisation have brought forth many new innovative computer systems which are capable of supporting a large number of concurrent operations and activities. These parallel computing systems will undoubtedly create new research and development areas when they are built and programmed to attain their maximum cost-effectiveness and benefit society by revealing hitherto unknown solution strategies and applications. The advances realised to date represent little progress when we compare what is known about parallel computation with the corresponding body of knowledge for serial computation. Indeed, many challenging problems in the fields of programming languages and compilers must be solved before the advantages of the proposed parallel architectures can be fully exploited.

This book is divided into six parts covering the following topics: parallel and distributed computer systems, analysis of parallel programming systems, multiple instruction multiple data (MIMD) computer systems, single instruction multiple data (SIMD) computer systems, data flow processors and parallel computer algorithms. Each chapter of the book was originally prepared as documentation for lectures presented at the Advanced Course on Parallel Processing Systems at the University of Technology, Loughborough, England in September 1980. The aims and purpose of the advanced course were to accelerate the interchange of information in this increasingly important area and to examine in depth and provide discussion of problems amongst the scientists and computer professionals who may use parallel processor systems and those who design or program such systems. The original course material has been extensively revised for publication in its present form. The book aims to provide a coherent account of all major aspects of parallel processing and also to give an up-to-date account of recent activity in this area.

PART 1

Parallel and distributed computer systems

1 Innovative computer architecture – how to increase parallelism but not complexity

WOLFGANG HÄNDLER

1 Introductory remarks

'Parallelism' is used as a general term to characterize all the different kinds of simultaneity occurring in modern computers. In this general sense it includes pipelining. In the following text we have nevertheless to differentiate parallelism (in a more special sense) as opposed to pipelining. In cases where we refer to the general and overall meaning we will call it 'parallelism in general' or 'parallelism i.g.'.

Parallelism in general offers great opportunities regarding:

(*a*) improved overall performance
(*b*) improved availability and safety.

The second point cannot be covered sufficiently in this article. It is neverthe-less a key point in the evolution towards parallelism. With respect to the first point, we consider all those prerequisites that make it possible to improve performance. Evidently parallelism *per se* does not guarantee such an improve-ment, as some contemporary concepts show. So a case study of useful parallelism is given in section 3 and the ideas behind it in section 4. Section 2 gives a general overview and orientation with respect to all possible contemporary and future forms of parallelism.

The classical computer, as defined by Burks, Goldstine and von Neumann [1], consists of (see figure 1.1):

program-control or control unit (CU)
arithmetic unit or arithmetic and logic unit (ALU)
memory or storage unit
input/output unit (I/O).

Later versions of this classical concept made it possible for at least two of these units to work at the same time, which was not the case during the pioneer period. Machine words or numbers, normally stored in a hardware unit called a memory cell, are also referred to as parallel words in cases where such words are processed by taking all positions (or bits) at the same time. In this sense we find some forms of parallelism i.g. in early computers.

In this presentation we will centre more on all possible forms of parallelism i.e. that distinctly go beyond the word parallelism as used in the context of the 'parallel computers' of the fifties and the sixties.

True parallelism (of any kind) requires the existence of more than one unit working at the same time. Such units can be control units (CU), arithmetic and logic units (ALU), input/output units and memory units, while simultaneous operation of the latter certainly can result in a speedup of the overall operation, they nevertheless do not influence the structure of processing, as the other units can.

In a classical structure the control unit (CU) together with an arithmetic and logic unit (ALU) form a central processor unit or, simply, a processing unit (PU). Replicating either PUs themselves or the number of ALUs connected to each PU results in proper parallelism i.g. Making available many PUs means that many programs or many parts of one program can be processed at the same time, i.e. in parallel (figure 1.2). Connecting many ALUs with one CU means that many data words can be processed in parallel by one program, which this CU is interpreting (figure 1.3). The PU with many ALUs, therefore, is more powerful than one of the forementioned PUs with only one ALU each.

In contrast to this parallelism, pipelining also requires – as defined above – a multitude of resources like PUs or ALUs. While one set of data is processed by one of the resources, another set of data can be processed by another resource next to it, etc. In this sense the data words are flowing from one resource (PU or ALU) to the next one in a chain process. During the whole process n tasks are performed, e.g. one after the other on one set of data. $1n$ such sets may be in

Figure 1.1. The classical computer.

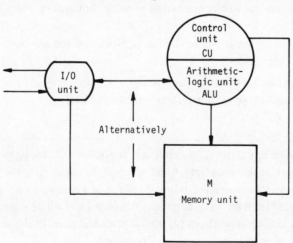

a 'pipeline' at the same time, where each one is at a different stage of the process.

Parallelism and pipelining can both be seen in three different logical levels:

	Parallelism	Pipelining
Program level	Multiprocessor	Macro-pipelining
Instruction level	Multiple ALUs (array processor)	Instruction pipelining
Word level	Multiple bits (wordlength, if greater than 1)	Arithmetic pipelining

With respect to pipelining these processing forms can be represented in block diagrams as shown in figures 1.4-1.6. Instead of differentiating three different

Figure 1.2. A multiprocessor, consisting of a common memory and several processing units.

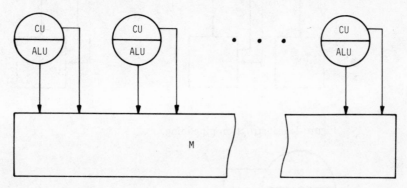

Figure 1.3. Parallel data processing of one program by several ALUs, controlled by one CU.

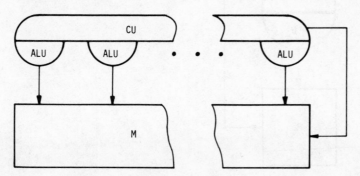

levels contemporary papers very often talk only about 'pipelining', which in many cases is not sufficient.

In cases where the multiplicity of hardware resources (e.g. ALUs) is n, one cannot gain an n-fold increase in performance by choosing an appropriate arrangement. This point will be considered in more detail in section 3.

With these six basic forms of parallelism i.g. (illustrated in figures 1.1–1.6) it is possible to introduce a classification scheme, which forms a starting point allowing us to build up a wide variety of composed computer structures, and which at the same time reflects historical as well as evolutionary aspects of these structures [2].

Figure 1.4. Macro-pipelining.

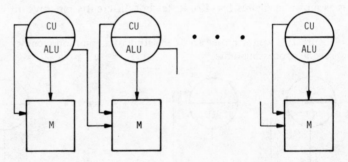

Figure 1.5. Instruction pipelining.

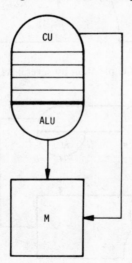

2   Classification and taxonomy of computer structures

A classification scheme has mainly to fulfil the following requirements:

(*a*) It must be possible to classify all existing as well as all foreseeable computer structures.

(*b*) It must differentiate essential processing structures.

(*c*) Any subject or computer structure must be assigned a unique classification.

Some existing classification schemes seem to violate just these rules [3]. They present only very rough categories, exclude viable structures and are not able to uniquely classify any kind of pipelining.

The Erlangen Classification System (ECS) largely avoids these disadvantages. It is mainly based on two points:

(*a*) It introduces a very simple, lucid but rigid triplet as a characterization for basic structures.

(*b*) It introduces operations +, * and v in order to make compositions of structures available and in order to represent a certain 'flexibility'.

In this context 'flexibility' (or 'versatility') is defined as the number of different operation modes in which existing hardware can be utilized.

Disregarding for the present the three types of pipelining we may define the Erlangen triplet [4]:

$$t = (k, d, w)$$

Figure 1.6. Arithmetic pipelining.

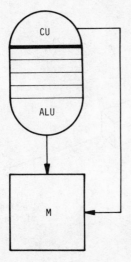

where

> k is the number of control units (CUs) interpreting a program
>
> d is the number of arithmetic and logic units (ALUs) controlled by one of the k control units
>
> w is the wordlength or number of bits handled in one of the d ALUs.

This characteristic can be seen as a point in a three-dimensional space (figure 1.7). It immediately follows that the characterized computer structure has k CUs of the same type and each one of the d ALUs (connected to each of the CUs) has to be of the same type. This homogeneity can also be seen with respect to the bits of a word in one of the d ALUs.

Simple computers of the Princeton type can be characterized by a triplet $t = (1,1,w)$ (see figure 1.7). Early Princeton computers had, e.g. 36-, 48- or 32-bit wordlength, so that we have $(1,1,36)$, $(1,1,48)$ or $(1,1,32)$ as triplets. The simplest possibility, which always seems to be possible, is the triplet $(1,1,1)$. Indeed this simplest form was realized in Europe during the fifties by van der Poël [5] and by T. Fromme [6], who called his computer the 'Minima'. More popular similar computers were called 'serial computers' at this time because the bits were processed one after another. The idea behind this very simple structure was to save hardware and money. Fast evolving hardware has since caused computer designers to change their point of view. A contributory fact was that

Figure 1.7. Three-dimensional representation of the elementary parallel-characteristic triplet of a computer of the Princeton type.

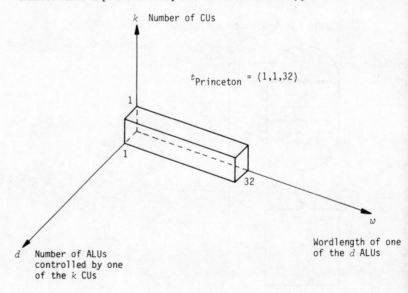

most control elements do not permit a serialization (sequentialization) without bringing about an additional complexity.

It has to be mentioned that the characterization by such very simple triplets is only valid if there is no autonomous I/O control, which in some cases can be programmed separately.

Having introduced these simple triplets or structures we can introduce combinations of structures such as really make up the contemporary computer generation. However, before we give some examples of such composites we have to direct our attention to all kinds of pipelining because these can be ingredients of a basic triplet or structure.

An elementary parallel-pipelining characteristic is an extended triplet

$$t = (k*k', d*d', w*w'),$$

where k, d, w are as defined above, and

k' is the number of control units (CUs) interpreting tasks of a program, whereby the data flow through these units (processor) is sequential: macro-pipeline

d' is the number of function units (ALUs) controlled by one CU and working on one data stream: instruction pipeline

w' is the number of levels or phases in an arithmetic pipeline.

Naturally the 'extended triplet' could be written in the form of a sextet. But such a form would be less readable, and the fact that the entities are well defined by the separating commas was decisive in the triplet style being adopted.

Simple examples of computers, which essentially correspond to the von Neumann type (Princeton type) but equipped with certain forms of pipelining, are as follows

CDC 7600 $\qquad t_{CDC\ 7600\text{-}CP} = (1*1, 1*9, 60*1) = (1,*9,60)$

in a simplified notation with the factor 1 dropped (see figure 1.8). Similarly figure 1.9 corresponds to

CDC STAR $\qquad t_{CDC\ STAR\text{-}CP} = (1,2,64*4)$

(where in the same manner the ones have been cancelled), and figure 1.10 is

TI ASC $\qquad t_{TI\ ASC\text{-}CP} = (1,4,64*8).$

The first example, CDC 7600 [7], is a representation of the central processor only. Otherwise we would have to add the notations for peripheral processor, front-end processor, etc., for which the appropriate operators are introduced later.

The notation $*9$ in $t_{CDC\ 7600\text{-}CP}$ means 'nine function units' which play the role of the ALU in this concept.

The notation $64*4$ in $t_{\text{CDC STAR-CP}}$ [8] means 'an arithmetic pipeline with four levels' working on 64-bit information. In the second position of the triplet the 2 signifies that two such pipelines are allocated.

The notation $64*8$ in $t_{\text{TI ASC-CP}}$ [9] accordingly means that arithmetic pipelines with eight levels are acting as ALUs. In the second position the 4 represents that four such arithmetic pipelines exist.

Figure 1.8. CDC 7600. Five 12-bit words from the peripheral processors are transferred into one 60-bit word of the central processor. The reverse transfer is done in a similar way.

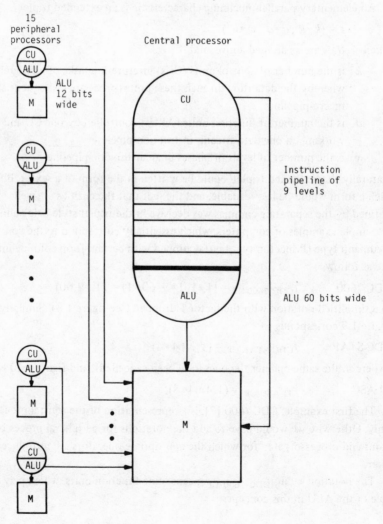

15
peripheral
processors

Central processor

CU
ALU

ALU
12 bits
wide

M

CU
ALU

M

CU

Instruction
pipeline of
9 levels

ALU

ALU 60 bits wide

CU
ALU

M

M

CU
ALU

M

It should be mentioned that in the last two examples the number of pipelines is optional. The numbers in these examples give the numbers for the full extension of each model.

With the given triplets all elementary structures can be characterized. Because the three parts of a triplet refer to a specific homogeneous structure, one has now to introduce composition rules to make possible the characterization of more complex structures.

With the basic triplets given above it is already possible to characterize either a multitude of (essentially) equal control units (CUs), each able to interpret a program, or a multitude of arithmetic and control units (ALUs), each able to process one data stream. If there are diverse elements instead of one triplet a composition of them has to be applied. For this reason we introduce the operators:

+ (plus) for the existence of more than one structure, in particular for diverse structures (because otherwise they might be united into one elementary triplet, as pointed out earlier), as an alternative for the data, whereby they may (normally) be processed, each item according to its specific nature on the best studied structure.

Figure 1.9. CDS STAR. Two ALUs each 64 bits wide. Arithmetic pipelines of 4 levels.

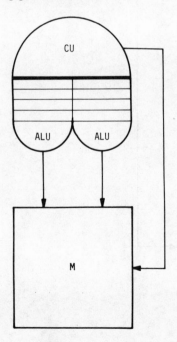

* (times) for the existence of sequentially ordered structures, whereby all
  data is (normally) processed through all structures, given by appropriate
  triplets.

At the same time both operators characterize the fact that more than one task
at a time may be executed in the overall structure. The operator + indicates
'parallel processing' (in the more specific sense) and the operator * means 'pipeline processing' or 'pipelining', which corresponds to the term 'macro-pipelining',
as formally introduced (section 1).

Nonhomogeneous structures characterized by compositions using + are very
infrequent while those characterized by compositions using * are more common
in use. The latter correspond for example to configurations with one central
processor and one peripheral processor or for example to configurations with

Figure 1.10. TI ASC. Four ALUs each 64 bits wide. Arithmetic pipelines
of 8 levels.

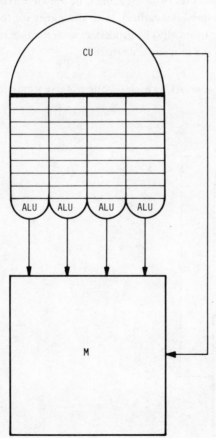

respectively more than one central processor and more than one peripheral processor. In these cases all data (and programs) are first processed normally by one of the peripheral processors and then by one of the central processors. The fact that the results or the output is forwarded to a peripheral processor is not taken into account by the notation to be introduced in the following.

Some examples follow to clarify the function of the operators + and *. The model CDC 7600 was given above only with respect to its central processor (CP). Adding the fifteen peripheral processors, which are a feature of this computer type, we obtain the following composition of triplets:

$$t_{\text{CDC 7600}} = (15,1,12) * (1,*9,60)$$

The second term is identical to the triplet formerly given for the CP. The first term stands for the peripheral processors, which forward the job stream as well as the data input stream (figure 1.8). Disregarding in this context the specific role of one of the peripheral processors (which processes the operating system) each entity of a program or of a data set will find its way through one of the peripheral processors into the central processor.

The example shows a nontrivial structure of customary architecture. The reader may try to characterize another structure that he is familiar with. One will recognize that most of the currently known structures may be represented. Nevertheless we shall disregard more complicated examples of the classification system in this introductory article: e.g. discussion of cases of data flow structures would consume a considerable space which could be more effectively used for other important points.

One such important point is the flexibility of a structure. We will use the term 'flexibility' synonymously with the term 'versatility' in this article. We mean by 'flexibility' that a given piece of hardware may be utilized in more than one way. In this sense most of the hardware of today is of flexibility 1, which means that no change can take place regarding how this hardware is used. For example, in a Princeton-type computer at any time a machine word is interpreted as a machine word, i.e. as a number, an instruction, or a piece of information of this length. In the new ICL-DAP configuration [10], where DAP means 'distributed array processor', the information stored in the DAP may be interpreted in different ways. In terms of the ECS classification we write:

$$t_{\text{DAP}} = (1,128,32) \vee (1,4096,1)$$

which means that the DAP hardware may be used in two ways.

The first possibility is to use 128 ALUs, each 32 bits wide. The second possibility is to use 4096 ALUs, each 1 bit wide (the minimum). So far the classification does not reflect the use and interconnection structure of memory blocks. Another characteristic fact of ICL-DAP configurations, namely that the

DAP hardware may also be used as a memory block only, cannot be represented.

But we have to discuss the expression for t_{DAP}. The two terms characterize alternatives in the sense that at one time only one of the two possibilities for which the two triplets are the representation may be utilized, because only one piece of hardware is existent.

This is apparently a difference from the formerly introduced operators + and *, where real hardware parts are connected together. The connector v therefore makes up another kind of operator. It mainly appears in the consideration of the expenditure of a given structure as characterized by a nonelementary expression.

Let us therefore consider the figures for an ICL-DAP configuration. Normally such a configuration consists of an ICL 2900 CP and the special DAP structure, for which the characterization has already been given. The composed structure may be written

$$t_{ICL\text{-}DAP} = (1,1,32) * [(1,128,32) \text{ v } (1,4096,1)].$$

While the expenditure for an ICL 2900, considering only active CPs and not the memory blocks, (essentially) amounts to the product $1 * 1 * 32 = 32$, the expenditure for the DAP amounts to only the product of one of its triplets, namely $1 * 128 * 32 = 4096$. In a really flexible equipment such a product must have the same value for all alternative terms (i.e. terms connected by v). DAP is an example of this. It is important to note that the terms connected by v reflect different modes of operation of the same equipment.

In order to show the power of the ECS classification system, more examples follow.

The well-known ILLIAC IV installation [11] originally consisted of one Burroughs B 6700 as a front-end machine plus the actual ILLIAC IV structure. This may be represented as

$$t_{B6700\text{-}ILLIAC} = (1,1,48) * (1,64,64).$$

This installation proved not to be a good combination in practice. Therefore another front-end combination was inserted later, replacing the B 6700. Because one DEC PDP 10 is not so powerful as the B 6700, two of them were used. Then the characterization in ECS is

$$t_{PDP10\text{-}ILLIAC} = (2,1,36) * (1,64,64).$$

The 2 in the first term means that all data is forwarded either in the first PDP 10 or in the second (in general not both). The second term stands for: 64 ALUs working with a wordlength of 64 bits.

Refinements of the representation in different directions are possible. The consideration e.g. of look-ahead features in ILLIAC may be handled in an appropriate d' factor (instruction pipeline).

In spite of the fact that the author has no information on the practical use of half-word operations in ILLIAC the appropriate ECS presentation would be

$$t_{\text{PDP10-ILLIAC}/2} = (2,1,36) * (1,128,32)$$

(ILLIAC IV descriptions refer to this operation mode). Using the notation for flexibility, as introduced earlier, we may write

$$t_{\text{PDP-ILLIAC}} = (2,1,36) * [(1,64,64) \vee (1,128,32)].$$

The second and the third factor are linked by v in order to indicate the alternative possibilities. The fact that this notation is used indicates that this is one piece of hardware used in two different ways. The 'operation mode' (1,128,32) might be interesting in cases where, for example, 128 is the number of elements in a vector and the wordlength of 32 bits is sufficient for computing.

In conformity with the consideration of the expenditure we may state that $1 * 64 * 64 = 1 * 128 * 32 = 4096$.

The second example refers to a less-known structure, which was developed by Sanders [12]. At the same time this structure serves to introduce a refinement of the ECS notation. The Sanders OMEN 60 computer has not been completed, as far as information is available. Nevertheless this structure is suited to the discussion of a new aspect. OMEN has two ALUs which are used alternatively, but only one CU interprets the single program. In this way the operation mode may be chosen according to the need of a program, either conventional or associative. The notation is then

$$t_{\text{OMEN 60}} = (1,1,16) + (0,64,1).$$

introducing a '0' for indicating nonexistence of a hardware unit, in this case a CU. The first term is the characterization of a standard PDP 11, which interprets all parts of the program. Some instructions are related to the second term, which represents a block of 64 ALUs, each one consisting of one-bit 'wordlength'.

The last notation characterizes a nonsymmetrical processor. In fact the PDP 11 is the more important part of the hardware, because it interprets the program, while the 'vertical processor'[1] (0,64,1) takes its control signals from the PDP 11.

In a case where we assume a device with the horizontal (or conventional) ALU and the vertical ALUs both related to a common superior CU, we would write

$$t_{\text{OMEN-symm}} = (1,0,0) * [(0,1,16) + (0,64,1)],$$

where the first term refers to a CU without any other parts of the computer and the second and third give the notation of two different ALU parts without the capability of interpreting a program.

According to the descriptions given by Sanders-Corporation and others [13], the two ALU parts are not allowed to access the common memory at the same time. $(0,1,16)$ accesses machine words in the conventional way, while $(0,64,1)$ calls up 'bit slices', for handling in a parallel or associative mode.

Having introduced the notation of zeros in the last example, we may add another remark. The classification system might be used to classify the history of digital computers in general and is therefore a real taxonomy. For example we have

$t_{\text{Abacus}} = (0,0,n)$, where n is the number of positions or bars with beads

$t_{\text{Desk calc}} = (0,1,n)$, where 1 stands for the 'logic' between the registers

and finally

$t_{\text{Prog controlled C}} = (1,1,w)$, where w is the wordlength.

The last triplet was the starting point of section 2, where we have demonstrated how more sophisticated structures could be composed.

So far we have given only examples of the classification of computer structures. This is helpful in some respects. Nevertheless the ECS notation is applicable also to algorithms or programs. A vector operation can be classified by a triplet $t_{\text{vect}} = (1,1024,32)$ if the number of elements of one of its vectors is 1024 and a 32-bit wordlength is sufficient for the required precision. The triplet stands for the typical vector operation such as vector multiplication and gives it for this very moment of operation. All other parts of a program, especially red tape or organizational parts have another characteristic, perhaps of the type $t_{\text{rt}} = (1,1,32)$, in order to indicate that a parallelization for this case cannot take place. But these details depend on the specific application. Characterizations of programs or algorithms therefore consist of sequences of triplets, where each one gives the computing hardware ideally needed for a certain period of the execution of a program.

The available hardware is known by giving an appropriate characterization. Such a characterization of hardware is essentially constant with respect to time. By contrast, as pointed out above, a program, or even more a certain job stream, shows an ever changing demand for hardware that may be applied to it. Therefore we finally have to search for an analysis that brings both these things together. In all cases, where there is a demand for hardware, which to some extent is not available, the triplets for a program must be divided into pieces. For example in the above mentioned case we have $t_{\text{vect}} = (1,1024,32)$ and if we assume that the ILLIAC IV is available for computation then we might utilize this computer in the half-word mode which we have described earlier. Then we have to consider the following fact:

$t_{\text{vect}} = (1,1024,32)$

has to be computed by

$$t_{PDP10\text{-}ILLIAC/2} = (2,1,36) * (1,128,32).$$

Disregarding for this restricted discussion the organizational aspects (for which we had to include the operation of one PDP10) we can handle the vectors (of 1024 elements each) by applying the ILLIAC half-word mode eight times $(128 \times 8 = 1024)$.

ECS, as we suggested in the foregoing discussion, is suited to characterize computer structure as well as algorithms and our further investigations are directed to the problem of describing both a given hardware and a given job stream.

The latter consideration makes it evident that the former definition of flexibility or versatility is suggestive. In all cases where hardware can be utilized in more than one way we have the possibility of making the best choice among the available operation modes, each given by a definite triplet.

In many cases the given hardware is not as powerful as the given program or job stream is demanding. Therefore the program has to be partitioned. In other cases the triplets of a program may be much 'smaller' than the available hardware. In these cases, therefore, we have to provide a permanent stream of jobs, which fill the hardware in a favourable way. An appropriate procedure could be called 'multiprogramming, second class', where hardware has to be partitioned rather than time to be parcelled out, as is done at present in time-sharing systems.

3   A case study in versatile parallel computer structure

In order to demonstrate some of the capabilities of ECS we will discuss the features, structure details and versatility of the 'Erlangen General Purpose Array'[2] project, which a group of computer scientists at the University of Erlangen–Nürnberg and the AEG-Telefunken Corporation has been implementing since 1978 [14]. The project is sponsored by the German Federal Ministry of Research and Technology with grants of about four million US dollars so far. At the end of this section the present state of the project will be pointed out to some extent.

The main ideas of EGPA have first of all to be explained. These ideas are discussed in a more philosophical sense in section 4.

Basic elements of the EGPA structure are the following:

(a) Princeton processor
(b) memory unit
(c) multiport unit, in direct connection with (b).

A pilot implementation, which will be discussed at the end of this section, containing five AEG-Telefunken type 80-60 processors, five memory units and

five multiports is an absolute minimum configuration with respect to the basic
ideas of EGPA (figure 1.11).

For architecture of EGPA configurations we combine one of each basic
element to make up one EGPA-unit. With such EGPA-units it is possible to build
up configurations of different sizes without changing the concept, the topology
of interconnections or the technological design.

The discussion will centre on two main points. First the processor in an
EGPA-unit is enabled by firmware to function also as a parallel and associative
processor very similar to a Goodyear **STARAN** computer [15]. In this sense the
infrastructure of the EGPA-unit is changed or made flexible (see section 2 on
flexibility or versatility). An appropriate structure for the interconnection of
such EGPA-units is required to ensure achievement of the two advantages of
parallelism, namely (compare section 1):

(*a*) improved overall performance
(*b*) improved availability and safety.

Evidently some preconditions with respect to programming and to the operating

Figure 1.11. EGPA PYRAMID. Minimal configuration, pilot implementation 5 × AEG-TFK 80-60.

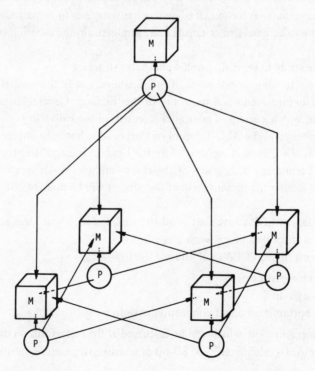

system have to be fulfilled before these advantages can be achieved in EGPA. All other basic requirements are created by specifying the topology.

The discussion starts with the structure of present-day processors. By definition a processor is a combination of one CU with a number of ALUs. In the case of a Princeton processor there is only one ALU and in some publications this structure is also called the 'classical universal computer' (or processor) [1]. In this context it is not important whether the processor is one of von Neumann's time, which consisted of an ALU with three to five specialized registers, or one of the later versions in which a set of 'general purpose' registers is available. Even stack processors can be included in the following discussion. Nevertheless we will restrict ourselves to a more abstract form of processor and will not discuss special processor versions.

An ALU for a classical structure consists of, say, 32 binary positions. Micro-operation signals cause the logic of the ALU to switch and to combine the machine words stored in two registers of this ALU. In additions (or subtractions) the sum (difference) is built up by a carry procedure and normally all positions are connected with their immediate neighbours in order to compute the final sum. A carry pyramid even considers a larger amount of positions in order to accelerate the process of addition (subtraction etc.). Also in the case of shifts we have a connection between neighbouring register positions.

Nevertheless, there is a great number of instructions which do not include the neighbourhood with their sequence of signals. In this way each one of the positions does not touch its neighbours. For example logic operations like the 'intersection' or the 'union' (a position-wise 'and'-operation or 'or'-operation) are of this kind. Descriptions of these elementary operations are very simple because there is only the need to describe the operation with respect to one position i. No signals go from position i to position $i+1$ or $i-1$ ($i = 1, 2, 3, \ldots, 32$).

Thus we can consider the ALU consisting of 32 single ALUs of wordlength '1' and the following 'relation' holds (figure 1.12)

$$1 \times w\text{-bit parallel word ALU} \equiv w \times 1\text{-bit ALUs}$$
$$+ \text{carry logic} + \text{shift logic}$$

where w is the wordlength.

This means that one can utilize the existing hardware also in an operation mode where 32 serial (1-bit) processors are available. Data processing is now sequentially executed bit by bit but for 32 items at the same time. Because the information has to be vertically stored in the conventional primary store (memory block) authors have sometimes called this operation mode 'vertical processing' [16].

This entirely new operation mode has some striking advantages. A factor of improvement between three and fifty can be gained by 'vertical processing' [17]. Naturally not all problems may be solved in a parallel or associative mode as realizable by 'vertical processing'. Some of the advantages are as follows:

(1) Entirely new algorithms are appropriate and efficient under 'vertical processing'. In most cases a program to solve a problem is suited either to sequential processing or to parallel processing but not to both to the same extent. Therefore one has to search for other, sometimes new, algorithms which solve the problem appropriately in parallel. Simple transformations to do this are very seldom available. The produced program is not an efficient one in such a case. The research concerning 'parallel algorithms' will probably be the key problem of the coming decades. In very important cases it will not be sufficient to say that an algorithm exists or that a problem is computable in the sense of Turing's concept. It has rather to be investigated whether an algorithm is parallel in its very nature or how a problem may be developed into such an algorithm [18].

(2) Vertical processing allows the handling of an arbitrary wordlength (while conventional or 'horizontal' processing is essentially bound by the machine word). Using microprogramming it is possible to build up efficient instructions such as compare w numbers with one given number and indicate which of them are greater and which of them are smaller, producing an appropriate pattern in a predetermined register of w bits, where w is the wordlength in the conventional (horizontal) sense. In the context of vertical processing it means that w items are processed, one bit of each of the w items at the same time. In the description of the above instruction the 'wordlength' of the items was not mentioned. Because it is related to the length of vertical information one should use another term for

Figure 1.12. Consideration of an ALU of wordlength '32' as consisting of 32 single ALUs of wordlength '1'.

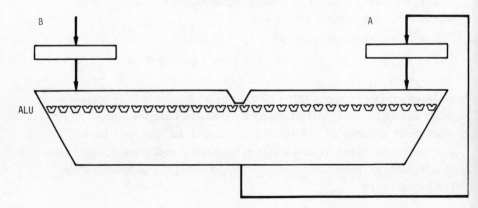

it. We consider the length of a piece of vertical information as an information length. The proposition of point (2) means that the 'information length' may be arbitrary and is only related to a counting process, which runs synchronously with the specific arithmetical or logical process. The whole process is cyclic and fully controlled by the microprogram that is responsible for this instruction. The number of bits that denotes the information length has to be brought into a register before the cyclic process can commence.

(3) Execution of a vertical instruction may be broken off after possibly a few bit-slices (in vertical processing this means machine words) when a given item cannot be found in memory (criterion for this is that the 'resolution mask' has become 'zero' in all positions, e.g. 32 positions). For a great proportion of problems comparisons and tests of the 'greatest number' kind are to be performed, or a certain item or name is searched for. In this case 'associative processing' takes place. Given a certain set of items, in our discussion preferably w or 32, we are interested in those items that fulfil a certain condition. Insofar as we have not processed any information all w or 32 items are candidates that may fulfil the condition. As we proceed – bit by bit – the number of candidates diminishes in normal cases. A '1' in position i at the end of the operation means that the item vertically stored in this position fulfils the criterion. Two extremes are possible. It is possible that all positions finally show '1s'. In this case all items meet the condition. On the other hand it is often the case that all positions finally show '0s', i.e. all items fail to meet the condition. Apparently this latter case cannot take place if we have asked for a maximum (or minimum). As an example let us assume that we are searching for a female first name (of an author for instance): Emily. By examining the bit-position denoting sex we immediately exclude the male candidates. The remaining '1s' indicate all female authors after this step, which is only related to one bit-position or a machine word in vertical processing. Further investigations have to proceed with 'E' (a group of 6 or 8 machine words), with 'm' (next group of 6 or 8 machine words), with 'i' (third group of 6 or 8 machine words), etc. The case where there are no female authors whose first name begins with 'E' is probably very infrequent. But if it does happen, then after the first step the 'resolution mask' becomes '0' and we break off the process. In most cases, however, we will have a certain number of '1s', namely those indicating 'Eileen', 'Elinor', 'Elizabeth', 'Emily', 'Ethel', 'Eve' and 'Evelyn'. 'Emily' naturally is only one of them. Then if we ask for the second character 'm' it is clear that the resolution mask now holds only '1s' in positions where 'Emily's have been found. This is the time we may break off the process in which the number of all fetches from memory and the number of elementary operations is much smaller than in the conventional, horizontal programming, case. The main reason is that in conventional programming (where each item is identical with one

or even more machine words) we have to exhaust the given list of items before we can give a statement about the existence of 'Emily' (which could be the last of all machine words). In such a way associative processing proves to be much more efficient than conventional processing. In the context of the last example ('Emily') it is worth making a further comment. Let us assume that typical German (female) first names are also taking part in our 'competition'. In this case we have to include such names as 'Emilie' and 'Emanuela' and therefore we would accordingly have to extend our consideration. Nevertheless, the statement that associative processing is more efficient in this respect than conventional processing, remains valid.

(4) The proportion of instruction fetches is very low compared with the proportion of cyclically and most efficiently processed data-slices, which do not demand new instruction fetches. 'Vertical instructions', whether working in parallel or associatively on w items to find a subset or the items fulfilling a certain criterion are always stored in the conventional manner, i.e. horizontally. They are interpreted according to the conventional instruction fetch of program control. However, it calls for a microprogram that is directed to vertically stored information and which has to be interpreted bit by bit (or machine word by machine word with respect to the hardware) according to the given instruction (operation). The microprogram may operate in a cycle, because all bits underlie the same operation. This process ends only when a counting process, which gives the length of information under investigation and which has to be placed into a defined register before the operation, is exhausted. Because an instruction fetch takes place only once, this is more efficient the longer the information length is. One could argue that this improvement can also take place if microprograms are designed for a conventional processing cycle searching (or testing) a certain set of data. But this does not hold true, since for an average searching (or testing) process a sequence of instructions has to be taken to execute the desired operation. In conventional processors without vertical processing this can only be done by a sequence of real instructions or by a microprogram. Then any loop contains more than one instruction, which results in full instruction fetches, while the whole cycle for vertical processing results in only one microprogram loop. In such a way we really lower the number of instruction fetches considerably.

Sometimes people say that the same number of information bits has to be called for, whether a conventional process or a vertical process is performed. But – apart from point (3) as already discussed – the vertical process results in a more regular structure of information, independent of the machine wordlength. Composition rules for operations that perform a searching or testing process are very simple for vertical processes, as will be pointed out in later publications.

For this presentation we restrict ourselves to a table of figures which may be achieved by introducing vertical processing (figure 1.13).

So far we have dealt with a single processor and what improvement in performance may be obtained by introducing vertical processing. One processor means that w items (e.g. $w = 32$ as wordlength) may be processed at a time (in parallel), but sequentially bit after bit. This is already efficient; nevertheless such a pro-

Figure 1.13*a*. A microprogrammed 64-bit processor with its main memory. Vertical processing is implemented by special microprograms. 64 (e.g.) items are stored, accessed and processed simultaneously, i.e. in a word-parallel and bit-sequential mode. Two vectors A and B are stored.

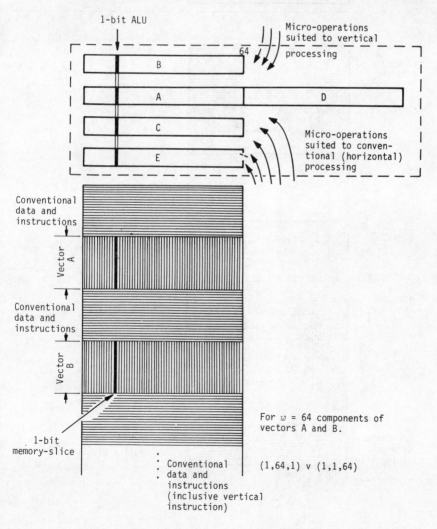

For w = 64 components of vectors A and B.

$(1,64,1)$ v $(1,1,64)$

Figure 1.13*b*. Example of an associative operation on a conventional microprogrammable processor with vertical processing. 64 objects, e.g. items related to books are stored.

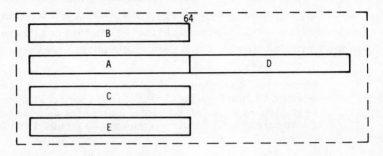

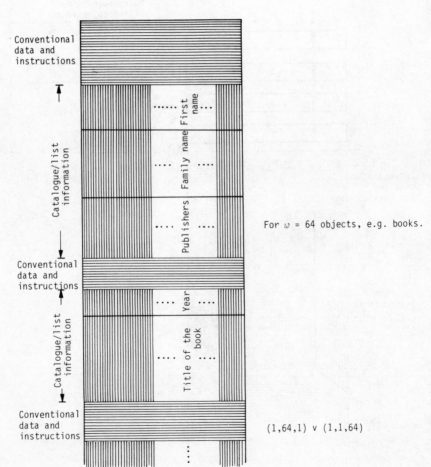

For w = 64 objects, e.g. books.

$(1,64,1) \lor (1,1,64)$

cedure is cumbersome if we have more than 32 items, which in all practical cases will occur. In such cases we can chain elementary vertical processes of the form we have described for w items, e.g. $w = 32$. It would not be elegant to go back to sequentiality to achieve what speedup there is to be reached by parallelism. Investigations in the context of the EGPA project proved the practicality of introducing a multiplicity of processors.

When we started section 3 we mentioned that two points were to be discussed. The first one, changing the infrastructure of one processor by the introduction of vertical processing, has already been covered. The second is now to extend the concept to a viable multiprocessor structure.

It is not sufficient just to have a pool of processors and to have connections somehow between them. EGPA is a concept which is based on computational considerations and needs but avoids the embarrassment of costly cross-bar switches which connect each processor with all others. This would amount to an increase of costs by $n(n - 1)/2$, or approximately n^2.

Instead we admit only a restricted connectivity for the EGPA-unit (see the description earlier in this section). Then the problem is to find an appropriate topology, viable in the sense that it allows us to compute most application programs efficiently without causing difficulties and delays regarding the exchange of data. The topology of 'restricted neighbourhood' ensures at the same time that costs (or expenditure) and complexity are not increasing unlimitedly with a growing number of processors.

For well-known applications we want to have connections available for the exchange of data. In such cases, where a data exchange takes place less frequently we may take into account that not a direct transfer is available, but instead transfer is made across a chain of processor connections.

Decisive for the connection of EGPA-units is the multiport, which is an integral part of an EGPA-unit. Cross-connections make it possible either to change the workload or to dynamically 'repair' a configuration under operation (see section 1). Assuming an elementary pair of EGPA-units (figure 1.14), the workload of a processor as well as the load of a memory block may be changed by an appropriate arrangement, determining which one of the processors has to perform a certain program and where the program has to be located.

Regarding a repair in the sense of a 'fault-tolerant' behaviour of the configuration we have to provide a radical change of the workload under the condition that one of the four connection lines of the two processors or one of the two memory blocks becomes inoperative.

With this universal connection principle in mind a rectangular array may be composed where each processor has access to its immediate neighbours in northern, eastern, southern and western directions (figure 1.15). Regarding the

Figure 1.14. Elementary pair of EGPA-units.

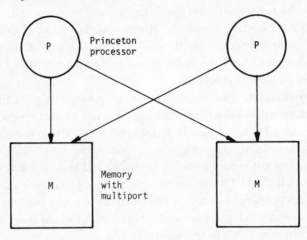

Figure 1.15. Processor connections to adjacent memory blocks
N, S, E, W; connections are closed to a toroid.

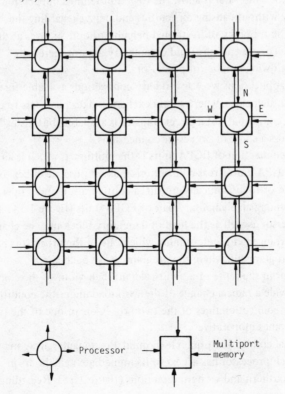

fact that a processor is connected to its 'own' associated memory block (by definition of an EGPA-unit) this topology results in a connection scheme where each processor has access to five memory blocks and each memory block is connected to five processors of the same layer.

Most common applications like the solution of partial differential equations by relaxation methods may be based on rectangular arrays, taking one processor, for example, to perform the iteration steps for one grid point. Boundary conditions may also be taken into consideration, disabling processors on the boundary and introducing instead given constant boundary values. But many other applications which make use of this topology are being investigated.

A worst case consideration would be if we assume that the connections are not utilized at all. This situation might take place when many terminal users want to 'log in' and the operating system (which will be described later) allocates each one a separate processor of the array. Instead of time-sharing we realize a space-sharing situation.

The latter two cases, the relaxation method and many terminal users, may be considered as extreme situations. In the first case the 'communication' of the processors with their environment is maximal, while in the second case the 'communication' disappears completely. If in the case of a relaxation all processors synchronously access data words from 'north' and thereafter from 'east' etc. then there is no competition regarding the multiports. In other cases a competition might take place. Nevertheless the number of processors and the number of memory blocks are equal (according to the description of an EGPA-unit earlier), and for that reason at least the average competition is very low [19].

So far we have left the operating system out of consideration. With this consideration and obeying the principle of 'space-sharing', where some processors are devoted to application programs and some others to the operating system, the resulting configuration is a pyaramid [20] (figure 1.11).

The lowest layer is the already described array fully devoted to application programs. All other layers are predominantly devoted to the operating system. In certain cases these layers may take over in a transitory role for the application programs, taking intermediate results from all processors of the working area (lowest layer) and composing them to a final result. But this special case may be disregarded in this presentation.

Nevertheless it has to be mentioned that the operating system (OS) as just described has to be specified more exactly as the global OS. In a multiprocessor configuration like this EGPA-pyramid one has also to provide a local OS associated with each processor. This local OS cares for all operations, enabling the single processor to accept information or to broadcast information from or to its neighbours. The global OS on the contrary carries out all operations and services, which in similar patterns are known from conventional computers and which are related to the overall functioning of the pyramid.

Summarizing, one may consider two directions of actions in the EGPA-pyramid. One is mainly going on at the lowest level, also called the working area, and is concerned with the horizontal exchange of data.

The process may be simply described in such a way that processors working on an application program and needing data from their neighbours may call this data by using appropriate addresses, which specify memory locations in the neighbourhood. This happens on a word-by-word basis. In this way the address attains a new meaning. It serves to move data in the desired direction, while normally in conventional computing it only serves to transfer the data to the active part of the processor and back again to the same part of memory. In EGPA the data exchange in the lowest level is based on the direct word-by-word transfer rather than on block transfer. The other direction is devoted to the exchange of control data, status information and input/output information. The exchange of this data is going on mainly in the vertical direction and links the different layers of the pyramid. In this context block transfers, mainly in the context of input/output, are not excluded.

The upper levels of the pyramid are responsible for the flow of input/output and for all services or tasks for which the conventional operating system is known. Space-sharing as defined above takes place in the way that the different tasks of an OS are distributed onto the different processors of the upper levels of the pyramid. The lowest level, the working area, is responsible for the execution of the actual application programs, for which the forementioned OS processors of the upper levels are preparing the schedule. The concept changes only slightly, whether the lowest level contains 4, 16, 64, 256 or even more processors. In such a way EGPA computers of different computing power may be realized. In section 4 we will refer to this concept as 'size modularity' as opposed to the 'family concept' of conventional computers [20].

The modularity of the EGPA levels has some further properties. Each array apparently contains 4, 16, 64 or, in general, 4^n EGPA-units ($n = 1, 2, 3, \ldots$). As described earlier these units are combined into a rectangular array with connections to the north, east, south and west. These are closed to form toroids by connecting the northern and southern 'edges' and in the same way the eastern and western 'edges'. This statement is not meaningful in the case $n = 1$. Closing the connection topology of one layer into a toroid has been conceived to provide the opportunity which such a configuration offers with respect to 'fault tolerance' in bigger configurations with 64 or more processors in the working area. Using the geometrical idea of the toroid, one may state that in case of one failure at the 'surface' of the toroid, the global OS may relocate the map from tasks onto processors so that a 'healthy' rectangular array may be built up. For the applications discussed earlier in the context of 'relaxation methods' it was important to have a rectangular array available.

We are at present working with a minimum pyramid, consisting of five EGPA-units, as mentioned before (figure 1.16). Research is concerned with all aspects of the operating system, with applications of different structures and with performance evaluation.

Supplementing section 2, we characterize the EGPA structure by giving the ECS notation. It is, as a general concept,

$$t_{\text{EGPA general}} = [(1,1,32) \vee (1,32,1)] \qquad \text{top}$$
$$* \; [(4,1,32) \vee (* \, 4,1,32) \vee (4,32,1)] \qquad \text{second layer}$$
$$* \; [(16,1,32) \vee (* \, 16,1,32) \vee (16,32,1)] \qquad \text{third layer}$$
$$* \; [(64,1,32) \vee (* \, 64,1,32) \vee (64,32,1)] \qquad \text{fourth layer}$$
$$\vdots \; \text{etc.}$$

Figure 1.16. Pilot configuration EGPA, University of Erlangen-Nürnberg (compare structure of Figure 1.11), consisting of 5 processors AEG-Telefunken Type 80-60. First frame to the left contains the Monitor III (Hardware) which is laid out to evaluate a variety of measurements in multiprocessors, in particular in EGPA.

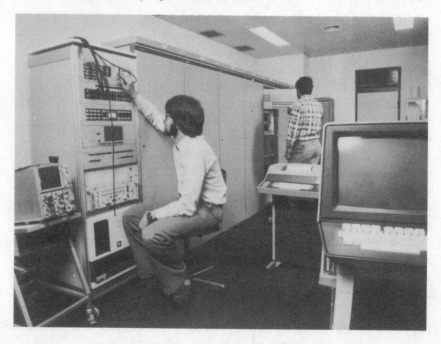

The lowest row characterizes the working area. The last term in each row characterizes the alternative, which is given by the operation mode 'vertical processing' but with each one of the say 64 processors autonomously working in this mode computing a separate maximum or minimum etc. At least this reflects the ECS notation with respect to the hardware facts. Of course it would be desirable to make available e.g. $(1,2048,1)$ instead of $(64,32,1)$ (for the fourth layer). The hierarchical structure of EGPA gives us the hope that there are procedures, involving the higher level layers, which efficiently approximate this desired structure $(1,2048,1)$.

In case we are not successful in this respect we have to consider hardware aids to reach our goal of having available an overall vertical procedure. Bitslice microprocessor technology seems to make a viable solution possible.

The restricted pilot configuration, which is available at present may be characterized by

$$t_{\text{EGPA pilot}} = [(1,1,32) \vee (1,32,1)] * [(4,1,32) \vee (* 4,1,32) \vee (4,32,1)].$$

All important points regarding the general concept of EGPA will be investigated.

4   The burdensome track to parallelism

First attempts to get a higher computing performance by parallelism go back to the year 1957 [21]. Therefore the question arises, why the approach of parallelism i.g. has not been generally introduced in view of the striking improvements in overall performance, availability and safety.

The central nervous system of man gives an example of an excellent parallel system. This system has not been understood up to now and there are doubts about the possibility of fully understanding it. But there is no doubt that computer scientists may learn from it [22].

Another example of parallelism is the analogue computer, particularly in the form of a feedback system, as described by Thompson (later Lord Kelvin) in 1876 [23]. The principle of analogue computation is much better understood than the data processing in man is. All integrators of an analogue computer are working at the same time, i.e. in parallel. It is very interesting in this context that some authors propose to directly transfer the concept of analogue computing into a multiprocessor configuration (e.g. [24]), where each processor takes over the role of an integrator. However, this principle may apparently only be applied to problems where the analogue computer is applicable. Generally speaking, the principle holds only for differential equations, not for the broad field of applications in which the digital computer proves to be so successful today.

The mentioned two fields give only suggestions in a most restrictive way how to proceed towards parallelism. Other paths must be investigated.

When the discussion about parallelism came up early in the sixties, people very often argued that increasing complexity would prevent evolution in this direction. Later the 'competition' between single von Neumann computers and multiprocessors was settled by referring to Grosch's law and to Minsky's conjecture. Therefore it seems to be worthwhile to briefly outline these two statements, which seem to confuse computer people very often [25].

Grosch's law says that the computer power of the performance of one processor increases with the square of the expenditure (figure 1.17). If this is the case then it is naturally useless to design multiprocessors. Apparently with two processors we have to spend four times the price and get only a twofold performance. This could be done much better by designing a processor with about 1.41 times the expenditure of the processor we considered at first. Therefore consideration of parallelism took place only for military applications for a rather long time; here security and availability are indispensable.

Also discussed is Minsky's conjecture, which claims that by reason of the necessary data exchange in parallel computing devices, where n is the parallelity, the performance equals only about $\log_2 n$, if one device has the performance 1 (figure 1.18). Computers with two, three or four processors, which were in operation during the sixties and seventies, seemed to prove this 'conjecture'.

Figure 1.17. Grosch's law.

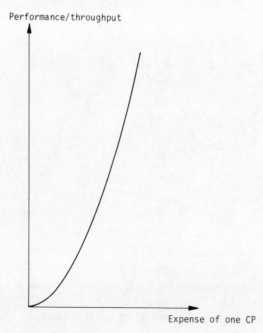

Performance/throughput

Expense of one CP

With their more or less conventional OS, the performance was considerably degraded in fact.

The statements of Grosch and Minsky sound very discouraging and they are very often cited in order to show that parallelism is not rewarding at all. Nevertheless both are refutable. The arguments for refutation are based on the following points, though a complete presentation cannot be given in this paper. On the one hand Grosch's law cannot be valid in the upper region, because then the influence of the speed of light and the possible smallness of integrated circuits strongly limit a further speedup (figure 1.19). Therefore the curve instead shows a reverse tendency in the upper region. Then we may spend more and more money, but will not earn a performance as predicted by Grosch's law. Therefore it was sometimes claimed by some authors that computer manufacturers have prescribed Grosch's law for their pricing policy in their 'family of computers'. By doing this these manufacturers wanted to give a certain stimulus for the purchase of all models of their family, while otherwise the models of the upper region would not be bought (if the price reflected reality with respect to the lower models). The whole expenditure is covered in such a way as given in figure 1.20, referring to the entire family of computers in question.

Figure 1.18. Minsky's conjecture.

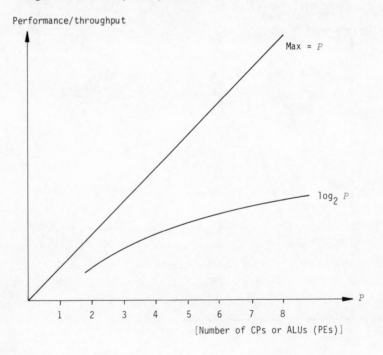

Performance/throughput

Max = P

$\log_2 P$

P

1   2   3   4   5   6   7   8

[Number of CPs or ALUs (PEs)]

Figure 1.19. Grosch's law, extended.

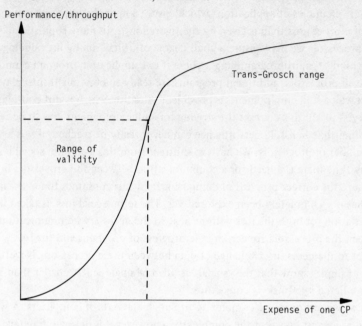

Figure 1.20. Price/expenditure policy for a computer family.

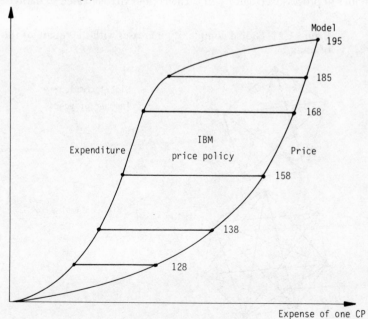

On the other hand it may be shown with respect to Minsky's conjecture that there are examples of applications which ensure a much higher degree of utilization of n processors than is given by the figure $\log_2 n$. In more sophisticated multiprocessors we may ensure a good degree of utilization by introducing a new kind of 'multiprogramming', where if one application program cannot utilize all processors, additional programs are ready to be brought into play. In such a way a 'full employment' is possible, a situation which is not considered by Minsky at all. In this context the striving for 'full employment' has to be restricted by noting that an n-fold performance can never really be reached, if n is again the number of processors. We have to subtract from this a certain 'social loss'. At any time there is a need for a communication between the processors in order to ensure the correct progress of computing, and this consumes time. 'Social loss' has not completely been explored yet. The term 'social loss' is taken in this presentation for both the loss with respect to the necessary communication between the processors concerning the progress of programs and the loss with respect to the necessary exchange of data between these processors. Nevertheless some examples show that this 'social loss' can be made much smaller than the loss predicted by Minsky's conjecture.

Now we return to the complexity of parallel layouts of computers. A widespread argument says that the complexity – however it is defined in detail – increases with the square of the number of units and in particular with the number of processors (figure 1.21). The complexity is related to hardware

Figure 1.21. Global complexity increases with the square of the number of units.

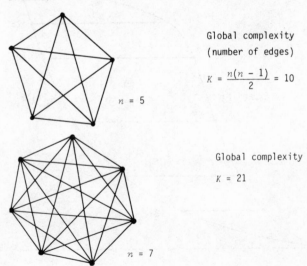

Global complexity
(number of edges)

$$K = \frac{n(n-1)}{2} = 10$$

$n = 5$

Global complexity

$K = 21$

$n = 7$

connections of the units (i.e. buses, rings, etc.) on one hand and to traffic problems on the other hand (i.e. congestions, competition, etc). This measure of complexity (proportional to n^2) arises from the American National Standard X3.12-1970 where it is stated: 'A multiprocessor is a computer employing two or more processing units under integrated control'.

Interpreting this standard in the seventies some authors have stated that: 'A multiprocessor has two or more processors, having access to one common memory, while private memory blocks are not excluded'. This would mean that a multiprocessor is viable only if n, the multiplicity or parallelity, is very small. One can show that based on contemporary technology e.g. six processors are already loading a bus to such an extent that no more traffic of information is possible and therefore only performance equivalent to four processors may be obtained. This figure may change according to circumstances but behave in a similar way. Multiprocessors with four processors seem insufficient and also the addition of, let us say, three processors would not bring a breakthrough. The only way to overcome the problem of intolerable complexity is to depart from the principle of '... one common memory ...' and to a certain extent '... processing units under integrated control ...'. Rather a better and more viable principle is to demand only a chain of units, which enable the computer to exchange data and status information between processors arbitrarily, but eventually across a number of chained units (figure 1.22).

Therefore the disastrous principle of full connectivity has to be replaced by the principle of 'restricted neighbourhood', which may also be called the principle of 'constant local complexity'. With an increasing number of units it cannot be permitted to enlarge the number of connections with which a unit is connected to its neighbours (figure 1.23). This principle, which ensures limited complexity

Figure 1.22. Information exchange across a number of chained units.

Memory blocks

Processors

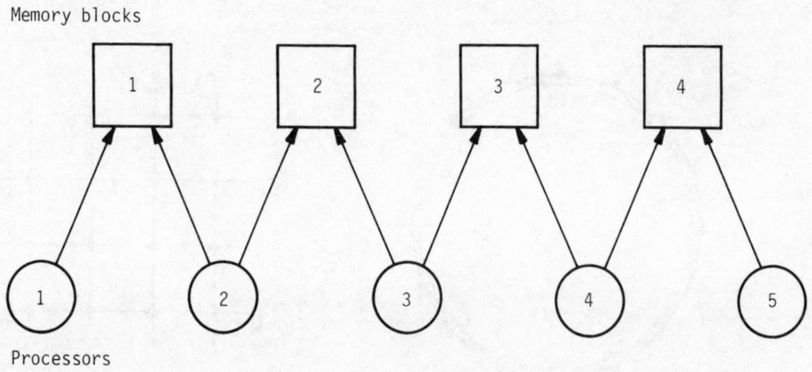

at any location of the structure, is independent of the technological solution (bus etc.), so far. But certainly we presented a solution in section 3, which is based on the concept of multiport in the context of project EGPA and which is technologically and conceptionally a feasible structure.

Last but not least we are very often confronted in architectural discussions with the 'trauma of unavoidable specialization'. In this context it is argued that if we want to have a performance of an order of magnitude higher than that of a Princeton processor we have to restrict ourselves to a small class of applications. In fact several examples from the seventies seem to prove that most powerful computers are always 'special purpose computers'. In this context we may cite concepts or structures like SOLOMON, ILLIAC IV, Goodyear STARAN, PEPE etc. Because of their specialized character'these computers need in addition a 'host' to operate them. But this does not hold true, as we have shown in sections 2 and 3. Even if our example of 'vertical processing' is only one of the possible structures other authors like Estrin [26] and Burks [27] have developed similar concepts to overcome inflexibly stiff computer structures.

Interpreted in terms of the ECS classification, we saw in section 2 that

Figure 1.23. The principle of 'restricted neighbourhood' or 'constant local complexity'.

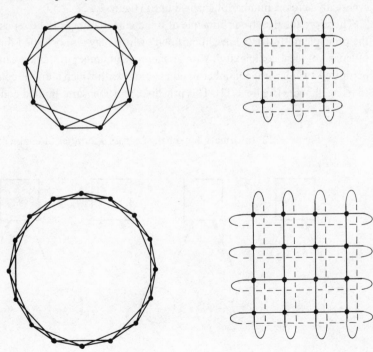

'flexibility' or 'versatility' is equivalent to the existence of more than one triplet connected by v, which is the same as if we have more than one point in a three-dimensional classification space. In section 3 we presented EGPA as an example of a flexible structure. In both sections we pleaded for flexibility in this sense, which is equivalent to a multiple utilization of hardware.

In all the foregoing examples we showed how obstacles may be overcome in computer architecture. In other areas it is not easy to see how to proceed. This is the case with programming languages. A large research programme for at least two decades will be necessary to explore new languages, which are not prohibitive with respect to 'parallel thinking'.

A good starting point for the following considerations could be the statement of Benjamin Whorf [28] that languages pave the way for thinking. Other authors say that the words of a language and the construct of a language are the vehicles for thoughts. In this sense it depends on the 'vehicles' what can be transferred by using a language.

In terms of programming languages this means that it depends on the language and its constructs how a program finally looks. At the same time the efficiency of a program in running time is dependent on the nature of such a language. The efficiency may be quite different from application to application. Nevertheless the influence of a language is very strong, even if it is not conscious to us. An example to show this follows.

We assume that a sum $Y(N)$ and partial sums $Y(I)$ have to be calculated according to

$$Y(0) := 0$$
$$\textbf{for } I = \textbf{step } 1 \textbf{ until } N \textbf{ do}$$
$$Y(I) := Y(I-1) + A(I)$$

If we examine this problem we are inclined to solve it by a loop structure proceeding in N steps as all computers do today. We do not readily see another way to calculate the N numbers (partial sums) $Y(I)$ $(I = 1, 2, 3, \ldots, N)$. Nevertheless a simple consideration shows that only $\log_2 N$ steps are necessary. Instead of $N = 8$ steps therefore only $\log_2 8 = 3$ steps (see figure 1.24) are needed.

Already in this example it would be troublesome to describe how a compiler should proceed in order to transform the expression above into the $\log_2$ shortened form. Other expressions would be even worse. Nevertheless some progress has been obtained with a compiler, which is capable of transforming at least some basic expressions of that kind.

Generally speaking for this section the influence of mathematical and linguistic tradition, definitions and possibly simply prejudice is very strong and some simple ways to make parallel computer structures effective might be hidden to our view today.

5 Summary and outlook

In section 1 an introduction was given for parallelism in general as distinguished from the more special parallelism with pipelining. While parallelism i.g. is a collective name, parallelism and pipelining are both embodiments in contemporary computer architecture, which can appear in a combined form. From these two embodiments post-Princeton structures are being developed, by com-

Figure 1.24. Parallel configuration schema:

$$\text{for} \quad Y[0] := 0 \quad N := 8$$
$$\textbf{for } I = 1 \quad \textbf{step } 1 \textbf{ until } N \textbf{ do}$$
$$Y[I] := Y[I - 1] + A[I]$$

where today's HLL (higher level languages) admit only a sequential proceeding in N steps.

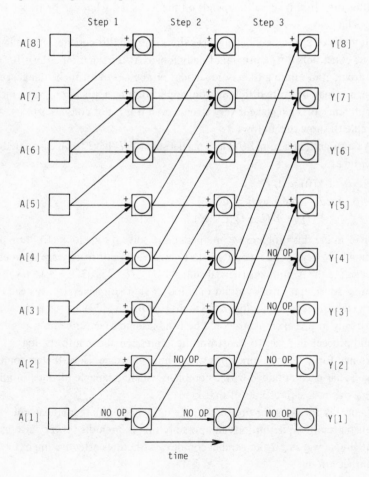

parison with which conventional Princeton structures resemble single-celled beings.

In section 2 an ordering scheme was offered which allocated each structure of all possible computers a point in a classification space or (for so-called flexible structures) a set of points in this space.

In such a way historic computers, existing contemporary computers, and all future computers one can think of are to be classifiable. In particular it is possible to classify complicated composed structures consisting of a number of possibly quite different processors. The classification scheme called the Erlangen Classification System (ECS) is so far mainly suited to classify structures of control units (CUs) and arithmetical and logical units (ALUs) and their interrelationships. Extensions are intended to include memory connections as well as data exchange networks. This latter area is not covered in this presentation.

In section 3 a case study was presented. The versatile EGPA project was described to clarify contemporary architectural considerations and mainly to give an example of 'versatility' (flexibility), a term that was introduced in section 2. In this sense versatility is the multiple utilization of hardware in the form of different operation modes or different kinds of interpretation. EGPA is supposed to be a most viable research vehicle and allows sophisticated and diversified investigations.

In section 4 more general points of view were given. Obstacles and prejudices were investigated in order to give ideas for their surmounting. The last point seems to be worth investigating in more detail. It says that the reason for a certain stagnation in computer architecture is not the lack of technology but a mental block where traditional ideas, language, standards etc. of different disciplines come together. This mental attitude is also able to explain the archaic thinking with respect to programming and use in terms of Princeton computers over at least thirty years (compare also [29]).

The last point should be made more forcibly by giving an example, probably known to the psychologist. Let us assume that a brain twister has been given, which demands a certain shape is partitioned (figure 1.25) into four congruent parts. Also assuming that the participants are not familiar with the solution of that particular brain twister one would try to solve the task by inserting lines in different ways. It seems one is very close to the solution if one gets a partition with four similar shapes (figure 1.26). But these shapes are not congruent, as is required. Therefore in this test participants continue with their trials. A particular consideration could be stating that twelve squares can be designed from the given shape. Dividing by four, one has three squares, which may possibly form the elementary shape we are searching for. Many other considerations may be thought of until the proper solution is found (figure 1.27).

The 'game' continues now. The psychologist makes a remark like: 'Now we are coming to a more difficult task. A shape of a slightly different kind has to be divided into five congruent parts.' Now it is interesting to see that most participants begin to proceed in exactly the same way they did with the first task. In such a way they get e.g. four squares (figure 1.28) or they insert 45-degree lines again. Nevertheless they fail to find the only possible simple solution, which consists of four straight parallel lines dividing the given square into five con-

Figure 1.25. A brain twister: the shape should be partitioned into four congruent parts.

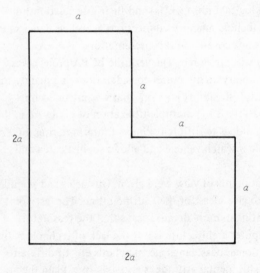

Figure 1.26. Partition into four similar, but not congruent, shapes.

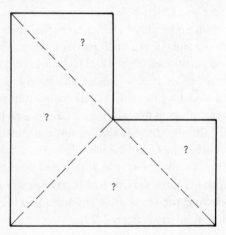

gruent strips. An equivalent solution may be found if the lines are turned through 90 degrees.

The reader may try to perform the test with his family or friends. He will probably have similar experiences that after the first part of the test the participant or participants seem to have passed over to a very strange 'state', in which they are not capable of solving the second part of the test. This would not be the case if the test were performed in the reverse direction. The participants would definitely solve the very easy task immediately.

The situation in computer science and particularly in computer architecture seems to be very similar in some respects. For approximately thirty years of

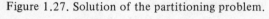

Figure 1.27. Solution of the partitioning problem.

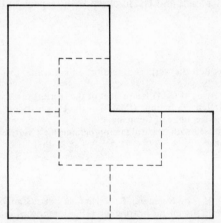

Figure 1.28. The shape should be partitioned into five congruent shapes.

research all considerations started with the classical Princeton computer and with the kind of programming utilizing it. People have learned to think as a consequence in terms of multiprogramming, time-sharing, front-end computers etc., which in reality are answers to problems, while they have forgotten the problems.

In the context of computer architecture it seems to be important to strengthen the consciousness on the one hand with respect to the real problems and on the other hand to the present-day technological possibilities which have entirely changed the scene. Extensive research has to be done in this field for at least the next two decades.

Acknowledgements

I am obliged to the pleasant help of my staff and in particular to Dr A. Bode, R. Kilgenstein, P. Schapelt and U. Hercksen with respect to the final version of this publication.

Notes

1 The available descriptions call it the 'vertical processor'. In our context we would prefer to say 'vertical ALUs'.
2 Erlangen General Purpose Array (EGPA) is a project of the Institut für Mathematische Maschinen und Datenverarbeitung (IMMD) of the University of Erlangen-Nürnberg, Federal Republic of Germany.
3 The term must not be confused with 'vertical microprogramming', 'vertical migration' and similar terms.

References

[1] Burks, A. W.; Goldstine, H. H.; von Neumann, J.: 'Preliminary discussion of the logical design of an electronic computing instrument' (1946), reprinted in: Randell, B. (ed.): *The Origins of Digital Computers*, Springer (1973), pp. 371–85
[2] Händler, W.: 'On classification schemes for computer systems in the post-von-Neumann-era', in *Proceedings of the 4th GI-Jahrestagung 1974*, Lecture Notes in Computer Science, Springer (1975), pp. 439–52
[3] Händler, W.: 'The impact of classification schemes on computer architecture', in *Proceedings of the 1977 International Conference on Parallel Processing*, IEEE, New York (1977), pp. 7–15
[4] Händler, W.: 'Zur Genealogie, Struktur und Klassifizieren von Rechnern', *Arbeitsberichte des IMMD*, 9, 8 (1976), 1–30

see also:

Bode, A.; Händler, W.: 'Classification d'architectures parallèles: introduction de la notation ECS et application au projet EGPA, RAIRO Informatique, *Computer Science*, 12, 4 (1978), 317–31
[5] van der Poel, W. L.: 'A simple electronic computer', *Applied Science Research*, 2 (1952), 367
[6] Poesch, H.; Fromme, T.: 'Programmorganisation bei kleinen Automaten mit innerem Programm', *ZAMM*, 34 (1954), 307–8
[7] Thornton, J. E.: *Design of a Computer: the Control Data 6600*, Foresman and Company, Glenview, Illinois (1970)
[8] Hintz, R. G.; Tate, D. P.: 'Control Data Star-100 processor design', in *COMPCON 72*, IEEE, New York (1972)

[9] Watson, W. J.: 'The TIASC – a highly modular and flexible super computer architecture', in *AFIPS FJCC 72*, AFIPS Press (1972), pp. 221–8

[10] Reddaway, S. F.: 'An elementary array with processing and storage capabilities', in *International Workshop on Computer Architecture, Grenoble (June 1973)*, pp. 1–25

[11] Barnes, G. H.; Brown, R. M.; Maso Kato et al.: 'The ILLIAC IV computer', *IEEE-Trans.*, C-17, 8 (1968), 746–57

[12] Thurber, K. J.: *Large Scale Computer Architecture*, Hayden Book Company (1976)

[13] Enslow, P. H. Jr. (ed.): *Multiprocessors and Parallel Processing*, Comtre Corporation, John Wiley and Sons, New York (1974)

[14] Händler, W.; Hofmann, F.; Schneider, H. J.: 'A general purpose array with a broad spectrum of applications', in *Proceedings of the Workshop on Computer Architecture*, IFB, Springer, Vol. 4 (1975), pp. 311–35

[15] Batcher, K. E.: 'Staran Series E', in *Proceedings of the 1977 Intern. Conference on Parallel Processing*, IEEE, New York (1977), pp. 140–3

[16] Händler, W.: 'Unconventional computation by conventional equipment', *Arbeitsberichte des IMMD*, 7, 2, University of Erlangen–Nürnberg (1974)

see also:

Händler, W.; Klar, R.: 'Fitting processors to the needs of a general purpose array (EGPA)', in *Proceedings of Micro-8*, IEEE/ACM, Chicago (1975), pp. 87–97
Bode, A.: 'Vertical processing: the emulation of associative and parallel behavior on conventional hardware', in *Proceedings of EUROMICRO '80*, Sami, Thompson, Mezzalira (eds.), North-Holland, London (1980), pp. 215–20

[17] Albert, B.; Bode, A.; Jacob, R.; Kilgenstein, R.; Rathke, M.: 'Vertikalverarbeitung: Beschleunigung von Anwenderprogrammen durch mikroprogrammierte Assoziativbefehle', in *Proceedings of 'Hardware für Software'*, Hauer, Seeger (eds.), Teubner (1980), pp. 114–23

see also:

Bode, A.; Händler, W.: 'Parallel and associative processing by extending a microprogrammed general purpose processor', to be published

[18] Kuck, D. J.: *The Structure of Computers and Computation*, John Wiley and Sons, Inc. (1978), Vol. I

[19] Hercksen, U.; Klar, R.; Kleinöder, W.: 'Hardware-Measurements of Storage Access Conflicts in the Processing Array EGPA', in *Proceedings of the 7th International Symposium on Computer Architecture, La Baule (1980)*, pp. 317–24

[20] Händler, W.: *Aspects of parallelism in computer architecture: Parallel Computers – Parallel Mathematics*, Feilmeier (ed.), North-Holland, Amsterdam, New York, Oxford (1977), pp. 1–8

[21] Leiner, A. L.; Notz, W. A.; Smith, J. C.; Weinberger, A.: 'PILOT, the NBS Multicomputer System', in *Proceedings of the Eastern Joint Computer Conference (1958)*, pp. 71–5

[22] Keidel, W. D.: *Sinnesphysiologie, Teil 1: Allgemeine Sinnesphysiologie, Visuelles System*, Springer Verlag, Berlin (1971)

[23] Thompson, Sir W.: *Proceedings of the Royal Society*, Vol. XXIV (1876), 271

[24] Korn, G. A.: 'Back to parallel computation: proposal for a completely new on-line simulation system using standard minicomputers for low-cost multiprocessing', *Simulation* (Aug. 1972), 37–45

[25] Thurber, K. J.; Patton, P. C.: 'The future of parallel processing', *IEEE, Transactions on Computers*, C-22 (Dec. 1971), pp. 1140–3

[26] Estrin, G.: 'Organization of computer systems: The fixed plus variable structure computer', in *Proceedings of WJCC (1960)*, pp. 33–40

[27] Burks, A.: Personal communication

[28] Whorf, B. L.: *Language, Thought and Reality*, MIT Press, Massachusetts (1963)

[29] Backus, J.: 'Can programming be liberated from the von Neumann style? A functional style and its algebra of programs', *CACM*, 21, 8 (1978), 613–41

2 Parallel control in distributed systems – a discussion of models

PHILIP H. ENSLOW Jr and TIMOTHY G. SAPONAS

Summary

Parallel processing has been a popular approach to improving system performance through several generations of computer systems design. Although it is not usually characterized as a 'parallel' processing system, a distributed processing system has the inherent capability for highly parallel operation. In order to capitalize on the potential performance improvements achievable by a distributed system, major parallel control problems must be solved. Central to the issue of parallel control is the design and implementation of distributed and decentralized control. A study of models for decentralized control has been initiated with this survey.

1 Background

1.1 Goals of computer system development

It is somewhat remarkable that the goals motivating most computer system development projects have remained basically unchanged since the earliest days of digital computers. Perhaps the most important of these long-sought-after improvements are the following:

1 Increased system productivity
  Greater capacity
  Shorter response time
  Increased throughput
2 Improved reliability and availability
3 Ease of expansion
4 Graceful growth and degradation
5 Improved ability to share system resources

These goals are not expressed in absolute numbers, so it is not surprising that they continue to apply even though phenomenal advances have been made in many of the areas such as speed, capacity, and reliability. What is noteworthy is how little progress has been made in areas such as modular growth, availability, adaptability, etc.

It seems that each new major systems concept or development (e.g., multi-programming, multiprocessing, networking, etc.) has been presented as 'the answer' to achieving all of these goals. 'Distributed processing' is no exception to this rule. In fact, many salesmen have dusted off their *old* lists of benefits and are marketing *today's* distributed systems as the answer to all of them. Although some forms of distributed processing appear to offer great promise as a means of making significant advances in many of the areas listed, the state of the art, particularly in system control software, is far from being able to deliver even a significant proportion of these benefits today.

1.2   Parallel processing systems

An important theme of computer system development work at both the 'system organization' and 'system software' levels has been *parallel processing*. It is important to note that parallel processing has been supported by both hardware and software.

Since the early days of computing a direction of research that has offered high promise has been that of 'parallel computing'. Work in this area dates from the late 1950s which saw the development of the PILOT system at the National Bureau of Standards. The PILOT system consisted of 'three independently operating computers that could work in cooperation' [Ensl74]. It is interesting to note that the development of parallel systems led to the development of other tightly-coupled systems such as the Burroughs B-825 and B-5000, the earliest examples of the classical multiprocessor. Other development paths saw the introduction of systems such as SOLOMON and the ILLIAC IV, examples of other forms of tightly-coupled processors.

1.2.1   Tightly-coupled computer systems

During the 1960s and 1970s activities in the development of parallel computing, specifically multiple computer systems, were focused primarily on the development of tightly-coupled systems. These tightly-coupled systems took the form of classical multiprocessors (i.e. shared main memory) as well as specialized computation systems such as vector and array processors. There was also significant activity in the development of loosely-coupled multiple computer systems as exemplified by the attached support processor concept. In the latter part of the 1970s vector and array processors were being connected to general computational systems and utilized as 'attached support processors'. In any event the specialized nature of the services provided by these 'ASP' systems exclude them from consideration as possible approaches to providing general-purpose computational support such as that available from tightly-coupled processors functioning as multiprocessors.

Although the concept of tightly-coupled multiprocessor systems seems like a valid approach to achieving almost unlimited improvements in performance with the addition of more processors, such has not been the result obtained with implemented systems. It is the very nature of tight-coupling that results in limitations on the improvements achievable. These limitations manifest themselves in the following ways:

1 The direct sharing of resources (memory and input/output primarily) results in access conflicts and delays in obtaining use of the shared resource.

2 User programming languages that support the effective utilization of tightly-coupled systems have not been adequately developed.

3 Any inefficiencies present in the operating system seem to be greatly exaggerated in a tightly-coupled system.

4 The development of 'optimal' schedules for the utilization of the processors is very difficult except in trivial or static situations. Also, the inability to maintain perfect synchronization between all processors often invalidates an 'optimal' schedule soon after it has been prepared.

Tightly-coupled systems certainly do have a role to play in the total spectrum of computer systems organization; however, their limitations should certainly be considered.

1.2.2 Loosely-coupled systems

Loosely-coupled systems are multiple computer systems in which the individual processors communicate with one another at the input/output level. There is no *direct* sharing of primary memory, although there may be sharing of an on-line storage device such as a disk in the input/output communication path. The important characteristic of this type of system is that all data transfer operations between the two systems are performed as input/output operations. The unit of data transferred is whatever is permissible on the particular input/output channel being utilized, and, in order to complete a transfer, the *active* cooperation of both processors is required (i.e., one must execute a READ operation in order to accommodate another's WRITE operation).

An important characteristic of loosely-coupled systems is that one processor does not have the capability to 'force' another processor to do something. It can deliver data across the interconnecting I/O path; however, even if that data is a request (or demand) for a service to be performed, the receiving processor, theoretically, has the full autonomous right to refuse that request. The reaction of processors to such requests for service is established by the operating system rules of the receiving processor, not by the transmitter. It is possible to have a system which is physically loosely-coupled but logically tightly-coupled due to the rules embodied in the operating system, e.g., a permanent master/slave relationship is defined.

1.2.3   Computer networks

A computer network can be characterized as a loosely-coupled multiple computer system in which the interconnection paths have been extended by the inclusion of data communications links. Fundamentally there are no differences between the basic characteristics of computer network systems and other loosely-coupled systems other than the data transfer rates normally provided. The transfer of data between two nodes still requires the cooperation of both parties and there is no inherent cooperation required between processors other than that which they wish to provide.

1.2.4   Distributed systems

Although there is a large amount of confusion, and often controversy, over exactly what is a 'distributed system', it is generally accepted that a distributed system is a computer network designed with some unity of purpose in mind. The components included in the system have been interconnected for the accomplishment of some identified common goal.

2   Introduction to FDPS

2.1   Motivation for an FDPS

Distributed processing systems are purported to provide a number of benefits including extensibility, integrity, performance, and resource sharing [Ensl78, Jens78]. The extensibility of these systems can be realized in several different forms. They might provide modular and incremental growth allowing for flexibility in the system's configuration, or they might support expansion in both capacity and in adding new functions. Finally, it might provide for incremental replacement or upgrading of system components (both hardware and software).

An increase in performance is also expected from a distributed system. The user should observe faster response time and an increase in system throughput. In addition, the utilization of system resources should be higher as a result of the ability to perform load balancing. A distributed system should also permit the sharing of data between cooperating users, making available specialized resources found only on certain processors. In general, a distributed system should provide more facilities than can be offered by any system composed of a single processor [Hopp79].

Most of these goals have been attempted in one form or another by various systems (e.g., multiprocessors, network machines). None of these, though, provides all the benefits cited above. To achieve all these goals, we advocate the development of Fully Distributed Processing Systems (FDPS).

2.2   *Definition of an FDPS*

A Fully Distributed Processing System (FDPS) as defined by Enslow [Ensl78] is distinguished by the following characteristics. First, an FDPS is composed of a multiplicity of general-purpose processors (i.e., processors that can be freely assigned to various tasks as required) physically connected by a network providing communication by means of a two-party protocol. The executive control in an FDPS must unify all logical and physical resources providing system transparency (i.e., services are requested by 'service name' rather than by a network address). System transparency is designed to aid rather than inhibit and, therefore, can be overridden. In other words, a user who is concerned about the performance of a particular application can provide system-specific information in order to guide its control. Finally, both the logical and physical components of an FDPS should interact in a manner described as 'cooperative autonomy' [Clar80, Ensl78]. This means that the components operate in an autonomous fashion requiring cooperation among processes for the exchange of information. In a cooperatively autonomous environment, the components are afforded the ability to refuse requests for services. This could result in anarchy except for the fact that all components follow a common master plan expressed by the philosophy of the executive control.

2.3   *Implications of the FDPS definition*
2.3.1   *Nature of an FDPS*

Several characteristics of an FDPS have an impact on the design of the executive control, including system transparency, cooperative autonomy, and extremely loose coupling. System transparency means that the FDPS appears to a user as a large uniprocessor which has available a variety of services. Services may be obtained by naming the desired service without specifying any information concerning the details of its physical location. The result is that the control is left with the task of locating all instances of a particular resource and choosing the instance to be utilized.

Cooperative autonomy is another characteristic of an FDPS affecting executive control. Both the logical and physical resource components of an FDPS are designed to operate in a cooperatively autonomous fashion. Thus, the control must be designed in such a manner that any resource is able to refuse a request even though it may have accepted the message containing the request. Degeneration into full anarchy is prevented by the criteria followed by all resources in the determination of whether a request may be rejected.

Another important FDPS characteristic that affects the design of the executive control is the extremely loose coupling of both physical and logical resources. The processors of an FDPS are connected by communication paths of relatively low bandwidth. (The direct sharing of memory between processors is prohibited.) This implies that the sharing of information among components on different processors is greatly curtailed, and the control is forced to work with information that is often out of date or inaccurate.

2.3.2   Why not a centralized control?

One of the first questions that comes to mind in the discussion of an FDPS is why a centralized method of control is not appropriate. In centralized systems the processes comprising the control share a coherent and deterministic view of the entire system state. An FDPS, though, contains only loosely-coupled components, and the communication among these components is variable and subjected to time delays. This means that one cannot guarantee that all processes will have the same view of the system state [Jens78].

A centralized control also presents problems in the area of fault-tolerance in the form of a single critical element, the control itself. This obstacle, though, is not insurmountable for strategies do exist for providing fault-tolerance in centralized applications. For example, Garcia-Molina [Garc79] describes a scheme for providing fault-tolerance in a distributed data base management system with a centralized control. These approaches typically assume that failures are extremely rare events and that the system can tolerate the dedication of a relatively long interval of time to reconfiguration. These restrictions are usually unacceptable to the basic control mechanism.

Finally, the issue of performance must be addressed. An application utilizing distributed resources is expected to utilize a large quantity of resources for control purposes. If control is realized in a centralized manner a large bottleneck will be created in the form of the node housing the control. A distributed and decentralized approach enables the bottleneck to be broken by dispersing the control decisions among multiple components on different nodes.

2.3.3   Distributed versus decentralized

This paper advocates utilizing a distributed and decentralized approach to control in an FDPS. There is a very important distinction between the terms 'distributed' and 'decentralized'. A distributed control is characterized by the location of its physical components on different nodes. This means there are multiple loci of activity. In a decentralized control, on the other hand, control decisions are made independently by different components. In other words, there are multiple loci of control. A distributed and decentralized control thus has physical components located on different nodes that are capable of making independent control decisions.

3 FDPS system models
3.1 Introduction

Models serve extremely important, if not essential, roles in the development of complex systems. This is especially true for systems in which the effects of complexity are further complicated by inconsistencies, ambiguities, and incompleteness in the use of the terms that are employed to describe the structure, as well as the operation of the systems involved and the components thereof. Suitable models are valuable tools to support and clarify such discussions. When examining or using any model it is equally important to recognize that it may have been prepared or developed for a specific purpose (e.g., logical or physical description, simulator design, implementation guide, etc.) and may not be totally suitable for other uses.

3.1.1 Why a new model?

Since the concepts of 'full distribution' were first conceived over four years ago members of the FDPS project have been plagued by severe problems in explaining the significance of various aspects of the definition of an FDPS. Most of these problems have been caused by the difficulties in clearly communicating the extremely important differences between 'fully' distributed systems and those that are merely 'distributed'. These problems in understanding often appear to result from the 'listener' incorrectly equating certain aspects of FDPS operation with those of a 'similarly appearing' distributed system. Such misunderstandings are not totally unreasonable, for some of the most significant differences are quite subtle. One highly desirable effect anticipated from 'new' system models is to prevent, or at least make more difficult, these undesirable associations with existing system concepts.

3.1.2 Approaches to modelling

There are a number of approaches that may be followed in the development of a system model, and the selection of the approach to be taken is based on intended uses for the model and the nature of the system being modelled.

There are basically six different types of models:

1 Physical structure model: Depicts the manner in which the various hardware and software components are *partitioned and packaged.*
2 Logical structure model: Focuses on the *functionality* provided by the hardware and software components and how they may be logically organized into modules.

3 Scenario or flow chart model: Depicts the *sequence of processing actions* taken on the data.

4 Interaction model: Focuses on the *interactions between processing entities* - services provided to or received from adjacent layer entities and the protocols governing the communication and negotiations that can occur between nonadjacent layers (see figure 2.1).

5 Analytic model: Focuses on the *performance of complete systems or subsystems.* Often the external performance characteristics of the system being modelled are available.

6 Simulation model: Depicts a system or subsystem by *modelling as close as possible the operations that it performs.* Provides more internal detail than an analytic model.

The various types of models discussed above *do not represent different ways to accomplish the same task.* Although there is some common information found in or derivable from two or more, each is actually focused on quite different aspects of the system description.

3.2 Other models

Although the work on FDPS models has certainly been strongly influenced by the numerous existing 'models' of multiprocessors, multiple computer systems, and computer networks, there has been very little influence from other 'distributed system' models since few have been developed to the

Figure 2.1. Protocols and interfaces.

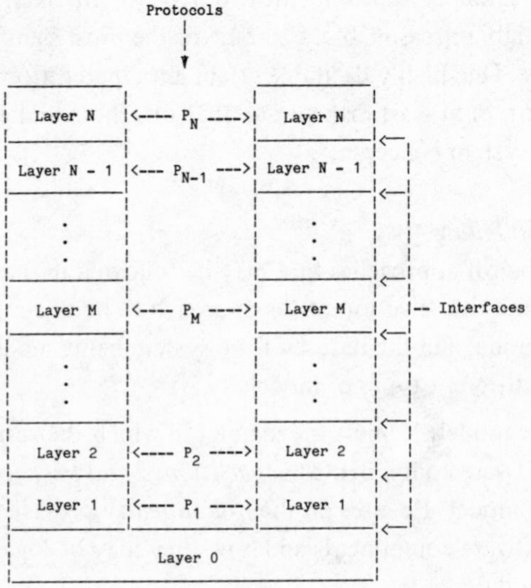

point that they can be closely analysed. One model that has had a great deal of influence on the development of the FDPS models, at least in guiding the manner in which these models are presented, is the 'Reference Model for Open System Interconnection' developed by the International Standards Organization (ISO) Study Committee 16.

3.2.1 The ISO Reference Model for OSI

The ISO Reference Model, a layered-interaction model, is being prepared to establish a framework for the development of standard protocols and interfaces as appropriate for the interconnection of heterogeneous nodes in a computer network. The ISO model is a 7-layer structure as shown in figure 2.2.

Although the ISO Reference Model has been influential in providing ideas and concepts applicable to a layered model of an FDPS, there are two major factors limiting its direct applicability:

The ISO model is almost totally concerned with communication between the nodes of a network. Some references are made to higher level protocols in the applications layer, but these are not a part of the OSI model.

Although it is not explicitly stated there appears to be a general assumption in the OSI model of a degree of coupling that is tighter than that anticipated for an FDPS. (This comment also applies to nearly all of the current network architectures – even those that include application layer protocols.)

Figure 2.2. The ISO Reference Model for OSI.

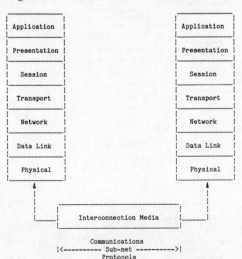

3.2.2   Protocol hierarchies

As stated above, the ISO Reference Model addresses only a subset of the protocols and interfaces that will be found in a complete distributed system. A more complete picture is shown in figure 2.3.

3.3   The FDPS models
3.3.1   The FDPS logical model

The current version of the FDPS logical model is organised into five layers above the 'physical interconnection' layer (figure 2.4). The important or significant characteristics of this logical model are:

1 It is also a rudimentary layered-interaction model; however, to be useful, the interaction model must delineate more layers.

2 The network operating system has been divided into two parts based on functionality and responsibilities:

   (*a*) The local operating system (LOS) is responsible for the detailed control and management of the users and resources at that node.

   (*b*) The distributed operating system (DOS) is responsible for interactions between this node and all others.

Figure 2.3. A complete protocol hierarchy.

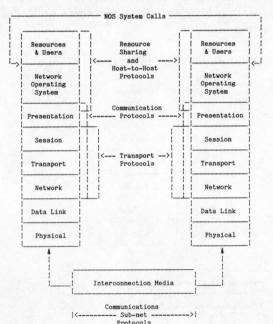

3 The correlation of FDPS layers and ISO layers is

FDPS layers	ISO layers
Users and resources	
Local operating system	Application
Distributed operating system	
Message handler	Presentation
	Session
	Transport
Message transporter	Network
	Data link
	Physical

3.3.2 The FDPS physical model

A physical model for the FDPS operating systems is shown in figure 2.5. This is a good example of how logical models and physical models may differ. In figure 2.5 the division between the LOS and DOS layers of the logical model runs horizontally through the MANAGERS.

3.3.3 FDPS interaction model

All the individual layers of the FDPS interaction model have not yet been identified; however, a more detailed list of the protocols that may be

Figure 2.4. Logical model of a control.

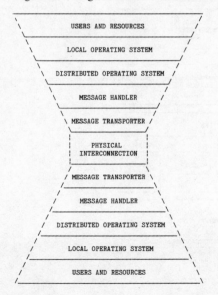

loosely related to figure 2.3 is given in figure 2.6. This list of protocols is especially significant to the FDPS research project since it identifies those specific area in which design work must be done.

4   Issues of control

Before examining specific aspects of control in an FDPS, a look at various issues of control is appropriate. There are basically three issues that need examining; the effect of the dynamics of an FDPS on the control, the nature of the information the control element must maintain, and the principles to be utilized in the design of the control.

4.1   Dynamics

Dynamics is an inherent characteristic of the operation of an FDPS. Aspects of dynamics can be found in the workload presented to the system, the availability of resources, and the individual work requests submitted. The dynamic nature of each of these provides the control with many unique problems.

Figure 2.5. Physical model of an FDPS network operating system.

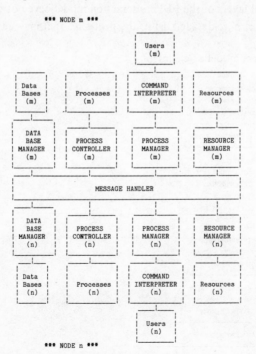

4.1.1 Workload presented to the system

In an FDPS work requests can be generated either by users or active processes and can arrive at any processor. Such work requests can potentially require the use of resources on any processor. Thus, the control must be able to respond to requests arriving at a variety of locations from a variety of sources. Each request may require system resources located on any node. One of the goals of the system is to respond to these requests in such a manner that the load on the entire system is balanced.

4.1.2 Availability of resources

Another dynamic aspect of the FDPS environment concerns the availability of the resources of the system. As mentioned above, a request for a system resource can originate from any location in the system. In addition, there may be multiple copies of a resource or possibly multiple resources that provide the same functionality (e.g., there may be functionally equivalent **FORTRAN** compilers on several nodes). Since resources are not immune to failures, the possibility of losing existing resources or gaining both new and old resources exists.

Figure 2.6. Classifications of computer network protocols.

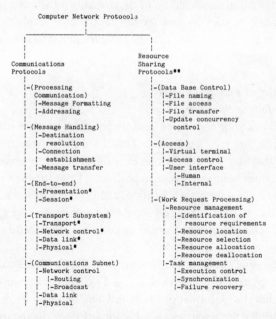

```
        Computer Network Protocols
       _____|_____
      |                               |
      |                               |
      |                         Resource
Communications                  Sharing
Protocols                       Protocols**
      |                               |
      |-(Processing                   |-(Data Base Control)
      |  Communication)               |   |-File naming
      |  |-Message Formatting         |   |-File access
      |  |-Addressing                 |   |-File transfer
      |                               |   |-Update concurrency
      |-(Message Handling)            |       control
      |  |-Destination                |
      |  |  resolution                |-(Access)
      |  |-Connection                 |   |-Virtual terminal
      |  |  establishment             |   |-Access control
      |  |-Message transfer           |   |-User interface
      |                               |       |-Human
      |-(End-to-end)                  |       |-Internal
      |  |-Presentation*              |
      |  |-Session*                   |-(Work Request Processing)
      |                               |   |-Resource management
      |-(Transport Subsystem)         |   |   |-Identification of
      |  |-Transport*                 |   |   |   resource requirements
      |  |-Network control*           |   |   |-Resource location
      |  |-Data link*                 |   |   |-Resource selection
      |  |-Physical*                  |   |   |-Resource allocation
      |                               |   |   |-Resource deallocation
      |-(Communications Subnet)       |   |-Task management
      |  |-Network control            |       |-Execution control
      |  |  |-Routing                 |       |-Synchronization
      |  |  |-Broadcast               |       |-Failure recovery
      |  |-Data link
      |  |-Physical


 * Classifications (layers) defined by the ISO and CCITT
   Network Architecture Models

 ** A preliminary list for FDPS's
```

Therefore, the control must be able to manage system resources in a dynamic environment in which the availability of a resource is unpredictable.

4.1.3 Individual work requests

Finally, there is the dynamic nature of the individual work requests. As mentioned above, these work requests define, either directly or indirectly, a set of cooperating processes to be invoked. Any of these processes may be command files which contain additional work requests. The main problem is to control these processes and do so in such a manner that the inherent parallelism of the operation is exploited to the maximum. In addition, the control must also handle the situation in which one or more of the processes fail.

4.2 Information

All control systems require information in order to function and perform their mission. The characteristics of the available information is one aspect of fully distributed systems that results in the following somewhat unique control problems:

> Because of the nature of the interconnection links information on hand is *always out of date.*
>
> Because of the autonomous nature of the operation of all components each processor can make 'its own decision' as to how to reply to an inquiry; therefore, there is always the *possibility* that information received is *incomplete or inaccurate.*

5 Characteristics of a control model

5.1 Basic operations of the control

The applications to be considered here are presented to the control in terms of a work request that specifies a series of tasks and their connectivity. The tasks to be executed may consist of either executable programs or command files. The control has three basic operations to perform: (1) information gathering, (2) work distribution and resource allocation, and (3) task execution. These operations need not be executed in a purely serial fashion but may take a more complex form with operations executed simultaneously or concurrently as the opportunity arises.

Examination of the basic operations in further detail (figure 2.7) reveals possible variations in the handling of work requests. Two steps exist in information gathering – (1) collecting information about task requirements for the work request and (2) identifying the resources available for satisfying the request. Information gathering is followed by the task of distributing the work and allocating resources. If this operation is not successful, three alternatives are available. First, more information can be gathered in an attempt to formulate a new work distribution. Second, more information can be gathered as above, but this time the requester will indicate a willingness to 'pay more' for the resources (this is referred to as bidding to a higher level). Finally, the user can simply be informed that it is impossible to satisfy his work request.

5.2   *Information requirements*

In accomplishing the operations mentioned above, the control must maintain two types of information: information about system resources and information about the structure of the set of tasks required to satisfy the work request. System resource information records the utilization of the system's resources. The task set information is specific to each individual work request and identifies the tasks identified in the work request and the connectivity of these tasks.

Each work request identifies a set of cooperating processes to be used to satisfy the request. These processes are referred to as 'tasks', and the collection

Figure 2.7. Work request processing.

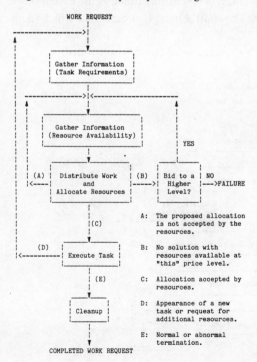

of these tasks is called a task set. The task set control information is collected in a structure, the task graph, which contains information describing the needed resources (files, processors, and special peripheral devices) and the connectivity (for purposes of interprocess communication) of the individual tasks comprising the task set.

The control must also maintain information on all system resources (processors, communication lines, files, and special peripheral devices). This information will include at a minimum an indication of the availability of resources (available, reserved, or assigned). Pre-emptible resources (e.g., processors and communication lines) capable of accommodating more than one user at a time may also have associated with them utilization information designed to guide the control in its effort to perform load balancing.

5.3   Information gathering

Upon receiving a work request the first task of the control is to gather information on the resources needed to satisfy the work request (figure 2.8) and the resources available to fill these needs (figure 2.9). Each work request includes a description of a series of tasks and the connectivity of those tasks. Associated with each task is a series of files. One is distinguished as the execution file and the rest are input/output files. The control must first determine which files are

Figure 2.8. Information gathering (resources required).

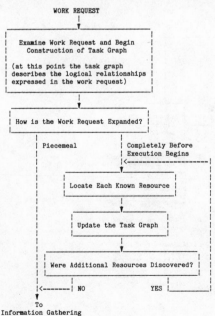

needed. It must then examine each of the execution files to determine the nature of its contents (executable code or commands). Each task will need a processor resource, and those tasks containing command files will also require a command interpreter.

The control must also determine which of the system resources are available. For non-pre-emptible resources the status of a resource can be 'available', 'reserved', or 'assigned'. A reservation indicates that a resource may be used in the future and that it should not be given to another user. Typically, there is a time-out associated with a reservation that will result in the release of the reservation if an assignment is not made within a specified time interval. An assignment, on the other hand, indicates that a resource is dedicated to a user until the user explicitly releases the assignment. Pre-emptible resources may be accessed by more than one concurrent user and thus can be treated in a different

Figure 2.9. Information gathering (resources available). 1: Resources reserved during information gathering. 2: No resources reserved. 3: Some resources may be reserved. A: General, for all resources. B: To meet specific task/job requirements. C: Replies cover information on resources available only. D: Replies cover information on the total status. E: Broadcast only significant changes. F: Periodic broadcasts at regular intervals.

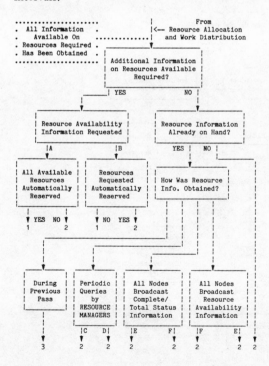

manner. For these resources the status may be indicated by continuous values
(e.g., the utilization of the resource) rather than the discrete values described
above.

5.4   *Work distribution and resource allocation*

Another decision of the control concerns the allocation of system
resources (figures 2.10 and 2.11). This process involves choosing from the available resources those that are to be utilized. This decision is designed to achieve
several goals including load balancing, maximum throughput, and minimum
response time. It can be viewed as an optimization problem similar in many
respects to that discussed by Morgan [Morg77].

Once an allocation has been determined, the processes comprising the task set
are scheduled and initiated. If a process cannot be scheduled immediately it may
be queued and scheduled at a later time. When it is scheduled, a process control
block and any other execution-time data structures must be created.

Figure 2.10. Resource allocation and work distribution.

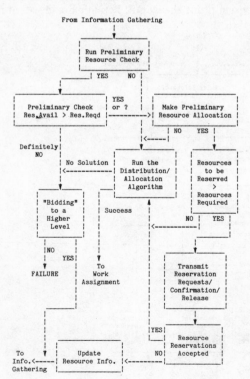

5.5   *Task execution*

Finally, the control must monitor the execution of active processes. This includes providing interprocess communication, handling requests from the active processes, and performing process termination. The tasks associated with interprocess communication include buffering messages and synchronizing communicating processes. The latter task is necessary to protect the system from processes that flood the system with messages before another process has time to absorb the messages. Active processes may also make requests of the control. These may take the form of requests for additional resources or possibly additional work requests. Work requests may originate from either command files or files containing executable code.

The termination of processes must be detected by the control. This includes both normal and abnormal termination. Any process needing to be informed of the termination must be so notified, open files closed, and other loose ends cleaned up. When the last of the processes of a work request has been terminated, the control must inform the originator of the request of its completion.

Figure 2.11. Work assignment.

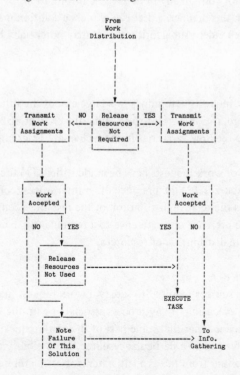

5.6 Fault recovery

If portions (tasks) of the work request are being performed on different processors, there is inherently a certain degree of fault recovery possible. The problem is in exploiting that capability. The ability to utilize 'good' work remaining after the failure of one or more of the processors executing a work request depends on the recovery agent having knowledge of the location of that work and the ability of the recovery agent to re-establish the appropriate linkages to the new locations for the portions of the work that were being executed on the failed processor.

6 Characterization of work requests

One of the goals of an FDPS is the ability to provide a hospitable environment for solving problems that allows one to utilize the natural distribution of data to obtain a solution which may take the form of an algorithm consisting of concurrent subalgorithms. The expression of the solution will be in terms of a work request that describes a series of cooperating processes, the connectivity of the processes (how the processes communicate), and the data files utilized by the processes. The description of the processes and data files reference logical entities and thus do not contain any node-specific information. By formulating work requests in this manner, a user can express a solution in terms of logical, configuration-independent subalgorithms that may potentially be executed concurrently.

6.1 Characteristics

The nature of work requests determines to a large extent the functionality of the control. Therefore, it is important to examine the characteristics of work requests and further to see how variations in these characteristics impact the strategies of control.

Five basic characteristics of work requests have been identified: (1) the visibility of references to resources; (2) the presence of an interprocess communication specification; (3) the relative distribution of the resources comprising the work request; (4) the presence of a reference to a redundantly maintained resource; and (5) the absolute distribution of resources.

6.1.1 Visibility of references to resources

References to the resources required to satisfy a work request may either be visible prior to the execution of any process associated with the work request or embedded in such a manner that some part of the work request must be executed to reveal the reference to a particular resource. The visibility of a resource reference results either from the explicit statement of the reference in

the work request or a declaration describing the reference that may be located
with little effort over that needed to locate the resource containing the reference.
An example of the latter means of visibility is a file system in which external
references made from a particular file are identified and stored in the 'header'
portion of the file. The identity of a reference can be obtained by simply
accessing the first portion of the file.

The greatest impact of the resource reference visibility characteristic occurs in
the construction of task graphs and the distribution of work. The timing of
resource reference resolution determines when the various parts of a task graph
can be constructed and which processes are required to take part in the construction procedure. Similarly, some work cannot be distributed until certain details
are resolved. For example, consider a system where resource references are not
resolved until execution time. If process X calls process Y, the control will not
be able to consider Y in the work distribution decision that must be made before
X can begin execution. The significance of this constraint imposed by characteristics of the work requests is that certain work distribution decisions may not be
'optimal' because total information is not available at the time the decision is made.

6.1.2   Interprocess communication

Another characteristic of the work requests is the presence or absence
of interprocess communication. The presence of interprocess communication
will affect both the work distribution decision and the control required during
execution. Experience has demonstrated that communication costs can be high,
and therefore the presence of interprocess communication is an important fact
that must be considered in a work distribution decision. In addition, if there is
communication between the processes of a work request, the control will have
to provide the means for passing messages, buffering messages, and providing
synchronization to insure that a reader does not underflow and a writer does
not overflow the message buffers.

6.1.3   The relative distribution of resources

How the resources of a work request are distributed (on the nodes of
the FDPS) relative to each other affects both the construction of task graphs and
the control required during execution. In certain models the presence of distributed resources results in the construction of task graphs, which pertain to
a particular work request, on multiple nodes. These task graphs may be replicated versions of the same task graph or multiple task graphs that, taken
together, describe the complete work request.

This distribution also affects how execution control is provided. The important issues here are controlling the activation of processes, controlling the

termination of processes and the associated cleanup operations, detecting failures and then recovering, and reporting results to users and processes requiring termination information. Each of these issues can be approached in a variety of ways resulting in a number of different control models.

6.1.4   *References to resources with redundant copies*

In an FDPS certain resources may exist as redundant copies for reasons of performance or fault-tolerance. The presence of references to these resources in a work request affects the work distribution decision by providing alternative choices for certain resources. In addition, the presence of redundant resources introduces the problem of maintaining the consistency of the resources. This may be accomplished by a concurrency control or a simple resource locking scheme

6.1.5   *The absolute distribution of resources*

The final work distribution characteristic to be considered concerns the absolute distribution of the resources referenced in the work request. The concern here is whether the resources that are referenced reside on the same node where the work request arrived or on another node or nodes. These differences lead to variations in task graph building as well as work distribution and execution control.

6.1.6   *Summary of work request characteristics*

There are thirty-two different combinations possible for the characteristics discussed above. It should be noticed, however, that several of these combinations are impossible because they contain conflicting characteristics. These conflicts demonstrate that the characteristics are not independent, but they do represent distinct issues that significantly affect the design and operation of the control. Therefore, their study is important to achieving a better understanding of control in an FDPS.

7   **Variations in control models**

Having described the functionality required of a control for an FDPS, we can now investigate the different variations available for realizing that functionality. The basic issues upon which different models can be based include the nature of how and when a task graph is constructed, the maintenance of resource availability information, the allocation of resources, process initiation, and process monitoring.

7.1.   **Task graph construction**

The task graph is a data structure used to maintain information about a task set. The nodes of a task graph represent the tasks of the task set, and the arcs represent the hierarchical relationships between tasks and the connectivity or flow of information between tasks. There are basically three issues in task graph construction: (1) who builds the task graph, (2) where the copies of the task graph are stored, and (3) when the task graph is built.

The identity of the component or components involved in the construction of a task graph is an issue that presents three basic choices. First, a central node can be responsible for the construction of all task graphs for all work requests. Another choice is for the control component on the node receiving the work request to construct the task graph. Finally, the job of building the task graph can be distributed among several components. In particular, the nodes involved in executing individual tasks of the work request can be responsible for constructing those parts of the task graph which they are processing.

Another issue of task graph construction concerns the location of the copies of the task graph. One possibility is to maintain a task graph representing the complete task set. This may be stored on only one node or redundant copies may be maintained on several nodes. The nodes containing the copies may be nodes specifically assigned the responsibility of maintaining task graphs or they may be the nodes that are executing part of the work request. Alternatively, the task graph could be divided into several subgraphs and these maintained on several nodes that may or may not be involved in the execution of the work request. Thus, there are basically two different issues: (1) a task graph can be maintained either as a single unit or as a series of subgraphs, and (2) a task graph or its subgraphs can be maintained either on nodes specializing in the maintenance of task graphs or nodes involved in receiving, or executing parts of a work request.

Finally, there is the issue concerning the timing of task graph construction in the sequence of work request processing. Two choices are available: (1) the task graph can be constructed completely, as far as possible, before execution is begun, or (2) the task graph can be constructed incrementally as execution progresses.

7.2 Resource availability information

Another issue upon which control models may vary is the maintenance of resource availability information. The main issues here are concerned with which components maintain this information and where it is maintained. The latter question includes the possibility of maintaining redundant availability information. A particular model need not uniformly apply the same technique for maintaining resource availability information on all resources. Rather, the technique best suited to a particular resource class may be utilized.

The responsibility for maintaining resource availability information can be delegated in a variety of ways. The centralized approach involves assigning a single component this responsibility. In this situation, requests and releases of resources flow through this specialized component which maintains the complete resource availability information in one location.

A variation of this technique maintains complete copies of the resource availability information at several locations [Caba79a,b]. Components at each of these locations are responsible for updating their copy of the resource availability information. This requires a protocol that insures the consistent operation of all components. For example, two components should not release a file for writing to different users at the same time. To provide this control, messages containing updates for the information tables must be exchanged among the components. In addition, a strategy for synchronizing the release of resources (e.g., passing a baton which permits the holder to release resources [Caba79a,b]) is required.

Another approach exhibiting more decentralization requires dividing the collection of resources into subsets or classes and assigning separate components to each subset. Each component is responsible for maintaining resource availability information on a particular subset. In this case, requests for resources can only be serviced by the control component responsible for that resource. Resources may either be named in such a manner that the desired manager is readily identifiable or a search for the appropriate manager can be utilized where control is passed from component to component until a component capable of providing service is discovered.

Pre-emptible resources which can be shared by multiple concurrent users (e.g., processors and communication lines) do not necessarily require the maintenance of precise availability information. For these resources, it is reasonable to maintain only approximate availability information because such resources are rarely exhausted. The primary concern in these instances is degraded performance.

7.3   *Allocating resources*

A major issue in allocating resources is concurrency control. It is possible in a hospitable environment to ignore concurrency control. In other environments this becomes an important issue that is made even more difficult in the FDPS case due to the loose-coupling inherent in this type of system. The control has basically two approaches to solving this problem. One is to introduce the concept of a reservation, which entails allowing a user to reserve a resource prior to the actual allocation and thus provide the work distribution component with reserved resources. The other technique involves making the work distribution without any reservations. In the latter case if the chosen resources cannot be allocated, the control can either wait until they can be allocated or attempt a new work distribution.

7.4   Process initiation

Several issues arise in process initiation. Chief among these is the distribution of responsibility. One possibility is to place a single component in complete charge of the entire task graph. It supervises separate components that are responsible for the execution of individual processes comprising the task graph. This hierarchy can be carried one step further to provide a control in which the component assuming responsibility for the complete task graph supervises components responsible for disjoint pieces of the task graph that further supervise components in charge of individual processes. The distribution of responsibility need not necessarily take a hierarchical form. For example, there may be no single component assuming responsibility for the complete task graph, but rather multiple components may exist that take charge of disjoint subgraphs of the complete task graph.

Regardless of the distribution, at some point a request for the assumption of responsibility by a component will be made. A component may reasonably deny such a request for two reasons: (1) the component does not possess enough resources to satisfy the request (e.g., there may not be enough space to place a new process on an input queue), or (2) the component may not be functioning. The question that arises concerns how this denial is handled. One solution is to keep trying the request either until it is accepted or until a certain number of attempts have failed. It is also possible to attempt to formulate a new work distribution decision that is made with the new knowledge that a certain component failed to accept a previous request.

7.5   Process monitoring

The task of monitoring the progress of the processes comprising the task set consists of two parts, providing interprocess communication (IPC) and handling requests. It is assumed that IPC is provided by means of ports [Balz71, Have78, Suns77, Zuck77] and that special control components called port managers are responsible for managing IPC. The issues here include the buffering of messages and the synchronization of communicators. To allow communicators the opportunity to execute in parallel, there needs to be some buffer space associated with each port. The nature and location of this space leads to different control designs. Another problem facing the control is that of synchronizing the communicators. This is necessary to prevent an overactive writer from utilizing a large amount of buffer space before its corresponding reader can remove some of the messages.

The task of monitoring processes also involves processing requests generated by the executing tasks. These may be either requests for additional resources (e.g., an additional file) or new work requests. One question concerns the selection of the control component to receive the request and assume responsibility for seeing that the request is satisfied. If the request is a work request, there is also the question of how the new task set is to be associated with the existing task set. The new task set could be combined with the old one creating a new and larger task set, or it could be kept separate from the old set with the only connection to the old set being the task that originated the new work request.

7.6 Process termination

When a process terminates there is always some cleanup work that must be accomplished (e.g., closing files, returning memory space, and deleting records concerning the process from the control's work space). In addition, depending on the reason for termination (normal or abnormal), other control components may need to be informed of the termination. The nature of the cleanup and the identity of the control components that must be informed of the termination is determined from the design decisions resulting from the issues discussed above.

7.7 Examples

To better appreciate the issues of control in an FDPS, it is appropriate to examine an example of work request processing on an FDPS. The work distribution decision that is utilized is the simple one that distributes processes in such a manner that they execute on the same nodes that house the files containing their code. In example 1 (figure 2.12) the following symbols are utilized:

[ ]   visible external reference
{ }   embedded external reference
$(n)A$ responsibility delegated from node n
$A(n)$ responsibility delegated to node n
$a\text{--}\rangle b$ IPC from process a to process b
$A,B,\dots$ uppercase letters indicate command files
$a,b,\dots$ lowercase letters indicate executable files
u,v,w,x,y,z indicates data files

This example has resources spread across two nodes. There is an IPC link between two processes that reside on different nodes. Since all resources do not reside on the source node, negotiation is required to transfer responsibility for a portion of the task graph. In addition, the presence of the IPC link requires that control be organized to handle the communication across nodes. A more detailed view concerning the details of work request processing is provided by two figures. Figure 2.13 outlines the basic steps involved in work request processing, and

Figure 2.12. Example 1.

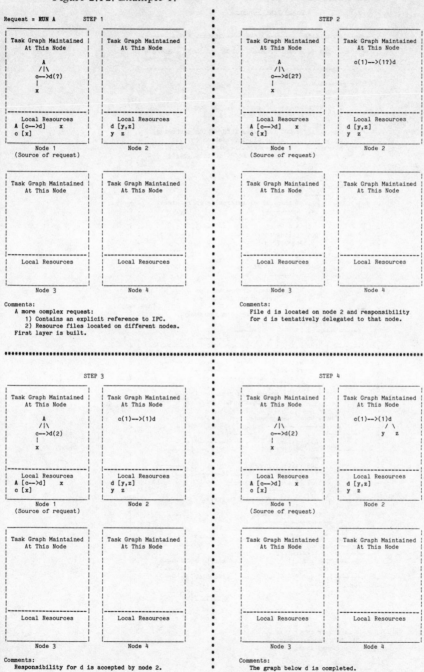

```
Request = RUN A        STEP 1                                          STEP 2

 Task Graph Maintained    Task Graph Maintained          Task Graph Maintained    Task Graph Maintained
    At This Node             At This Node                    At This Node             At This Node

         A                                                        A                  c(1)-->(1?)d
        /|\                                                      /|\
     c-->d(?)                                                 c-->d(2?)
       |                                                        |
       x                                                        x

 ----------------------   ----------------------         ----------------------   ----------------------
   Local Resources          Local Resources                Local Resources          Local Resources
 A [c-->d]     x           d [y,z]                        A [c-->d]     x           d [y,z]
 c [x]                     y  z                           c [x]                     y  z

       Node 1                  Node 2                           Node 1                  Node 2
   (Source of request)                                     (Source of request)


 Task Graph Maintained    Task Graph Maintained          Task Graph Maintained    Task Graph Maintained
    At This Node             At This Node                    At This Node             At This Node




 ----------------------   ----------------------         ----------------------   ----------------------
   Local Resources          Local Resources                Local Resources          Local Resources


       Node 3                  Node 4                           Node 3                  Node 4
Comments:                                                Comments:
 A more complex request:                                  File d is located on node 2 and responsibility
   1) Contains an explicit reference to IPC.              for d is tentatively delegated to that node.
   2) Resource files located on different nodes.
 First layer is built.
```

```
          STEP 3                                                    STEP 4

 Task Graph Maintained    Task Graph Maintained          Task Graph Maintained    Task Graph Maintained
    At This Node             At This Node                    At This Node             At This Node

         A                  c(1)-->(1)d                          A                  c(1)-->(1)d
        /|\                                                     /|\                    / \
     c-->d(2)                                                c-->d(2)                 y   z
       |                                                        |
       x                                                        x

 ----------------------   ----------------------         ----------------------   ----------------------
   Local Resources          Local Resources                Local Resources          Local Resources
 A [c-->d]     x           d [y,z]                        A [c-->d]     x           d [y,z]
 c [x]                     y  z                           c [x]                     y  z

       Node 1                  Node 2                           Node 1                  Node 2
   (Source of request)                                     (Source of request)


 Task Graph Maintained    Task Graph Maintained          Task Graph Maintained    Task Graph Maintained
    At This Node             At This Node                    At This Node             At This Node




 ----------------------   ----------------------         ----------------------   ----------------------
   Local Resources          Local Resources                Local Resources          Local Resources


       Node 3                  Node 4                           Node 3                  Node 4
Comments:                                                Comments:
 Responsibility for d is accepted by node 2.              The graph below d is completed.
```

Figure 2.13. Basic steps in work request processing.

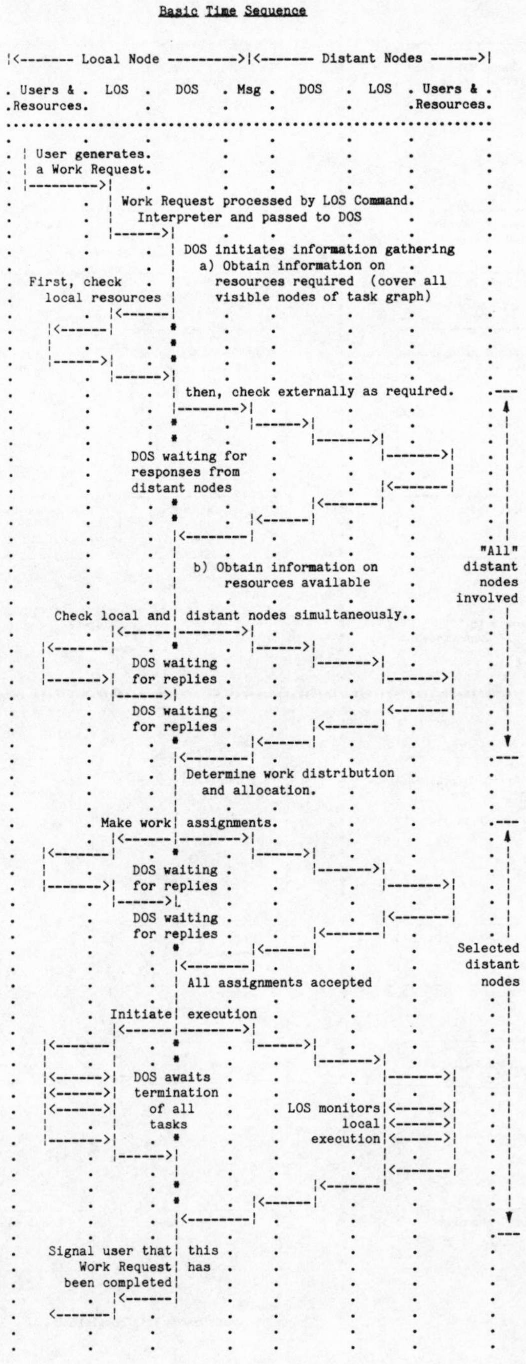

```
                         Basic Time Sequence


|<------- Local Node ---------->|<------- Distant Nodes ------>|
. Users & . LOS  .  DOS  . Msg .  DOS  .  LOS  . Users & .
.Resources.       .       .     .       .       .Resources.
..........................................................
 .        .       .       .     .       .       .       .
 . | User generates.      .     .       .       .       .
 . | a Work Request.      .     .       .       .       .
 . |-------->|     .       .     .       .       .       .
 .        .  | Work Request processed by LOS Command.     .
 .        .  | Interpreter and passed to DOS      .       .
 .        .  |------>|     .     .       .       .       .
 .        .       .  | DOS initiates information gathering .
 .        .       .  |   a) Obtain information on  .       .
 .        .       .  |      resources required  (cover all .
 . First, check   .  |      visible nodes of task graph)   .
 . local resources |  |<------|  .       .       .       .
 .        . |<------|  •     .     .       .       .       .
 .        . |       •  .     .     .       .       .       .
 .        . |------>|  .  •  .     .       .       .       .
 .        .       .  |------>|     .       .       .       .
 .        .       .  | then, check externally as required. .---
 .        .       .  |-------->|   .       .       .       . ▲
 .        .       •  .  .  |------>|       .       .       . |
 .        .       .  .     .   |------->|  |-------->|      . |
 .        .       . DOS waiting for .     .       |------->| . |
 .        .       . responses from .      .       .       . |
 .        .       . distant nodes  .      .  |<-------|    . |
 .        .       •  .     .       .   |<-------|  .       . |
 .        .       .  .   |<-------|      .       .       . |
 .        .       .  |<---------|  .     .       .       . |
 .        .       .  |       .     .     .       .       "All"
 .        .       .  | b) Obtain information on   . distant
 .        .       .  |    resources available     . nodes
 .        .       .  |       .     .     .       . involved
 . Check local and| distant nodes simultaneously.. . |
 .        . |<------|-------->|    .     .       .       . |
 . |<-------|  .  •  .  |------>|   .       .       .       . |
 . |       .  DOS waiting .     .   |------->|      .       . |
 . |------->| for replies .     .     .       |------->|    . |
 .        . |------>|     .     .     .       .       .       . |
 .        .       . DOS waiting .     .     .       .       . |
 .        .       . for replies .     .  |<-------|    .       . |
 .        .       •  .     . |<-------|   .       .       . ▼
 .        .       .  |<---------|   .     .       .       .---
 .        .       .  | Determine work distribution .       .
 .        .       .  |    and allocation. .       .       .
 .        .       .  |       .     .     .       .       .
 . Make work| assignments.  .     .     .       .       .---
 .        . |<------|-------->|    .     .       .       . ▲
 . |<-------|  .  •  .  |------>|   .       .       .       . |
 . |       .  DOS waiting .     .   |------->|      .       . |
 . |------->| for replies .     .     .       |------->|    . |
 .        . |------>|L    .     .     .       .       .       . |
 .        .       . DOS waiting .     .     .       .       . |
 .        .       . for replies .     .  |<-------|    .       . |
 .        .       •  .  |<-------|    .       .       . Selected
 .        .       .  |<---------|   .     .       . distant
 .        .       .  | All assignments accepted   . nodes
 .        .       .  |       .     .     .       .       . |
 . Initiate| execution .     .     .     .       .       . |
 .        . |<------|-------->|    .     .       .       . |
 . |<-------|  .  •  .  |------>|   .       .       .       . |
 . |       .  .     .     .   |------->|   .       .       . |
 . |<------>| DOS awaits .     .     .       |------->|    . |
 . |<------>| termination .     .     .       .       .       . |
 . |<------>| of all .     . LOS monitors|<------>|    .       . |
 . |       .  tasks .     .     local|<------>|    .       . |
 . |------->|  .  •  .  execution|<------>|    .       . |
 .        . |------>|     .     .     .       .       .       . |
 .        .       .  |     .     .     .       .       .       . |
 .        .       .  •     .     .  |<-------|    .       . |
 .        .       .  .   |<------|    .       .       . |
 .        .       .  |<---------|   .     .       .       . ▼
 .        .       .  |     .     .     .       .       .---
 . Signal user that| this .     .     .       .       .
 . Work Request| has .     .     .     .       .       .
 . been completed|  .     .     .     .       .       .
 .        . |<------|     .     .     .       .       .
 . <-------|  .     .     .     .     .       .       .
 .        .       .  .     .     .     .       .       .
```

Figure 2.14. An example of work request processing.

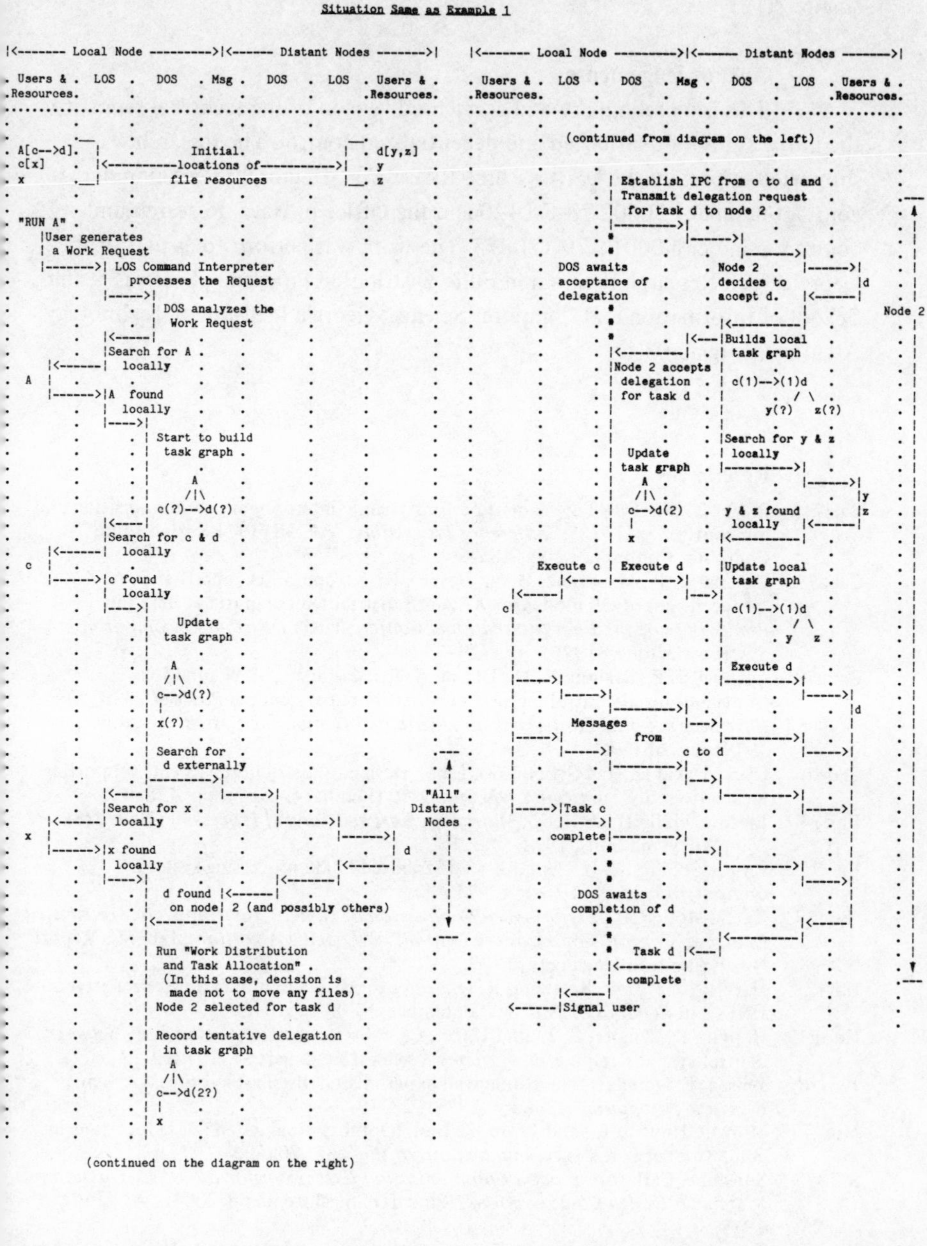

Situation Same as Example 1

```
|<------- Local Node ---------->|<------ Distant Nodes -------->|      |<-------- Local Node ---------->|<------ Distant Nodes ------->|
. Users & . LOS  . DOS  . Msg . DOS  . LOS  . Users & .           . Users & . LOS  . DOS  . Msg . DOS  . LOS  . Users & .
.Resources.      .      .     .      .      .Resources.           .Resources.      .      .     .      .      .Resources.
...............................................................   ...........................................................
.                .          .         .       .        .               (continued from diagram on the left)    .
. A[c-->d].    |           Initial.      .          |   d[y,z]   .      .        .      .     .      .      .      .
. c[x]    .    |<-----------locations of----------->|    . y     .      .        .      .     .      .      .      .
. x       .__| .    file resources        |__. z           .      .        .  | Establish IPC from c to d and .
.              .          .         .       .        .      .      .        .  | Transmit delegation request    .   .--
. "RUN A"  .              .         .       .        .      .      .        .  | for task d to node 2  .      .   . A
.  |User generates        .         .       .        .      .      .        .  |---------->|        .      .      . |
.  | a Work Request       .         .       .        .      .      .        .     •       . |------->|       .   . |
.  |------->| LOS Command Interpreter        .      .      . DOS awaits .   Node 2 . |------->|------->|      . |
.           |  processes the Request          .      .      . acceptance of .   decides to          |d    . |
.           |------->|            .       .        .      .      . delegation    .   accept d.  |<------|      . Node 2
.                   . | DOS analyzes the    .        .      .      .     •       .      . |<------------|       .   . |
.                   . |  Work Request        .        .      .      .     •       . |<---|Builds local        .   . |
.           |<------|          .       .        .      .      .      .     •       . | task graph        .   . |
.           |Search for A .        .       .        .      .      . |<------------| .          .      .      . |
. |<------|  locally    .        .       .        .      .      . |Node 2 accepts |         .      .      . |
. A |           .          .       .        .      .      . | delegation  .  c(1)-->(1)d     .      . |
. |------->|A found     .        .       .        .      .      . | for task d  .   . / \            .      . |
.     |   locally    .        .       .        .      .      . |          .     y(?)   z(?)        .   . |
.     |---->|        .        .       .        .      .      . |          .      .      .      .      . |
.          . | Start to build  .        .      .      .      . |Search for y & z  .      .      . |
.          . | task graph .      .        .      .      . | Update   . | locally     .      .      . |
.          . |         .       .        .      .      . | task graph . |------------>|     .      . |
.          . |    A   .        .       .        .      .      . |    A    .      . |------->|      . |
.          . |   /|\  .        .       .        .      .      . |   /|\   .      .      .  |y    . |
.          . | c(?)-->d(?)      .        .      .      . | c-->d(2)  . y & z found   .   . |
. |<------|          .       .        .      .      . |          . locally  |<------|      .|z    . |
. |Search for c & d .        .       .        .      .      . |          . |<------------|       .   . |
. c |<------| locally   .        .       .        .      . Execute c . Execute d .  |Update local        .   . |
. |------->|c found    .        .       .        .      .  |<-----|---------->|  . | task graph        .   . |
.     | locally     .        .       .        .      . |<----->|        .  |----->|        .      .      . |
.     |---->|        .        .       .        .      . c|       .        .   . c(1)-->(1)d     .      . |
.          . |  Update  .        .       .        .      . |          .      .   . | / \             .      . |
.          . | task graph .      .        .      .      . |          .      .   .  . y   z .          .   . |
.          . |         .       .        .      .      . |          .      .   . | Execute d .          .   . |
.          . |    A   .        .       .        .      . |------->|      .   . |---------->|       .      . |
.          . |   /|\  .        .       .        .      . |       |----->|      .      . |------->|      . |
.          . | c-->d(?)  .        .      .        .      . |          .  |------->|      .      .      .|d    . |
.          . |  |    .        .       .        .      . |          .      .   . |---------->|       .      . |
.          . | x(?)  .        .       .        .      . | Messages  . |--->|        .      .      . |
.          . |         .       .        .      .      . |------->|   from   .      . |------->|      . |
.          . | Search for .      .        .      . .---   . |          .  c to d   .   . |------->|      . |
.          . | d externally .    .        .      . . |    . |          .  |------->|      .      .      . |
.          . |---------->|   .       .        .      . . |    . |          .      .   . |------->|      . |
.     . |<----|          . |------->|      .      . "All" . |------->|      .      .   . |------->|      . |
.          . |Search for x .      .   |       . Distant . |------->|Task c  .      .   . |------->|      . |
. |<------|  locally  .        . |------->|   . Nodes .  complete|---------->|      .      .   . |------->|      . |
. x |<------|        .       .        |------->|   . |   .         •       . |------->|      .      .      . |
. |------->|x found   .        .       .        .|d  . |   .         •       . |---------->|       .      . |
.     | locally     .        .       |<------|    . |   . DOS awaits .      .   . |------->|      . |
.     |---->|        .        .       .        . . |   . completion of d    .      .      .      . |
.          . | d found |<------|   .        .      . . |   .         •       . |      . |<------------|       . |
.          . | on node| 2 (and possibly others)     . |   .         •       . Task d |<---|        .      . |▼
.          . |<---------|  .       .        .      . . ▼   . |---------->|      .      .   . .--
.          . |         .       .        .      .    .---   . | complete  .      .      .      .
.          . | Run "Work Distribution   .        .      .      . |<-----|          .      .      .
.          . | and Task Allocation". .      .        .      . <------|Signal user .      .      .
.          . | (In this case, decision is   .      .      .      .      .      .      .      .
.          . |  made not to move any files) .    .      .      .      .      .      .      .      .
.          . | Node 2 selected for task d  .      .      .      .      .      .      .      .      .
.          . | Record tentative delegation .      .      .      .      .      .      .      .      .
.          . |  in task graph   .        .      .      .      .      .      .      .      .      .
.          . |    A    .        .       .        .      .      .      .      .      .      .      .
.          . |   /|\   .        .       .        .      .      .      .      .      .      .      .
.          . | c-->d(2?)  .      .        .      .      .      .      .      .      .      .      .
.          . |  |    .        .       .        .      .      .      .      .      .      .      .      .
.          . | x    .        .       .        .      .      .      .      .      .      .      .      .

 (continued on the diagram on the right)
```

figure 2.14 depicts the steps needed to process the work request for example 1 (figure 2.12).

Acknowledgements

This is a preliminary and condensed version of the technical report for the initial study of distributed and decentralized control. The research was supported in part by the US Air Force RADC Post-Doctoral Program under contract number F30602-78-C-0120 and the Office of Naval Research under contract number N00014-79-C-0873. The work was performed as part of the Georgia Tech Research Program in Fully Distributed Processing Systems at the School of Information and Computer Science, Georgia Institute of Technology, Atlanta, Georgia 30332.

References

Balz71   Balzer R. M., 'PORTS – A method for dynamic interprogram communication and job control', in *AFIPS Conference Proceedings* Vol. 38 (1971 Spring Joint Computer Conference): pp. 485–9.

Caba79a Cabanal, J. P., Marouane, M. N., Besbes, R., Sazbon, E. D., and Diarra, A. K., 'A decentralized OS model for ARAMIS distributed computer system', in *Proceedings of the First International Conference on Distributed Computing Systems* (October, 1979): pp. 529–35.

Caba79b Cabanel, J. P., Sazbon, R. D., Diarra, A. K., Marouane, M. N., and Besbes, R., 'A decentralized control method in a distributed system', in *Proceedings of the First International Conference on Distributed Computing Systems* (October, 1979): pp. 651–9.

Clar80   Clark, David D., and Svobodova, Liba, 'Design of distributed systems supporting local autonomy', in *COMPCON Spring 80* (February, 1980): pp. 438–44.

Ensl74   Enslow, Philip H., Jr. (ed.), *Multiprocessors and Parallel Processing*, New York: John Wiley and Sons, 1974.

Ensl78   Enslow, Philip H., Jr., 'What is a "distributed" data processing system?' *Computer* (January, 1978): 13–21.

Garc79   Garcia-Molina, H., *Performance Comparison of Update Algorithms for Distributed Database, Crash Recovery in the Centralized Locking Algorithm*, Progress Report No. 7, Stanford University, 1979.

Have78   Haverty, J. F., and Rettberg, R. D., 'Inter-process communications for a server in UNIX', in *COMPCON Fall 78* (September, 1978): pp. 312–15.

Hopp79   Hopper, K., Kugler, H. J., and Unger, C., 'Abstract machines modelling network control systems', *Operating Systems Review* 13 (January, 1979): 10–24.

Jens78   Jensen, E. Douglas, 'The Honeywell experimental distributed processor –An overview', *Computer* (January, 1978): 28–38.

Morg77   Morgan, Howard L., and Levin, K. Dan, 'Optimal program and data locations in computer networks', *Communications of the ACM* 20 (May, 1977): 315–22.

Suns77   Sunshine, Carl, *Interprocess Communication Extensions for the UNIX Operating System: I. Design Considerations*, Rand Technical Report R-2064/1-AF, June 1977.

Zuck77   Zucker, Steven, *Interprocess Communication Extensions for the UNIX Operating System: II. Implementation*, Rand Technical Report R-2064/2-AF, June, 1977.

PART 2

Analysis of parallel programming systems

3 Techniques to exploit parallelism

JEAN-LOUP BAER

1 Introduction

The two most often cited incentives for the design and use of multi-processor systems are increased performance and reliability. Greater security, graceful degradation and enhancement are factors which are also frequently mentioned [JONE 80]. The purpose of this chapter is more limited. It is to indicate how efficiency, i.e., performance gain or speed-up, can be obtained through the use of multiprocessing, defined as the simultaneous processing of two or more portions of the same program by two or more processing units. We include in the notion of 'program' the instantiation of several similar processes as in the classic reader–writer problem.

We place ourselves at the application program level but we are not oblivious to the underlying architectures and operating systems. In the same sense that a programmer should be aware of the management of the memory hierarchy of its installation [MORR 73], a multiprocessor user must take into account the new dimensions brought forth by the multiplicity of the computing units and their interconnections as well as be cognizant of the potential overheads incurred by the sharing of common resources and synchronization.

Algorithms and data structures which have been designed for conventional uniprocessor systems cannot be blindly transposed to multiprocessor architectures without experiencing inefficiencies in processor utilization and limited improvement of performance. Our goal is therefore to present some techniques which, when applied, will lead to processes and data structures better tailored to parallel processing environments. The exploitation of parallelism that we are dealing with will be at the modeling and algorithm design levels.

When designing programs for multiprocessor systems we have to distinguish between the adaptation to parallel environments of large tasks already encountered in uniprocessors and the creation of new algorithms specific to particular architectures. When the point of departure is an existing program, some modeling process can be applied to discover which parts of the original program can be partitioned into concurrent tasks and what the ensuing conflicts in data references might be. This approach is treated in section 2 with Petri nets and extensions as the primary modeling tool. In the case of algorithms and data structures tailored to their execution environment the target architecture is of great importance. This is even more so if the final product is to be a hardware special-purpose unit. In section 3 we show, by example, the range of cooperation which can be achieved from 'total' (or synchronous algorithms) to 'null' (competitive or asynchronous algorithms). Section 4 is devoted to a brief treatment of cooperative algorithms. Section 5 covers the basic techniques to achieve concurrency in a competitive environment. This is illustrated by showing the exploitation of these techniques on a common example, namely concurrent search and insertion in balanced tree structures. Section 6 is a summary of the guidelines given in this chapter.

2   Modeling for parallel systems
2.1   Introduction

Numerous models for describing parallelism in computer systems have been proposed in the last fifteen years. Depending on the intended application, we find models (schemes) aimed mostly at formal descriptions and hence suitable for correctness analysis [MILL 73] and models more attuned to the description of large systems, less formal and more akin to parallel flowcharts [BAER 77a]. Our bias here is towards the second category, i.e., we take a pragmatic approach requiring as a first quality of the models that they be descriptive of the control and data flows they represent. This leads us towards graph models to which we can assign various levels of interpretation.

Because this technique is deemed most appropriate for large tasks, the processing units in the target architecture must be full CPUs rather than functional units such as adders or multipliers. In other words, the unit of computation, or the granularity of the decomposition, will be a block of statements (or in some instances a procedure) rather than an arithmetic expression or an assignment statement.

Among the tools which have been used to represent parallelism, Petri nets and their extensions have been quite popular. Operating systems, compilers, communication protocols and distributed data base update algorithms are some of the applications whose control flows have been modeled with (extensions of) Petri nets. Since the literature on Petri nets is quite abundant (e.g. see [PETE 77]) we restrict ourselves to a brief and informal introduction.

2.2   Petri nets and extensions – a brief introduction

A Petri net consists of a set of places corresponding to conditions which may hold in the system, a set of transitions representing events which may occur, and a set of directed arcs connecting places to transitions and transitions to places. A place may contain tokens which signify the holding of the corresponding condition. Graphically, places are denoted by circles; transitions, by bars; and tokens by dots inside a place. A net has associated with it an initial marking (the number of tokens initially assigned to each place in the net). A transition may fire when all its input places (places linked to the transition by an arc directed from the place to the transition) are full (contain a token). After firing, a token is removed from every input place and a token is added to every output place. The firing of a transition corresponds to the occurrence of the event. Sequences of transition firings are called execution sequences. An execution sequence represents a simulation of the system being modeled, with the initial marking being the initial conditions. A first generalization of Petri nets is to allow weights to be associated with each arc, indicating the number of tokens to be removed or added for enabling and completion of a transition. Figure 3.1 illustrates these concepts (the weight of an arc is 1 unless otherwise indicated).

A Petri net is safe if a place cannot hold more than one token at any time (extension to k-safe is immediate). A marking M' is reachable from marking M if there exists an execution sequence which starts from the initial state M and terminates with the state M'. The set of all reachable markings from M is denoted $r(M)$. A transition t is live for a marking M if for all markings $M'' \in r(M)$ there exists an execution sequence which reaches marking M'' where t can fire. A Petri net is live if all its transitions are live. Two firable transitions are in conflict if they share a common input place. The liveness property is related to the absence of deadlock, that of safety to the boundedness in the use of resources, and conflicts are used to model synchronization constraints as well as predicates.

As we see below there are limitations in the modeling power of Petri nets. Some extensions have been used. The price to be paid is the undecidability of many formal properties unless we restrict the nets to be safe: in which case we have finite state models.

Figure 3.1. Petri net firing rule.

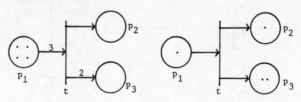

Initial marking: p_1 contains 4 tokens   after the firing of t

p_2 and p_3 are empty

t is firable since p_1 contains more

than 3 tokens

The usual programming language constructs are easily depicted by Petri nets. It is sufficient to introduce a transition on each arc of a flowchart and let the nodes be places to obtain a Petri net representing a program. But the basic interpretation of the roles of transitions and places is not followed. In general, the modeling will be performed in such a way that transitions will correspond to executable statements and places will act as deciders, besides having their usual meaning of condition holders. Figure 3.2 shows a Petri net representation of a **do while** and of an **if then else**.

Non-deterministic constructs such as guarded commands can also be modeled but in a somewhat cumbersome fashion. Note, however, that it is easy to show the parallel evaluation of all the guards.

This leads us to show how well suited Petri nets are to represent *partitioning* of tasks. Figure 3.3 gives a representation of the ALGOL-like program:

> **parbegin**
> > *S1*: **parbegin**
> > > *S1.1*: **begin** ... **end**;
> > > *S1.2*: **begin** ... **end**;
> >
> > **parend**;
> > *S2*: **begin** ... **end**;
> > *S3*: **begin** ... **end**;
>
> **parend**

Figure 3.2. Petri net representation of some programming language constructs.

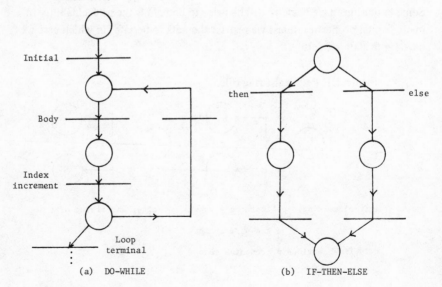

(a) DO-WHILE

(b) IF-THEN-ELSE

Modeling of sharable subprograms, procedures or co-routines as well as the modularization of the nets are more challenging problems. We shall return to some of these difficulties shortly. But on the other hand, Petri nets are extremely valuable for the representation of process synchronization and mutual exclusion. For example, a semaphore can be represented as an input place shared by the transitions (critical sections) which are to be mutually exclusive. Figure 3.4 illustrates this approach. Generalized semaphores can also be represented without difficulty.

Figure 3.3. Parallelism model by Petri nets.

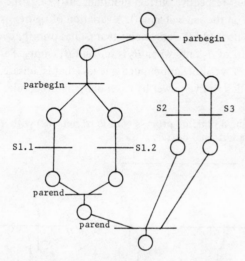

Figure 3.4. Mutual exclusion.

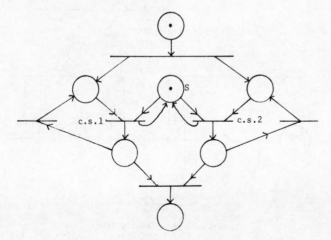

Another major technique to represent parallelism, namely *pipelining*, can be easily represented with Petri nets. This is shown in figure 3.5. Note that one can vary the number of buffers between stages but the representation can become cumbersome (this same problem arises while modeling a bounded buffer or guarded commands).

A major limitation in the modeling power of Petri nets is their incapacity to 'count' the number of tokens on a place or, equivalently, to test whether a place is empty. The following example [KOSA 73] illustrates this deficiency. Two producers P_1 and P_2 produce items and deposit them in buffers B_1 and B_2 respectively. Two consumers C_1 and C_2 remove elements from B_1 and B_2 and are not allowed to access their respective buffers simultaneously (e.g., the access to the two buffers could be on the same channel). A variation of figure 3.4 could model this situation. Let us now add the constraint that C_1 has priority over C_2, i.e., C_2 can consume elements of B_2 only when B_2 is full and B_1 empty. Petri nets cannot model this situation if we allow unbounded queues (that is, unsafe nets). We can remove this lack of descriptive power by extending the firing rule.

Figure 3.5. Modeling a pipeline process with Petri nets. (*a*) with a single latch. (*b*) with an additional buffer.

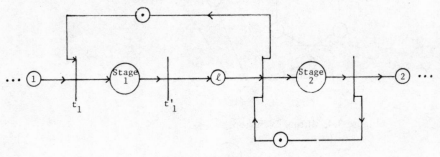

(a) With a single latch

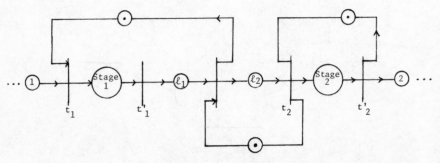

(b) With an additional buffer

Agerwala [AGER 73] has introduced inhibitors (arcs with a dash) which allow the testing of emptiness of a place. Now the priority problem is represented easily (see figure 3.6) but this added property has given to Petri nets the same power as Turing machines. Hence liveness and safety are undecidable for these extended nets.

Instead of an inhibitor which represents a NOT condition, we can extend the firing rule to allow disjunctive logic as shown in figures 3.7a and 3.7b, where + means EOR. The **if then else** of figure 3.2b takes the form of figure 3.7c. A descriptive advantage is that decision-making events are modeled as transitions. More interpretation can be added with switches, a special type of place which determines which of two output places receives a token when a transition with disjunctive 'output' logic fires. This is especially useful for modeling exception conditions or the termination of a process. But introducing an additional control variable and a predicate on that variable can serve the same purpose.

The next extension, token absorbers, is useful for 'killing' redundant processes (note that *redundancy* or *duplication* is an important technique for exploiting parallelism) and for leaving the net in a properly terminating condition (PT). PT nets are defined such that for all executions these nets are left in a predetermined terminal marking [BAER 73]. To see why this property is extremely valuable, consider a modularization of the net, for example in various pipeline stages as in figure 3.5. There we want to find the same initial conditions each time the transitions t_1 for stage 1 or t_2 for stage 2 fire. This implies that t'_1 and t'_2 must leave their respective subnets in properly terminating conditions. The following example shows another use of token absorbers (represented as dashed arcs in the figures). Two processes P_1 and P_2 are available to search a linear table for a given key. P_1 starts at the low end of the table and P_2 at the high end, and each ends in the middle. (There are better algorithms as will be discussed later.) As soon as one process has found a matching entry, the other should quit (or not start).

Figure 3.6. Modeling priority via Petri nets with inhibitors.

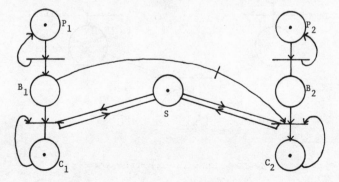

Figure 3.8 shows an extended Petri net of the two processes (the token absorbers from P_2 have not been shown).

If we had n processes instead of 2, figure 3.8 would become rapidly intractable. Colored Petri nets [JENS 79] are useful tools for avoiding this 'spaghetti' effect. Moreover, they can model program re-entrancy and the instantiation of several identical processes [BAER 77a]. In this extension, places contain bags of colored tokens. They are connected to the transitions by labeled arcs. The labels are

Figure 3.7. Petri nets extended with disjunctive logic. (*a*) when *t* fires, only one of p_2, p_3, p_4 will receive a token. (*b*) *t* is firable only if one of p_1, p_2, p_3 contains a token. (*c*) **if then else** with disjunctive logic.

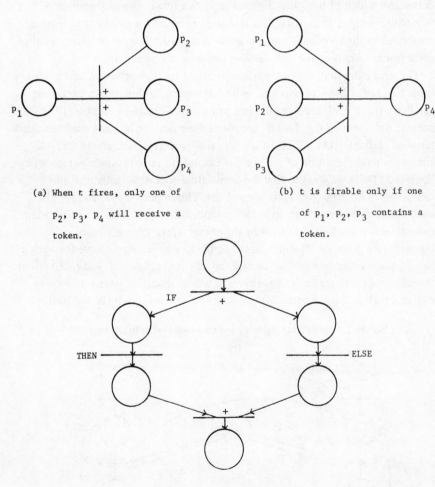

(a) When t fires, only one of p_2, p_3, p_4 will receive a token.

(b) t is firable only if one of p_1, p_2, p_3 contains a token.

(c) IF-THEN-ELSE with disjunctive logic

either sets of colors or free variables. The firing rules are modified as follows. If (p_i, t) is labeled with set N_i, then t can be enabled only if p_i contains at least one token of each color belonging to N_i and the firing will remove one token of each color. If (t, p_j) is labeled with N_j, then the firing of t will deposit on p_j one token of each color belonging to N_j. This is shown in figures 3.9a and 3.9b with 3.9c being the equivalent Petri net construct.

If one or more arcs are labeled with a free variable x, then this free variable may be bound to any color belonging to N_i, and the firing rule is applied as if all these arcs were labeled with this color (see figures 3.10a and 3.10b). If several bindings allow the firing of t, then not only do we have a choice but also several bindings can be performed and several instances of the transaction can fire provided there are enough tokens (see figures 3.10c and 3.10d).

As an example of the use of this model, consider the broadcast of a message by some process P_o to n processes $P_1, P_2, \ldots, P_n$, each identified by a different color. Let $N = x_1, x_2, \ldots, x_n$ be the set of these colors and let x_i be the color associated with P_i. Each P_i performs the same algorithm on its own data and

Figure 3.8. Extended Petri nets with disjunctive logic and token absorbers.

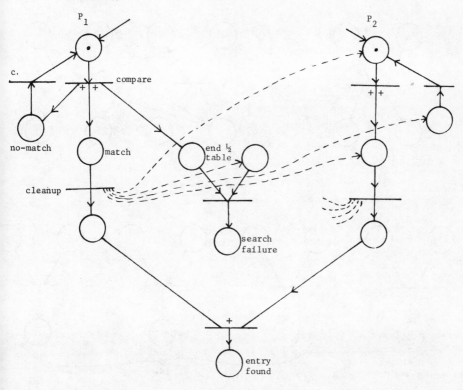

Figure 3.9. Firing rules for colored Petri nets (labeled arcs).

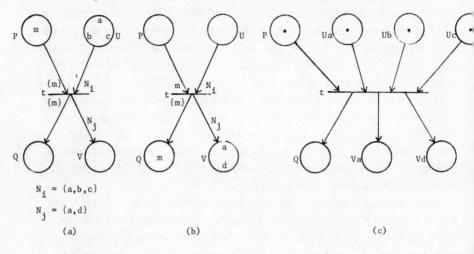

$N_i = \{a,b,c\}$

$N_j = \{a,d\}$

(a)   (b)   (c)

Figure 3.10. Colored Petri nets with free variable labels.

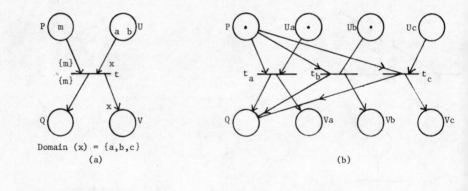

Domain $(x) = \{a,b,c\}$

(a)   (b)

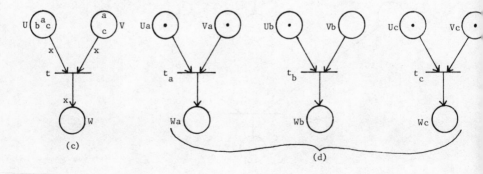

(c)   (d)

either acknowledges positively (A^+) or negatively (A^-). P_o then performs task Y if all answers are positive or task Z if at least one answer is negative. The colored Petri net of figure 3.11 represents this situation with only a single net for P_i since all other processes P_j $(1 \leqslant j \neq i \leqslant n)$ have the same structure.

2.3 Modeling experience

Rather than cataloging other extensions such as constraints on the subsets of places which can be full concurrently or timing attributes for transition firings, we present some conclusions reached from having modeled a non-trivial sequential program (a compiler [BAER 77b]) and subsequently modified it so it could be run as a three-stage pipeline process. (Incidentally, we found that a 2:1 speed-up could be obtained with three processors for error-free compilations.)

Modularity

Our first observations pertain to the role of modularity. Modular sequential programs might not be best suited for the detection of parallelism or

Figure 3.11. Example of modeling with colored Petri nets.

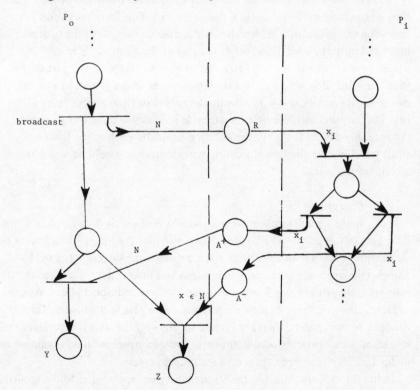

for the design of a new parallel system. For example, potential parallelism might be hidden by the modularization of processes. This is particularly true when checking for data independence. It becomes necessary to expand modules to determine whether there exist data dependencies between the body of the procedure represented by the module and the context of each call. Different synchronizations at each call might be needed in order to fully exploit some inherent parallelism.

From our limited observations on the compiler example, as well as by perusing other programs, it appears that the modularity of the model will tend to follow the structure of the code. This points out the need for language extensions so that the parallelism in the problem may be explicitly expressed and the structure of the program may be oriented toward parallel processing.

The other side of the coin on modularization is what methods can be used in order to partition a large system into smaller subsystems. The problem arises in the graph model when we want to represent events and conditions at two different levels of detail. The usual way of handling hierarchical modeling is to represent a subnet by a single transition in the higher level net (e.g., transitions t'_1 and t'_2 in figure 3.5) and require that the form of the input and output control flow be the same in the subnet and the single transition. In other words, the transition expands into a net which is self-contained except for the original input and output places. However, if the goal of the modeling is to describe a large parallel system, it is advantageous to be able to represent a part of the total net which describes a significant logical phase of the system as a module, even though there exist synchronization signals to or from another part of the net. Thus, we would advocate a hierarchy of models where, in this particular instance, the details of the synchronization would be given at the first level while possibly only the fact of existing synchronization would be noted at the second level of detail.

Data graphs

In the compiler model we associated a very simple data graph with the Petri net control graph (we also used disjunctive logic, switches – which were not that helpful – and token absorbers). Each data structure was represented by a single (square) place with input and output arcs linking data places to transitions. Naturally, transition firing was not affected by these additional places. As can be expected, the simplicity of the data graph is a weakness in the model. The uniform handling of structured data is inadequate for showing the data independence of two transitions operating on disjoint partitions of a structure and for gaining an understanding of the operations on a structured object.

In her thesis, Carla Ellis [ELLI 79] tried different approaches to the modeling of data in this context. In addition to the primitive 'square' places model, she investigated the use of three other techniques that we summarize now.

The shared data model is patterned loosely after monitors. The primitive model is extended by having all related data cells enclosed within a class box. Special places (denoted by triangles) represent accessing procedures with restrictions provided textually. Exclusive access inside a class is not assumed. The role of these restrictions is closely related to that of assertions in a correctness proof; but the textual components do not significantly help in expressing parallelism.

The second approach is derived from AMBIT/G, a graphical programming language for the manipulation of directed graphs. Pattern matching rules, assumed indivisible, are called in connection with transitions in the accompanying Petri net. The strong point of this approach is that it can describe very well the structure of the data and transformations on the structure. On the other hand the total interpretation is not appropriate for the analysis of some formal properties such as determinacy.

The last data model is based on Venn diagrams. It is motivated by the fact that a commonly used technique in the design of parallel algorithms which manipulate shared data is the decomposition of a large structure into independent subsets of data items. For example, in a compiler the lexical analysis can add new entries of a given block in the symbol table while previous entries from an independent block are used by the parser or the code generator. As stated by Ellis, the underlying philosophy is that the dynamic partitioning of data among processes may be more important for parallel systems than other characteristics such as type or structural configuration. The Venn diagram paradigm describes well the conceptual relationships among the data items (e.g., variable scoping is succinctly and adequately described).

One conclusion reached by this study of data models is similar to one of those attained by studying the role of modularity, namely that we should have a hierarchy of models. Each model would emphasize one aspect of the process. A primitive data graph or a shared class model would be convenient for determinacy analysis. An interpreted model could be useful in showing structural relationships while a Venn diagram approach is more fitting for correctness arguments and for providing a (limited) amount of insight for parallelization issues.

Levels of interpretation

Our final comments on the modeling of parallel systems deal with the level of interpretation in the modeling process. We have already touched upon this subject while we were presenting alternatives for data models. The level of interpretation depends on the goals of the modeling with some of the possibilities being description, simulation, and analysis for formal properties such as proper termination. It is reasonable to imagine that during the course of a modeling project all of these may become desirable.

We consider the model as a schema, i.e., a triple consisting of a set of data locations or variables, a set of operators each with an input set of data cells and an output set, and a control. The interpretation specifies the computational functions and the decision-making functions associated with the operators, the domain of values which a variable may assume, and initial values. Uninterpreted models allow for mathematical analysis whereas interpreted models are more satisfactory for simulation, detailed description, and data-dependent correctness questions. The amount of information which may be present in partially interpreted models can vary a great deal. Partial interpretation is necessary if both descriptive and analytic power are desired, but the level of the interpretation may lie anywhere in the wide range between 'slightly' interpreted to 'almost completely' interpreted.

A Petri net with the extension of disjunctive logic and the input and output data cells specified for each transition is completely uninterpreted. A degree of interpretation is given by the labeling of transitions with names representing the functions performed. The model becomes increasingly more interpreted as the labeling becomes more like a procedural definition of the function performed by the transition. A complete procedural definition for each transition yields a nearly completely interpreted schema.

At various stages in our experiment different levels of (partial) interpretation were required. In our initial modeling effort, when the goal was to learn about the compiler, a moderate amount of interpretation was sufficient with transitions described by a blend of procedural definition and simple labeling. A more nearly complete interpretation was required for the investigation of the integrity of data structures and as a basis for simulation. On the other hand a much lower level of interpretation was given during the design stage for the specification of new algorithms and checking for proper termination. The interesting property of the extended Petri net model is that it can consistently handle such a variety of purposes. The reason behind this flexibility is that the interpretation is separate from the control and data flow graphs and can be ignored for the sake of analysis.

In conclusion, modeling from an existing sequential program should be seen solely as a first approach. The next step is to start anew and redesign parts of the program so that it is better tailored to its new environment.

3 Designing parallel algorithms: from competition to cooperation

Designing algorithms for multiprocessor systems is greatly influenced by the target architectures (see [BAER 80*a*] for a sample of these). If we have a multifunctional unit processor such as a CDC 6600, we might leave all optimizations to the compiler. In the case of a pipeline or vector computer, compilers should be able to generate 'vector code' but not indiscriminately because of the influence of the set-up and flush times. However, the compiler optimization is not sufficient and algorithms have to be changed so that they take advantage of the pipelining. For example, lexical analysis of source programs is better handled in these organizations as a multipass process: one pass could remove blanks, another find operators, another find matching pairs of parentheses, etc. When an array processor of the ILLIAC IV type is considered, programming is far from being a simple matter. Algorithms must be developed to keep all processors as busy as possible under the constraints of lock-step computations. There it is mandatory, for efficiency reasons, to design specific algorithms and to tailor data structures to the environment. In addition, programmers and analysts should be provided with high-level language constructs which reflect this SIMD (single instruction, multiple data) architecture. With MIMD (multiple instruction, multiple data) multiprocessors such as C.mmp and Cm*, the architecture imposes fewer constraints. However, care must be taken in the placement of code and data in order to avoid undue overhead caused by the interference between accessing shared resources (mainly primary memory) and synchronization. Replication of code and localization of data close to the processor accessing it most often are required in order to obtain substantial performance improvements [JONE 80].

In this section our aim is to show, via an example, that for a given task there exist variations, in the algorithm and in the target architectures, that can greatly influence the performance improvements. The emphasis will be on the range of cooperation and synchronization required between the processes assumed to be implemented on individual homogeneous processors.

The example is based on the idea of batch searching and consists of variations on the theme of binary search. The binary search algorithm is twisted to fit given architectures or, conversely, the process can be seen as the design of an architecture tailored to the algorithm. The basic system consists of p processors (Pc) and m interleaved memory modules (Mp). A Pc–Mp switch allows connections between Pc's and Mp's. The memory holds an ordered table of n elements ($n \gg m$). The Pc's perform table look-ups as requested by external users. It is implied that there are always requests pending. We present some possible organizations for a special-purpose unit whose function is to answer these search queries. Analyses of the performance of each organization are developed in a forthcoming paper and will only be summarized here [BAER 80b].

In the first organization, the Pc's compete freely for access to the Mp modules. Each processor, when free, takes a request from the queue and performs the usual binary search. The table is stored in Mp in such a way that element X_i ($i = 1, 2, \ldots, n$) is in module M_j with $j = i \bmod m$. At the completion of the search the Pc becomes free again and repeats the same algorithm on the next request. As can be seen, there is no Pc synchronization. However performance can be degraded in an unbearable fashion by memory interference. For example, if $m = 2^k$ (a reasonable choice for ease in interleaving) and $n = 2^q - 1$ then the ratio ρ of the number of comparisons with one operand in the most often referenced module to the total number of comparisons is:

$$\rho = \frac{q-k}{q} \quad \text{for an unsuccessful search and}$$

$$\rho \simeq \frac{q-k}{q-1} - \frac{1}{m(q-1)} \quad \text{for a successful search.}$$

To give an idea of the skewness of the distribution of references, for $n = 1023$ and $m = 4$ we have $\rho = 0.8$ for an unsuccessful search and $\rho = 0.86$ for a successful one. Thus in this 'worst' case, over 80% of the time only one processor will be able to progress towards completion of its query. Of course on the average, i.e., for a number of different values of n, the competition for memory cycles out of the same module will not be this fierce but nonetheless greater than assuming that each memory module has a uniform probability of access.

A second, radically different, approach is to have as much cooperation between processors as possible. To realize this, we insist that the requests be sorted and processed in batches, that is, the query performed by P_i for value v_i is such that $v_i \leqslant v_{i+1}$, $0 \leqslant i \leqslant p-1$. The target architecture has the SIMD structure depicted in figure 3.12 with P_i storing in L_i and R_i the current bounds of its search interval. All Pc's access Mp concurrently (hence with possibility of conflict) and determine their new L_i and R_i. Then, we set

$$L_i = \max (L_i, L_{i-1}) \quad \text{and} \quad R_i = \min (R_i, R_{i+1}).$$

An initial interpolation is performed so that all processors do not access the middle of the table simultaneously in the first step of the binary search.

An interesting feature of this algorithm is that a processor may progress, i.e., reduce its interval of search, although it has not been able to access memory. However, the performance of the algorithm is degraded by two factors. First, the initial interpolation search might be detrimental. Second, and more important, the sorting constraint requires that all queries be finished before a new batch of p requests may be processed. Nevertheless, simulations show an improvement over the competition organization and no 'worst' case degradation.

In the third method, we completely suppress memory interference and use implicit synchronization. In this gentleman's agreement, each Pc accesses a favored memory module (say M_i for P_i) until $(R_i - L_i) < m$ for all i. This takes $\lceil \log (n/m) \rceil + 1$ steps. Then in the $(m-1)$ successive steps P_i accesses modules

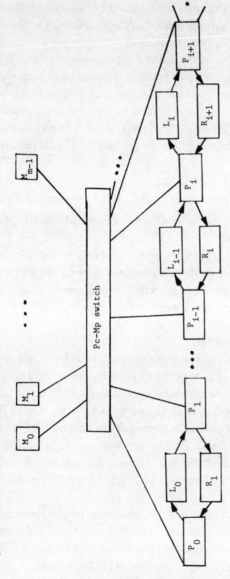

Figure 3.12. A cooperative organization.

$M_{(i+1) \bmod m}, M_{(i+2) \bmod m}, \ldots, M_{(i+m-1) \bmod m}$. Thus the whole process takes $(\log n - \log m + m)$ steps (about 20% faster on the average than in the previous method).

Although memory interference is avoided and synchronization limited to a minimum, we still have the major inconvenience of waiting for the last Pc to be finished. Moreover, it seems that some explicit transfer of information between adjacent Pc's could be advantageous.

We can combine features of the last two organizations as follows. Each Pc accesses Mp modules as in the linear search of the gentleman's agreement algorithm so that a free processor can start its search process at any time. Furthermore, P_i writes L_i, R_i and v_i in three registers accessible from its neighbors P_{i-1} and P_{i+1} (the Pc's form a ring). When P_j starts processing a new query, it sets L_j to 1, R_j to n and v_j to the search key. Then it performs the following:

> if $v_j \leqslant v_{j+1}$ then $R_j := R_{j+1}$ else $L_j := L_{j+1}$;
> if $v_j \leqslant v_{j-1}$ then $R_j := min\ (R_j, R_{j-1})$ else $L_j := max\ (L_j, L_{j-1})$;

An improvement of 25% over the gentleman's agreement algorithm has been observed with this method.

It is quite possible that further improvements could be found. However, our goal here was simply to demonstrate the range of cooperation which can be injected to avoid memory interference while keeping synchronization at a sensible level. The next two sections dwell more on these aspects.

4   Cooperative algorithms

As we saw in the previous section, cooperation between processors for the accomplishment of a given task can vary greatly. Some architectures have embedded facilities for implementing cooperation. It can be at the basic hardware level as in pipeline machines or an interconnection network as in an ILLIAC IV-like architecture. The interconnection network can be simplified into a hierarchy of buses as in Cm*. And, finally, primary memory can be the only means to share data information as in C.mmp. While common memory may at first glance appear less attractive, it might be quite sufficient for a small amount of sharable data.

Let us see how these architectural constraints can be of influence in the design of algorithms. We proceed once more by example. Consider the cooperative search of section 2 as represented by the Petri net of figure 3.8. The information relative to P_2 required by P_1 is two flags indicating whether P_2 has found the entry or whether P_2 has finished searching its half-table. Two identical flags set by P_1 are required by P_2. The algorithm (for P_1) is:

P1. found := *false* ; *P1. finished* := *false* ; *half* := $\lfloor(beginning + end)/2\rfloor$;
index := *beginning* ; *found* := *P1. found* ∨ *P2. found* ;
while *index* ⩽ *half* ∧ ⌐ *found* **do**
    begin *linear search* ;
          if *success* **then begin** *P1. found* := *true*;
                          exit (*success, P1*)
               end ;
       index := *index* + 1 ; *found* := *P1. found* ∨ *P2. found*
    end ;
if ⌐ *found* **then begin** *P1. finished* := *true*;
                if *P2. finished* **then exit** (*failure, P1*)
        end ;

where the name of the process in **exit** indicates which of P_1 and P_2 will retain control. Note that there is still a little bug in this program since P_1 and P_2 could finish at the same time and both call **exit**. The correction is left as an exercise for the reader.

Evidently, this scheme can be improved. First a Boolean flag 'found' could be shared. More importantly, one should provide for the possibility of a process to continue its search as long as the entry has not been found, that is, an arbitrary half-table split is to be avoided. This implies that each process be cognizant of the other's progress, i.e., '$P_2.index$' must be consulted by P_1, and conversely. Still another method is to have a common '*index*' for both processes. Access to '*index*' must be on a mutual exclusion basis since both processes can read and write this shared variable. How much overhead is spent in this protocol is an interesting question. For a detailed study of this question the reader is referred to [OLEI 78] which uses a simple root-finding algorithm as a vehicle for the evaluation. Note that if we had n ($n > 2$) processes sharing the searching task, this last method might be the only viable one (but beware of memory interference as shown in the previous section!).

What if the table were ordered? It has been shown that a cooperative Fibonacci search is optimal for two processors [KUNG 76] and for a two-stage pipeline processor [WELL 74]. The method is as follows. Let $ONE(L)$ be the state where one process tests an element within the correct interval of length L and $TWO(L)$ the state where both processes are within the correct interval. Since this testing involves a single comparison (and is terminated when $L \leqslant 1$) there is no point in 'killing' the outside process in state ONE since this might take longer than just letting it end its (non-useful) computation. The initial step is $TWO(L)$ with P_1 testing at element $L \cdot \phi^2$ and P_2 at $L \cdot \phi$ where ϕ is the reciprocal of the golden ratio ($\phi + \phi^2 = 1$). If P_1 finishes first and finds that the element should be at its left then we pass to state $ONE(L . \phi^2)$. If P_1 finishes first and finds that the correct element is at its right, we pass to state $TWO(L . \phi)$. A similar analysis holds for P_2 finishing first. When we are in state $ONE(l)$ then if P_1, which tests within l, finishes first we pass to $ONE(l, \phi)$ or $ONE(l . \phi^2)$. If P_2 finishes first, we pass to $TWO(l . \phi)$. The whole computation follows one path in the computation tree of figure 3.13.

Here cooperation is reduced to knowledge of the current state and the associated lower and upper bounds of the correct interval. As in the previous examples, up-to-date information is not critical. For example, if in our first scheme P_1 finds an entry and P_2 tests 'found' before P_1 sets 'P_1.*found*', then the only resulting factor is an extra iteration for P_2. This (advantageous) lack of rigorism is true also in most numerical algorithms involving *relaxation* procedures.

Finally, the distinction between static and dynamic partitioning, within the realm of cooperation, has to be made. Extending the Fibonacci search to more than two processors requires changes in the algorithm (definition of states) and in the data structure (the Fibonacci binary search tree must be transformed into an appropriate *n*-ary tree). But this can be done only when the value of *n* is known, and hence is called '*static* partitioning'. On the other hand, any number of processes can search concurrently an unordered linear table by using

Figure 3.13. State diagram for a cooperative Fibonacci search.

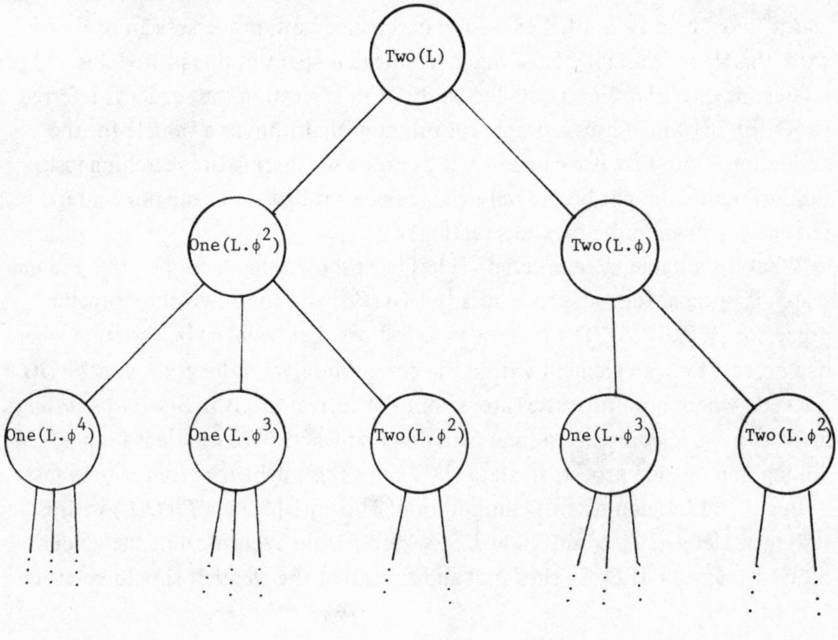

a common *'index'*. A better example which is both *dynamic* and *hierarchical* is a parallel QUICKSORT. A master performs the first split and orders a slave to QUICKSORT one of the two subarrays while it (the master) continues with the other subarray. The splitting continues recursively until either the array is sorted or there are no more free processors, in which case the maximum parallelism is not obtained. The process is more dynamic than in the previous example since processors can be released and reattached to the computation later and is hierarchical since we have a master–slave relationship. This latter quality is often the mark of dynamic partitioning.

5   Concurrency in a competitive environment

There exist many instances where cooperation in a multiprocessing system cannot be enforced smoothly. When several processes wish to access or modify a common resource (e.g., shared variables, secondary memories holding a common data base, access to a bus or communication link) critical sections or the like are necessary. The competition can be refereed with various degrees of severity. Consider the case of several Pc's, each with its own private cache, which access some common variables in Mp. In order to have consistent data, several alternatives can be proposed. From the most drastic to the most lenient, some of them are:

(*a*) Forbid writable data to be transferred into caches (implementable with read/write bits in Mp).

(*b*) Lock writable data so that only one processor at a time has exclusive access (in its cache) to it (implying some kind of critical section protocol).

(*c*) Have caches monitor each other so that changes to common data in one of them invalidates the corresponding entries in the others. This becomes rapidly technologically infeasible as the number of caches grows. Another solution of the same type is to have the writing Pc broadcast the change to all other Pc's. This creates contention on the communication links.

(*d*) Have all Pc's proceed as if they were sole owners of the data they modify. After completion of the unit of processing (defined somewhat arbitrarily) a check is made to see whether correct values of the data were used. If yes, the computation continues, otherwise it is rolled back. This is certainly not easily implementable at this level of the architecture (unless the amount of sharing is extremely small) but becomes plausible if one replaces caches and Mp by distributed processors with Mp sharing a common data base on secondary memory.

At a higher level in the system, i.e., when software processes are the units of granularity, there is no real equivalent to solution (*a*). A great deal of effort has been expended on finding ways to minimize the amount of locking of solution (*b*). As we shall see, optimistic solutions as in (*d*) can become very attractive.

Solution (c) with timestamping is implementable in local network organizations.

In order to introduce methods for reducing the locking overhead, our vehicle of study will be a specific reader–writer problem, namely a search-and-insertion procedure for balanced searched tree structures. We shall not dwell on the details of the algorithms, which vary according to the particular data structures (see, e.g., [KNUT 73]), but look at several procedures that have been used with the goal of obtaining as much concurrency as possible between the reader and writer processes.

Let K be the queried (reader) or inserted (writer) key. We denote by I-path the search (reader) or insertion (writer) path and by c-node the node on the I-path during insertion which is such that rebalancing will be limited to the nodes (and their brothers) on the I-path below this c-node. The synopsis for a reader process is as follows. Starting with a 'current' pointer to the root node a local search for K is performed. If K is found the process terminates, otherwise the appropriate 'son of current' (abbreviated 'son') is determined. The process continues recursively with 'son' replacing 'current' until success or until the I-path reaches a leaf. For a writer, the same procedure is applied (with failures and success being the inverse) and the c-node is determined at the same time. (Note that a node on the I-path may qualify temporarily as a c-node and then be removed from this position by one of its 'safe' descendants.) When the I-path reaches a leaf, K is inserted and rebalancing (from c-node down or up to c-node) is performed.

In a multiprocessing environment, we insist first that if a reader R_i searches for key K_i which is in the tree prior to R_i's instantiation, then R_i should be successful. And second, when all writers have completed their insertions, the tree should be balanced according to the original specifications.

In order to meet these requirements, we can enforce the following locking protocols. The readers must be allowed to search locally and determine the appropriate 'son' without being disturbed by other processes. Hence the protocol to progress along the I-path (assuming that 'current' is locked):

> search-locally (success or son);
> if success then unlock (current) and exit (success)
> else (in this order) lock (son), unlock (current) and set current to son.

A writer W_j in the I-path building phase proceeds similarly but must also take care of the c-node. The protocol for finding the place of insertion has for main body (assuming K_j is not in the tree and that 'current' is not a leaf):

> search-locally (son); lock (son); set current to son;
> if current is safe release all locks held by W_j on the ancestors of current.

This protocol can readily be improved by observing that readers should not lock out each other. *Multiple locking* can be used to that effect. Readers *r*-lock nodes while writers *w*-lock. A *w*-lock node is inaccessible to any other process while an *r*-lock node can be concurrently *r*-locked by another reader (we assume a FIFO discipline for processes wishing to access nodes, so that writers are not starved). The technique can be pushed further in this particular application [BAYE 77]. While building its *I*-path, a writer should not prevent readers from accessing the subtree of root *c*-node. To do this a writer *a*-locks the *I*-path (from *c*-node down). This *a*-lock is compatible with *r*-locks and incompatible with *a*-locks and *w*-locks (i.e., only one writer is allowed on the critical *I*-path). When it is time for rebalancing, *a*-locks are converted top-down to *w*-locks.

This technique can be refined further by bounding the number of nodes *w*-locked at any given time. Auxiliary 'tricks' are necessary (for another presentation of similar ideas see [KWON 80]). First, we can *modify the data structures* with redundancy (adding a key-pointer pair or a brother pointer), or by allowing the data structure to be temporarily degraded (e.g., allow more than the regular number of sons for leaves) as long as it returns to its original specifications when all processes have terminated. With some of these modifications, *concurrent reading and writing* in a node can be implemented following the original ideas of [LAMP 77]. Readers follow the *I*-path top-down and read the contents of nodes from left to right while writers in their rebalancing phase proceed bottom-up and from right to left. Information can be read more than once because of collision between a reader and a writer but there is no loss and no skipping. In this case, the only time when a node has to be *w*-locked is when some extra pointers have to be deleted. Before doing so, though, readers have to be chased from the 'current' node otherwise they could be misdirected. This is realized by the protocol:

> w-lock(father); a-lock(father); w-lock(current); perform modifications;
> unlock(current);

The *w*-locking of the father empties this node of readers. This step is necessary because some reader *r*-locking father can take a very long time between finding its appropriate son and actually locking that son (for further details see [ELLI 80]). The same paradigm can be used if a redundant copy of the restructured subtree (from *c*-node down) is built bottom-up by the writer. Then a top-down change of pointers as above is performed, *w*-locking only one node at a time.

Concurrency among writers can be enhanced by using *pipelining* and *demon processes*. Writers behave like readers until they reach a leaf. At that point they *a*-lock it and either insert the key if there is room for it or place it in an ordered linked list of keys waiting to be inserted and which will force the tree to be restructured. Then these writers quit and let specialized processes perform the restructuring. Since only a bounded number of nodes need to be *w*-locked these demon processes can be pipelined [ELLI 80].

This last method is a first approximation of what we could call *'optimistic* algorithms'. Such an approach is as follows [BAYE 77]. Writers proceed as readers until they find the appropriate leaf, which they *w*-lock. If the key can be inserted without restructuring, it is done so. Otherwise, the writer starts anew from the root using another protocol which will insure a satisfactory restructuring. This method is especially good if the probability of restructuring is small, e.g., if the nodes can contain a large number of keys, and in a virtual memory environment with the bulk of the data structure on a secondary memory device, since, in the second pass, the *I*-path will already (with high probability) be in primary memory. The use of such methods should certainly be encouraged when the probability of roll-back is small and when both roll-backs and retries are relatively easy and not too time-consuming.

Certainly, we have not covered all possible techniques to program multi-processing systems efficiently in a competitive environment (not even all for our particular application). However, it is hoped that those we have reviewed will give a fair idea of the range of possibilities.

6   Conclusion

In this paper we have indicated several techniques to exploit parallelism at the modeling and algorithmic levels. We have considered two separate cases depending on the point of departure. If the goal is to design parallel programs starting from some existing sequential environment then the use of a graph model indicating control and data flows and able to express the concepts of partitioning, pipelining, replication and process synchronization appears appropriate. Petri nets and extensions are good tools for this methodology. On the other hand, if new algorithms and data structures are to be defined to accomplish specific tasks, then it is mandatory (for efficiency reasons) to take into account the target architectures. We have shown the degrees of cooperation that could be achieved from total competition to high levels of information transfer. Some cooperative techniques, where the amount of information transferred is limited, have been examined with their effect on memory interference and synchronization overhead being a primary concern. We have introduced the concepts of static and dynamic partitioning in this context. In the case of independent processes (and processors) competing for common resources, we have shown some methods used to reduce the amount of required locking. Various techniques such as multiple locking, pipelining, concurrent reading and writing, redundancy, demon processes and optimistic algorithms have been examined within the context of a particular application.

It is not claimed that all possible methods have been reported herein. But it is hoped that the contents of this paper will provide a good start towards cataloging useful techniques for the exploitation of multiprocessor systems.

Acknowledgements

This work was supported in part by NSF grant MCS-76-09839. I am indebted to Ms Blair Rice for her help in drawing the figures.

References

[AGER 73] Agerwala, T. and M. Flynn, 'Comments on capabilities, limitations and "correctness" of Petri nets', in *Proc. 1st Symp. on Comp. Arch.*, 1973, pp. 81–6

[BAER 73] Baer, J.-L., 'Modeling for parallel computations: A case study', in *Proc. 1973 Sagamore Comp. Conf. Parallel Processing*, 1973, pp. 13–22

[BAER 77a] Baer, J.-L. and J. Jensen, 'Simulation of large parallel systems: Modeling of tasks', in *Proc. 3rd Int. Symp. on Modeling and Performance Evaluation*, Oct. 1977, pp. 53–73

[BAER 77b] Baer, J.-L. and C. Ellis, 'Model, design, and evaluation of a compiler for a parallel processing environment', *IEEE TSE, SE-3, 6*, Nov. 1977, 394–405

[BAER 80a] Baer, J.-L., *Computer Systems Architecture*, Computer Science Press, 1980

[BAER 80b] Baer, J.-L., H. C. Du, and R. E. Ladner, *Binary Search in a Multiprocessing Environment* TR 80-11-01. University of Washington, October 1980

[BAYE 77] Bayer, R. and M. Schkolnick, 'Concurrency of operations on B-trees', *Acta Informatica*, 9, 1977, 1–22

[ELLI 79] Ellis, C., 'The design and evaluation of algorithms for parallel processing', Ph.D. Diss., Univ. of Washington, 1979

[ELLI 80] Ellis, C. S., 'Concurrent search and insertion in 2–3 trees' *Acta Informatica*, 14, 1980, 63–86

[JENS 79] Jensen, K., *Coloured Petri Nets and the Invariant Method*, DAT. MI-PB-104, Aarhus Univ., 1979

[JONE 80] Jones, A. K. and P. Schwarz, 'Experience using multiprocessor systems – a status report', *Computing Surveys*, 12, 2, June 1980, 121–66

[KNUT 73] Knuth, D., *The Art of Computer Programming, vol. 3, Searching and Sorting*, Addison-Wesley, 1973

[KOSA 73] Kosaraju, S., 'Limitations of Dijkstra's semaphore primitives and Petri nets', in *Proc. 4th Symp. on O.S. Principles*, 1973, pp. 122–6

[KUNG 76] Kung, H. T., 'Synchronized and asynchronous parallel algorithms for multi-processors', in *Algorithms and Complexity: New Directions and Recent Results*, Acad. Press, N.Y., 1976, pp. 153–200

[KWON 80] Kwong, Y. S. and D. Wood, 'Concurrent operations in large ordered indexes', *Proc. 4th Int. Symp. on Progr.*, Lecture Notes in Computer Science, 83, 1980, pp. 207–22

[LAMP 77] Lamport, L., 'Concurrent reading and writing', *CACM*, 20, 11, Nov. 1977, 806–11

[MILL 73] Miller, R., 'A comparison of some theoretical models of parallel computation', *IEEE TC, C-22,8,* Aug. 1973, 710–17

[MORR 73] Morrison, J. E., 'User program performance in virtual storage systems', *IBM Systems Journal*, 12, 3, 1973, 216–37

[OLEI 78] Oleinick, P. N., 'The implementation and evaluation of parallel algorithms on C.mmp', Ph.D. Diss, Carnegie-Mellon Univ., 1978

[PETE 77] Peterson, J., 'Petri nets', *Computing Surveys*, 9, 3, Sept. 1977, 223–52

[STON 78] Stone, H. S., 'Sorting on STAR', *IEEE TSE, SE-4*, Mar. 1978, 138–46

[WELL 74] Weller, D. L. and E. S. Davidson, 'Optimal searching algorithms for parallel pipelined computers', in *Parallel Processing*, Lecture Notes in Computer Science, 24, 1974, pp. 291–305

4　Transformations of sequential programs into parallel programs

G. ROUCAIROL

Summary

Considering successively two syntactic equivalences of program schemas, we describe two transformations of sequential into parallel programs such that these equivalences are preserved. In order to reach maximal concurrency, these transformations are based on the use of a 'generalized queue realization'. This mechanism provides a means to control the concurrent execution of different steps of a loop. This is obtained by maintaining in different queues the relative order of events conditioning the execution of different occurrences of instructions. In particular it is shown how these queues are used to implement a 'data-driven' process of execution.

1　Introduction

The intrinsic complexity of describing concurrency leads us naturally to the investigation of the automatic transformation of sequential programs into parallel ones. Numerous studies have been devoted to this topic; Baer (BA 73) and Kuck (KU 73) conducted important surveys about the different proposed methods. From a general point of view these methods can be divided into two complementary classes:

(*a*) *Local transformations* try to point out the inherent concurrency of some particular task, taking into account the semantics of particular operators: Fortran DO loops (KU 75); commutativity, distributivity and associativity of arithmetic operations (BA 73); or the semantics of data structures such as simultaneous accesses to parallel hyperplanes of an array (LA 75).

(*b*) *Global transformations*, based upon a syntactical analysis of a sequential program, modify its control structure deeply in order to allow concurrent execution of instructions using distinct variables.

The transformations we are going to describe belong to this latter class.

Most global transformations which have been proposed in the literature are implicitly based on an equivalence of programs formalized by Keller (KE 73). Therefore we are going to introduce this equivalence in the framework of

a general model of parallel programs and to recall the transformation which
allows us to reach maximal concurrency for this equivalence. Afterwards we
shall introduce a weaker equivalence which allows us to compare programs with
different sets of variables. The 'parallelization' transformation which preserves
this equivalence demonstrates particularly 'pipeline'-like concurrency and a 'data-
driven' process of execution.

2   Definitions

2.1   Parallel program schemas

Following Karp & Miller (KA 69) and Keller (KE 73) a parallel program
schema may be defined as a couple $S = (S_C, S_I)$ where:

(a) S_I is a data-flow schema which defines the operators of the program and
the variables they use. It is built from:

A set $B = \{a, b, c, \ldots\}$ of operators.

A set $M = \{m_1, m_2, \ldots\}$ of variables.

For each operator $b \in B$, an ordered set of input variables

$$D(b) = \{d_1, \ldots, d_{i(b)}\}$$

and an ordered set of output variables

$$R(b) = \{r_1, \ldots, r_{j(b)}\}.$$

(Initially we consider that each variable is a scalar whose content is
globally accessed; this aspect will be changed in the last section of the
chapter.)

(b) S_C is a control schema which defines the (partial) order of execution of
the operators of the data-flow schema. It is described as a 4-tuple $S_C = (Q, q_0, \Sigma, \tau)$
where:

Q is a set of states,

q_0 an initial state,

$\Sigma = \cup_{b \in B} \Sigma(b)$ is an alphabet,

$\Sigma(b) = \{b_1, \ldots, b_{k(b)}\}$ is an alphabet of possible distinct terminations of
operator b. (Each operator b appears as a $k(b)$-ary test.)

τ is a partial function $\tau: Q \times \Sigma \to Q$ called the transition function.

Example

A 'while-loop' containing the simultaneous execution of two operators
a and b may be represented by the schema in figure 4.1. Such a schema may
model the parallel flowchart shown in figure 4.2.

Remark

In order to simplify, we consider in this model that each operator is instantaneously executed. This restriction can be avoided by decomposing each operator into a 'beginning operator' and an 'ending' operator having in common a variable which is an output of the former and an input of the latter.

2.2 Computations of a schema

The term 'computation' of the schema S is used to describe every finite word accepted by the terminal state or every infinite word accepted by the automaton defined by the control schema (more precisely every infinite word satisfying the 'finite-delay' property, see Karp & Miller (KAR 69)). We shall denote by $C(S)$ the set of computations of a schema S.

Figure 4.1.

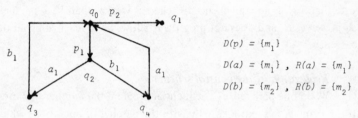

$$D(p) = \{m_1\}$$
$$D(a) = \{m_1\} \;,\; R(a) = \{m_1\}$$
$$D(b) = \{m_2\} \;,\; R(b) = \{m_2\}$$

Figure 4.2.

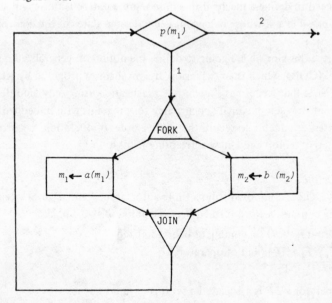

2.3   Equivalence of schemas

Let R be any equivalence relation over a set of computations. We say that two schemas S and S' are R-equivalent and we write $S \equiv S'(R)$ iff for every $x \in C(S)$ there exists $y \in C(S')$ such that $(x,y) \in R$ and vice versa.

2.4   Maximal concurrency

For a given equivalence of schemas the notion of maximal concurrency may be defined from a preorder relation 'more concurrent than'. A schema S is said to be more concurrent than a schema S' for the equivalence R $(S' \leqslant_R S)$ iff:

$$S \equiv S'(R)$$
$$C(S') \subseteq C(S)$$

Intuitively this means that the control schema of S allows more combinations than that of S' for scheduling the executions of the operators; therefore it defines more freedom and so contains more possibilities of concurrency.

Note that if R' is an equivalence of schemes weaker than R, a 'parallelization' which preserves R' and does not preserve R allows us to reach a higher degree of concurrency.

2.5   Realization of the control schema

When one parallelizes a sequential program the number of states of its control schema grows exponentially with the number of operations which can be executed concurrently. Moreover, this set of states is not necessarily finite.

So we need to define a mechanism whose representation is finite and as concise as possible and whose behaviour generates the states of the control schema.

To achieve this aim we are going to define the notion of 'generalized queue realization' (GQR), which is an extension of a mechanism proposed by Keller (KE 73). (Note that Keller has shown that a realization using only 'counters' is not sufficient to reach maximal concurrency for programs with imbedded loops, since counters are unable to record the relative order of operations occurring in the next step of a loop and a new activation of this loop.)

Definition

A GQR is composed from a finite automaton $\mathfrak{P}$ and a set of queues $\mathfrak{F}$. Each queue contains a word formed over the union of two alphabets:

$\Gamma_b = \{\bar{a} | a \in B\}$ (beginning of operators) and
$\Gamma_e = \{\bar{a} | a \in B\}$ (end of operators).
$\Gamma = \Gamma_b \cup \Gamma_e$.

To each operator $a \in B$ is associated a set $I(a)$ of input queues.

The behaviour of this particular automaton follows the following rules:

(1) A control state q is composed from a state of the automaton $\mathfrak{P}$ and the content of the queues.

(2) An operator a is said to be *enabled* in a state q iff for each input queue F of a there exists a word $x \in (\Gamma - \{\bar{a}\})^*$ and a symbol $\pi \in \Gamma_e$ such that $x\pi\bar{a}$ is a prefix of the content of F.

(3) The execution of the operator a leads successively to the following operations:

for every queue F the replacement of the first occurrence of $\bar{a}$ (if it exists) by $\tilde{a}$;

possibly a transition of the automation $\mathfrak{P}$ for which some words may be appended to the end of the queues.

Example

Realization of the control schema of figure 4.1

$$\mathfrak{F} = \{F_1, F_2, F_3, F_4\}$$

with

$$I(a) = \{F_1\}, I(b) = \{F_2\}, I(p) = \{F_3, F_4\}$$

as initial configuration of the queues:

$$F_1 : \bar{p}, F_2 : \bar{p}, F_3 : \tilde{\alpha}\bar{p}, F_4 : \tilde{\alpha}\bar{p}$$

Where $\tilde{\alpha}$ is an extra symbol supposed to belong to Γ_e and used to initiate the mechanism described above. The finite automaton is described by figure 4.3. The control schema generated by this realization is then represented by the infinite graph shown in figure 4.4, which accepts exactly the same set of computations as the graph in figure 4.1.

Remark

According to the behaviour of a GQR, it is not necessary to keep in a queue F a prefix $x \in \Gamma_e^*$ if there exists a symbol $\sigma \in \Gamma_e$ such that $x\sigma$ is also a prefix of the content of F.

Using this simplification we may obtain a finite control schema for the preceding example.

Figure 4.3.

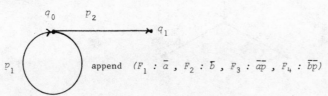

3   K-equivalence

3.1   Definition

K-equivalence defined by Keller (KE 73), allows us to compare schemas with an identical data-flow schema. It is based on the comparison of the execution ordering of operators which share either an input and an output variable or just an output variable. This notion of sharing of variables is expressed by a symmetric relation ρ defined over the set of operators:

$$(a,b) \in \rho \text{ iff } D(a) \cap R(b) \neq \emptyset \text{ or}$$
$$D(b) \cap R(a) \neq \emptyset \text{ or}$$
$$R(a) \cap R(b) \neq \emptyset$$

We denote by $\bar\rho$ the reflexive closure of ρ.

Then the K-equivalence of two computations x and y is defined by:

$$(x,y) \in K \text{ iff for every } (a,b) \in \bar\rho$$
$$E(\Sigma(a) \cup \Sigma(b), x) = E(\Sigma(a) \cup \Sigma(b), y)$$

where $E(A, z)$ with $A \subseteq \Sigma$ denotes the word obtained from z by erasing symbols which do not belong to A.

Figure 4.4.

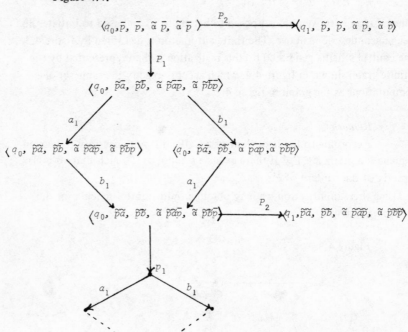

Example

For the relation $\rho = \{(a, b), (b, c), (a, d)\}$ the following computations are equivalent:

$$x = a_1 b_1 c_1 d_1 d_1,$$
$$y = a_1 d_1 b_1 d_1 c_1,$$
$$z = a_1 b_1 d_1 d_1 c_1, \ldots$$

3.2 Transformation

Let us consider a sequential schema S whose set of states is finite. One can show (KE 73) that maximal concurrency may be reached by retaining from the control schema of S only the sequentiality of execution of operators linked by ρ, taking into account the fact that the execution of an operator cannot be anticipated on the execution of the test which controls this operator in S. We are going to give as an example a transformation which generally allows maximal concurrency.

Let us consider the following simple program which computes the number of permutations of p items among n:

> $data\ (N, P);$
> $X: = N\ (a)\ ;\ Y: = 0(b)\ ;\ Z: = 1\ (c)\ ;$
> **while** $Y \leqslant P - 1\ (p)$ **do**
> $\qquad\qquad Y: = Y + 1\ (d)\ ;$
> $\qquad\qquad Z: = Z * X\ (e)\ ;$
> $\qquad\qquad X: = X - 1\ (f)\ ;$
> $\qquad\qquad$ **od** ;
> $A: = Z\ (f)\ ;$
> **result** $(A)\ ;$

This program corresponds to the sequential schema shown in figure 4.5. The relation ρ is $\{(a, e), (a, f), (b, p), (b, d), (c, e), (c, g), (d, p), (e, f), (e, e), (e, g), (f, f), (d, d), (e, a), (f, a), \ldots\}$.

The GQR which allows maximal concurrency for this program is defined as follows:

(1) For each pair of couples (a, b) and (b, a) belonging to $\bar{\rho}$ there is associated a unique queue $F_{a,b}$ in $\mathfrak{F}$ and for each operator $b \in B$
$I(b) = \{F_{a,b}\ \text{or}\ F_{b,a} \in \mathfrak{F}\}$.

(2) The finite automaton $\mathfrak{P}$ is built from the sequential control schema by conserving uniquely the terminal states and the states in which are accepted symbols of tests. (An operator p is a test iff $|\Sigma(p)| > 1$). The transitions of this automaton are labelled by **append** operations defined by the following rule: for

a transition from the state q_i to the state q_j of $\mathfrak{P}$, one appends to a queue $F_{a,b}$ a word $x \in (\{\bar{a}, \bar{b}\})^*$ corresponding exactly to the sequence of symbols belonging to $\Sigma(a) \cup \Sigma(b)$ accepted between the states q_i and q_j of the sequential control schema.

For the preceding example we obtain the schema shown in figure 4.6. The initial content of the file is determined by the preceding rule applied to the symbol encountered between q_0 and q_1:

$$F_{a,e} : \tilde{\alpha}\bar{a}, F_{a,f} : \tilde{\alpha}\bar{a}, F_{b,p} : \tilde{\alpha}\bar{b}\bar{p}, F_{b,d} : \tilde{\alpha}\bar{b}, F_{c,e} : \tilde{\alpha}\bar{c}, F_{c,g} : \tilde{\alpha}\bar{c}$$

Figure 4.5.

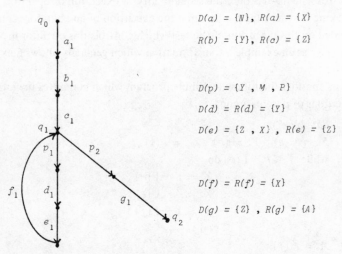

$D(a) = \{N\}, R(a) = \{X\}$

$R(b) = \{Y\}, R(c) = \{Z\}$

$D(p) = \{Y , M , P\}$

$D(d) = R(d) = \{Y\}$

$D(e) = \{Z , X\} , R(e) = \{Z\}$

$D(f) = R(f) = \{X\}$

$D(g) = \{Z\} , R(g) = \{A\}$

Figure 4.6.

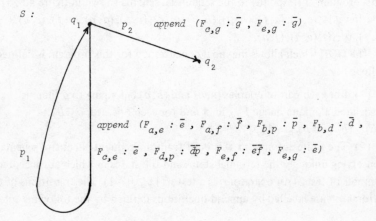

$S :$

q_1 p_2 *append* $(F_{c,g} : \bar{g} , F_{e,g} : \bar{g})$

append $(F_{a,e} : \bar{e} , F_{a,f} : \bar{f} , F_{b,p} : \bar{p} , F_{b,d} : \bar{d} ,$

$F_{c,e} : \bar{e} , F_{d,p} : \overline{dp} , F_{e,f} : \overline{ef} , F_{e,g} : \bar{e})$

(We have not considered queues like $F_{a,a}, F_{b,b}, \ldots$ because they are redundant in this example.)

If we consider a partial order between occurrences of operators induced by some precedence relation in time we can visualize the amount of concurrency obtained for two steps of the iteration shown in figure 4.7.

4   *U*-equivalence

4.1   Definition

U-equivalence is based on the comparison in two computations of value transmissions between occurrences of operators [RO 74, 78].

If x is a computation, we say there is a value transmission from the nth occurrence of symbol a_k to the pth occurrence of symbol b_h in x iff

the nth occurrence of a_k precedes the pth occurrence of b_h,

a variable m is an output of operator a and an input of operator b,

there is no other assignment of m between these two occurrences of a and b.

If m is the ith output of a and the jth input of b we write:

$$(a_k, n) - u(x, i, j) - (b_h, p).$$

(b uses a value produced by a.)

Figure 4.7.

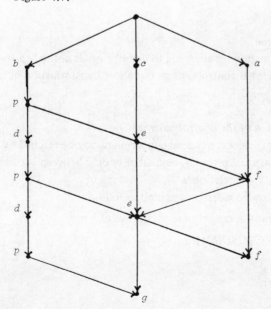

Then we say that two computations x and y are equivalent, $(x,y) \in U$, iff

for every $b \in B$ $E(\Sigma(b),x) = E(\Sigma(b),y)$

for any $(i,j) \in \mathbb{N}^2$ the relation $u(x,i,j)$ is identical to the relation $u(y,i,j)$.

Example

Let $x = a_1 b_1 c_1 d_1 e_1 f_1$ be a computation of a schema whose data-flow schema is such that:

$$R(a) = \{m_1\} = D(b) = D(d),$$

$$R(b) = R(d) = \{m_2\} = D(c) = D(e),$$

$$R(c) = \{m_3\}, R(e) = \{m_4\}, D(f) = \{m_3, m_4\}:$$

Let us consider the computation $y = a_1 d_1 b_1 e_1 c_1 f_1$ of a schema whose data-flow schema differs from the preceding one in the following way:

$$D(c) = R(b) = \{m_2'\}, D(e) = R(d) = \{m_2''\}.$$

Then we can deduce that $(x,y) \in U$.

It is clear that this equivalence is weaker than the preceding one, moreover it allows us to compare schemas with different sets of variables but with the same set of operators.

4.2 Transformation

The transformation we are going to describe needs not only a transformation of the sequential control schema but also a transformation of the data-flow schema.

4.2.1 Transformation of the control schema

For the U-equivalence, maximal concurrency may be reached by retaining from the sequential program, sequentiality only between occurrences of operators linked by some relation 'u'.

The GQR which allows concurrency is built as follows:

(1) For any operator b the set of input queues of b is

$$I(b) = \{F_{b,i} | i \in [1, |D(b)|]\}$$

and

$$\mathfrak{F} = \bigcup_{b \in B} I(b),$$

We shall use the following notation: let $F_{b,i}$ be any queue, $Op(F_{b,i})$ is the set of operators, including b, which have an output variable which is the ith input variable of b.

(2) The finite automaton $\mathfrak{P}$ is built as in the preceding transformation, and its transitions are labelled with append operations defined by the following rule: for a transition of $\mathfrak{P}$ between a state q_i and a state q_j, one appends to a queue $F_{b,i}$ a word $x \in (\{\bar{a}|a \in Op(F_{b,i})\})^*$ which corresponds exactly to the sequence of symbols belonging to

$$\underset{a \in Op(F_{b,i})}{\cup} \Sigma(a)$$

accepted between the states q_i and q_j of the sequential control schema.

For the example we obtain the following GQR:

$$I(a) = \{F_{a,1}\}, \quad I(b) = \{F_{b,1}\}, \quad I(c) = \{F_{c,1}\},$$
$$I(p) = \{F_{p,1}\}, \quad I(d) = \{F_{d,1}\}, \quad I(e) = \{F_{e,1}, F_{e,2}\},$$
$$I(f) = \{F_{f,1}\}, \quad I(g) = \{F_{g,1}\}.$$
$$Op(F_{a,1}) = \{a\}, \quad Op(F_{b,1}) = \{b\}, \quad Op(F_{c,1}) = \{c\},$$
$$Op(F_{p,1}) = \{p, b, d\}, \quad Op(F_{d,1}) = \{d, b\}, \quad Op(F_{e,1}) = \{e, c\},$$
$$Op(F_{e,2}) = \{e, a, f\}, \quad Op(F_{f,1}) = \{f, a\}, \quad Op(F_{g,1}) = \{g, c, e\}.$$

The initial content of the queues is:

$$F_{a,1} : \bar{\alpha}\bar{a}, \quad F_{b,1} : \bar{\alpha}\bar{b}, \quad F_{c,1} : \bar{\alpha}\bar{c}, \quad F_{p,1} : \bar{b}\bar{p}, \quad F_{d,1} : \bar{b},$$
$$F_{e,1} : \bar{c}, \quad F_{e,2} : \bar{a}, \quad F_{f,1} : \bar{a}, \quad F_{g,1} : \bar{c}.$$

For two steps of the iteration, the concurrency which is obtained may be visualized as in figure 4.9. If we compare this graph to the preceding one we can verify that arrows from e to f have disappeared.

Figure 4.8.

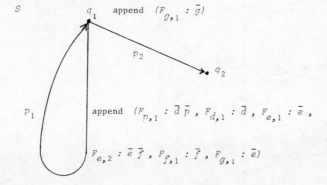

4.2.2   Transformation of the data-flow schema

Looking at the preceding example we notice that the operator f may go faster than the operator e, and the advance which can be taken by f is unbounded. So in order to maintain in the parallel schema the 'u' relations existing in the sequential program we are going to define a principle of single-assignment of the variables by each occurrence of the execution of an operator.

First we replace each variable of the sequential schema by an unbounded one-dimensional array. The addressing mechanism of such arrays uses the following:

> Let q be a state reached by a GQR and $F_{b,i}$ be a queue associated with a variable m;
>
> $nb(q, d, F_{b,i})$ is an integer which counts the number of occurrences of symbols in $F_{b,i}$ preceding the first occurrence of $\bar{d}$;
>
> only those symbols corresponding to operators which have m as an output variable are counted;

so this integer counts exactly the number of times the ith input of operator b is assigned in the sequential schema before the next occurrence of d.

Now we can state the addressing rules. Once an operator b is enabled in a state q

> (1) it uses in the array corresponding to its ith input the value located in the value located in the $nb(q, b, F_{b,i})$ item of this array.

Figure 4.9.

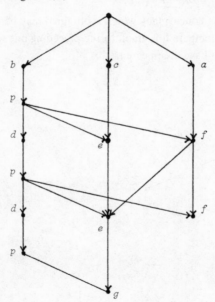

(2) it produces in the array corresponding to its jth input a value located in the $nb(q, b, F_{c,k}) + 1$ item of this array, where $F_{c,k}$ is any queue such that the kth input of c is the jth output of b in the sequential program.

Example

We consider the array X corresponding to the variable X in the preceding example.

When the first occurrence of a is enabled, queues $F_{e,2}$ and $F_{f,1}$ each contain a prefix of the form $\bar{a}$, so the value computed by a is located in the first item of X.

When the first occurrence of e is enabled $F_{e,2}$ contains a prefix of the form $\bar{a}\bar{e}\bar{f}$ or $\bar{a}\bar{e}\hat{f}$ so $nb(q, e, F_{e,2}) = 1$ and e uses the first item of X.

When the first occurrence of f is enabled, a prefix of $F_{f,1}$ is of the form $\bar{a}\bar{f}$, so f uses the first item of X; moreover $F_{e,2}$ contains a prefix of the form $\bar{a}\bar{e}\bar{f}$ or $\bar{a}\bar{e}\hat{f}$; consequently $nb(g, f, F_{e,2}) = nb(q, f, F_{f,1}) = 1$ and the second item of X is assigned by f.

When the second occurrence of e is enabled, $F_{e,2}$ contains a prefix of the form $\bar{a}\bar{e}\hat{f}\bar{e}\bar{f}$ or $\bar{a}\bar{e}\hat{f}\bar{e}\hat{f}$, then $nb(q, e, F_{e,2}) = 2$ and e uses the second item of X.

And so on.

References

(BA 73) J. L. Baer 'A survey of some theoretical aspects of multiprocessing' *A.C.M. Computing Surveys*, **5**, 1, 1973

(DE 74) J. B. Dennis 'First version of the data-flow language' in *Proc. of the first Symposium on Programming. Paris 1974. Lect. notes in Comp. Sc 19* Springer-Verlag

(KA 69) R. M. Karp & R. E. Miller 'Parallel program schemata' *J.C.S.S.* **3**, 2, 1969

(KE 73) R. M. Keller 'Parallel program schemata and maximal parallelism' *J.A.C.M.* **20**, 3, 4, 1973

(KU 75) D. J. Kuck *Parallel processors architecture, a survey* Sagamore Conference on Parallel Processing, Syracuse University Press, 1975

(LA 75) L. Lamport *Parallel execution on array and vector computers* Sagamore Conference on Parallel Processing, Syracuse University Press, 1975

(LO 79) L. Logrippo 'Renamings, maximal parallelism, and space-time tradeoff in program schemata *J.A.C.M.* **26**, 4, 1979

(RO 74) G. Roucairol 'Une transformation de programmes séquentiels en programmes parallèles' *First Programming Symposium. Paris 1974. Lect. Notes in Comp. Sc. 19* Springer-Verlag

(RO 78) G. Roucairol 'Contribution à l'étude des équivalences syntaxiques et transformations de programmes parallèles' Thèse d'Etat, Institut de Programmation, Université Pierre et Marie Curie, Nov. 1978

5 Representation of parallelism in computer programs

SHIRLEY A. WILLIAMS

1 Introduction

The development of multiprocessors has enabled the throughput of computation to be increased over that for serial processors. In order that serial programs may utilise the speed of multiprocessors it is necessary to be able to examine such programs and indicate where there is potential parallelism. In this chapter a method of detecting parallelism in Algol-type programming languages will be presented. This method, which is based on studying variable usage, will then be extended to illustrate proposed language features that will enable the programmer to express the inherent parallelism in the problem being encoded.

1.1 Processor memory

It will be assumed here that each processor of the multiprocessor has attached to it a private memory in which copies of the data it is using can be kept. When a process has been completed, all its non-private data is available to be copied into a shared memory.

The implementation of the multiprocessor need not be as simple as the above suggests. Indeed as Mead and Conway (1980) point out it must be recognised that communication is expensive and computation is not, so an efficient scheduling strategy and a hierarchical arrangement of processors may be used to emulate the above.

2 Detection of parallelism

It is proposed that a serial program will be divided into sections between which possible execution ordering of relationships will be examined for parallelism.

Suitable program areas that can be considered for formulation into sections include:

  (i) Individual statements
 (ii) Groups of assignment statements
(iii) Blocks of an Algol-type program
(iv) Iterations of a loop

(v) Conditional statements

(vi) Execution of a procedure after a call.

The term 'process' will be used to describe these sections. A process itself may be composed of other processes and so the size of a process is somewhat arbitrary. Here it is assumed that the size of a process will be chosen to reflect the parallelism in the problem while realising that communication between processors is expensive and so ensuring that processes are not too small.

For each process (P_i) input and output sets can be formulated, such that:

I_i represents the set of all locations for which the first operation in P_i involving them is a fetch.

O_i represents the set of all locations that are stored to in P_i.

2.1 Relationships between processes

The relationships that may exist between n processes $P_1, P_2, \ldots, P_n$ will not be considered. Assuming that a serial program, containing $P_1, P_2, \ldots, P_n$ is written such that P_{i+1} is always executed immediately after P_i, for all i such that $1 \leqslant i < n$. Then four distinct relationships may be considered to exist between n processes. These are:

(1) *Contemporary.* Processes $P_1, P_2, \ldots, P_n$ can be executed at the same time and the locations used accessed in any order.

(2) *Prerequisite.* Process P_i must fetch what it requires before P_{i+1} stores its results, for all i such that $1 \leqslant i < n$.

(3) *Conservative.* Process P_i must store its results before P_{i+1} does, for all i such that $1 \leqslant i < n$.

(4) *Consecutive.* Process P_i must be completed before P_{i+1} commences, for all i such that $1 \leqslant i < n$.

There are a number of other relationships that may be deemed to exist between processes. Although these are not relevant to converting serial programs to run on multiprocessors with private memories, two examples will be given:

(5) *Commutative.* The set of processes $P_1, P_2, \ldots, P_n$ may be executed in any order but once a process has commenced it must be completed before any other process can commence.

(6) *Synchronous.* Processes $P_1, P_2, \ldots, P_n$ must all fetch their inputs before any process stores its results.

The reader may like to consider what other relationships are possible.

Using the input and output sets of processes it is possible to develop tests to determine which relationships, in addition to consecutive, exist between a group of processes $P_1, P_2, \ldots, P_n$. Details of how these tests can be derived are given in Evans and Williams (1980) and the tests are summarised in table 5.1. It can be seen that any relationship in the table contains all the conditions for the relationships beneath it, thus it will be possible to systematically establish the 'strongest' relationship that exists between a group of processes. Similarly the tests for a small group of processes $P_k, \ldots, P_m$ are a subgroup of the tests for a larger group $P_1, P_2, \ldots, P_n$, where $1 \leqslant k < m \leqslant n$. Thus it is possible to establish the relationships for small groups of processes and then use that information to help derive the relationships for a larger group. Iterative loops are a special case of this and several 'short cuts' are given in Evans and Williams (1980) for establishing the relationships between iterations of loops.

2.2   Example

A simple example of detecting the relationships between processes will be presented here (more detailed examples appear in Evans & Williams (1980)). Consider these two statements that appear adjacently in a program:

$a \leftarrow b \uparrow n$;

$b \leftarrow c \uparrow n$

Assuming each statement may be executed as a separate process then the assignments to a and b can be processes P_1 and P_2 respectively. The input and output sets are:

I_1: b, n $\qquad$ O_1: a

I_2: c, n $\qquad$ O_2: b

The relationship between the processes is known to be at least consecutive and using the input and output sets it is possible to test for the other relationships.

Table 5.1. *Conditions necessary for a given relationship to exist between n serial processes $P_1, P_2, \ldots, P_n$*

Relationship	Tests
Contemporary	$I_k \cap O_l = \emptyset^*$ $O_k \cap (O_{k+1} \cup \ldots \cup O_n) = \emptyset^+$
Prerequisite	$O_k \cap (I_{k+1} \cup \ldots \cup I_n) = \emptyset^+$ $O_k \cap (O_{k+1} \cup \ldots \cup O_n) = \emptyset^+$
Conservative	$O_k \cap (I_{k+1} \cup \ldots \cup I_n) = \emptyset^+$
Consecutive	No conditions necessary as the processes are presented as being executed in this order

$\emptyset$ denotes the empty set
* for all k such that $1 \leqslant k \leqslant n$ and for all l such that $1 \leqslant l \leqslant n$ and $k \neq l$
+ for all k such that $1 \leqslant k < n$

Conservative

$$O_1 \cap I_2$$
$$a \cap (c, n) = \emptyset \qquad P_1 \text{ and } P_2 \text{ are conservative}$$

Prerequisite

$$O_1 \cap O_2$$
$$a \cap b = \emptyset \qquad P_1 \text{ and } P_2 \text{ are prerequisite}$$

Contemporary

$$I_1 \cap O_2$$
$$(b, n) \cap b = b \qquad P_1 \text{ and } P_2 \text{ are not contemporary}$$

Thus process P_1 must always fetch what it requires before P_2 stores its results.

3   Parallel programming

The test described in the previous section are one method of converting serial programs to run on multiprocessors. However if a problem is still to be programmed it may be worth considering a parallel implementation of it (Jones and Schwartz, 1980). Here a different facet of the tests will be presented, which will enable the user to write parallel programs.

Early proposals for parallel programming facilities (e.g. Algol 68) allowed communication via inspection and updating of common store. However this approach was said to create severe problems in the construction of correct programs and difficulties in the actual implementation. As a result of these doubts most of the recent proposals allow for direct communication between specified processes (e.g. Hoare, 1978). The method proposed here will be based on the memory arrangement given at the beginning of this chapter, which is similar to the concept of common store but easier to implement. This method will be particularly suited to representing the type of parallelism found in large scale simulations and numerical problems. It will be shown that proving the correctness of these programs will not be unduly difficult.

Consider a system where a process commences by reading the values of all non-local inputs it will need and taking private copies of them. The process then performs its operations using only local copies of variables. Finally any non-local variables that have been changed are made available for copying back to their non-local locations.

The reading of locations is non-destructive and there is no way of detecting that something is being read. Writing is destructive and if a read of a location was to occur during a write to it the value read is non-deterministic. Similarly if two or more processes write to one location at the same time the value left is non-deterministic.

The order of execution of these processes will be controlled by a series of calls which will constrain when processes can receive their inputs and transmit their outputs. A call of a group of processes may itself be considered as a process having inputs and outputs which will be passed to its subprocesses. The format of these calls will depend on the surrounding language, which will not be defined here. An illustration of the use of these calls will be presented in an Algol-type notation.

The six relationships (1) to (6) mentioned earlier are all suited to user definition of parallelism.

A suitable format for the calls would be to name the relationship and to follow this by the list of processes connected by it; along with each process name would be a list of its non-local inputs and outputs. Process definitions can then appear elsewhere using local names for both the inputs that will be received and the outputs that will be transmitted.

3.1   Example

A simple example of how a parallel construct could be programmed in this notation will now be given. Consider two processes that each take two inputs and transmit one output:

process *hcf*	**process** *lcd*
inputs $x1, x2$	**inputs** $y1, y2$
outputs $x3$	**outputs** $y3$
↑	↑
operations	operations
↓	↓

If a programmer wished to call *hcf* and *lcd* both with the same inputs a and b, the outputs going in to a and b respectively, then this could be effected by:

call synchronous (*hcf* (**in** a, b **out** a), *lcd* (**in** a, b **out** b))

3.2   Correctness

It is generally accepted that proving the correctness of non-trivial programs is difficult. This difficulty is exacerbated by the introduction of parallel programming because of the non-determinism that may occur when two or more processes may access one location at the 'same time'.

This method ensures that all the inputs and outputs to a process are listed. Additionally the relationships between processes are specified such that it is feasible to identify when inputs or outputs or both may be accessing a location at the 'same time'. It is thus possible to detect which variables will be affected by non-determinism, due to parallel programming, by forming the intersections of the appropriate input and output sets. This information can be used during the program construction phase to ensure non-determinism is not unknowingly introduced into the program. Furthermore the knowledge of non-determinism can be assimilated into a program representation and an established serial technique (such as symbolic execution) can be applied to verify the correctness of the program.

4 Conclusions

This chapter has considered programs in a multiprocessor environment. A number of areas have been dealt with only briefly and some areas (in particular optimisation and transformation) have been completely omitted. This is not because the author considers these areas to be unimportant but only to concentrate attention on the importance of studying variable usage in a multiprocessor environment. When serial programs are to be run on a multiprocessor studying the variable usage will enable detection of where operations may be executed in parallel. It would also appear that by considering variable usage it is possible to express parallelism in a manner that does not endanger the construction of correct programs.

Acknowledgements

This research was supported by the Science Research Council initially as a studentship and more recently by a postdoctoral research fellowship. The author would like to thank a number of colleagues at both Loughborough and Reading for useful discussions and suggestions.

References

Evans, D. J. and Williams, S. A. (1980) 'Analysis and detection of parallel processable code', *Computer Journal*, **23**, 1, 66–72
Hoare, C. A. R. (1978) 'Communicating sequential processes', *C.A.C.M.*, **21**, 8, 666–77
Jones, A. K. and Schwartz, P. (1980) 'Experience using multiprocessor systems – A status report', *Computing Surveys*, **12**, 2, 121–65
Mead, C. and Conway, L. (1980) *Introduction to VLSI Systems*, Addison-Wesley

6   Proof of protocols in the case of failures

C. GIRAULT

1   Introduction

The management of distributed algorithms is based on the reliability of an underlying transmission protocol. It is essential to show how such a protocol may work even in the case of the most usual transmission failures: erroneous messages, lost messages, and crashes of sites. The first problem needs only some tests in the protocols but the last two are difficult. Known models and proofs avoid dealing with the superfluous messages eventually created by the required repetitions and with the complexity of asynchronous crashes and recoveries.

To obtain more than a superficial confidence, the assumptions about all failures must be carefully stated and it is necessary to give a precise description of the parallelism involved in asynchronous events at the sites. We obtain here an adequate modelling of a classical protocol by means of Petri nets in order to prove its reliabilit

The paper is organized as follows. The different types of transmission failures are considered in section 2, as well as some needed hypotheses on the network rules. Section 2 gives a Petri net model of the alternate bit protocol allowing any losses and repetitions. A very concise version is then presented using coloured Petri nets. Elementary structural properties of these nets are derived by means of linear algebra. Section 4 analyses the model behaviour in detail by examining the graph structure of all possible model states. The proofs concerning this graph structure and the protocol properties are given in section 5. Finally, the site crashes are studied and also the use of unalterable supports for recoveries. A very complete model is thus obtained and its behaviour is analysed.

2   Types of failures
2.1   Erroneous messages

We are not concerned with the quality of the error detection codes but only with the control of the needed repetitions. Therefore we assume that every erroneous transmission of a message is detected and in particular that no error can modify the control fields contained in the messages. The erroneous message is deleted; it will be repeated but without superfluity [BOCHMANN 77]. Thus this problem appears only as a particular case of the next one.

2.2   Lost and superfluous messages

Presumptions of losses of messages are given by time out mechanisms and thus repetitions may be forced. The 'alternate bit protocol' correctly manages these repetitions. However, in order to avoid the difficulties caused by superfluous messages, known descriptions and proofs assume that the time out delays are chosen long enough for alarms to occur only when losses are effective [AZEMA 81, BOCHMANN 77, 79, HOFFMANN 80, JARD 80]. Unfortunately this is not realistic, since messages may simply have been delayed by overload of the intermediate network nodes or of the terminal stations.

Conversely it is sufficient to assume that the messages are always received in the order of emission. This FIFO (first in, first out) constraint, not needed in the absence of superfluity, is verified for direct communication and more generally for circuit switching networks without reconfiguration. Under this very important hypothesis we will prove the correct behaviour of the protocol even with superfluous repetitions. Moreover, in spite of the intricacy of the parallel treatment of errors, we will finally obtain a very intuitive explanation of this behaviour as well as rather unknown side properties.

2.3   Crashes of sites

Crashes need the keeping of crucial information in non-volatile supports to avoid a complete restart. The received message, its number and the control state must be written in an atomic manner. Conversely in the model this writing and all the transmission operations must form divisible sequences with respect to crashes, and occurrences of crashes must be allowed in any intermediate state with the deletion of all volatile data.

3   Modelling of the protocol

The 'alternate bit' protocol may be used to control the exchange of messages between two stations Σ and Σ' directly or indirectly connected in both directions. The messages may wait in buffers but, if not lost, they are assumed to be always received in the emission order. Thus the ordered sets of buffers constitute two streams Λ from Σ to Σ' and Λ' from Σ' to Σ.

The principle of the protocol is that each station Σ or Σ' manages its own private bit B (or B') whose value is packed with every sent message to serve as a control bit. The changes of the control bits in a stream of messages are used to acknowledge the messages that have been sent in the opposite direction. When an awaited acknowledgement does not arrive in time, due to some loss or delay, a time out mechanism enforces the repetition of the message sent.

3.1 Petri net modelling

Let us now give a first description of the protocol by means of Petri nets [PETERSON 77, BRAUER 79]. The net of figure 6.1 is composed of four parts, two for the stations Σ and Σ' and two for the streams Λ and Λ'.

When Σ is ready to get a new message from its environment, and if B has the value '0', the state of Σ is represented by a token in the place S. The message is packed with the value of B and may be denoted by M. It is sent in the stream Λ by the transition s that also makes Σ pass to the state W and arms the clock of Σ with a delay Θ.

If B has the value '1' we replace S, M, s, W in the above procedure by $\bar{S}, \bar{M}, \bar{s}, \bar{W}$.

Figure 6.1.

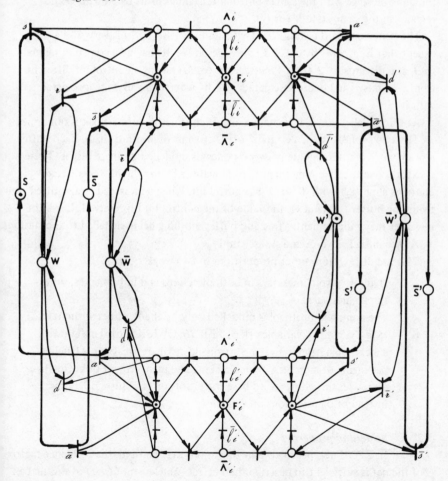

Σ now waits for a response from Σ' and thus scans the responses delivered via the stream Λ'. A message is denoted by M' (or $\bar{M}'$) according to the value of the control bit that Σ' has packed with it.

If this control bit is equal to the private bit B, the response is not an acknowledgment but only a superfluous message. Thus the transition d only discards this response M' from Λ' (or $\bar{d}$ discards $\bar{M}'$) and Σ remains in the same state with the clock still armed.

Otherwise the response is an acknowledgement. Thus the transition $\bar{a}$ accepts $\bar{M}'$ (or a accepts M'): the response is removed from Λ', the message given to the environment, the clock disarmed and Σ passes from state W to $\bar{S}$ (or from $\bar{W}$ to S), alternating the value of its private bit B.

When in state W (or $\bar{W}$) the time Θ is out, Σ repeats by the transition r (or $\bar{r}$) the same message with the same control bit, again arms its clock with Θ and remains in the same state W (or $\bar{W}$).

The behaviour of the station Σ' (with states W', $\bar{W}'$, S, $\bar{S}'$) is very similar except that Σ' accepts by a' (or $\bar{a}'$) messages M (or $\bar{M}$) having a control bit equal to B' and discards by $\bar{d}'$ (or d') messages $\bar{M}$ (or M) having a control bit different from B'. Thus a' and $\bar{d}'$ are associated with W' whereas $\bar{a}$ and d are associated with W.

At the initialization Σ is in state S and Σ' in state W' but its clock is not armed.

The two subnets Λ and Λ' model FIFO streams of arbitrary sizes. Each buffer (for instance in intermediate network nodes) is modelled by three places. There is exactly one token among them that indicates whether the buffer is free or contains a message with '0' or '1' as control bit. When a message is transmitted from one buffer to the next, the value of the control bit is preserved. Losses of messages may independently free any buffer, nothing being signalled to the stations.

At the initialization Λ and Λ' are empty.

This net differs from other propositions in two ways:

1. It allows several messages in both directions and in particular, super-fluous messages.
2. The complete protocol is modelled only by the Petri net without external control variables [KELLER 76, OWICKI 76]. This allows a clear separation between control and auxiliary treatments (such as packaging of messages, error checking and management of buffers). Moreover this allows us to base the proofs on structures of graphs instead of on assertions on variables.

3.2   Structural properties

In a Petri net, provided that transitions may be fired, the incidence matrix C of the net is sufficient to describe their effect. An element $C(p,t)$ of this matrix is the difference between the number of tokens placed and removed by the transition t in the place p.

Let $k = (k_i)$ be any integer vector solution of the linear system $C \cdot k = 0$ with $k_i \geqslant 0$. Such k_i may be considered as the numbers of occurrences of each transition in a sequence of firings that does not modify the marking. Here this system shows that all such sequences must contain an equal number of all the transitions $s, a', \bar{s}', \bar{a}, \bar{s}, \bar{a}', s', a$. Moreover they may be fired in this order. But we have still to prove that this is always possible.

Let $w = (w_i)$ be any integer vector solution of the linear system $w^T \cdot C = 0$ with $w_i \geqslant 0$. Such w_i may be considered as the weights of places such that the weighted sum of the tokens in the places remains invariant by any firing. The solutions show that there is always exactly one token in the set $S, W, \bar{S}, \bar{W}$, one in the set $S', W', \bar{S}', \bar{W}'$ and one in each set like $F_i, \Lambda_i, \bar{\Lambda}_i$ or $F_i', \Lambda_i', \bar{\Lambda}_i'$. These invariants may be interpreted as follows: $\bar{\Sigma}$ and Σ' are processes and each buffer is well managed.

Moreover we may introduce extra places to obtain more invariants. For instance, with a host emitter place E, a host receiver place R' and a dummy place L for losses (see figure 6.2), it appears that the number of tokens in the set $E, \Lambda_0, \ldots, \Lambda_n, R', L$ and similarly in $\bar{E}, \bar{\Lambda}_0, \ldots, \bar{\Lambda}_n, \bar{R}', \bar{L}$, $\bar{E}', \bar{\Lambda}_0', \ldots, \bar{\Lambda}_n', \bar{R}, \bar{L}'$, $E', \Lambda_0, \ldots, \Lambda_n, R, L'$ are invariants: all non-lost messages emitted with a given control bit are still in the stream or have been received without change of this bit.

However these structural properties are not sufficient to prove that any message sent and eventually repeated will be accepted exactly once. These invariants would be satisfied if, for instance, the first message M_0 were lost, the next $\bar{M}_1$ accepted, the next M_2 and its repetition M_2 accepted. Thus we will have to study in detail the behaviour of the net. Before that let us give a new version of our model.

Figure 6.2.

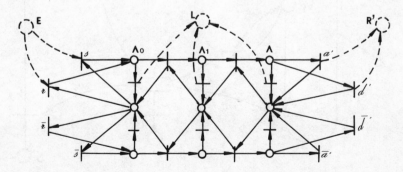

3.3   Coloured Petri net model

In order to obtain a concise description we now use coloured Petri nets [JENSEN 79, PETERSON 80] that appear also as a simplified case of predicate-transition nets [GENRICH 79]. In our case the tokens will only be coloured by '0' or '1'. For the states of the stations the colours indicate the values of the managed private bits, for the messages the colours indicate the values of the packed control bits. In our case the arcs are labelled by a free variable x or its opposite $\bar{x}$. For a given firing of a transition this variable must be bounded by either '0' or '1', in order to determine the colours of the tokens carried by the arcs. If x is for instance bounded by '0', then all the arcs labelled by x will carry only '0' tokens and those labelled by $\bar{x}$ only '1' tokens. In figure 6.3, if W contains a '0' token then x must be bounded also by '0' to allow the firing of either

Figure 6.3.

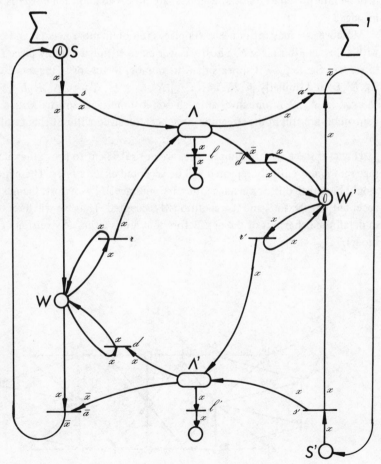

d or *a*: *d* fires if a '0' token may be got from Λ leaving unmodified the token in
W, *a* fires if a '1' token is got and the '0' token in W is replaced by a '1' token in S.

Starting from the previous model, the use of colours allows us to combine the
places such as S and $\bar{S}$ or W and $\bar{W}$. For a further simplification we use FIFO
places for Λ and Λ': in such places, coloured tokens may only be got in the
order in which they have been put. To allow any number of repetitions, these
places may contain an unbounded number of tokens. The protocol is now
modelled by the simple net of figure 6.3, where, at the initialization S and W'
contain a '0' token and all other places are empty.

4   Behaviour of the protocol

The parallelism induces a very complex graph of the states of the
system. We now need notations to make understandable all the possible func-
tionings of the whole net and to prove its properties.

Because we assume that the order of messages emitted by Σ or Σ' is preserved,
it is convenient to use words λ or λ' on the alphabets $M, \bar{M}$ or $M', \bar{M}'$ to
describe the contents of Λ and Λ'.

4.1   Patterns of states

We shall prove that Λ and Λ' may only contain messages of one type,
possibly followed by messages of the other type. As Λ contains some M followed
by some $\bar{M}$ or vice versa, λ may only have one of the two patterns $M^* \bar{M}^*$ or
$\bar{M}^* M^*$ (where an asterisk indicates any number, possibly zero, of repetitions).
More precisely, we have to consider the lack of some symbols and to split M^*
into $M^+ \cup \epsilon$ (where $^+$ indicates any non-zero number of repetitions and ϵ the
empty word). Let us denote by π the pattern of λ: $\pi \in M^+ \bar{M}^+, \bar{M}^+ M^+, M^+, \bar{M}^+, \epsilon$.
Similarly π' is the pattern of λ'.

Let $\sigma \in S, \bar{S}, W, \bar{W}$ and $\sigma' \in S', \bar{S}', W', \bar{W}'$ be the states of Σ and Σ'.
A global state of the system is thus a quadruple $\langle \sigma, \sigma', \lambda, \lambda' \rangle$ and its pattern is
$\langle \sigma, \sigma', \pi, \pi' \rangle$ where π and π' are the patterns of λ and λ'.

4.2   The reachability graph and its quotient

The reachability graph G of the whole system has for nodes, all the
states $\langle \sigma, \sigma', \lambda, \lambda' \rangle$ that may be obtained from the initial state $\langle S, W', \epsilon, \epsilon \rangle$ by any
successive firings of transitions. In this graph G, there exists an arc labelled by
a transition t from one state to another if and only if the firing of t derives the
second from the first.

Because the size of G grows quickly with the maximum number of allowed
repetitions we prefer to draw its quotient graph Q, whose nodes are the equivalence classes of states having the same pattern. In Q there is an arc, labelled by t,

from one pattern to another if and only if the firing of t derives some state of the second pattern from some state of the first pattern. For instance $\langle S, W', M^+, \epsilon \rangle \xrightarrow{a'} \langle S, \bar{S}', M^+, \epsilon \rangle$ and also $\langle S, W', M^+, \epsilon \rangle \xrightarrow{a'} \langle S, \bar{S}', \epsilon, \epsilon \rangle$ because $\langle S, W', M^{k+1}, \epsilon \rangle \xrightarrow{a'} \langle S, \bar{S}', M^k, \epsilon \rangle$ with either $k > 0$ or $k = 0$. The size of this graph Q remains constant, whatever the allowed numbers of repetitions.

5 Proof of the protocol

The initial pattern $\langle S, W', \epsilon, \epsilon \rangle$ is in fact only a particular case of $\langle S, W', \bar{M}^*, M'^* \rangle$ where there remain $\bar{M}$ messages in Λ, M' messages in Λ' and moreover Σ' may be repeating M' messages. Thus we start the construction of Q from this more general pattern and we will then consider the initialization. This section will prove that Q is made of linked subgraphs each one composed of nodes having the same σ and σ'. We begin by studying the detailed structure of the first two subgraphs $\mathbf{S}$ ($\sigma = S, \sigma' = W'$) and $\mathbf{A}'$ ($\sigma = W, \sigma' = W'$).

We have now to study the assertions that govern the structure of $\mathbf{S}$ and $\mathbf{A}'$. This structure is described in figure 6.4, where, for the sake of clarity, we have not drawn the loops that do not change the patterns. Figure 6.5 shows the two complete projections of this part of Q on the subsystems $\langle S, S', \Lambda \rangle$ and $\langle S, S', \Lambda' \rangle$. Then we will prove that Q effectively has the structure shown in figures 6.4 and 6.6.

· Let $k, \bar{k}, k', \bar{k}'$ be the numbers of messages $M, \bar{M}, M', \bar{M}'$.

Lemma 1

If at the entry in $\mathbf{S}$ ($\sigma = S, \sigma' = W'$) there are no M messages in the stream Λ and no $\bar{M}'$ messages in Λ' ($\pi \subset \bar{M}^*, \pi' \subset M'^*$), then the following properties are verified:

1. The patterns π and π' are preserved by the firings $r', \bar{d}'$ only allowed inside $\mathbf{S}$ and by the losses.
2. Since $\bar{s}$ and $\bar{r}$ are not allowed, $\bar{k}$ cannot increase and may only decrease by $\bar{l}$ or $\bar{d}'$.
3. Since both r' and l' are allowed, k' may be modified in any direction.
4. The firing of s from $\sigma = S$ is always possible, whereas $\sigma' = W'$ cannot change since there is no M in Λ ($\pi \subset \bar{M}^*$).

Corollary 1

$\mathbf{S}$ may always be left but only by an s transition that leads to $\mathbf{A}'$. At the exit of $\mathbf{S}, \pi \subset \bar{M}^*M \subset \bar{M}^*M^*$ and $\pi' \subset M'^*$.

Lemma 2

If at the entry in $\mathbf{A}'$ ($\sigma = W, \sigma' = W'$) there are no $\bar{M}'$ messages in the stream Λ' and if all the $\bar{M}$ messages precede the M ones in the stream Λ ($\pi \subset \bar{M}^*M^*$,

$\pi' \subset M'^*$) then the following properties are verified:

1. The patterns π and π' are preserved by the firings $r, d, r', \bar{d}'$ only allowed inside $\mathbf{A}'$ and by the losses. Here the FIFO hypothesis is sufficient to avoid the shuffle in Λ of the newly generated M messages with the still remaining $\bar{M}'$ messages.

2. Since both r' and l' are allowed, k' may be modified in any direction.

3. Since $\bar{s}$ and $\bar{r}$ are not allowed, $\bar{k}$ may only decrease by $\bar{l}$ or $\bar{d}'$ until $\pi \subset M^*$ is definitely obtained.

4. Because of the FIFO hypothesis, the a' transition cannot fire before all the $\bar{M}$ messages have been lost or discarded and $\pi \subset M^*$ ($\bar{k} = 0$).

Figure 6.4.

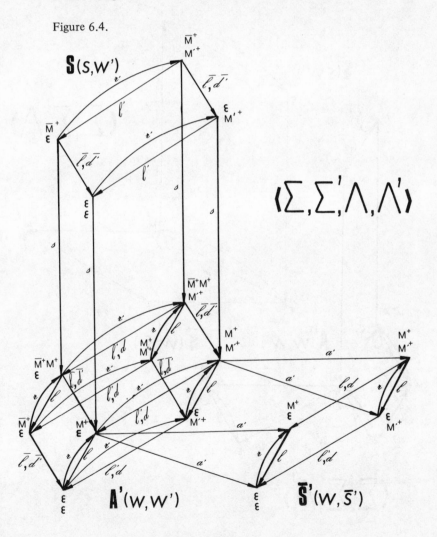

5. Because of the losses, π may become ϵ, but by the regular repetitions π may always be M^+ ($k > 0$) again.
6. Thus the firing of a' from $\sigma' = W'$ will certainly become possible; whereas $\sigma = W$ cannot change since there is no $\bar{M}'$ in Λ' ($\pi' \subset M'^*$).

Corollary 2

$\mathbf{A}'$ may always be left but only by an a' transition that leads to $\bar{\mathbf{S}}'$ ($\sigma = W$, $\sigma' = S'$). At the exit of $\mathbf{A}'$ $\pi = M^*$ and $\pi' = M'^*$.

Figure 6.5.

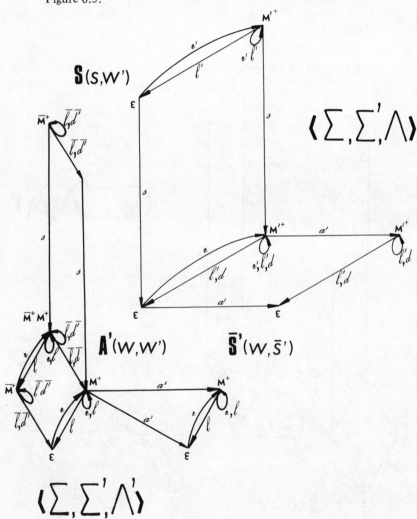

Theorem 1

From the pattern $\langle S, W', \bar{M}^*, M'^* \rangle$ the only possible behaviour of the system is the repetition of purely sequential moves from one subgraph to the next according to the following scheme:

$S \xrightarrow{s} A' \xrightarrow{a'} \bar{S}'$:   change Σ and Σ', $B' = \bar{B} = 1$

$\bar{S}' \xrightarrow{\bar{s}'} \bar{A} \xrightarrow{\bar{a}} \bar{S}$:   change back Σ and Σ', $B = B' = 1$

$\bar{S} \xrightarrow{\bar{s}} \bar{A}' \xrightarrow{\bar{a}'} S'$:   change Σ and Σ' again, $B' = \bar{B} = 0$

$S' \xrightarrow{s'} A \xrightarrow{a} S$:   change back Σ and Σ' again, $B = B' = 0$.

The proof results from circular application of corollaries 1 and 2. The only parallelism between Σ and Σ' occurs inside each subgraph. The complete structure of the graph Q is thus obtained (see figure 6.6).

Thus the Petri net is live: in any state there is a sequence that allows the firing of any transition. All the states like $\langle S, W', \bar{M}^*, M'^* \rangle$ are home states: they may always be re-entered and they allow the system to reach any other correct state.

Figure 6.6.

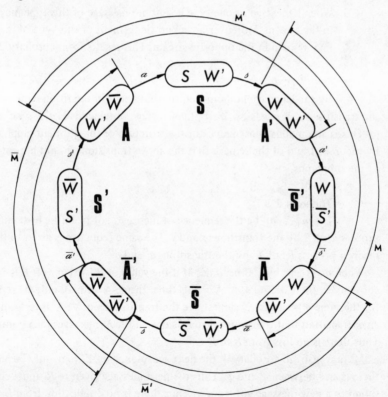

At the exit of all subgraphs like **A**, partial proper termination is obtained: there are no $\bar{M}$ in Λ and no $\bar{M}'$ in Λ'.

Remark

The initial state $\langle S, W', \epsilon, \epsilon' \rangle$ with the clock of Σ' disarmed satisfies the conditions of theorem 1. Moreover it allows us to obtain any state described by the patterns.

Only $\langle W, W', M, \epsilon' \rangle$ may be obtained at the first entry in $\mathbf{A}'$, $\langle W, \bar{S}', M^*, \epsilon \rangle$ at the first entry in $\bar{\mathbf{S}}'$, $\langle W, \bar{W}', M^*, \bar{M}' \rangle$ at the first entry in $\mathbf{A}$, and then with complete generality $\langle \bar{S}, \bar{W}', M^*, \bar{M}'^* \rangle$ at the entry in $\bar{\mathbf{S}}$.

Corollary 3

1. No stream contains more than one group of messages of one type followed by one group of the other type. This results from the preservation of all the patterns (and hence from the FIFO hypothesis).
2. There are never more than three types of messages in the whole network.
3. When a message of one type is sent, no message of this type may remain in the stream. Moreover no acknowledgement of this type of message may remain in the opposite stream. This results from corollary 2.

Corollary 4

By the language homomorphism that keeps in the firing sequences only the transitions $s, \bar{s}, a, \bar{a}, s', \bar{s}', a', \bar{a}'$, the language obtained is $(s\, a'\, \bar{s}'\, \bar{a}\, \bar{s}\, \bar{a}'\, s'\, a)^*$.

This is an obvious consequence of the structure of the quotient graph Q given by theorem 1 and of the remark that the above transitions do not appear in any of the subgraphs.

Theorem 2

Let $m_1 \ldots m_i$ be the sequence of messages got from the host emitter process E of Σ by the transitions s and $\bar{s}$. The same sequence is given to the host receiver process R' of Σ' by the transitions a' and $\bar{a}'$.

When m_i is sent by E it becomes M if the value of B is 0 (or $\bar{M}$ if B is 1). By corollary 2, there are no M in Λ at this time. Inside $\mathbf{A}'\, M$ may only be repeated for the same m_i because Σ cannot fire the transitions s or s'. $\mathbf{A}'$ is left only by an a' transition that transmits m_i to R' since all the M messages in Λ contain m_i. Thus there is no loss from E to R'.

Moreover, from corollary 4, the next acceptance by Σ' may only be an $\bar{a}'$, and there is an $\bar{s}$ between a' and $\bar{a}'$. Thus the next message given to R' must correspond to a new message got from E. Thus there is no duplication from E to R'.

Corollary 5

When Σ accepts m_i' from Σ' and gives it to its receiver R, this is also an acknowledgement that the last message m_i sent by Σ has effectively been given to R'. When m_i is sent, by corollary 2 there are no $\bar{M}'$ in Λ' if the value of B is 0 (or no M' if the value of B is 1). The $\bar{M}'$ awaited by Σ results from an $\bar{s}'$ that follows an a'. By theorem 2, a' gives m_i to R' and this $\bar{s}'$ gets m_i' for the same value of i. By theorem 2 again, Σ will give m_i'. Thus the numbering of the received messages that serve also to acknowledge agrees with the numbering of the emitted messages.

Discussion

Our analysis has proved that, even with losses and superfluous repetitions the alternate bit protocol is correct. The Petri net model conveniently describes the parallelism of operations on the two streams Λ and Λ'. Because they are almost independent, the reachability graph of the model may be simply considered as the Cartesian product of the graphs describing the two subsystems $\langle \Sigma, \Sigma', \Lambda \rangle$ and $\langle \Sigma, \Sigma', \Lambda' \rangle$. The introduction of state patterns is here powerful enough to study the behaviour and the properties of even an unbounded Petri net.

The FIFO hypothesis on the streams is very important. However, it is a sufficient but not necessary condition for the correctness. In fact it is only necessary to be able to test if there remains no message of some type in the whole network medium. This may be easily modelled by Petri nets with inhibitor arcs which forbid the firing of a transition while some of its input places are not empty. From a practical point of view the implementation of such a test is too complicated for the sake of only attaining a greater flexibility.

The understanding of this simple protocol and of its working hypothesis is the necessary basis for enabling us to generalize the proof when, as in the international standard for High Level Data Link Control procedures (HDLC), several types of messages may be sent in advance in each direction. The model has been easily generalized for HDLC and its correctness proof obtained by G. Berthelot.

6 Modelling of station crashes

We now finish our study of the reliability of the alternate bit protocol by showing how to deal with station crashes.

The recovery is based on the preservation of the most essential information during the crashes. A decomposition of the protocol in more elementary actions is needed to deal with the incidence of crashes at any time. We show how to introduce in our model this preservation, the occurrence of crashes and the recovery procedure. However, we do not give here the proof of the reliability of

the complete model. An example of a similar proof has been published for the
related problem of crashes during the update of a distributed data base [BAER 81].

6.1   Preservation of information

When a station crashes then all data and states of processes are lost. The
recovery procedure is based on the keeping of inalterable information in non-
volatile supports like disks or tapes. These supports, called logs, may be written
in an indivisible manner with respect to crashes. The information together with
an error detecting code are written on a free block. If this writing is achieved
without a crash the information may then be correctly read. Otherwise an error
will be detected, the recovery procedure will try to read the information, and the
previously stored block will be used instead of the incorrect one. Of course, the
recovery procedure also needs a volatile copy of the log, but it does not matter
if a new crash occurs during this procedure: since the log state is not destroyed,
the procedure will only be started again.

Thus, after a crash the logs are the only information that can be used. Therefore all the process states associated with the same log state must be considered
as equivalent. As the log writings are costly, they must be restricted to the crucial
changes of the process. Here, a writing is obviously needed each time the private
bit of a station is alternated and the accepted message given to the host receiver.
Our model will use the minimum number of log writings.

We do not want to model the treatment of crashes in the environment of
a station, but only the recovery of the station itself. Thus we assume that its
emitter and its receiver are reliable. Moreover, the message number may also be
kept in the log and thus it does not matter if the station requests the same
message from the emitter several times or gives the same message to the receiver
several times.

The use of logs may be conveniently modelled in a Petri net by introducing
places associated with the log states. A token is moved from some log place L or
changed in colour by some transition modelling the writing of a log. During
normal operations this token represents information superfluous to the one
determined by the process state. However in the case of a crash, this token
remains unchanged. On the subsequent recovery the choice of the new state
will depend on the position and the colour of this token. Our model combines
the detailed net of the station, the very simple net that keeps trace of the log,
and all the crash and recovery transitions (see figure 6.7).

6.2   Modelling of crashes and recoveries

Crashes can occur at any time but their incidence on low level sequences
of instructions is not very meaningful. It is sufficient to allow their occurrences

between the following operations: getting a message g, preparation of a sending s, or of a repetition r, output to the other station o, input from the other station i, test for discarding d or acceptance a, transmission of a message to the receiver t and finally log writing wl or log reading rl.

When a crash occurs, the state of station Σ as well as the copy of its private bit are lost. Therefore for each state place, a transition c may remove any coloured token from that place and put a colourless token in a special place C. A crashed station is thus modelled by a colourless token in the place of C, a coloured one in L and no token in the other places. Moreover any message

Figure 6.7.

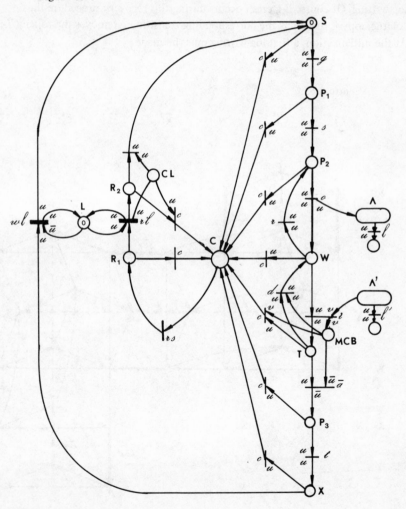

buffered or being processed by Σ is lost. Therefore in such a case, the transition c also removes any token corresponding to the internal information of Σ. For instance, after an input the station has a copy of the message control bit (MCB in figure 6.7) in order to test it (state T); a crash may remove both tokens, whatever their colours. All new arriving messages will be ignored but this is already modelled by the losses in Λ'.

The recovery start rs is modelled by moving the colourless token from C to the place $R1$. By the log reading rl, a volatile copy of the log CL is taken. This allows us to find again the lost colour of Σ (and also the number of the current message for communicating with the environment). Nothing else being known, the only thing to do is to restart all the operations, beginning just after the last log writing. Of course if a crash occurs during this recovery procedure the volatile copy is lost, thus the corresponding transition c removes the token CL. At the initialization, a first log writing must be made.

Figure 6.8.

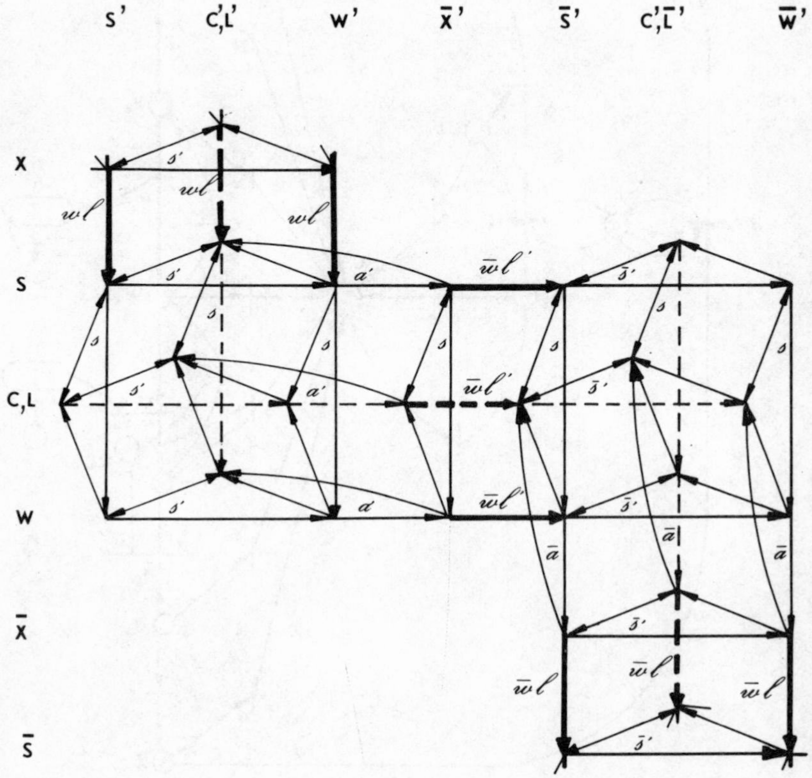

6.3   *Behaviour of the protocol*

In this section we neglect the intermediate states by identifying
R_2, S, P_1, P_2 with S, W, T with W, P_3, X with X, R_1, C with C. We combine
L with C in order to distinguish the value of the log in case of crashes.

Figure 6.9.

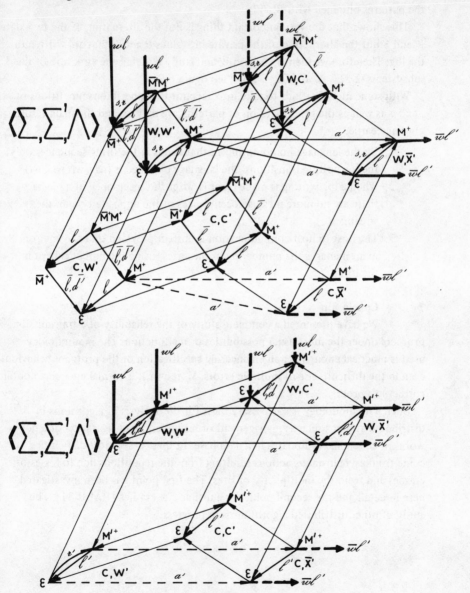

The schema of figure 6.8 shows the incidence of crashes on the states of the stations. Of course when only one station has crashed, the other may continue to have some more changes of state. The recovery creates new situations, for instance pairs of states like S, S'. Also, more general patterns may now be obtained. For instance, sequences like $\langle S, W', \bar{M}^+, M'^+\rangle \xrightarrow{s} \langle W, W', \bar{M}^+M^+, M'^+\rangle \xrightarrow{c} \langle CL, W', \bar{M}^+M^+, M'^+\rangle \xrightarrow{rl} \langle S, W', \bar{M}^+M^+, M'^+\rangle$ associate with S, S' (or S, W') all the patterns obtained with W, W'.

This shows that the very important thing is not the alternation of the two states W and S but the alternation of the private bit values B and $\bar{B}$ that are written on the log. Therefore we identify S with W and study in detail the structure of the subsystems $\langle \Sigma, \Sigma', \Lambda \rangle$ and $\langle \Sigma, \Sigma', \Lambda' \rangle$; see figure 6.9.

With some modifications to take into account the superfluous repetitions of s and a as well as the generalization of patterns, we may extend the main results obtained earlier:

1. By the language homomorphism that keeps in the firing sequences only the log writing transitions, the language obtained is $(\overline{wl}', \overline{wl}, wl', wl)^*$.
2. When a log writing is made (that is, after the acceptance of a message) there are no more message occurrences of the opposite type in the stream.
3. The host to host communication is correct provided that the environment manages the numbering of messages (using the numbers kept in the logs).

7   Conclusion
We have presented a complete study of the reliability of a transmission protocol under the most usual possibilities of malfunction. The methodology used is practical enough for an engineering specification of the protocol behaviour even in the difficult case of multiple errors. Moreover it is formal enough to obtain correctness proofs.

Such a methodology is a necessary basis for the analysis of algorithms in distributed systems such as management of resources, reconfiguration of a network, or coherence of updates in a data base. In these cases most difficulties come from asynchronous actions resulting from the repetitions due to losses or crashes and from the multiplicity of sites. The first point has been investigated here in detail and the second point for multiple site crashes [BAER 81]. The study of other distributed algorithms is in progress.

References

Azema, P. 'Application des réseaux de Petri à l'étude des mécanismes de communication' in *7th Ecole de Printemps d'Informatique Théorique: Réseaux de Petri et parallélisme*, éd. Roucairol, G., Colleville, May 1980 (to appear LITP-ENSTA, University of Paris, VII, 1981)

Baer, J. L., Gardarin, G., Girault, C., Roucairol, G. 'The two step commitment protocol, modeling, specification and proof methodology', *5th International Conf. on Software Engineering, I.E.E.E., San Diego, March 1981*

Berthelot, G., Terrat, R. 'Modernisation d'un protocole de transport par réseaux de Petri', *5th Summer School 'Programming 80', Primorsko, Bulgaria, June 1980*

Best, E. 'Atomicity of activities' in *Proceedings of the Advanced Course on General Net Theory of Processes and Systems, Hamburg, October 1979*, ed. Brauer, W., Lecture Notes in Computer Science, 84, Springer Verlag, 1980, pp. 235–50

Bochmann, G. V. *Architecture of distributed systems*, Lecture Notes in Computer Science, 77, Springer Verlag, 1979

Bochmann, G. V., Jecsei, J. 'A unified method for the application and verification of protocols' in *Information Processing 77*, ed. Gilchrist, B., IFIP, North Holland Publishing Company, 1977

Brauer, W. (ed.) *Net Theory and Applications, Proc. of the Advanced Course on General Net Theory of Processes and Systems, Hamburg, October 1979*, Lecture Notes in Computer Science, 84, Springer Verlag, 1980

Danthine, A. 'Protocol representation with finite state models' *I.E.E.E. Transactions on Communications*, **28**, 4, April 1980

Genrich, H. J., Lautenbach, K. 'The analysis of distributed systems by means of predicate transition nets' in *Semantics of Concurrent Computation, Evian, 1979*. Ed. Kahn, G. Lecture Notes in Computer Science, 70, Springer Verlag, pp. 123–46, 1979

Hoffmann, M. G. 'Hardware implementation of communication protocols, a formal approach' in *7th Annual Symposium on Computer Architecture, La Baule, May 1980, SIGARCH Newsletter*, 8, 3, ACM-IEEE, 1980, pp. 253–63

Jantzen, M., Valk, R. 'Formal properties of place transition nets' in *Proceedings of the Advanced Course on General Net Theory of Processes and Systems, Hamburg, October 1979*, ed. Brauer, W., Lecture Notes in Computer Science, 84, Springer Verlag, 1980, pp. 165–212

Jard, C. *Description et validation de protocoles, présentation de quelques techniques sur un exemple particulier*, BIGRE. Bulletin 19, June 1980, IRISA – Rennes, pp. 11–19 (internal report)

Jensen, K. *Coloured Petri nets and the invariant method*. DAI MI-PB-104, Aarhus University, October 1979, pp. 1–27 (internal report)

Keller, R. M. 'Formal verification of parallel programs' *Communications of the A.C.M.* **19**, 7, July 1976, 371–84

Memmi, G., Roucairol, G. 'Linear algebra in net theory' in *Proceedings of the Advanced Course on General Net Theory of Processes and Systems, Hamburg, October 1979*, ed. Brauer, W., Lecture Notes in Computer Science, 84, Springer Verlag, 1980, pp. 213–24

Merlin, P., Farber, D-J. 'Recoverability of communication protocols: implications of a theoretical study' *I.E.E.E., Transactions on Com.*, September 1976, 1036–43

Owicki, S., Gries, D. 'Verifying properties of parallel programs: an axiomatic approach' *Communications of the A.C.M.*, **19**, 5, May 1976, 279–85

Peterson, J. 'Petri nets' *Computing Surveys*, 9, 3, September 1977, 223–52

Peterson, J. 'A note on coloured Petri nets' *Information Processing Letters*, **11**, 1, August 1980

PART 3

The Loughborough MIMD parallel processor system

7 The organisation and use of parallel processing systems

I. A. NEWMAN

1 Introduction

Although the term 'parallel processing systems' is normally only used to describe a small number of rather esoteric research oriented 'machines', it could be used with accuracy to describe a very large number of existing commercially available 'mainframe' computer systems. This chapter sets out to identify those advantages of parallel processing that have already been realised and those that are yet to be realised and discusses the work being undertaken in the Department of Computer Studies at Loughborough University to resolve some of the remaining problems.

The first part of the chapter describes possible organisations for parallel processing systems and identifies several levels at which parallelism can occur. The reasons for adopting a parallel processing solution to a problem are identified and the problems associated with the different organisations are noted.

The second part of the chapter describes an experimental system designed and implemented at Loughborough University to investigate different ways of exploiting parallelism. The final part of the chapter examines the problems of obtaining greater reliability in multiprocessor systems and identifies some of the solutions within the context of the experimental system described earlier.

Throughout the chapter, it is assumed that a parallel processing system exists when several operations contributing to the solution of a single problem can take place simultaneously. The operations being performed could be the same or different and the criterion for simultaneity is that an operation, in this sense, should be a single hardware instruction or some subdivision of an instruction. This constraint is required to eliminate multiprogramming on a single processor, which gives the appearance of parallel processing if time divisions of the order of seconds are considered.

2 Organisation of parallel processing systems

The organisation of a computer system can be examined at many levels of detail and from many points of view. Three obvious subdivisions within the structure of a computer system are hardware, system software and applications software. The types of parallelism that can exist at the hardware level and their effect on the structure of operating systems and other system software are examined below. The interrelationship of hardware and operating system structure on the applications programmer and the user is also discussed.

2.1   Parallelism in hardware

At the lowest hardware levels processing information in parallel is the norm, all 8 bits in a byte (or 16, 24, 32, etc. bits in a word) being processed simultaneously in most instructions on most computers.

Instruction pipelining is another form of parallel processing within conventional hardware. In this case either distinct sections within the decoding and execution of an instruction are carried out simultaneously or the decoding and execution of several instructions is overlapped. For both forms of pipelining the hardware must be designed to ensure that no value can be used in one instruction or in part of an instruction if it is being changed by an operation which should have occurred earlier in the sequence of instructions being executed. The hardware must achieve the same effect as if there had been no overlapping and this form of parallelism is therefore invisible to all programs running on that hardware, except for any increase in execution speed which may occur through the operation of the pipeline.

The same criterion does not, necessarily, apply to another example of parallelism in conventional hardware. Autonomous peripheral transfers, initiated by an instruction, or instructions, executed by the main processor but actually running under the control of a separate 'processor', can frequently access the memory that is available to the main processor, at the same time. If the main processor utilises an area of memory where a transfer is in progress the result could be unpredictable.

Nevertheless many existing computer systems comprise a main or 'central' processor which executes the application programs and one or more other general purpose processors (often with different architectures) to manage groups of peripherals, such as discs or communication lines. The processors typically communicate using designated areas of the main memory of the central processor and all transfers are under the control of 'trusted' programs to ensure that the potential for erroneous operation is not realised. Generally, the processors managing the peripherals have a fixed program loaded and act as slaves for the central processor which can itself only interact with them while running under the control of the operating system. Such computers are clearly examples of multiple instruction multiple data (MIMD) architecture (Flynn, 1966) although this is invisible to programmers at all but the operating system level. This structure is not usually described as a multiple processor architecture because no application programmer has any reason to be aware of the actual nature of the hardware.

Parallel processing systems where the hardware organisation is visible to programmers, and thus exploitable by them, will either comprise several separate processing units each capable of executing separate instructions independently, or several identical processing units simultaneously executing the same instruction, or, possibly, some combination of the two types. The second type of organisation is clearly classifiable as the single instruction multiple data (SIMD) type while the first is the MIMD type if the processors operate sequentially or possibly some different classification in the case of data flow machines (Syre, chapter 13; Treleavan, chapter 14).

Within the general class of MIMD systems there is a wide range of physical interconnections between the processors. The most integrated, or tightly coupled system comprises several processing units sharing the same memory while the most 'loosely coupled' comprises totally separate computer systems linked by slow speed communication lines. The characteristics of the linkage are the speed and bandwidth of any link and the extent of shared memory. Strictly, shared memory could be regarded as a very fast, high bandwidth, communication line provided the use of such memory is restricted to communication. However, it requires a different type of management from a communication line, so that it is more useful to consider shared memory as a separate mechanism.

At the hardware level a number of reasons can be advanced for implementing parallel processing systems:

(*a*) Additional speed: this prompted parallel rather than serial architectures originally, also pipelining and autonomous peripheral transfers. It is also the reason behind the implementation of the vector and array processors of the SIMD type. Two subclasses of speed can be distinguished: greater system throughput and greater execution speed for one program.

(*b*) Ease of implementation: as an example, general purpose processors were used to manage groups of peripherals rather than special purpose hardware being designed and implemented because it was quicker and easier (more cost-effective).

(*c*1) Greater reliability: often used in conjunction with reason (*a*) above. It would frequently be possible to achieve greater speed by using faster components but only if either a lower reliability level, or a much higher cost, were acceptable (absolute speed limits are, in any case, now being reached).

The above reasons apply, in general, to any parallel processing system. For

MIMD systems, in particular, additional reasons offered are:

(c2) Greater reliability: graceful degradation with processing continuing in the event of the failure of one of the duplicated components.

(d) Modular expansion: the addition of extra processing units as and when needed to meet load requirements. (This also includes the addition of special purpose processors to meet specialist requirements.)

2.2   System software for parallel systems

As has been noted earlier, where the hardware has concealed the parallelism, as in pipelining, the designer of the system software has no special decisions to make.

For all other hardware organisations two types of decision must be taken:

(1) how the hardware capabilities are to be exploited in the system software itself (if at all);

(2) whether to reveal the parallel architecture to the user (application programmer) or conceal it from him.

The outcome of the decisions depends largely on the reason for configuring the parallel processing system in the first place.

For those systems where ease of implementation or overall system throughput was the criterion the system programmer would normally use the facilities provided by the hardware and then conceal them from everyone else, giving the appearance of a uniprocessor system to all application programmers. Concealment would also be appropriate if the reason for configuring the system were overall reliability where components are replicated to ensure that there is a high probability of one remaining operational at all times.

It would, however, probably be thought counterproductive to conceal the parallelism if the reason for configuring the system was to provide higher execution speeds within a single program. In many examples of this type of machine it may also be difficult, if not impossible, for the system software to use the available parallelism effectively. The hardware is configured to be suitable for solving a particular class of problems and most system software is not of that class.

As a general rule, the MIMD systems are more likely to have been configured for ease, overall speed or overall reliability whereas the SIMD systems are generally designed for high execution speed on particular classes of problem.

The majority of the larger mainframe systems (IBM 370 and 303X, ICL 1900 and 2900, CDC 6600 and 7600) are MIMD systems which are organised at the system programming level so that they appear as uniprocessors to all other programmers.

The system software organisation used to manage parallelism again depends on the reason for configuring the system and the interface that is required for the application user. With many SIMD systems the system software simply ignores the parallel architecture, passing it directly to the application programmer to manage as best he can. However, although this in theory allows the application programmer to gain the maximum benefit from the parallelism with no system software overhead, it also passes on the burden of programming. Any parallel system is inevitably more difficult to program than a uniprocessor system and passing the architecture on unadulterated can lead to a considerably longer development time for programs with potentially very little benefit (execution speeds of the same order as for a uniprocessor) if the algorithm chosen is not suited to the hardware structure. The alternative is to provide some system software which wholly or partially conceals the parallelism. Typically, compilers may be provided which can translate vector or array operations, such as in APL or in some FORTRAN extensions, directly into the appropriate hardware operations. The maximum speed of the hardware is not normally obtainable using such compilers; on the other hand development times are decreased significantly.

There is a much wider range of organisational possibilities for system software on an MIMD machine. As noted earlier for SIMD systems, it is necessary to realise that programming a multiprocessor system explicitly is a great deal more difficult than programming a uniprocessor to carry out the same task since synchronisation between paths must be considered (Woodward, chapter 9). Thus, most application users would normally only choose to attempt to program the system in this way where no other choice was available to them (i.e. they either needed the speed within one task or the reliability of having several processors carrying out the same task to improve the chance that one will complete it). Coupling this structure with the normal reasons for providing MIMD systems, as already stated, means that the system software is normally organised to totally conceal the parallelism from other users of the hardware.

Two basic organisational possibilities exist for managing multiprocessor systems. The system can be hierarchical with functional division of tasks amongst the processors and a master–slave relationship between any pair of processors.

Alternatively every processor can be basically autonomous, communicating with the others on a basis of equality.

In the first case there is effectively a single system even at the system software level, with the set of data structures which are utilised by the software being spread over all the processors. In the second case it is possible to have either one system with the data structures being common to all the processors, or many systems with each processor having its own system software and its own separate data structures. On one hand application programs are processed by the system as a whole with resources including a processor being allocated as required from the totality of resources available, while on the other hand each processor has its own work load and application programs are managed by a particular processor which normally satisfies the requirement for the job from within its own resources.

The system software organisations are usually associated with particular hardware organisations. Master–slave hierarchies are used where there is an obvious 'central processor' with specialised processors carrying out specific tasks as in the large batch systems already mentioned. Several processing units sharing memory and peripherals as in the Plessey 250 system (Williams, 1972) would normally be run under a single operating system with shared data structures. A loosely coupled network of processors distributed physically at several locations would be a prime candidate for a structure with separate, largely autonomous, systems. Nevertheless there is no logical necessity to relate system software structure to hardware structure. It would be perfectly possible to partition the common memory and run a tightly coupled shared memory system as if it comprised autonomous processors. It would also be possible to run a collection of loosely coupled, distributed processors as if it were a single system with shared data structures and one pool of work. However, although it is possible and useful to separate the system software structure from the hardware structure a serious mismatch between them is likely to lead to a very ineffective overall system.

2.3   Parallelism at application programming level

As has already been stated programming a parallel system is substantially more difficult than programming a uniprocessor. Thus most users have no incentive to design their algorithms deliberately for a multiprocessor system. Clearly if they can write their programs ignoring the multiprocessor nature of the system and then gain the advantages through some action of the system (hardware or software) they will be happy to do so but this requires no special effort on their part. The only clear reasons for programming for a parallel processor are higher speed on a single problem or greater reliability for obtaining results to a problem. For greater reliability alone it would appear that the simplest solution is to replicate the same job on several systems and compare the results, thus requiring a minimum of interaction and a minimum of special programming. However, this solution is wasteful of resources, and it is possible to conceive of a combination of reliability and speed which would necessitate a solution utilising the flexibility of a multiple processor system. It should be noted, however, that increasing the reliability at the software level consumes other resources, resulting in a lower overall throughput.

3 Research in parallel systems at Loughborough

Section 2 described a number of organisations for parallel processing systems. It is clear that MIMD systems organised with functional specialisation for overall throughput are highly successful since most manufacturers have adopted this structure. It is also clear that SIMD systems are very useful for solving the special class of problems for which they are designed. Finally, networks of autonomous processors connected via communication lines, such as the ARPANET have been successfully established and have been operating for a number of years.

The problems of very tightly coupled and very loosely coupled MIMD architectures have been extensively researched. However, intermediate levels of coupling at the hardware and software level and 'mismatch' coupling (loosely coupled hardware and tightly coupled software or vice versa) have not been so widely studied.

Two particular aspects which have been selected for further work in the Department of Computer Studies at Loughborough University (supported by funds from the Science Research Council) are:

(1) A multiprocessor system with substantial shared memory on which each processor operates autonomously most of the time but can co-operate with one or more others in executing a particular program.

(2) Several separate computers with different hardware architectures, loosely coupled together, appearing to the users as a single computer system under some circumstances.

The first project is intended to investigate the possibility of combining several smaller machines to get the overall work throughput of a larger machine at a lower cost and with a higher reliability. It is assumed that most tasks (programs) submitted to the system as a whole would be capable of being executed satisfactorily on one of the processors running independently of the others, but a few of the tasks would require faster processing than could be provided by one computer alone. The overall design chosen to meet these objectives is a system comprising several processors each with enough private memory and peripherals to be capable of processing tasks effectively, together with shared memory and possibly other shared resources.

The software managing the separate computers must cooperate in allocating the shared resources (including memory) but a suitable balance of resources that are shared and those that are replicated on each machine should enable the overall resource utilisation to be optimised. Data structures in the shared memory which are accessible to programs running on all the individual processors provide the capability for cooperation with several processors being used to speed up the execution of a single task.

The research has been used to demonstrate the feasibility of such a design using production systems running the manufacturers' software to which a small number of modifications have been made. The initial research vehicle was a dual Interdata 70 system each machine having 32 Kb of private memory and 32 Kb shared and one machine having a 10 Mb disc (figure 7.1). Although limited this did demonstrate that speed-up factors of better than 1.8 could be achieved for individual tasks using suitably designed algorithms. A second research vehicle has since been established comprising four Texas 990/10 systems each with 96 Kb private memory and with 64 Kb shared memory and a 50 Mb shared disc, with one of the processors having a separate 10 Mb disc (figure 7.2). Each processor runs under the powerful DX10 uniprocessor operating system which has been modified to permit the processors to run independently and yet to cooperate in running programs with data in shared memory. This system has already been used to demonstrate that the familiar $1:1.8:2.3:1.8$ factors for 1, 2, 3 and 4 processors running on the same problem with all resources shared does not apply to this configuration since the shared memory is accessed relatively infrequently, provided the application program algorithms are designed sensibly.

The research has involved solving the problems of making minimum modifications to the operating systems to achieve satisfactory cooperation and of designing a coordination algorithm to work on unmodified hardware (Slade, chapter 8; Woodward, chapter 9). It has also involved the design and implementation of suitable algorithms for exploiting the parallelism and the design of tools for estimating potential parallelism (Newman & Woodward, 1977) and for measuring performance of the algorithms (Barlow, chapter 10).

Further research on the project is concerned with completing the implementation of parallel processing on the Texas system, designing algorithms for the configuration and measuring their performance, and investigating the overall throughput of the system with alternative methods of managing the shared resources. Of particular interest in this context is the management of information on the

Figure 7.1. Dual Interdata 70 system.

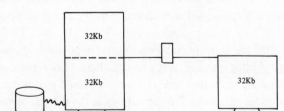

shared disc. Is it best for this to be handled by one processor with which the others communicate or should they coordinate to determine who obtains access?

The second project was concerned with one of the major obstacles to the successful exploitation of networks. On most existing networks comprising different processors, each processor has its own operating system and job control language and there is, in addition, a network job control language. This combination makes it very difficult for an individual user to make the best use of the available resources since he needs to know details of several systems. The alternative is to implement the same (machine independent) job control language on every machine and allow the user to specify the requirements of his job in a standard way without needing to be aware of the machine with which he is communicating. This approach was taken on a network comprising the two Interdata systems referred to earlier, and a PDP 11/40 which was also in the department.

The UNIQUE machine independent command language (Newman, 1980) was implemented on top of the existing operating system on both the Interdata and the PDP 11 computers. The machines were linked using 2400 baud asynchronous

Figure 7.2. Four-processor Texas Instruments 990/10 system.

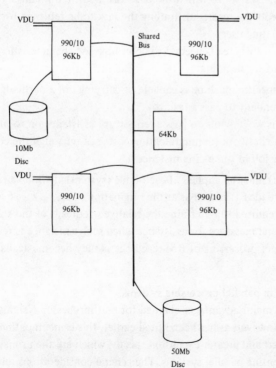

communication lines and file transfer and virtual terminal protocols were implemented. Terminals are connected to a specific machine and it is assumed that most tasks will be processed on the machine to which they are input. The command language allows the required sequence of operations, the scheduling constraints and an estimate of the necessary resources to be specified. The commands supplied by the user to describe a task that he wishes to perform are analysed by a command language compiler and the resource and constraint information is passed to the task scheduler on the machine. This scheduler decides whether the task can be completed within the constraints on that machine. If the task can be processed it is scheduled in the normal way, if it cannot help is sought from the other machines in the network. The scheduling requirements of the task are broadcast with a general request for help and replies are awaited. If only one reply is received the task is passed to that machine (the partially compiled job control and any required files are transmitted) while if several replies come one of the respondents is selected and the task is transmitted. If no reply is forthcoming within a short period the user is informed that the task cannot be processed at the present time and is given the opportunity of revising the constraints or resubmitting the task later. Whenever a task is moved between machines the system to which the task was submitted retains a copy of the request and expects the results of running the task to be returned for transmission to the originating user.

Further research in this area is needed to determine the characteristics of alternative algorithms for deciding:

(*a*) whether a specific machine is capable of carrying out a particular task;
(*b*) which respondent to pass a task to;
(*c*) whether it is worthwhile to pass a request for assistance on to other nodes in the network (communication costs can outweigh the cost of running the job in some circumstances).

Algorithms for (*c*) must be applied at each node (system) at which a request arrives, when it is broadcast, as well as at the originating node.

Research is also required to determine the relative overheads of the strategy of broadcasting general messages for assistance when such assistance is required, against notifying other processors of free resources as they become available.

4   Reliability in parallel processing systems

One of the major advantages claimed for multiprocessor systems is greater reliability. However, as has been noted earlier, this is incompatible with increasing throughput and greater execution speeds, which are the primary reasons for implementing parallel systems. The general considerations relating to reliability of computer systems are outlined briefly in section 4.1 below and then some specific problems and solutions related to MIMD systems comprising processors with some private and some shared resources are discussed.

4.1   General considerations

The reliability of a computer system is generally described in terms of the percentage of time for which the system is operational relative to the maximum time it could have been operating, and is normally thought of as relating to catastrophic hardware errors. However, more precisely, reliability is a measure of the probability of obtaining correct *outputs* for a particular task executed on the system within a given time (or a normalised sum of the probabilities for a variety of tasks). To provide a 'completely reliable' system all erroneous results would need to be detected, the processing would need to be reinstated to a position before the error occurred and the work would then need to be completed. Since it is only possible to detect and recover from errors which have been *anticipated*, and even this may involve an inordinate amount of work, practical systems will only give a high degree of protection against certain classes of faults. Completely reliable systems are unobtainable, however much is spent attempting to achieve them.

There has been a substantial amount of research work carried out in investigating the provision of protection against various types of malfunction (both software and hardware) in a conventional single processor system (Randell & Anderson, 1979) but this has not yet been consolidated into practical systems on any scale because of the cost and because of the loss of performance which is inevitably associated with checking for correct outputs. For most computer users the perceived risk of very occasionally obtaining incorrect results, or of not obtaining results at all, is acceptable, i.e. the reliability of existing hardware and software is quite adequate for their needs.

The few users who have tried to achieve greater reliability have been concerned with real-time applications where errors could be extremely costly. Typical solutions to the problem of protecting against complete failure of a computer system have been to duplicate the hardware and software and keep the second system running 'warm', replicating the work done by the first system. Malfunctions in the primary system are then detected manually and recovery is effected by switching over to the secondary system. This can of course be done automatically, providing it is possible to ensure that the error detection circuits cannot themselves be faulty and cause switching to take place from a 'good' processor to a failing processor. Since this cannot be guaranteed it is more usual to run the two machines in parallel doing identical work and detect errors by noting any inconsistency between the results. This leaves a decision on whether to continue, and if so, with which processor, to the humans in charge. Three identical systems have been used in very special applications with the outputs being compared with 'voting' logic, but even this begs the question of the action to be taken where two processors agree and one differs, and totally ignores the possibility of errors in the voting logic itself. (The naive approach of switching off the system and calling the engineer when one processor appears to be faulty results in three times as much 'down time' as would occur on a single processor.)

There has been very little practical or theoretical work done on reliability in multiple processor systems where the processors are carrying out different work, since such systems are normally configured to obtain the maximum speed-up, and this is incompatible with providing error checking and recovery capabilities. The Tandem Non-Stop system is the obvious counterexample, but even this does not provide protection against applications software malfunction; only against certain classes of hardware error (the risk of operating system error is minimised by providing some self checking and by keeping it simple).

4.2 Reliability on the Loughborough MIMD system

Some indication of the difficulty of providing reliability in MIMD systems can be obtained by examining some work on the system at Loughborough. The cost of providing automatic detection of and recovery from the complete failure of a processor was investigated, and this was extended to theoretical investigation of the algorithms required to detect and recover from the failure of one or more processors in a system with several processors and some shared memory. The coordination algorithms were modified to enable the demise of one processor to be detected and recovery of any shared resources being used by that processor to be effected. Two methods of 'death' detection were investigated. The first involved postulating that the processors would be connected by hardware in a ring, and each processor would periodically send an interrupt to its successor and receive an interrupt in reply. If the reply did not occur within a fixed time then the successor was deemed to have failed and recovery action was initiated. This method had the disadvantage that it required manual disconnection of the interrupt path from the defunct successor and reconnection to the new successor if further failures were to be detected; alternatively higher connectivity could be used provided death detection, or more strictly recovery, could still be performed by only one processor at any time. The second method of detecting failure was to provide two locations in common memory for each processor, one containing the time as seen by that processor, the other the 'time increment' within which an update to the time would occur. The processors were then arranged in a software ring and each periodically checks that the time shown by its successor is consistent with its own. This method has the advantage of not requiring special hardware nor manual intervention to reconfigure after one processor fails. Of course, neither method protects the system against partial hardware failures which still allow the 'alive' reply to be given, or against intermittent failures, where a processor apparently 'dies', has its resources removed and then comes back to life and uses the resources which are now owned by one of the other processors. Also the whole system fails if the shared memory fails.

The modifications to the coordination algorithm to permit the detection of this limited form of processor failure and to recover shared resources owned by a defunct processor do not, in themselves, permit the safe completion of a task running several parallel paths which use shared resources.

Consider a simple example in which there are four separate variables for which new values are to be calculated and the new values do not depend on the original values. It would be possible to set up four separate parallel paths each calculating the value of one variable (although in practice it would not be cost-effective to do so, the overheads of setting up the parallel paths far outweighing the gains).

Each path has three 'stages':

(1) commence;
(2) calculate variable;
(3) indicate completion.

Clearly, all three stages must be completed for all four paths before this section of the program is complete. Also, it is obviously possible to restart a path if the processor which is executing it fails before indicating completion.

However if the new value of the variable is dependent on the old value of the same variable then restarting would be satisfactory if the failure occurs between stages (1) and (2) but would be disastrous if the failure occurred between steps (2) and (3).

The 'obvious solution' of adding an extra flag, which is set to 'false' until step (2) is completed and then to 'true', does not actually help since it would still be possible for the failure to occur between step (2) and the setting of the flag. In any case, actual algorithms do not update only one variable: usually a number of variables need to be updated and their values must be kept self-consistent.

The method adopted to overcome the problem of ensuring reliability against processor failure on the Loughborough systems is to modify the application programs so that the values of all variables to be changed in a parallel path are stored before the path is commenced. In the event of failure during execution of the path, the original values of the variables are then restored before execution is recommenced. Executing modified programs with a simple implementation of the revised coordination algorithm adds about 25-30% to the execution time.

4.3   A general mechanism for the protection of data integrity against processor failure

The method of 'checkpointing' variables before embarking on a parallel path is only satisfactory where there is a complete separation of variables between the paths (data partitioning). Wherever two or more paths can interact through a shared variable, which is managed as a shared resource separately from the paths themselves, this mechanism is unsuitable.

If a path commences, updates the shared variables and then fails, it is clearly not possible to reset the shared variable to its value before the path started because this loses all record of updates performed by other paths between the time the failed path started and when its failure was detected. Neither is it possible to continue as if the path has been completed. The solution in this case could be to treat obtaining the value of the shared variable, and storing that value in a variable which is local to the path, as a separate step independent of the parallel path itself which then commences by storing the values of the other variables.

The 'access shared variable' path itself now contains several stages. In the case where a shared variable must take all values between 1 and 50 it could comprise:

   (a)   obtain access to the variable (claim resource);
   (b)   read current value;
   (c)   if value exceeds 50 release resource and exit;
   (d)   store value in path local variable;
   (e)   add 1 to value;
   (f)   store value in shared variable;
   (g)   release resource.

Stages (b) to (f) would not necessarily all be distinct but would involve several machine instructions.

It would be necessary to protect the value of the variable before starting on the path so that it could be restored in the event of failure, but this involves gaining access to the shared variable and moving it to a local variable (which is stages (a), (b), (d), (g) of the path already described). Furthermore, if the resource is released between storing the value and gaining access for update another processor may also commence the 'gain access to store variable before updating' procedure. In this case if one of the processors completes its update and the other processor fails during its update, recovery action would lead to the loss of the first update.

The general solution to the problem is to use 'point updates' such that all interconnected actions appear to take place as a single action which will always have either completed or not have started. With shared memory such an action is writing to a single memory location. Where several locations need to be changed it is clearly not possible to do this directly and even with a single location it is not possible to both complete the change and indicate that it is complete in a single write to the location to be changed.

The answer is twofold:

(*a*) Use pointers to variables rather than the variables themselves in the data structures.

(*b*) Never update any variable value *in situ.* Always copy the new value to a new location then change the pointer.

This solution is based on the principle that a single link list can have a new entry added or an old entry deleted in a self-consistent way by changing one pointer.

Three examples of the use of this procedure in practice are given below:

4.3.1 Single shared variable

Allocate three locations: one for a pointer, the other two for two values of the variable. An update uses the pointer to determine which of the two locations holds the current value, calculates the new value, places it in the other location, and then changes the pointer. The act of changing the pointer is indivisible and at all stages up to there it is safe to restart. It is only then necessary to remember the original state of the pointer to determine whether the update is complete. One possible convention which simplifies this is to designate one of the two locations as the normal location and extend the update routine to include copying the updated value to the first location and then resetting the pointer to the first location. The 'normal' state is thus both value locations containing the same value and the pointer pointing to the first location, but an update has occurred and the procedure can be completed by another processor once the pointer has been changed.

4.3.2 Several shared variables containing related data

In this case each variable is allocated two value locations and there is a pointer value for the whole table. The normal state is with each pair of variables having the same value and the global pointer indicating that the first variable value is correct in every case. Update then proceeds on each variable in turn with updated values being placed in the second location. Once all updates have been completed the global pointer is reset. The update is complete once the table pointer is changed but before this the initial values are still all available in the first locations, so restarting is safe. In recovery the table pointer is taken to indicate the state of the table.

4.3.3   A data structure containing variable length records of related data

In this case each data record is pointed to by a pair of pointers which normally both point to the same record, and there is a global 'structure pointer' indicating that the first pointer is 'correct'. Records are updated by generating the new version of the record in a new place. The second pointer is then changed to point at the updated record. Once all updates are completed the structure pointer is changed to indicate that the second pointer is now correct. The update is completed by copying back the new pointer values to the first pointers and resetting the structure pointer.

It can be seen that this method will generalise to any data structure. It also has the advantage that in non-failure situations involving several readers and one updater, it permits the readers to obtain self-consistent values of the data without needing to coordinate, even though an update is in progress. The sole criterion is that the reader must be willing to obtain a set of values which may shortly become obsolete, but there are many situations in which this is acceptable.

5   Conclusions

There are many successful examples of MIMD systems with both tightly coupled and loosely coupled organisations at hardware and software levels. There are also several successful SIMD systems designed to process particular types of work. In the case of the SIMD systems and the tightly coupled MIMD systems execution speed of individual programs or of the whole workload is the main criterion for choosing a parallel architecture although convenience in implementation may play a part. Programming for parallel systems is more difficult than programming for uniprocessor systems and this has led to the parallelism being concealed on most existing MIMD systems.

However, research is now being undertaken into combining the advantages of the greater speed to be obtained from the explicit use of parallelism with the greater throughput and greater reliability that could be obtained with a system comprising several nearly autonomous processors and concealed parallelism. Initial results from these investigations have been most encouraging and further work is being undertaken.

References

Flynn, M. J., 'Very high speed computing systems' *Proc. IEEE*, **54** (12), 1901-9 (1966)

Newman, I. A., 'Developments in the UNIQUE machine independent command language' in *Command Language Directions*, ed. D. Beech, North Holland, pp. 65-79 (1980)

Newman, I. A. & Woodward, M. C., *The Reliable Sharing of Passive Resources in a Multiprocessor Environment*, Dept. Computer Studies, Loughborough University, Research Report No. 45 (1977)

Randell, B. & Anderson, T. (Eds.), *Computing System Reliability*, Cambridge University Press (1979)

Williams, K., 'System 250 – Basic concepts', in *Computer Systems & Technology, IERE Conference Proceedings, No. 25*, pp. 157-68 (1972)

8 Implementing parallel processing on a production minicomputer system

A. J. SLADE

1 Introduction

In recent years a great deal of effort has been directed towards developing parallel computers and algorithms to run on them. Most of the machines in service are of the single instruction multiple data (SIMD) type.[1,2] Such systems have been designed for efficient parallel processing on a particular type of problem and cannot be used effectively on a more general workload.

An alternative is the multiple instruction multiple data (MIMD) type machine where processors can execute 'blocks' of code independently. Parallel processing in this 'block' format is then an extension of multiple processing of independent tasks to include time ordering constraints and data sharing or transfer between tasks.

One such system, where the data sharing between 'blocks' is achieved through processors sharing a region of memory, has been constructed.[3] This system preserves the time ordering relationships by use of specialised 'lockout' hardware on the shared memory.

In this chapter an implementation of parallel processing on a two processor shared memory system with no special hardware will be discussed. Synchronisation or time ordering is based on the use of the abstract resource ring,[4] a software protection mechanism which enables multiple processors to reliably access and update any shared resource.

The system as delivered by the manufacturer is described in section 2. The structure of a parallel program and a set of user constructs which can be used to define this structure are discussed in section 3. Sections 4 and 5 go on to describe the practical details of implementation and modifications made to achieve a simple user interface and efficient use of processors.

2 The initial configuration

The hardware is based on the Interdata model 55 dual processor illustrated in figure 8.1 and described in reference 5. The model 70 processor has 32K bytes of memory while the original model 50 processor (now upgraded to a second model 70 processor) has 64K bytes of memory. (For convenience and brevity the two processors will be referred to as *A* and *B* respectively.)

For this application the system is configured so that processor *A* can directly address 32K bytes of the memory on processor *B*. Both processors thus have 32K bytes of 'private' memory (addressed as bytes 0-32K−1) and 32K bytes of shared memory (32K-64K −1). Each location of the shared memory is referred to by the same address in the two processors.

Processor *B* has a disc attached which can transfer into any of the 64K locations of *B*. A disc operating system (DOS) is provided which will run in system *B* but is not designed to control the dual processor configuration. A number of utilities are also provided, as are compilers for Fortran and machine code.

3   Parallel program structure

A segment of a parallel program has graphical representation of the form shown in figure 8.2 where left before right time ordering holds. Several points are important to the implementation of this structure:

(i)   Each path $(S_1, P_1, \ldots)$ must be executed by only one processor no matter how many processors are attached to a job, otherwise stability of the results cannot be assured. A consequence of this is that when one

Figure 8.1. Model 55 configuration.

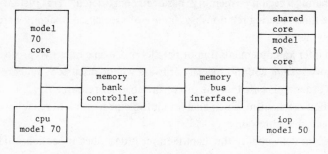

Figure 8.2. Segment of a parallel program.

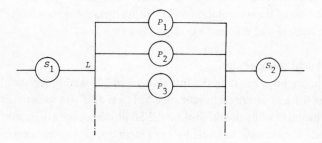

processor takes up a path all others must be 'informed' and locked out of that path.

(ii) Only after all preceding paths have been checked as completed can a given path be started, i.e. $P_1, \ldots, P_n$ must be completed before starting S_2.

(iii) Variables used by $P_1, \ldots, P_n$ but defined in S_1 must be made available to the processors executing these segments and all variables set by $P_1, \ldots, P_n$ and used in S_2 must be made available to the processor that executes S_2.

(iv) Data defined in S_1 and required in S_2 must be made available to the processor executing S_2.

In order to program such conceptual structures the user will want to define, in a simple way, where the parallel paths start and end. Parallel paths can consist of 'identical' or different code and so we allow users to indicate identical paths as follows:

```
        DOPAR      1  I=1,N
        .
        .
        'code using index I'
        .
        .
  1     PAREND
```

and different paths by

```
        FORK       1,2,3,...
  1     'code for path 1'
        .
        .
        GOTO 100
  2     'code for path 2'
        .
        .
        GOTO 100
  3     'code for path 3'
        .
        .
  100   JOIN
```

In the first case the analogy with the Fortran DO loop is clear, while the second case is equivalent to the computed GOTO in Fortran. This latter construct has been widely discussed (see for example Brinch Hansen[6]), while the former has also been proposed elsewhere (Wallach[7]).

Two structures with nested parallelism are illustrated in figure 8.3. Only nesting organisations of type (*a*) are allowed in our implementation, and although this is a restriction the author believes it incurs no loss of generality.

4 Implementation considerations

There are a number of ways in which the system could have been developed to implement parallel programming. The way that was chosen was based on three assumptions:

   (i) Both processors execute a copy of the same program. The program is loaded into the private memory of each processor.

  (ii) To take account of point (iii) of section 3, data common to parallel paths is held in shared memory.

 (iii) The processor executing a path immediately before a DOPAR or FORK will execute the path following the corresponding PAREND or JOIN. This takes a case of point (iv) of section 3 and together with the path nesting restriction stated above implies that subroutine calls and returns are made by the same processor.

The remaining requirements for the implementation of parallel processing are those of points (i) and (ii) of section 3 which both relate to the ability to ensure correct time ordered execution of the paths. This is achieved using the abstract resource ring[3].

The ring administers a set of abstract resources that are available to all the processors in the system. However only one processor at a time can 'possess' a resource; the others, if they want it, are forced to wait for it until it is given to one of them by the possessing processor. By transferring a resource on a giving as opposed to a taking basis one can ensure a resource is possessed by only one processor at a time.

The system is initialised so that the resources are arbitrarily allocated to one processor.

The ring structure is implemented in terms of two Fortran callable subroutines:

     GETRES (I)

which obtains exclusive use of the resource I and

     PUTRES (I)

which relinquishes ownership of the resource I.

In the current implementation there are eight abstract resources and thus eight resource rings.

5 Implementation details

In operation the user programs are developed, compiled and then written to disc on system *B*. The application program and ring control routines are then

Figure 8.3. Two structures with nested parallelism.

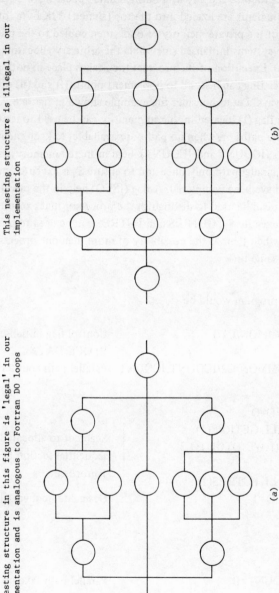

(a)

The nesting structure in this figure is 'legal' in our
implementation and is analogous to Fortran DO loops

(b)

This nesting structure is illegal in our
implementation

loaded into the bottom (private) 32K bytes of memory attached to processor B. The ring data structure and any user defined data appearing in Fortran COMMON statements are loaded into the top (shared) 32K bytes of B's memory. The contents of the private memory of B are then copied to the private memory of A and both systems initialised (including the arbitrary allocation of the abstract ring resources). Execution of the program then takes place in both processors.

The resource ring can be used to implement points (i) and (ii) of section 4 in a number of ways. Let us consider the example shown in figure 8.2.

A dynamic flag (I) located in shared memory can be used to route processors to the allowable paths or, when no paths are available, to keep them in an idling loop. Counters (ICOUNT and JCOUNT), held in shared memory, can be used to allocate each parallel path only once and to ensure S_2 is executed only after P_1, P_2 and P_3 have been completed. A flag (ISEQ) held in the private memory of each processor can be used to distinguish the processor that executes S_1 and thus get it later to execute S_2. GETRES and PUTRES can be used to protect updates to these flags when there is the possibility of more than one processor trying to do this at the same time.

A suitable program would be

	COMMON/C1/I	Control flag initialised to O in BLOCK DATA
	COMMON/C2/ICOUNT,JCOUNT	Parallel path counters
C		
	ISEQ=O	
	CALL GETRES(1)	Segment to allocate following sequential section to only 1 processor
	IF (I.WE.O) GOTO 2	
	I=−1	
	CALL PUTRES(1)	
	ISEQ=1	Designate 'sequential' processor
	.	
	.	
	.	
	S1	
	.	
	.	
	.	
	ICOUNT=0	Parallel path take up counter
	JCOUNT=0	Parallel path finished counter
	I=1	Bring all processors to start of parallel section

C

```
    10   CALL GETRES(1)
         ICOUNT=ICOUNT+1
         IF(ICOUNT.GT.3) GOTO 14
         GOTO (11,12,13),ICOUNT
    14   I=-1
         GOTO 2
    11   CALL PUTRES(1)
         .
         .
         P1
         .
         .
         GOTO 20
    12   CALL PUTRES(1)
         .
         .
         P2
         .
         .
         GOTO 20
    13   CALL PUTRES(1)
         .
         .
         P3
         .
         .
    20   CALL GETRES(1)
         JCOUNT=JCOUNT+1
         IF (JCOUNT.LT.3) GOTO 10
         CALL PUTRES(1)
```

C

```
         I=2
    30   IF (ISEQ.EQ.O) GOTO 2
         I=-1
         .
         .
         S2
         .
         .
         I=3
    99   STOP
```

Ensures each path is only taken up once by protecting take up with a resource allocation

First parallel segment

Second parallel segment

Third parallel path

Checks path completion

All processors are tested to find the 'sequential' one and then when found all remaining ones are locked in the idle loop.

```
C
    2    CALL PUTRES(1)
         IF(I.LT'1.OR.I.GT.3) GOTO 2    Idling loop with control switch
         GOTO (10,30,99),I
C
         END
C
         BLOCK DATA
         COMMON/C1/I
         DATA I/0/
         END
```

As can be seen, large amounts of code are required to ensure stable and 'correct' execution of the code. When extended to nested loops separate counters and sequential indicators have to be set up for each level of nesting, vastly increasing the complexity of the additional code. In extreme cases the original algorithm can become insignificant in comparison to this additional code.

This can be greatly reduced as far as the application program is concerned by introducing two macro calls, FORK and JOIN:

```
         :        }S1
         :
   10    FORK 11,12,13
   11    CONTINUE
         :        }P1
         :
         GOTO 20
   12    CONTINUE
         :        }P2
         :
         P2
         GOTO 20
   13    CONTINUE
         :        }P3
         :
         GOTO 20
   20    JOIN
         :
         :        S1
```

The macros generate the code given earlier.

Although this procedure makes it easier to program the algorithms and appears to go part way towards the desired user interface it has some inherent disadvantages:

(*a*) Each processor is dedicated to the current task even though it might not be doing any useful work (it will be performing the loop at label 2).

(*b*) If the parallel segments arise in a FUNCTION or SUBROUTINE then the idling processors which are looping in code in the MAIN program have to be routed into the correct position in the FUNCTION using a variable entry FUNCTION call from the MAIN. Handling all this correctly requires the user to place macros in the calling sequence routines right through to the FUNCTION call itself.

The above problems can be overcome by restructuring the method of allocating paths to processors. Instead of viewing the problem as one task with several processors, a more general approach is to consider the parallel job as one which creates other tasks during its execution. As an example consider the task illustrated in figure 8.2. This can be described as five separate tasks S_1, P_1, P_2, P_3, S_2. Initially only S_1 is available for running, then, when the point labelled L is reached, S_1 is finished and P_1, P_2, P_3 can be started; when all three of these are finished S_2 can be started.

These tasks may then be scheduled for execution on one of the processors. A unified scheduling algorithm was, therefore, devised to administer the distribution of the tasks between the processors. The scheduler maintains a block of information, called a task control block (TCB), for each task known to it. The scheduler is called by the processors when any parallel statement is encountered (FORK, JOIN, DOPAR, PAREND) and will result in the addition or deletion of TCBs from the list maintained by the scheduler. The list is then searched for the first available task which can be executed by the processor. If no task is found the processor can be switched to processing other work using normal multiprogramming techniques.

The information contained in a TCB must give

(1) the start address of the path,
(2) some codification of the precedence relations controlling when it can be executed,
(3) the processor(s) which may execute the path (see note (iii) of section 4).

The implementation of a suitable structure will now be examined in more detail.

5.1 Start address

Fortran labels are not valid subroutine parameters and therefore cannot be passed from the program to the scheduling list, for example by using CALL

FORK(11,12,13) etc. This problem can be overcome by expanding the macro

FORK 11,12,13

to

    CALL FORK(3)
    GOTO 13
    GOTO 12
    GOTO 11

where the parameter of CALL FORK is the number of parallel paths being created by the call. The start points of the paths will now be the GOTOs and since their addresses relative to the address of the CALL FORK(3) can be trivially calculated, the start addresses for the paths can be calculated in the subroutine FORK and inserted in the TCB. (The subroutine FORK must of necessity be written in machine code.)

5.2 Precedence relation

Parallel paths, once encountered on the FORK macro, can be executed by any processor. Only the path following the JOIN macro has to await execution – until this macro has been executed by each of the paths referenced on the corresponding FORK macro. This precedence condition can be handled by placing the label of the JOIN macro on the FORK macro, namely FORK 11, 12, 13; 20 (for our previous example).

The entry for a path contains a unique path identifier, the path identifier of the parent task, the start address of the path (calculated from the label as shown in 5.1) and a precedence count which is set for zero for all paths following the FORK (P_1, P_2, P_3 in figure 8.2) and to the number of parallel paths for the path following the JOIN (i.e. 3 for S_2 of figure 8.2). Paths can then be taken up whenever their precedence count is zero, and when taken up have their identifier and parent identifier copied to the executing processor. When a processor executes a JOIN it can, from the parent identifier it has, find the correct precedence counter to decrement. The need for all this information becomes apparent on consideration of the nesting of FORKs and JOINs.

5.3 Processor selection

As mentioned above, any processor may execute a path generated by a FORK. However, in our implementation, to maintain the correct setting of variables the processor continuing after a JOIN must be the processor which issued the corresponding FORK (all variables which are not used in the parallel paths are stored in private memory, those 'private' variables used in paths S_1 and required again in S_2 but not used in $P_1, \ldots, P_n$ will have the correct values only in the copy of the program stored in the private memory of the processor that executed path S_1). Since the TCB for the path following the JOIN is created when the corresponding FORK is encountered, it is trivial to place the name (number) of the processor in the TCB to enforce this processor selection.

The parallel loop commands

> DOPAR 1 I=I1, I2, I3
> :
> :
> 1   PAREND

are implemented in a very similar manner to the FORK and JOIN. Here, clearly, the number of tasks to be added to the scheduler list is calculated from values of I1, I2 and I3 and the start addresses of the parallel paths are all identical and equal to the first statement after DOPAR, while the label following the DOPAR gives the address of the equivalent JOIN.

5.4   Initialisation

The processor initialisation phase, mentioned earlier, initialises the scheduler list to contain a single TCB pointing to the start of the main segment of the application program with a precedence count of zero.

6   Conclusion

The methods described above are independent of the number of processors in the system.

A two processor system has been in use at Loughborough since the middle of 1976. In that time various algorithms incorporating parallel sections have been tried and figures for slowdown due to memory clashing and processor synchronisation obtained. Full details of the information obtained can be found in Barlow & Evans.[8]

The system at present requires a fairly extensive loading procedure and is inflexible in operation to the extent that both (all) processors are effectively dedicated to the one task. This situation is acceptable in a dedicated environment but if a system is required for general processing as well a more flexible organisation is required. As by no means all problems are susceptible to a parallel solution, a better approach to the problem would be to embed parallel processing in the more general concept of distributed processing. The problems of inter-task communication in a general multiprogramming computer have been, in general, solved and combining this with a network linking the cooperating machines will provide a more general vehicle for parallel processing. The Department of Computer Studies at Loughborough is at present developing a distributed processing network incorporating the already working parallel processing system. In this case the scheduler mentioned earlier will form part of the system scheduler in each machine, thus linking the creation of tasks from within the parallel program to the list of tasks known to the underlying operating system and allowing multiprogramming in conjunction with the parallel processing.

References

1 G. H. Barnes et al 'The ILLIAC IV computer' *IEEE Trans. Comput.* **C-17** 746–57 (1968).
2 K. E. Butcher 'STARAN/REDCAP hardware architecture' in *Proc. Sagamore Conf. on Parallel Processing* pp. 147–52 (1972).
3 C. G. Bell and W. A. Wulf 'C.mmp A multi-mini processor' *AFIPS Conference 41*, p. 765 (1972).
4 I. A. Newman and M. C. Woodward *Reliable Sharing of Passive Resources in a Multiprocessor Environment* Report 45 of Computer Studies Department (1977) Loughborough University of Technology.
5 *Model 55: Dual Memory Bank Controller, Information Specification.* Interdata Inc (1971) New Jersey 07757, U.S.A.
6 P. Brinch Hansen *Operating System Principles* Prentice-Hall Englewood Cliffs, New Jersey (1973).
7 Y. Wallach 'Parallel-processor systems in power-dispatch' *IEEE Summer Power Meeting, California*, 1974; papers C74-3349 and C74-3356.
8 R. H. Barlow and D. J. Evans *Performance of a Dual Minicomputer Parallel Computer System* Report 43 of Computer Studies Department (1977) Loughborough University of Technology.

9 Coordination

M. C. WOODWARD

1 Introduction

Within a parallel processing system, we have several operations at a particular level occurring simultaneously, for example numerous multiplications in an array processor or several parallel paths in an MIMD (multiple instruction, multiple data) system. Some mechanism is required whereby these operations may coordinate.

We may usefully classify parallel processing systems according to the means whereby this coordination is derived. Two major classes can be distinguished:

(i) Those relying upon hardware functions for coordination.

(ii) Those relying upon software functions for coordination.

2 Coordination by hardware

Into group (i) fall the SIMD (single instruction, multiple data) systems, including the array processors. These systems consist of many small arithmetic processors attached to a host computer. The arithmetic processors are coordinated by virtue of being clocked by a common timing signal. That is, while parallel operation is being utilised, all the arithmetic processors are performing their steps at the same rate and the host processor is waiting at the hardware level for their operation to cease.

Viewed in another way, we may say that coordination at the software level is not required, since there is only a single program counter (that of the host computer) within the system.

Further discussion of these systems will be left to other chapters. We will now concentrate on systems which rely upon coordination by software.

3 Coordination by software

The other major group of parallel processing systems is that of MIMD computers. We will consider why software coordination is required, the circumstances in which this requirement manifests itself, and some solutions to the problem.

Why is it required?

We may say that software coordination is required whenever the 'unit of parallelism' is at a higher level than that at which the hardware operates. With the array processor, the parallelism is achieved at the same level as the operation of the hardware (i.e. arithmetic functions), so software coordination is not required. A multiprocessor providing parallelism between sections of program requires software coordination, since the unit of parallelism consists of many instructions. It should be noted that whilst software coordination is required some hardware primitives may be used.

Why coordinate?

Within MIMD systems, the approach to parallelism is to execute blocks of instructions in parallel. These sections would, typically, be called parallel paths. Various proposals exist for expressing or determining where this parallelism should be.

The question 'why coordinate?' may be rephrased as 'what are we trying to do when we coordinate?'. In an attempt to answer this question we may consider some circumstances in which coordination (or synchronisation) is required.

(i) *When a path terminates.* If parallel paths are allowed to be created and to die during the execution of a parallel program then coordination is required when a path terminates.

(ii) *When information is passed between two paths.* One parallel path may produce results required by another. Coordination is required to enable the information transfer to take place.

(iii) *Access to shared resources.* Most, if not all, shared resources must be accessed in a controlled manner to prevent them being corrupted. These resources may range from shared data structures in a user program to a shared disc drive.

From these examples, we may answer the above question by saying that coordination is required when communication takes place. As will be seen from other chapters, however, certain classes of algorithms do not require coordinated communication. So, coordination is required whenever a path wishes to communicate with its environment. Consider the three examples again:

(i) Communication takes place with the scheduler of parallel paths.

(ii) Communication takes place with other parallel paths.

(iii) Communication takes place with any other path or task accessing the resource. These communications are of the form 'can I use the resource?' or 'I am using the resource'.

What mechanism may we use?

Two mechanisms whereby the communication may be achieved can be envisaged:

(*a*) message passing system
(*b*) via shared variables.

For the message sending system, it is possible to use communications hardware, e.g. networks. Systems have been developed which are based upon a message sending system, e.g. the Distributed Computing System (DCS) of the University of California. In this system, all the processors are connected to a communications ring. By using special hardware, the coordination has been passed to the hardware.

With shared variables, however, reliance cannot be put upon the hardware. The most common medium to hold shared variables is that of memory (core or semi-conductor). It should be noted that a message system could be based upon shared variables, the medium for transport being the shared memory, however the coordination problems are then only passed to the software handling the message system.

We will now consider some examples of algorithms which provide the required coordination. Consider, first, communication between paths of a parallel program (example (ii) above). The simplest way to coordinate is to use a flag to indicate the state of the communication variables. This is relevant when the communication will proceed in a known fashion. The flag will be initialised to indicate the first sender of information. As information is sent, the flag is altered to indicate that the reader may read the information. As long as the alteration to the flag is an indivisible operation, communication may become as complex as required.

However, a situation will arise when either the communication will become too complex or the originator of the communication is unknown. In these cases we have the situation of a shared resource ((iii) above). With a shared resource a more complex flagging system is required. The remainder of the discussion will be in the framework of gaining and releasing access to a shared resource.

Some multiprocessor systems contain special instructions to enable access to shared resources to be synchronised. Many of these are of the 'test and set' variety. A value is fetched from memory, inspected, and possibly changed. During the whole of the instruction the memory bus is held by the processor to prevent another accessing the memory. Dijkstra's proposal of a 'semaphore' provides a similar mechanism.

In a given situation, however, it may be undesirable to use such a hardware function, or the hardware may not provide such instructions. In such situations we are left with providing the synchronisation using only 'standard' read and store instructions. This problem was proposed by Dijkstra [1], and first solved by Dekker. Since then several solutions have been published. All these algorithms operate by using a complex flagging system.

Lampart [2] has developed an algorithm of this type which guarantees access to a shared resource on a first-come-first-served basis. Each processor requiring access to the resource has an associated numeric variable. The value of this variable indicates the order in which the processors (and paths which they are executing) may access the resource. Each time a processor wishes to access the resource it assigns a new value to the variable which is one more than the largest number of the other processors. Having derived its number, it then inspects the number of each processor until it is ranked earlier. Once all the other processors have been checked, it is then ranked first and may use the resource. Once the processor has finished with the resource, it assigns zero to the variable.

With this scheme, the resource is left 'unowned' while a processor is not using it. That is, there is no mutual organisation in accessing the resource, each processor having to inspect all others when it claims the resource. An alternative approach is to use a resource master technique in which one processor is responsible for the resource until the ownership is passed to another.

An example of this type is a scheme in use at Loughborough University. With this method, a single location is used to store the current owner and each processor is given a unique identification number. Processors which wish to use the resource indicate this within a flag and then wait until their number is placed within the owner location. When this occurs the processor is now master of the resource and is responsible for it. When a processor releases the resource it is its responsibility to pass the ownership to another processor requesting the resource. The flags will be searched (in any desired order) to discover the new owner. It should be noted that it is possible that no processor wishes to use the resource. In such circumstances the processor must attempt to dispose of the resource at a later time.

Each of these techniques has differing performance characteristics. The technique in which resources are freed performs best if there is low usage of the resource. As resource usage increases so the resource master technique gives better performance.

4 Representation of coordination

Many language constructs have been proposed whereby coordination may be achieved, e.g. monitors and critical regions. Whilst these constructs are elegant ways of representing communication and coordination, some lower level primitives are required to implement them. The use of one of the language constructs implies a (logical) shared resource, and the appropriate coordination may be applied.

5 Conclusion

With some parallel processing systems the problem of coordination does not arise; it is handled by the available hardware. However, with many MIMD systems coordination has to be provided. Depending upon the type of communication required various levels of coordination are available.

References

[1] Dijkstra, E. W. 'Cooperating sequential processes', Technological University, Eindhoven (1965), reprinted in *Programming Languages*, F. Genuys (ed.), Academic Press, New York (1968)

[2] Lampart, L. 'A new solution of Dijkstra's concurrent programming problem' *CACM,* 17, 8, (1974), 453–5

10 Performance measures for parallel algorithms

R. H. BARLOW

1 Introduction

In a recent paper Baudet (1978) considers the iterative solution of
the Laplace equation using a multiple instruction multiple data (MIMD)
type parallel computer, in fact the Cmmp machine at Carnegie Mellon
University.

The main development in his paper is that the usual solution methods, Gauss-
Jacobi and Gauss–Seidel, involve a level of synchronisation between the processors
that significantly reduces the parallel performance. He therefore considers asynchronous iterative schemes, demonstrating theoretically that they converge and
showing that they perform much better on the Cmmp than the aforementioned
synchronous methods.

However, in running the synchronised algorithms on a similarly structured
two processor parallel computer here at Loughborough (Barlow & Evans,
1978, 1980), we encountered only a small performance loss due to the
synchronisation overhead. Clearly this difference must be attributable to
a faster synchronisation tool on the Loughborough computer than on the Cmmp
machine.

What this difference highlights to us is the need to characterise overheads in
parallel programs in a system independent manner. In this way we can match
algorithm to machine, and also avoid the danger of rejecting an algorithm because
it performs badly on one particular computer system.

In this chapter we first discuss those features that characterise parallel processing as opposed to sequential processing. Then in section 3 we discuss how one
can provide system independent measures of these features. In section 4 we apply
this analysis to the performance of iterative solutions of the Laplace equation on
a parallel computer.

The analysis is restricted to algorithms intended for execution on multiple
instruction multiple data type computers. Similar considerations should apply
to single instruction multiple data (SIMD) computers, but lacking in experience
of SIMD computers and algorithms we have not attempted an analysis of such
systems.

2　　　　**Characterisation of parallel programs**

Parallel computing requires:

(i) multiple processors,

(ii) communication for data sharing,

(iii) synchronisation to allow unique data modification.

Associated with these three features of systems are three factors that affect the performance of parallel programs:

(*a*) the degree of parallelism in the program,

(*b*) accesses to shared data space impose an overhead,

(*c*) access to the synchronisation tool and the protected data structures impose an overhead.

A typical MIMD computer system is shown in figure 10.1. Essentially it is a collection of independent processing systems that have some hardware connection that allows them to communicate. Let us remark that although such systems usually feature a shared memory for fast communication it is not necessary and its presence, absence, or particular form in no way disturbs our analysis. The same general point holds for the synchronisation tool.

The three characteristic features of parallel computing (*a*), (*b*) and (*c*) above, have been widely recognised and discussed, but usually algorithms have been characterised by their potential parallelism (Chen & Kuck, 1975), and systems by their unit overhead for shared memory or synchronisation (Baskett & Smith, 1976). Rosenfeld (1969) discusses all three features and suggests that full attention to overheads (*b*) and (*c*) is required at the algorithm design stage in

Figure 10.1. Typical shared memory multi-mini system.

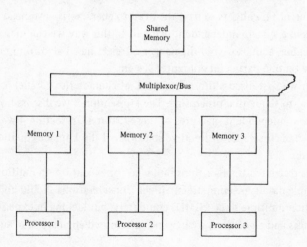

order to reduce them to a low level. Kung (1976) comments that in some cases parallel versions of an algorithm might run slower than the sequential due to the synchronisation overhead.

We contend that in the same way that parallel programs 'demand' the resource of m processors, they also demand the resource of x shared data accesses and y synchronisations. All three resource demands by the algorithm directly affect the potential performance of the algorithm and, as we shall see, each of the three limits the maximum performance attainable. One should therefore associate with parallel algorithms a system independent performance measure for each of these resource demands. In fact, it is not the synchronisation primitive alone that is the resource but it and the structure it protects, and if there are several logically independent structures each should have its own measure.

Together these measures would characterise the algorithm. When associated with the corresponding properties of a given system it will be possible to predict a total performance measure for the algorithm on that particular system.

3   Performance measures for parallel programs

All programs divide into sections that reflect the logical structure of the problem concerned. With respect to each section differing resource demands will be made and to reflect accurately what the potential performance might be (to discover bottlenecks in resource allocation) it is necessary to treat each section individually.

However, to obtain from this section-by-section analysis useful performance measures it is necessary to determine the relative importance, or computational complexity, of the various sections. Complexity can be given in terms of the number of computational operations in a section but because the computational complexity of individual operations differs greatly it is not always a useful measure. To supplement this measure we therefore decided to consider a second complexity measure based on the number of machine cycles required to compute a section. Clearly measures based on cycles are not machine dependent but because the balance of operation complexity and the relative speeds of processor and primary store are not changing greatly we are content to allow this failing to remain.

3.1   Potential parallelism

Inspection of a program leads quickly to an estimate of the number of parallel processes available in a given section of the program. This degree of parallelism is usually a function of system size and is clearly a measure of the potential parallelism in the section.

To combine the different potential parallelisms available from different sections we need a slightly different measure. This measure, called 'speedup', also reflects the fact that the parallel resource demand of the program is met by any $m \geqslant 1$ processor. It is the usual measure used to characterise potential parallelism in a program.

If $T(m)$ is the time taken by m processors to execute the parallel paths of a section then speedup is defined as

$$\text{speedup } (m \text{ processors}) = T(1)/T(m)$$

Using estimates for the computational complexity of the program one can combine the speedup factors from all the program sections.

Usually in calculating an overall speedup factor for m processors one assumes that they all execute at the same speed. The calculation is then usually quite simple. If a given parallel computing system has different speed processors then one can model the overall speedup using the different levels of parallelism from different sections together with the complexity estimate for each section.

An important point to note is that the speedup measure will contain the effects of what are commonly called synchronisation losses. Thus, if a program has a section with two parallel paths of equal length executed by two different speed processors, and the next sequential path can only be started after completion of the two parallel paths, then one of the processors will finish its path before the other. The first will then be forced to wait until the second has completed its path before either of them can start the next sequential path. This is a delay due to the need for the processors to synchronise themselves before starting the next set of paths (in this case the sequential one) but its effect is included in the speedup measure.

One assumption of the analysis above is that the amount of computation is independent of the number of executing processors. Useful algorithms exist in which the amount of computation is a non-deterministic function of the parallel execution (Kung, 1976).

3.2   Access to shared resources

Let us note that shared data is a shared resource. It can be classified into two types:

(i) Sensitive data: data structures to which access must only be granted to one processor at a time. Thus, a shared counter whose value must always correspond to the number of accesses made to it falls into this class. So too, does a scheduling list that the processors share.

(ii) Non-sensitive data: data structures which multiple processors are allowed to access or modify at the same time, or data structures which in one section are accessed by one processor while in a later different section are accessed by another processor.

All data is mapped onto physical storage resources that can only allow one access for each internal cycle. In addition, however, sensitive data structures are logical resources to which access must only be granted on a one-at-a-time basis for the complete access/modification cycle. Accesses to logical resources must be protected by a synchronisation tool (Dijkstra, 1968). Whether this access tool is a software or hardware construct is immaterial.

All accesses to a shared resource will involve an overhead having two components:

   (i) A component arising from the access mechanism to that resource: for example, shared data held on a shared disc or even in another processor's local memory space will take longer to access than a processor's local data.

  (ii) A component arising from processors competing for and being forced to wait on the availability of the shared resource.

Let us remark that if shared data is held over different physical resources then the analysis must proceed separately for each resource.

The access path to physical shared data might be a shared bus or shared memory module or a private memory module of another processor accessed through a processor-to-processor communication protocol.

For a logical shared resource the access mechanism is the synchronisation tool (although of course some physical path must eventually be used to access the data). Each logically independent shared data structure is a different shared resource and contention for that resource proceeds independently of any other resource, unless the computer system maps different shared resources onto the same resource access controller or synchronisation tool. In parallel multiprocessor parallel computer systems the scheduling list of currently known paths and their status is a shared resource to which access must be protected by the synchronisation tool.

Each shared resource has a limit to its availability. If the total demand rate from all the processes equals the resource availability then saturation has occurred and no more speedup can be achieved through using more processors. Thus the maximum number of processors that can be effectively used in parallel programs is limited independently by each shared resource according to

$$\text{maximum no. processors} = 1/(\text{demand rate} \times \text{resource cycle time}).$$

Thus the mean demand rate to a resource is an important measure of the best performance obtainable. We will now show that this demand rate also determines, together with system properties, any loss in performance arising from processes sharing resources.

If the access mechanism response time is independent of the number of competing processors then the access overhead is

demand rate to the resource × excess unit access time

where by excess we mean with comparison to the corresponding sequential algorithm.

Contention increases the overhead and is widely recognised to be a function of the number of competing processors and the temporal pattern of access to the resource. Models such as those of Baskett & Smith (1976) or Bhandarkar (1975) can predict the contention component from the number of competing processors and the mean rate of demand to the resource.

If the access mechanism, which is a system property, responds in time dependent on the number of competing processors, then the effect of this can be modelled in precisely the same way as the contention overhead above.

Obviously this analysis must be applied section-by-section to the algorithm using the complexity measure to determine the mean rate of demand to the resource from a given path.

In general, then, the algorithm gives the mean rate of demand to the resource and the number of competing processors (or at least the maximum number). The system determines the resource access properties. Together they yield bounds on the maximum number of processors that can be effectively used and an estimate of the overhead due to sharing a resource.

4 Application to the iterative solution of the Laplace equation

Consider the solution of the Laplace equation with Dirichlet boundary values discretised on a rectangular mesh to yield the five-point equation for each grid point as:

$$x_{i,j-1} + x_{i-1,j} - 4x_{i,j} + x_{i+1,j} + x_{i,j+1} = 0 \qquad (4.1)$$

from which one obtains the Gauss–Jacobi update formulae

$$x_{i,j}^{(n+1)} = (x_{i-1,j}^{(n)} + x_{i,j-1}^{(n)} + x_{i,j+1}^{(n)} + x_{i+1,j}^{(n)})/4 \qquad (4.2)$$

which relates the update of any point only to its four nearest neighbours. Clearly updates of all n^2 points are independent, assuming one stores all new values in a second grid. Parallel versions of the Gauss–Seidel and successive over-relaxation (SOR) schemes are derived in Barlow & Evans (1980): the Gauss–Jacobi method is chosen as our example here because it is simpler to identify the parallelism in that method.

Since the value of a point updated in one iterative cycle is used in the updates of its four nearest neighbour points in the next cycle it is clear that all grid values must be held as data shared between the processors or parallel processes. However, there is no possibility of either multiple processors trying to update the same value or of one processor using a value that is being updated by another parallel process.

This latter exclusion is achieved by having grids for new and old values and ensuring all updates in one cycle of iterations are complete before the next starts. The grid values are then not a sensitive data structure and access to them does not require protection by a synchronisation tool.

As mentioned earlier, however, the scheduling structure representing the parallel paths to the system is a sensitive shared data structure to which access can be granted to only one processor at a time.

A simple algorithm for this system that includes the convergence criteria is:

```
        SHARED U1 (N,N) U2 (N,N) ,N,NEW,BCONVG,EPS
        NEW=TRUE, EPS=. . .
   1    BCONVG=TRUE
        DOPARALLEL 100I=1,N
        DOPARALLEL 99J=1,N
        IF(NEW) GOTO 20
        U2(I,J)=(U1(I−1,J)+U1(I,J−1)+U1(I,J+1)−U(I+1,J))/4
        GOTO 30
   20   U1(I,J)=(U2(I−1,J)+U2(I,J−1)+U2(I,J+1)+U(I+1,J))/4
   30   IF(ABS(U1(I,J)−U2(I,J)).GT.EPS)BCONVG=FALSE
   99   PARALLEL END
  100   PARALLEL END
        NEW=.NOT.NEW
        IF (NOT BCONVG) GOTO 1
```

Each iterative cycle consists of a parallel section with $N_1 = n^2$ parallel paths each of complexity $C_1 = 7$ or 8 operations, and a sequential section of complexity $C_2 = 2$ operations, where $N_2 = 1$. The potential speedup S_1 from the parallel section when m processors are used is

$$S_1 = N_1/(\text{integer part of } (N_1 + m - 1)/m),$$

the potential speedup from the sequential path is $S_2 = 1$.

The overall potential speedup in each iterative cycle is then

$$S_T = (C_1 N_1 + C_2 N_2)/(C_1 N_1/S_1 + C_2 N_2/S_2)$$

which for this example if we assume m divides n^2 exactly is

$$S_T = (8n^2 + 2)/(8n^2/m + 2) \sim 0.8m \quad \text{for } m = n^2$$
$$\sim \quad m \quad \text{for } n^2/m \gg 1.$$

Let us now examine how accesses to the shared resources of shared data space and shared scheduling structure restrict the maximum speedup obtainable. Each parallel path makes $M_1 = 8$ accesses to shared data, giving a demand rate of $C_1/M_1 \sim 1$. If the physical resource holding the shared data cycles in p machine cycles then it becomes saturated when

$$m \text{ (processors)} = (C_1/M_1) \times \text{(mean operation time in machine cycles)}/p$$

and the speedup obtained from the parallel sections is limited by this figure. Assume, now, the scheduling resource cycles in r machine cycles then, since each parallel path makes $L_1 = 1$ accesses to the shared scheduling resource, this resource becomes saturated at

$$m \text{ (processors)} = (C_1/L_1) \times \text{(mean operation time in machine cycles)}/r.$$

These formulae become more realistic if one uses estimates for the time taken for the operations. Typical values are that real, integer and boolean operations take approximately 100, 15 and 5 machine cycles respectively to execute. The mean operation time is ~ 100 cycles for this problem. Thus shared data is accessed at a rate of 1 access per ~ 100 cycles and shared scheduling structure is accessed at a rate of 1 access per ~ 1000 cycles.

If we now consider the two processor parallel computer system at Loughborough University which holds shared data in a shared memory module which has a cycle time of 1 machine cycle, and where a parallel path scheduling resource takes 500 machine cycles to cycle it is clear that the maximum number of cooperating processors is limited to $(8 \times 100)/500 = 1.6$ by the scheduling resource and to 50 by the shared data resource (since access to real arithmetic data take 2 cycles on this system and thus $p = 2$ in the above formula.

Thus without attempting to run the algorithm or predict its performance losses due to accessing shared resources we have shown that the algorithm is unsuitable for this particular parallel processing system.

We therefore consider an alternative form of the algorithm. In equation (4.2) we now group all points on a row into a block. We obtain a set of simultaneous equations for the new values on a row expressed in terms of values on the two adjoining rows. In this algorithm updates to different rows are independent but updates within a row are dependent. The level of parallelism now equals the number of rows and the work within a path is now $8n$ operations. These block algorithms have the advantage of faster convergence than the point scheme. Of relevance here however is that the rate of access to the shared scheduling resource is now 1 per $8n$ operations, which converted into the maximum available speedup from this parallel section on the Loughborough system is $m = 1.6n$. Obviously losses in performance in accessing this resource are also drastically reduced with respect to the previous algorithm.

We can note that accesses to shared data are also reduced since for each row we make $2n$ accesses to neighbouring data, n accesses to the old values on the row and n accesses to the new values of the row. The convergence flag can be held in local data space and copied to the shared data space once all the tests have been completed on that row. Thus shared data accesses are reduced to 1 per 2 operations or 1 per 200 machine cycles.

Having shown that parallel processing is feasible with small numbers of processors for small n let us now try to predict the losses on the two processor Loughborough system due to the parallel algorithm having to share resources.

(i) Shared data resource: on the Loughborough system any access to shared data takes ~ 1 machine cycle longer than accesses to local data space and thus for this algorithm we have an access overhead of 2 cycles per 200 cycles $\sim 1\%$. Because the Loughborough system is asymmetric with respect to the shared and local memories of the two processors, contention losses are relatively complex to predict. Using a model of shared memory contention losses for this system given by Barlow & Evans (1978) one finds that at an access rate of 1 access per 100 cycles the contention losses are $\sim 0.25\%$ for two processors.

(ii) Shared scheduling structure: this feature is not required by the sequential version of the algorithm and thus if the parallel version makes 1 access per $8n$ operations (or $\sim 800n$ machine cycles) and the scheduler needs 500 machine cycles to execute we have an access overhead of $0.625/n$ or $\sim 4\%$ for a 15×15 system. To this must be added the access time to the synchronisation tool protecting this resource (750 cycles). Thus the access loss due to scheduling the system is $\sim 1.5/n \sim 10\%$ for a 15×15 system. Contention overheads due to the scheduling resource being occupied and thus not available would amount to $\sim 0.1\%$ using a simple model of random contention given by Barlow & Evans (1978). However this is increased by the non-linear access time to the software synchronisation tool in the presence of multiple processors. The operation of the synchronisation tool is explained in Newman & Woodward (1978). From discussion with the authors and our own experience the contention access overhead for control of a logical resource with this synchronisation tool will be about 70% of the access time at low and medium use rates but decreasing rapidly as saturation is reached: at saturation this synchronisation tool has almost no contention overhead! This applies to the synchronisation tool itself: the contention overhead from the resource being used will of course increase with increasing demand up to the saturation point.

In table 10.1 we give results (taken from Barlow & Evans, 1980) for the Gauss-Seidel version of this block algorithm. In all aspects except the maximum potential speedup the algorithm has the same properties as the Gauss-Jacobi scheme. The number of parallel paths is reduced from n to $n/2$ in this method due to the need to preserve the precise update order scheme required to achieve the convergence

Table 10.1. Results for Gauss–Seidel solution to the Laplace equation with Dirichlet boundary values

Interior size	Access rate to shared data	Access rate to scheduling	Access loss shared data	Access loss scheduling	Contention loss shared data	Contention loss scheduling	Two processor speedup
16 × 16	1:115 cycles	1:23K cycles	1%	6%	Not obtainable	5%	1.71
32 × 32	1:125 cycles	1:49K cycles	0.9%	3%	0.3%	2.5%	1.82

power of the method. The figures agree reasonably well with our estimates. Note that some potential speedup is lost because the speed of the two processors differs by 5% and thus at the end of each iterative cycle we will have one processor waiting on the other to finish.

5 Conclusions

We have shown the importance of considering all the resource demands of a parallel program. The ability of a given parallel computer system to meet the resource demands of a program limit only the effectiveness of the program on that system. However if all systems are roughly similar these measures provide guides to the algorithm designer as to which direction to go in developing a more suitable algorithm. On the other hand if all algorithms make roughly similar demands to some resource the measures guide the hardware designer to providing a system that can meet the resource demands of most algorithms.

We should add that estimation of these measures is not a difficult task: the level of difficulty is similar to that in providing a measure of complexity for a section of program.

Acknowledgement

This research was sponsored by the Science Research Council under its Distributed Computer Systems Research Programme.

Reference

Barlow, R. H. & Evans, D. J. (1978) 'Performance of a dual minicomputer parallel processing system' EUROCOMP 78, Online Conferences, Uxbridge
Barlow, R. H. & Evans, D. J. (1979) 'A parallel organisation of the bisection algorithm' *Computer Journal* 22, 267–9
Barlow, R. H. & Evans, D. J. (1980) *Synchronous and Asynchronous Iterative Parallel Algorithms for Linear Systems*, Internal Report, Dept. Computer Studies, Loughborough University (to appear in *Computer Journal*)
Baskett, F. & Smith, A' J. (1976) 'Interference in multiprocessor computer systems with interleaved memory' *CACM* 19, 327–34
Baudet, G. M. (1978) 'Asynchronous iterative methods for multiprocessors' *JACM* 25, 226–44
Bhandarkar, D. P. (1975) 'Analysis of memory interference in multiprocessors' *IEEE Trans. on Comp.* C24, 897–908
Chen, S' C. & Kuck, D'. J. (1975) 'Time and parallel bounds for linear recurrence relations' *IEEE Trans. on Comp.* C24, 701–17
Dijkstra, E. W. (1968) 'Cooperating sequential processors' in *Programming Languages* (F. Genuys ed.) Academic Press, New York pp. 43–112
Kung, H. T. (1976) 'Synchronous and asynchronous parallel algorithms for multiprocessors' in *New Directions and Recent Results in Algorithms and Complexity* (F. Traub ed.) Academic Press, New York
Newman, I. A. & Woodward, M. C. *Reliable Sharing of Passive Resources in a Multiprocessor Environment*, Internal Report, Dept. Computer Studies Loughborough University
Rosenfeld, J. L. (1969) 'A case study in programming for parallel processors' *CACM* 12, 645–55

PART 4

SIMD architectures and languages

11   High-speed machines and their compilers

DAVID J. KUCK

1   Introduction

By its nature, high-speed computation requires suitable algorithms, a fast machine, and a compiler to match the two. This paper discusses all three in an interrelated manner.

In section 2, a machine taxonomy and survey of existing high-speed computers is presented. It is suggested that the four fundamental methods described for speeding up a serial processor will continue to be used in various combinations in future supercomputers.

Section 3 presents a number of elementary building blocks out of which more complex algorithms can be constructed. These building blocks are characterized by the kinds of data structures they operate on. A discussion of how to speed up these building blocks is given and various related hardware features (including those of section 2) are discussed.

Finally, section 4 contains a discussion of transforming dependence graphs of sequential programs for high-speed machines. First, dependence graphs are discussed and in terms of these, the building blocks of section 3 can be defined. Then, transformations to remove dependences (and enhance speedup) are given. Finally, several abstractions of dependence graphs are discussed. These may be used in code generation for high-speed machines.

Section 5 contains several conclusions and gives references to further topics.

2   A machine taxonomy

Consider the problem of designing a computer that is faster than a traditional one containing a single processor, memory and control unit. To make the problem realistic, assume that the traditional machine is well designed and achieves high performance for the technology it uses. Furthermore, at any given time it is reasonable to assume that faster technology cannot be used; only architectural changes may be made to achieve faster performance. Four basically different approaches to the solution of this problem have been taken over the years, and many combinations of these approaches have also been used. Figure 11.1 illustrates a number of these and we will discuss this figure as a survey of high-speed computer systems as well as the principles upon which they are based.

In order to constrain this discussion, we will assume that faster performance is to be achieved on a monoprogrammed system. Thus, we really want to speed up the execution of each program presented to the system. The machines we will discuss can, of course, be multiprogrammed, but turnaround time, not throughput, will be the center of our attention here.

Figure 11.1. Architectural speedup techniques.

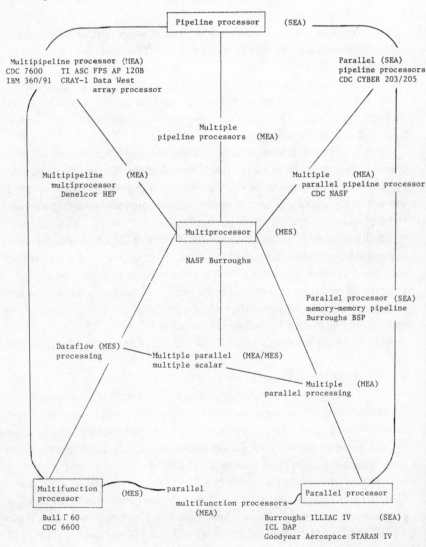

2.1 Multiprocessors

A straightforward approach to solving the above problem is simply to replicate the traditional machine many times and interconnect the ensemble. Every major computer manufacturer today has a multiprocessor system of some kind, but almost all of these are primarily intended to increase throughput by multiprogramming, not decrease the turnaround time for a single job. The Flow Model Processor (FMP) proposed by Burroughs is an exception that was designed for the NASA Numerical Aerodynamics Simulation Facility (NASF) study [LuBa80]. This machine has not been built, but its design goal (which has been met via simulation) was about one gigaflops (10^9 floating-point operations per second).

Several difficulties of such machines may be mentioned. First are the problems of interconnection and synchronization. Transmission of data and control information can be expensive in time or in hardware (or both if one is not careful). Also, compilation for such a system from traditional programs is a problem that has not been studied enough [KuPa79].

Since each processor in such a system executes a traditional scalar instruction set, we will refer to such a system as an MES machine (multiple execution scalar). In figure 11.1, we show multiprocessor systems at the center, with the Burroughs FMP as the illustrative example. While there are no existing high-performance machines of this type, such a system may have a good potential for ultimately providing the best possible architectural speedup.

2.2 Multifunction processor

In this approach, classically, a few of the functions of the traditional processor are replicated and the control unit is expanded accordingly to allow all the functional units to operate simultaneously. This saves some of the hardware incurred in a multiprocessor since only selected functional units are replicated. The CDC 6600 is a classic example of a multifunction processor [Thor70]. As higher levels of integrated circuits become available, saving processor hardware may not be as important as achieving layout regularity, so such architectural savings may be of less importance.

This type of organization may require complex interconnections and synchronization. Systems that were built in the past (e.g., the CDC 6600) had few enough functional units that these problems were minimal. To extend the approach to large numbers of functional units is more complex, however. Compilation for such a system is similar to that for a multiprocessor; it took CDC over ten years to produce a high quality (better object code performance than assembly language) Fortran compiler for the 6600.

Since this machine can execute a number of scalar operations simultaneously, we also refer to it as an MES system. Notice that figure 11.2 indicates that either the multiprocessor or the multifunction processor is potentially capable of unlimited speedup on most applications, given sufficient hardware parallelism. Very-high-speed versions of neither machine exist today; however, they do provide the best hope for the future. The fastest machines since the late 1960s have used pipeline and parallel processors, instead.

2.3 Parallel processing

Here we replicate processors as in the multiprocessor approach, but they are all driven by a common control unit. Thus, synchronization is handled centrally and is not much of a problem, but interconnecting the processors is very important in most applications; historically, the cost savings with this approach were important, but in the future that argument may be insignificant.

Several types of parallel machines have been built, including the ILLIAC IV [BBKK68] which contains an array of 64 fast, floating-point processors, and the ICL Distributed Array Processor (DAP) [Redd73] and the Goodyear Aerospace STARAN IV [Ensl74], both of which are arrays of bit-serial processors. We refer to these as SEA (single execution array) machines because each instruction is executed on a whole array of data at once.

Parallel processors are capable of achieving speedups proportional to the number of processors they contain, for a large number of applications. On the other hand, they are obviously less broadly applicable than an MES machine, in which a large number of differing operations may be carried out at once. We will explore the details of these distinctions in section 3.

2.4 Pipeline processing

In a sense this is the most economical way to speed up a traditional processor. The idea is based on the fact that the execution of many machine instructions consumes several clock periods, often using the same hardware iteratively. If such hardware is replicated serially (or 'unwound', see figure 11.2), a new pair of operands can be fed into the processor on each clock period. Instead of waiting for a whole operation to finish, we can have a number of them flowing through the processor at once. Of course, the speedup is now limited by the number of clocks required by individual operations (i.e., by the pipeline length). No interconnection or synchronization problems arise, however, assuming that we have a single pipeline system, and that the control unit complexity does not grow significantly when pipelining is introduced.

Pipelining has achieved great commercial successes, probably because of its simplicity. Many 'array processors' are built to enhance small computers with fast, floating-point capabilities. (This is a restricted use of the term 'array processor' that we will not use further in this paper.) About fifteen such systems are listed in [Robi79]. Some cost only a few tens of thousands of dollars. Because pipeline processors execute a single operation on a long sequence of data items we will refer to these as 'SEA processors' (as we did for parallel processors); see the top of figure 11.1.

2.5   *Combination processing*

The four architectural techniques described above are often used in various combinations in order to obtain even greater speedup over traditional systems. For example, the successor to the CDC 6600 was the CDC 7600 which basically added pipelining to the CDC 6600 architecture. In the mid 1970s, the CDC 7600 (with a 27.5 ns clock) was succeeded by the CRAY-1 (with a 12.5 ns clock) as the fastest available supercomputer; the CRAY-1 is also a multifunction pipeline processor [Russ78]. In fact, figure 11.1 shows half a dozen machines categorized as multipipeline processors and we designate them as MEA machines (multiple execution array). All these machines can execute more than one type of array instructions simultaneously. The Denelcor HEP [Smit78], shown in figure 11.1 on a link to pure multiprocessors, consists of a collection of multi-pipeline processors. The HEP is also an MEA machine in this sense, but has scalar instructions in contrast to the array instructions of most pipeline machines.

On the line between pure pipeline and parallel systems we show two other SEA machines, the CDC CYBER 203/205 and the Burroughs BSP (Burroughs Scientific Processor). The CDC machines (successors to the CDC STAR-100) obtain speeds beyond those provided by their 20 ns clock pipelines, by arranging several pipelines in parallel. Thus, a single vector addition may be broken into four parallel parts, each carried out on a separate addition pipeline. The

Figure 11.2.

Architectural comparisons

System	Processing	Control unit	Processor interconnection	Interprocessor synchronization	Potential speedup
Traditional	Serial	Single	No	No	1
Pipeline	Unwind serial	Expand single	No	No	Limited by pipeline length
Parallel	Replicate serial	Single	Yes	No	Unlimited on many applications
Multifunction	Replicate functions	Expand single	Yes	Yes	Unlimited on most applications
Multiprocessor	Replicate serial	Replicate single	Yes	Yes	Unlimited on most applications

Burroughs BSP consists of sixteen nonpipelined processors operating in parallel, but the instructions are such that a five-segment, memory-to-memory pipeline is formed by fetching, aligning, processing data, and then aligning, and storing the results.

It should be noted that on the link between pure multiprocessing and the CDC CYBER 203/205, we show the CDC proposal to NASA for the Numerical Aerodynamic Simulation Facility. CDC proposed a collection of CYBER 203/205-like machines to achieve 1 gigaflops (10^9 floating-point operations per second) in competition with the Burroughs FMP.

Between pure multifunction processors and multiprocessors, we show data flow processing in figure 11.1. This refers to a collection of related work aimed at achieving high-speed computation by extending the multifunction processor concept and introducing new programming techniques [Arvi80]. Proposals of this type all seem to be for MES machines.

A combination MES and MEA machine was proposed in [KuPa79] to extend the range of array machines to tightly-coupled multiprocessing for certain computations, while still taking full advantage of array instruction sets and array data accessing hardware on those computations well suited to array processing. This avoids some synchronization overhead and allows well understood array data alignment hardware to be used. Notice that several other combinations are shown in figure 11.1, but we will not discuss the others further here.

2.6 Summary

Reviewing figure 11.1, we see that the lower left corner contains MES machines while the right-hand side contains SEA machines. Between the two, encircling the center, we see a collection of MEA and combination MEA/MES systems. It seems clear that in the future more and more combination systems will be designed to execute multiple scalar and multiple array instruction sequences, as well as combinations of these. For more discussion and references about some of these machines see [Kuck78], [Ensl74]. Before discussing the performance potential of such machines, however, we must turn our attention to the types of computations to be performed on them.

3 Algorithm structures

Algorithms can be characterized in terms of the elementary building blocks they contain. The definitions of these building blocks can be given without regard to the structure of the computer on which the computation is to be carried out. Ultimately, however, hardware realities do arise and must be dealt with. Thus, our definitions will reflect certain computer structure capabilities of a very general nature.

This section is intended to be independent of particular programming languages. We have dealt mainly with numerical Fortran programs, but these ideas can be applied in a much wider context than that. We assume only that a dependence graph has been constructed for a given program or algorithm. In section 4 dependence graphs and their transformation will be discussed in detail. In this section we assume a graph has been presented to us and discuss how to execute it on various computer structures. We also assume that the graph represents a program or algorithm that has been written or transformed to perform well on a machine with a high degree of simultaneity (see figure 11.3). In section 4 will discuss how to transform sequential programs into parallel ones. In what follows we use 'program segment' to refer to that part (or all) of a program or algorithm in which we are interested.

3.1   *Loop-free program segments*

The first distinction we make is between program segments containing loops and those that do not contain loops. A loop may be specified by an explicit iteration statement (e.g., DO, FOR), by a conditional looping statement (e.g., WHILE), or by some kind of recursion construct (e.g., a recursive procedure call). Generally speaking, a program without a loop has a rather low running time on a serial machine, because a programmer must write a distinct statement for each computational time step. For this reason the speedup of loop-free program segments is sometimes disregarded. However, for the best possible overall program speedup, even loop-free program segments must be speeded up as much as possible.

In the simplest case a loop-free segment contains a single statement. For example, it may be an arithmetic or Boolean assignment statement or a conditional expression. If an assignment statement contains an expression of n atoms, then by various tree-height reduction methods, the expression can be evaluated in $O(\log n)$ steps [Kuck78]. Similarly, if a conditional expression contains n possible outcomes, then it can be transformed for evaluation in $O(\log n)$ steps [Kuhn79,80].

More generally, a loop-free program may contain a block of assignment statements (BAS), or a mixture of conditional expressions and assignments, or in a functional language a conditional expression with a collection of embedded arithmetic and Boolean expressions to be evaluated.

A BAS can be transformed to a set of independent assignment statements (see section 4); all can be evaluated simultaneously and each may be tree-height reduced. A collection of arithmetic and Boolean expression processors can be used to execute these quickly [KuPa79], [VaZi78], [Swan72]. A conditional expression may be speeded up by the compilation techniques mentioned above;

hardware for fast execution is also discussed in these three references. A collection of assignments and conditionals without cycles can be broken into a BAS followed by a conditional expression, followed by a BAS [Davi72], and then treated as above.

In figure 11.3 two special hardware devices are mentioned to handle these two cases. If no such hardware is available, then loop-free program segments must be executed sequentially. If a loop is given that contains scalars, we assume that after it has been transformed for parallel evaluation these scalars will be expanded to arrays; so we can relate scalar data to loop-free program segments as in figure 11.3.

Figure 11.3. Data, program and machine structures.

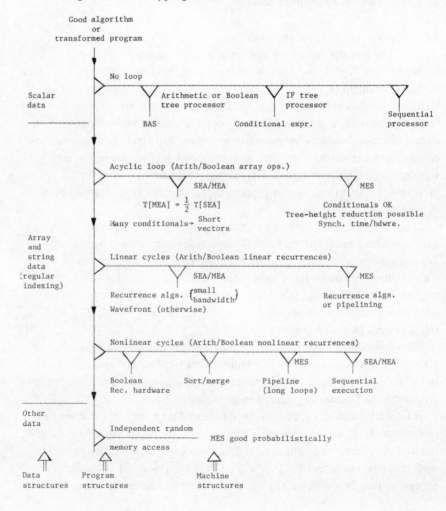

3.2 Loops

A program segment containing a loop may be one of three types: acyclic, linear cyclic, or nonlinear cyclic. A loop is said to have a cycle if data generated by a statement on one execution of the loop is passed back to the statement on some later execution of the loop. This cycle may involve one or more statements. A simple, one-statement example is to compute for $1 \leqslant i \leqslant n$:

$$x_i = a_i x_{i-1} + b_i x_{i-2} + c_i. \tag{1}$$

This statement leads to a *linear cycle* because the right-hand side is a linear combination of the left-hand side variable. A loop containing a linear cycle is called a *linear cyclic loop*. If a cycle is not linear the loop containing it is a *nonlinear cyclic loop*. If a loop contains no cycles it is called an *acyclic loop*.

3.3 Acyclic loop speedup

In order to speed up the computation of an acyclic loop exactly the same techniques can be used as for a program segment containing no loop, but now they may be applied simultaneously to a number of elements of a data structure. Thus, the effective speedup may be as high as the product of the speedup for one pass through the loop and the number of times the loop is executed. We have observed empirically in our measurements of FORTRAN programs that typically the additional speedup gained by allowing MEA operation (over SEA) is about a factor of 2.

Conditional expressions can complicate matters here, and the type of hardware being used must be considered. We can associate with each assignment statement in a loop a bit vector that indicates which elements of a data structure are to be computed, and the bits can be set by appropriate tests which may be carried out simultaneously. However, if there are many paths through a serial loop then these bit vectors may be very sparse. Thus an array machine – either parallel or pipeline – can suffer tremendous degradation in performance. In [BaGK80] a memory system to access dense vectors even in this case was proposed. On the other hand, a multiprocessor may be able to execute the program very efficiently with one loop iteration being carried out on each processor and conditional branching being carried out as in the original program. As indicated in figure 11.3, we may have to give some time and hardware to interprocessor synchronization in the MES case if data dependences extend from one iteration to the next.

3.4 Linear cyclic loop speedup

Consider a program segment that is a loop containing a maximal cycle of dependences. Whether there are one or more statements in the cycle it is straightforward to associate a linear system of equations with a linear cyclic loop. For example, from equation (1) we can derive

$$x = Lx + c, \tag{2}$$

where x and c are column vectors and L is a lower triangular $n \times n$ matrix with two subdiagonals (containing the as and bs). The *order* m of such a linear system or linear recurrence is the distance of the farthest nonzero diagonal from the main diagonal (2 in this case), and we denote such systems as $R\langle n, m \rangle$ linear recurrences. [Kuck78] explains that the solution, x, can be expressed as the product of n matrices (each containing one column of L) and c. This *product-form* algorithm can be used to solve linear recurrences of lower order in a fast

Figure 11.4.

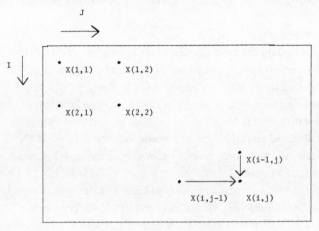

(a) Original X Array

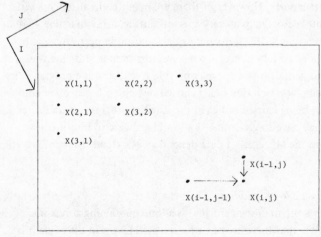

(b) Reindexed X Array

and efficient manner. As the order grows, the number of processors required to get high speedups may grow so large as to make the product-form algorithms inefficient. Nevertheless, for low-order systems, either SEA or MES machines may be used efficiently.

High-order systems often arise in practice from recurrences in multiply dimensioned arrays. For example, consider program 1:

```
DO   I ← 1, N
    DO   J ← 1, N
        X(I,J) ← X(I−1,J) + X(I,J−1) + C
    ENDO
ENDO
```

This is reminiscent of a program segment to solve a partial differential equation or to smooth a digitized picture. The X(I,J) array is illustrated in figure 11.4(*a*). If this loop were rewritten as a one-dimensional array, an $R\langle n^2, n\rangle$ system would result, and the number of processors required by the product-form algorithm for large *n* would be enormous.

As an alternative, the *wave-front* algorithm may be used here in a very efficient manner. This method was first discussed in [KuMC72] and was further discussed in [Lamp74] and [PaKL80]. The *wave-front* algorithm applied to program 1 would reindex the *X*-array as shown in figure 11.4(*b*) and would lead to program 2:

```
DO   I ← 1, N
    DO   SIM J ← 1, I
        X(I,J) ← X(I−1,J) + X(I−1,J−1) + C
    ENDOSIM
ENDO
    K ← 2
DO   I ← N + 1, 2N−1
    DO   SIM J ← K, N
        K ← K + 1
        X(I,J) ← X(I−1,J) + X(I−1,J−1) + C
    ENDOSIM
ENDO
```

Note that program 2 can be regarded as a sequence of 2N−1 vector operations.

For SEA machines, the wave-front method may only be applied to arrays of two or more dimensions, because it simultaneously computes all elements of lower dimensional arrays that appear in a given program. Thus, for high-order linear recurrences in one-dimensional arrays, we must use the product-form algorithms for limited numbers of processors; these achieve moderate efficiency, but not the highest possible speedup.

Given an MES machine, any high-order linear recurrence may be solved efficiently if it appears in a loop with many other statements, by use of the wave-front algorithm. To illustrate the idea, let us return to program 1 and expand the inner loop as in program 3:

$$
\begin{aligned}
&\text{DO} \quad I \leftarrow 1, N \\
&\qquad X(I,1) \leftarrow X(I-1,1) + X(I,0) + C \\
&\qquad X(I,2) \leftarrow X(I-1,2) + X(I,1) + C \\
&\qquad \vdots \\
&\qquad X(I,N) \leftarrow X(I-1,N) + X(I,N-1) + C \\
&\text{ENDO}
\end{aligned}
$$

By loop distribution [Kuck78], this becomes a sequence of N loops as shown in program 4:

$$
\begin{aligned}
&\text{DO} \quad I \leftarrow 1, N \\
&\qquad X(I,1) \leftarrow X(I-1,1) + X(I,0) + C \\
&\text{ENDO} \\
&\text{DO} \quad I \leftarrow 1, N \\
&\qquad X(I,2) \leftarrow X(I-1,2) + X(I,1) + C \\
&\text{ENDO} \\
&\qquad \vdots \\
&\text{DO} \quad I \leftarrow 1, N \\
&\qquad X(I,N) \leftarrow X(I-1,N) + X(I,N-1) + C \\
&\text{ENDO}
\end{aligned}
$$

Assume that N processors are available and the i-th distributed loop of program 4 is assigned to processor i. Since no computation may begin until its dependences are satisfied, the resulting *dependence driven* computation is as sketched in figure 11.5.

Several observations are now in order. First, note that the $2N-1$ time steps of figure 11.5 correspond to the $2N-1$ I-iterations of program 2, and exactly the same computational steps are carried out in each case. In figure 11.5 synchronization is carried out by an MES machine at the interprocessor level, while in the SEA case (program 2) the control unit that issues instructions keeps

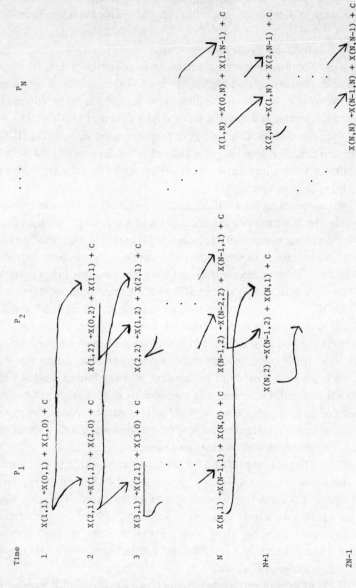

Figure 11.5. Dependence driven MES wave-front computation.

the system synchronized. Secondly, notice that the number of processors needed (and hence the speedup) is proportional to the number of statements in a loop. Notice that dependences between adjacent processors are sufficient to ensure proper execution ordering in both these cases, but it is sometimes necessary to provide for longer distance data passing and synchronization.

3.5 Nonlinear cyclic loop speedup

Some nonlinear recurrences can be rewritten in linear form and then the methods discussed previously may be used. Other algorithms containing nonlinear recurrences can be formulated directly on parallel hardware with significant speedups; sorting and merging are examples [Batc68] which lead to nonlinear Boolean recurrences. Other Boolean recurrences are discussed in [BaGK80]. These are the first four entries in figure 11.3 under nonlinear recurrences. Most nonlinear arithmetic recurrences, however, are difficult or impossible to speed up by such techniques.

When compiling for an SEA machine, nonlinear recurrences can sometimes be avoided by interchanging the order of loop execution (to get the index or indices involved in the nonlinearity to outer loops) and then sequentially executing enough outer loops to satisfy the nonlinear dependences between sequential iterations. If this technique does not work, then no speedup is possible for a nonlinear cyclic loop using an SEA or MEA machine as indicated in figure 11.3.

An MES machine can execute any nonlinear recurrence with speedup proportional to the number of cycles occurring in its loop (recall program 3). Notice that the method used in figure 11.5 works equally well whether the cyclic dependences of program 4 are linear or nonlinear. Also, notice that the individual loops in program 4 need not be identical. We say a loop is *pipelined* across an MES machine if it is broken into a number of smaller loops and one of these is assigned to each processor (see [PaKL80] for details). Again, the processor interconnection requirements for synchronization and data communication may be more complex for other programs.

It may be seen that figure 11.3 relates data structures, program structures, and machine structures. We have glossed over the notation of 'regular indexing' in figure 11.3 for the array or string data we have been discussing. What this means is that we assume data can be accessed quickly for processing, and hardware cost is reasonable. Many proposals exist for fast, relatively inexpensive, data alignment networks [Sieg80], and conflict-free array access memories have also been designed [LaVo80].

Without getting into hardware details, we can distinguish 'regular' indexing from 'other data' in figure 11.3 by examples. Arrays with subscripted subscripts that are not known until run time or list structures that are of arbitrary form and are modified by the program are examples of 'other data'. These may be stored in a parallel memory and accessed at random. If each processor in a multiprocessor generates addresses independently and they are uniformly distributed across the memories, good expected effective bandwidths can be achieved [BaSm76], [ChKL77]. Under similar assumptions, a stochastic shuffle network gives good expected effective bandwidth [PaKL80]. Much work is needed in this area to study various addressing patterns analytically and empirically. Notice that the three types of program structures for arrays with regular indexing can be repeated here, and many of the techniques discussed above may be used. However, it seems likely that some type of MES machine will be most effective in this case.

4　Dependence graph transformation

This section presents a framework for discussing compilers for high-speed machines. The idea is to isolate the algorithm or building blocks discussed in section 3. First we define five kinds of program dependence, how they arise in languages, and how to build a dependence graph. Then we sketch various ways of removing dependences – even from graphs that are derived in an exact way from a given program. This can lead to faster computations. Finally we discuss several abstractions of a program graph that can be used in code generation for supercomputers.

Recall that in figure 11.3 it was assumed at the top that a program was in a form that was suitable for fast computation. This could be human generated or derived from a program segment written in an ordinary programming language. By the methods of this section, dependence graphs of sequential programs may be transformed to serve as inputs to figure 11.3.

4.1　Dependences

Any algorithm that is formalized and expressed in a language (programming or natural) contains some kinds of dependences between the atomic operands and between the steps of the algorithm. Programmers generally pay little attention to the dependences in a 'pure' algorithm or to any 'artificial' dependences that they may introduce when expressing the algorithm in some language. Nevertheless, if a program is to be run on a machine with any kind of simultaneously operating subsystems, the dependences may be very important. In many cases, reducing the number of dependences leads to direct reductions in a program's running time.

Roughly speaking, there are four times at which dependences can be reduced: when a language is selected for implementing the program; when the program is transcribed into that language; when the program is compiled; and when it is executed. Most languages have an explicitly stated dependence between consecutive statements in the control flow graph (e.g., PASCAL, ALGOL, FORTRAN, SNOBOL, etc.). A few languages [AcDe79], [ArGP78] are defined so that some types of dependence are impossible and others are greatly reduced. Making the programmer responsible for reducing dependences imposes a difficult, if not impossible, task on the programmer. High-speed computer systems with multiple functional units or pipelines commonly employ a lookahead control unit that breaks dependences at execution time. We believe that compilers are quite well suited to solving this problem, and will discuss this approach.

Before proceeding, we will illustrate five dependence types with the example of program 5:

$$S1: A \leftarrow B + C$$
$$S2: B \leftarrow A * 3$$
$$S3: A \leftarrow 2 * C$$
$$S4: P \leftarrow B \geqslant 0$$
$$\text{IF P THEN S5: } D \leftarrow 1$$
$$\text{ELSE S6: } D \leftarrow 0$$

We say that S2 is *flow dependent* on S1 (which we denote S1 → S2) because of A, S2 is *anti-dependent* on S1 (S1 ↛ S2) because of B, S3 is *output dependent* on S1 (S1 ⊖→ S3) because of A, and S3 is *input dependent* on S1 (S1 ⊣→ S3) because of C. These are four kinds of *data dependence* and all assume that assignments are to be executed in the order of presentation. We say that S5 and S6 are *control dependent* on S4 (S4 ⊖→ S5 and S4 ⊖→ S6).

It is simple to give an algorithm that removes all flow, output, and anti-dependences from a block of assignment statements. For example, S1, S2, and S3 of program 5 can be rewritten as program 6:

$$S2': B \leftarrow (B+C) * 3$$
$$S3 : A \leftarrow 2 * C$$

Now S2' and S3 can be executed simultaneously (input dependence does not require an execution ordering), so multiple memory units and multiple functional units may be utilized. These two programs can be represented graphically by the dependence graphs of figures 11.6 and 11.7 respectively. Here we associate nodes with assignment statements.

If the goal is program speedup, however, we must deal with arrays as well as other data structures, depending on the language. The problem of discovering exact dependences in a block of assignment statements contained in one or more loops is difficult to solve, since dependence between two statements means that on one or more pairs of iterations there is a dependence.

The construction of a dependence graph for only scalar variables is a simple extension of the flow analysis technique [Hech77]. When a dependence graph is needed for a program that deals with arrays, other methods must be used if something other than an extremely conservative graph is needed. For certain subscript forms efficient and exact tests may be found. In [Bane76] and [BCKT79] the problem is discussed in detail. The data arc set analysis technique [Kuhn80] deals with a larger class of subscripts and yields exact results, but may be difficult to implement in a production compiler.

4.2 Arc removal

The penalty for including a spurious dependence is more severe inside loops, because cycles of dependence indicate some type of recurrence and these can consume much time (or hardware if solved in a fast way). Even using the best tests, there will be arcs in the dependence graph that can be eliminated by transforming the program. These transforms become more important as the quality of the dependence graph declines.

Figure 11.6.

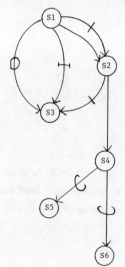

Figure 11.7.

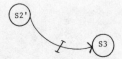

For the statements inside a loop, a compiler can eliminate dependences in two ways. First, if the dependence arcs to be eliminated are not in a cycle, we could use either the method illustrated above by program 6 or some simple renaming techniques. When the dependence arcs are in a cycle we must use other methods.

Output and anti-dependence arcs in cycles can be eliminated by the method of *expansion*. This method consists of transforming scalars into (possibly multi-dimensional) arrays and arrays into arrays of higher dimension. The dependence graph shown in figure 11.8 includes output and anti-dependence arcs involved in a cycle. It corresponds to program 7:

```
DO    I ← 1, N
      DO    J ← 1, M
S1:             C(I) ← X(I) + 1
S2:             A ← C(I) + 1
      ENDO
ENDO
```

By expanding scalar A and array C we obtain program 8:

```
DO    I ← 1, N
      DO    J ← 1, M
S1:             C′(I,J) ← X(I) + 1
S2:             A′(I,J) ← C′(I,J) + 1
      ENDO
ENDO
A ← A′(N,M)
C(∗) ← C′(∗,M)
```

Figure 11.9 shows the cycle free dependence graph of program 8. In general, expansion is not as straightforward as the previous example might lead one to believe. While it is theoretically possible to expand in every case, it is not reasonable to do so in some.

Figure 11.8.

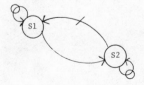

Control dependence cycles can be eliminated by solving Boolean recurrences. Consider, for example, program 9:

```
        DO    I ← 1, N
S1:           P(I) ← A(I−1) > 0
              IF P(I) THEN S2: A(I) ← C(I)
        ENDO
```

As shown in figure 11.10, there is a cycle involving a control dependence. Program 9 can be transformed into program 10:

```
        DO    I ← 1, N
S1:           P(I) ← (P(I−1) AND C(I−1) > 0) OR
                     (NOT P(I−1) and A(I−1) > 0)
        ENDO
        DO    I ← 1, N
              IF P(I) THEN S2: A(I) ← C(I)
        ENDO
```

The outcome of program 10 (the dependence graph shown in figure 11.11) is typical; a loop with a cycle including a control dependence becomes a Boolean recurrence (the first loop of program 10) followed by a loop without control dependence arcs. This transformation is useful because Boolean recurrences can

Figure 11.9.

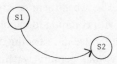

Figure 11.10.

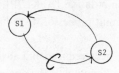

Figure 11.11.

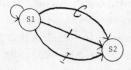

be recognized by a compiler and, in many cases, can be executed in parallel if the appropriate hardware is available [BaGK80].

4.3   Graph abstraction

Let us assume that a compiler has initially built a dependence graph and then transformed it to remove as many arcs as it can. We will assume that loop control has been distributed down to the level of cycles or single nodes in the dependence graph [Kuck78]. We will now discuss several *abstraction* transformations that make the program more suitable for execution on certain computer architectures in the sense that code generation is made easier and run-time performance is improved.

First, we discuss cycle removal. A flow dependence cycle can be replaced with a recurrence node. In many high-performance machines, there are several instructions to handle recurrences. For example, the CRAY-1, CYBER 203/205 and the TI ASC all have a number of *reduction* instructions (e.g., sum the elements of a vector). The Burroughs BSP has an instruction to solve any first-order linear recurrence. Code generation for most multiple arithmetic unit machines can be enhanced by using one of the well-studied linear recurrence algorithms [Kuck78], [Gajs81].

Cycles of flow, anti-, and output dependences may be removed in a similar manner (by treating the anti- and output dependences as flow dependences, then using a recurrence solver). This will give the correct results, but may waste time. The problem of breaking such cycles was discussed in section 4.2.

Given two or more nodes that are contained in loops, another type of abstraction may be performed on a dependence graph. Given two distributed nodes, if their index sets are identical, and if the dependences between them satisfy certain conditions, the nodes may be *fused* into one node with common loop control.

Loop fusion removes input dependences and is effective in restricting the use of critical resources at run time. For example, in a virtual memory system, it allows the multiple use of a page that has been fetched from secondary memory, thereby reducing the space–time product of the computation [AbKL79]. It also could be used to enhance a cache hit ratio or, in a multiprocessor, to reduce interprocessor communication [PaKL80].

At this point, the original dependence graph has been reduced and abstracted enough to be a DAG (directed acyclic graph), and scheduling of the operations defined by the nodes of the DAG can be done for various architectures. The nodes in each anti-chain of the DAG can be executed simultaneously. Furthermore, one of several recurrence algorithms available on the target machine may be chosen according to the resources and time available to complete that particular portion of the schedule. Other nodes could be transformed by tree-height reduction, if that is desirable.

5 Conclusion

This chapter presents the definitions of three machine types in section 2, and lists a number of real computer systems in this framework. Section 3 presents several algorithm building blocks and discusses how they can be executed on the machine types of section 2. Section 4 discusses how a given dependence graph may be transformed to remove cycles and then abstracted to obtain a directed acyclic graph for code generation.

These ideas may be applied to a number of real computer systems, and some are mentioned in the chapter. This has been done using the Parafrase system at the University of Illinois. Virtual memory space–time product can be reduced substantially by these ideas [AbKL79], since address locality is greatly enhanced. The application of the ideas in register-to-register pipeline systems is discussed in [KKLW80], and in this case register management becomes an important consideration. Memory-to-memory parallel systems were discussed in [KuMC72] and [KBCD74]. Recently we have studied MES systems, since they can perform well even when SEA and MEA systems do not [PaKL80].

Acknowledgements

I am indebted to Robert Kuhn, Bruce Leasure, David Padua, and Michael Wolfe for many of the ideas and some of the presentation used in this chapter. Vivian Alsip did a superb job of typing it under pressure.

References

[AbKL79] W. Abu-Sufah, D. Kuck and D. Lawrie, 'Automatic program transformations for virtual memory computers' in *Proceedings of the 1979 National Computer Conference*, pp. 969–74, June 1979.

[AcDe79] W. B. Ackerman and J. B. Dennis, *VAL – A Value-Oriented Algorithmic Language*, Preliminary Ref. Manual, Lab. for Comput. Sci. (TR-218), MIT, Cambridge, MA, June 1979.

[ArGP78] Arvind, K. P., Gostelow and W. Plouffe, *An Asynchronous Programming language and Computing Machine*, University of California at Irvine, Dept. of Comput. Sci. Rpt. No. 114A, Dec. 1978.

[Arvi80] Arvind, 'Decomposing a program for multiple processor systems' in *Proceedings of the 1980 International Conference on Parallel Processing*, pp. 7–14, Aug. 1980.

[BaGK80] U. Banerjee, D. Gajski and D. Kuck, 'Array machine control units for loops containing IFs' in *Proceedings of the 1980 International Conference on Parallel Processing*, pp. 28–36, Aug. 1980.

[Bane76] U. Banerjee, *Data Dependence in Ordinary Programs*, M.S. thesis, University of Illinois at Urbana-Champaign, Dept. of Comput. Sci. Rpt. No. 76-837, Nov. 1976.

[BaSm76] F. Baskett and A. J. Smith, 'Interference in multiprocessor computer systems with interleaved memory' *Comm. of the ACM*, 19, 6, pp. 327–34, June 1976.

[Batc68] K. E. Batcher, 'Sorting networks and their applications' in *Proceedings AFIPS Spring Joint Computer Conference*, 32, pp. 307–15, 1968.

[BBKK68] G. H. Barnes, R. M. Brown, M. Kato, D. J. Kuck, D. L. Slotnick and R. A. Stokes, 'The ILLIAC IV computer' *IEEE Trans. on Computers*, C-17, 8, pp. 746–57, Aug. 1968.

[BCKT79] U. Banerjee, S. C. Chen, D. J. Kuck and R. A. Towle, 'Time and parallel processor bounds for Fortran-like loops' *IEEE Trans. on Computers*, C-28, 9, pp. 660–70, Sept. 1979.

[ChKL77] D. Chang, D. J. Kuck and D. H. Lawrie, 'On the effective bandwidth of parallel memories' *IEEE Trans. on Computers*, C-26, 5, pp. 480-90, May 1977.

[Davi72] E. W. Davis, Jr., 'Concurrent processing of conditional jump trees' in Compcon 72, IEEE Computer Society Conference Proceedings, pp. 279-81, Sept. 1972.

[Ensl74] P. H. Enslow, Ed., *Multiprocessors and Parallel Processing*, Wiley-Interscience, New York, 1974.

[Gajs81] D. D. Gajski, 'An algorithm for solving linear recurrence systems on parallel and pipelined machines' *IEEE Trans. on Computers*, Mar. 1981.

[Hech77] M. S. Hecht, *Data Flow Analysis of Computer Programs*, Elsevier North-Holland, New York, 1977.

[KBCD74] D. Kuck, P. Budnik, S-C. Chen, E. Davis, Jr., J. Han, P. Kraska, D. Lawrie, Y. Muraoka, R. Strebendt and R. Towle, 'Measurements of parallelism in ordinary FORTRAN programs', *IEEE Computer*, 7, 1, pp. 37-46, Jan. 1974.

[KKLW80] D. J. Kuck, R. H. Kuhn, B. Leasure and M. Wolfe, 'The structure of an advanced vectorizer for pipelined processors' to appear in *Proceedings of COMPSAC 80, Computer Software & Applications Conference*, Chicago, Oct. 1980.

[Kuck78] D. J. Kuck, *The Structure of Computers and Computations*, Vol. I, John Wiley & Sons, 1978.

[Kuhn79] R. H. Kuhn, 'Fast evaluation of arbitary decision trees' in *Proceedings of the International Conference on Parallel Processing*, pp. 267-8, Aug. 1979.

[Kuhn80] R. H. Kuhn, *Optimization and Interconnection Complexity for: Parallel Processors, Single-Stage Networks, and Decision Trees*, Ph.D. thesis, Univ. of Ill. at Urb.-Champ., Dept. of Comput. Sci. Rpt. No. 80-1009, Feb. 1980.

[KuMC72] D. J. Kuck, Y. Muraoka and S. C. Chen, 'On the number of operations simultaneously executable in FORTRAN-like programs and their resulting speed-up' *IEEE Trans. on Computers*, C-21, 12, pp. 1293-310, Dec. 1972.

[KuPa79] D. J. Kuck and D. A. Padua, 'High-speed multiprocessors and their compilers' in *Proceedings of the International Conference on Parallel Processing*, pp. 5-16, Aug. 1979.

[Lamp74] L. Lamport, 'The parallel execution of DO loops' *Comm. of the ACM*, 17, pp. 83-93, 1974.

[LaVo80] D. Lawrie and C. Vora, 'The prime memory system for array access' in *Proceedings of the 1980 International Conference on Parallel Processing*, pp. 81-90, Aug. 1980.

[LuBa80] S. F. Lundstrom and G. H. Barnes, 'A controllable MIMD architecture' in *Proceedings of the 1980 International Conference on Parallel Processing*, pp. 19-27, Aug. 1980.

[PaKL80] D. A. Padua, D. J. Kuck and D. H. Lawrie, 'High-speed multiprocessors and compilation techniques' Special Issue on Parallel Processing, *IEEE Trans. on Computers*, C-29, 9, 763-76, Sept. 1980.

[Redd73] S. F. Reddaway, 'An elementary array with processing and storage capabilities' in *Proceedings of the International Workshop on Computer Architecture*, Grenoble, June 1973.

[Robi79] A. L. Robinson, 'Array processors; Maxi number crunching for a mini price' *Science*, 203, 12, pp. 156-60, Jan. 1979.

[Russ78] R. M. Russell, 'The Cray-1 computer system' *Comm. of the ACM*, 21, 1, p. 6372, Jan. 1978.

[Sieg80] H. J. Siegel, Ed., *Proceedings of the Workshop on Interconnection Networks*, Lafayette, Indiana, April 1980.

[Smit78] B. J. Smith, 'A pipelined, shared resource MIMD computer' in *Proceedings of the 1978 International Conference on Parallel Processing*, pp. 6-8, Aug. 1978.

[Swan72] L. A. Swanson, *Simulation of a Tree Processor*, M.S. thesis, Univ. of Ill. at Urb.-Champ., Dept. of Comput. Sci. Rpt. No. 503, Jan. 1972.

[Thor70] J. E. Thornton, *Design of a Computer, the Control Data 6600*, Scott, Foresman and Co., Glenview, Illinois, 1970.

[VaZi78] T. Vanaken and G. Zick, 'The X-Pipe: A pipeline for expression trees' in *Proceedings of the 1978 International Conference on Parallel Processing*, pp. 238-45, Aug. 1978.

12 Practical parallel processors and their uses

1 Introduction

One of the first theoretical descriptions of a parallel processing system is due to Richardson [8], who computed a weather forecast entirely by hand. The time taken was excessive so he proposed an operational forecasting factory: a hall staffed with 64000 'computers'. Each computer would deal with the column of atmosphere above a location on the earth's surface. The ensemble would be controlled by a director who coordinated the activity and kept the calculations in step; we may call this concept the Albert Hall computer. Judging from the date of Richardson's work, 1922, it is obvious that by a computer he meant a person probably equipped with a desk calculator but the basic principle is that of the modern single instruction multiple datastream (SIMD) machine.

The study of parallel systems was greatly influenced by the development of the ILLIAC IV system [7] and the research into algorithms has primarily concentrated on the use of that type of architecture. To give a basis for our discussion it is useful to consider a crude overview of the ILLIAC IV as a model machine. Figure 12.1 shows schematically the prime components which interest us. The major components are:

(*a*) a control unit which broadcasts identical instructions to the processing elements,

(*b*) a set of 64 processing elements (PE),

(*c*) a set of processing element memories (PEM), one per processing element, and

(*d*) a disc subsystem which can send data to and from the processing element memories and which can be loaded or unloaded from a central system which provides all external communication.

All the systems we shall consider will have roughly the same four components:

(*a*) a control unit as a single instruction source,

(*b*) a set of processors,

(*c*) a set of memories (one per processor), and

(*d*) a system for communication with external data sources.

The characteristics which will distinguish one system from another are primarily:

(*a*) the number of processing elements,
(*b*) the complexity of the operations supported by the processing element hardware,
(*c*) the interconnection paths between the processors,
(*d*) the size of the memory modules, and
(*e*) the communication paths to other host systems.

The ILLIAC IV has 64 processing elements, each being based upon a medium sized Burroughs mainframe computer, so the individual processors are powerful floating point units with a 64-bit word operation. The processing element memories each hold 1024 64-bit words. The disc system has a total capacity of approximately 16 million 64-bit words. For many applications it is found necessary to use the PE memories as working storage with the discs being used as

Figure 12.1. Overview of ILLIAC IV computer.

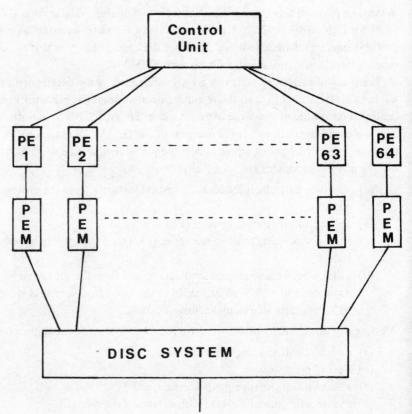

main data storage. An effect of this use of discs as major storage medium means that many implementation studies on the ILLIAC IV have been dominated by the need to optimise disc transfers rather than by the demands of parallel programming, and so the reader is warned against too ready extrapolation of ILLIAC IV experience to more modern systems.

As the processing element of ILLIAC IV has much in common with a standard processor it has become common to study the performance of theoretical parallel systems in terms of a number of concepts, two of the most common of which are 'speed-up' and 'efficiency'. The following definitions follow Kuck [6].

Let T_p be the time required to perform some calculation on a p processor machine. Then the speed-up factor over a uniprocessor is

$$S_p = T_1/T_p$$

and the efficiency is

$$E_p = S_p/p \leqslant 1$$

If p processors perform p times faster than a single processor then E_p will be unity, but in general one expects some degradation. The arguments behind the definitions of these quantities appear very reasonable and simple, so they are widely used, but as we shall discuss later there is reason to doubt their validity when applied to today's real multiprocessor systems.

In section 2 we will describe three multiprocessor systems: ICL-DAP, CIMSA PROPAL 2, and the proposed Goodyear MPP. In section 3 we will consider the programming language proposed for ICL-DAP and the effects of the architecture on a number of algorithms.

2   Some modern highly parallel processing systems
2.1   *General*

The advantages of the parallel processor seem to be greatest when applied to the solution of problems in matrix algebra or finite difference methods for the solution of partial differential equations. It is well known that many algorithms in these areas require the same types of operation to be repeated on large numbers of data items. If one can, in the case of a partial differential equation, allocate one processing element per cell then one would hope to be able to compute all cells simultaneously. Typical finite difference meshes are 50×50 or 100×100 so such an organisation would imply a requirement for 2500 or 10000 processor systems. Indeed if a three-dimensional $100 \times 100 \times 100$ problem were to be tackled it would appear that 10^6 or more processors could be needed. If one has fewer processors than cells it is necessary to make repeated operations in a fashion analogous to those done in a serial computer. The large degree of potential parallelism in real problems means that there is an urge to build systems with many more processors than the 64 of the ILLIAC IV system.

The requirement to build a system with one thousand or more processors leads to some very obvious physical constraints on the type of processor which is replicated many times:

> it must be physically small
> it must have low power consumption and
> it must be relatively cheap to make.

A natural result of these constraints is that the unit should be relatively simple. The first idea that might strike the reader is that their favourite microprocessor chip would satisfy the requirements and indeed it appears that nearly every university in the world has some project in which a number of microprocessors are connected together. If, however, one is trying to establish a single instruction multiple datastream system a mass produced microprocessor has some technical disadvantages which are primarily:

> (*a*) they were not designed to be used in large armies and
> (*b*) they replicate many times functions such as instruction decode, which in principle needs only to be done once.

For these and other reasons the current set of **SIMD** machines are not based on 8- or 16-bit off-the-shelf microprocessor chips but on even simpler bit-organised, special purpose processing elements. In order to better describe these systems it is probably best to start with the consideration of a specific system and describe alternative approaches in terms of modifications and improvements to this most basic design.

2.2   The ICL distributed array processor (DAP)

The DAP [1] is a good starting point for the discussion as it is the longest established of the designs and has the most elementary processing element. Figure 12.2 shows a schematic of a single DAP processing element and its associated memory module. The most important difference between this processing element and the ILLIAC IV processing element is that the organisation is based on a 1-bit word rather than a 64-bit word. The processing element for the DAP has three single word (i.e. 1-bit) registers A, Q, C, and an arithmetic unit (the adder) for performing arithmetic on data held in the memory or registers. The instruction set obeyed by the processing elements deals only with single word length operations and are therefore little more than fundamental Boolean operations. If it is required to use this type of processing element for complex operations (say 16-bit arithmetic), then a program is necessary which looks very like a multiple precision software routine for a system with longer word length.

As an example of the software consideration needed to drive bit organised processors we can examine more closely the task of addition of two 16-bit memory fields (X and Y) and placing the result in another 16-bit field (Z) held in the memory. Any competent programmer knows what has to be done to add two fields of 16 words precision on a word bit machine. The program would look something like the following (using a pseudo high level language)

```
CARRY: = 0
DO  LOOP  I = 1 TO 16
Z_i: = X_i + Y_i + CARRY
IF (OVERFLOW)  THEN CARRY:= UNIT
                ELSE  CARRY:= 0
LOOP: CONTINUE
```

This pseudo program is only valid if one is using an appropriate number representation and all types of complications may be necessary if one has twos complement form for negatives etc. The major lesson that we want to take from

Figure 12.2. DAP processing element.

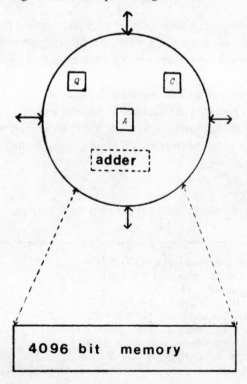

the example is the existence of at least three memory access cycles for every unit of precision so that the execution time will be proportional to the number of words (p) in our multiple precision arithmetic format.

The DAP's processing element supports single bit arithmetic by means of the adder, shown in figure 12.2. The add instruction sums the contents of the Q register, the C register and a selected word (bit) of the memory and leaves the 2-bit result in Q and C. The contents of C being the most significant bit can also be considered as the overflow indicator.

The addition of two fields of length p bits requires $3p$ memory access ($2p$ read access times for the bits X and Y and p write access times for the result Z). Hence it is a characteristic of the processing element that the operation time is a function of the precision of the arithmetic and the bit complexity of the operation. The bit complexity of an operation is unfamiliar to most computer users and leads to performance characteristics which are contrary to most users' experience. Table 12.1 shows approximate relative operation times for a DAP processing element. There are a large number of very important observations that can be made from studying table 12.1. Some of the most important are:

(a) fixed point arithmetic is usually very much faster than floating point arithmetic,

(b) short precision arithmetic is faster than long precision arithmetic (addition and data movement varies with the number of bits whilst multiplication, division and square root vary as the square of the number of bits),

(c) data movement is fast relative to floating point arithmetic,

(d) logical operations are very fast relative to arithmetic, and

(e) the relative magnitude of various operations is very different from the relative magnitude obtained from a word based processor with hardware floating point unit.

Table 12.1. Some relative operation times for a single DAP processing element.

Single bit Boolean operation (L1.AND.L2)	1
16-bit fixed point additions (I = J + K)	10
16-bit data movement (I = J)	6
32-bit fixed point addition (I2 = J2 + K2)	20
32-bit floating point addition (X = Y + Z)	180
32-bit floating point multiplication (X = Y *Z)	280
32-bit floating point square root (X = SQRT (Y))	250
64-bit floating point multiply (X2 = Y2 * Z2)	1000

The last point cannot be overemphasised. The development of hardware floating point arithmetic units has reached the stage where the time for a multiplication is usually only two or three memory access times. Also double precision arithmetic takes almost the same time as single precision arithmetic. The development of floating point hardware is so advanced that some manufacturers do not find it cost effective to provide a separate integer arithmetic unit but do integer arithmetic using the floating point hardware. The properties of floating point units have become so ingrained in many users' minds that they cannot conceive that there are alternative approaches, hence it is taken as axiomatic that square root must be performed using Newton–Raphson iterations and is therefore a costly operation. Table 12.1 shows that for a bit-organised system square root can be cheaper than multiplication and hence the research into algorithms which avoid square root operations is only necessary for a restricted type of computer – it is not the result of a fundamental property of arithmetic.

The speed of bit-organised PEs is relatively slow compared with modern high speed architectures – due primarily to the store access times. As it is fundamental to their design that the average memory processor transfer is only single bit then the operation times are ultimately controlled by the cycle times for access to the memory chips.

As a minor digression into technology it should be noted that the memory cycle time is the crucial parameter rather than the access time normally quoted. The cycle time is the minimum elapsed time between successive accesses and this is often three or four times longer than the, say, 50 nanoseconds which may be quoted as the access time for a high performance storage chip.

On the basis of an approximate 200 nanosecond cycle time the relative times in table 12.1 translate approximately to microseconds and hence a single processor is a low speed device.

The ICL-DAP installed at Queen Mary College, London, has 4096 such processors and so is a highly parallel SIMD system made out of many low speed units. The processing elements are arranged in a 64×64 matrix and receive a single instruction stream broadcast from a single unit called the master control unit. Figure 12.3 shows an overview of the interprocessor organisation. The figure shows 64 row highways and 64 column highways which can be used to transmit data either between processors or to the outside world.

The master control unit has eight 64-bit registers which are attached to the row and column highways and are used to select (or transmit) data from (or to) all processors in a row or column. Data may be transmitted to all processors simultaneously via the row or column highways or each processor may AND some data onto the highways to allow global enquiries to be made of the state of the processing elements.

A very important facilityof the processing element is achieved by the use of the single bit register *A* shown in figure 12.2. The register is called the activity register and can be used as a switch to permit processing elements to ignore certain instructions transmitted by the master control unit. Some facility (such as the activity register) to inhibit the operation of some processors in an SIMD system is essential. The reason is obvious: there are few algorithms which require the same operation in every processing element (e.g. one can only take square roots if the numbers are positive).

The usual method of programming the DAP is by using a high level language DAP-FORTRAN which is described briefly in section 3. An advantage of the use of high level languages is the ability to hide the low level architecture from the general user. The majority of DAP users do not need to know about the bit-organised nature of the computer as they use system code for the usual arithmetic operations. However, to give a feel for what low level programming is like

Figure 12.3. DAP interprocessor organisation.

6 4
Column Highways

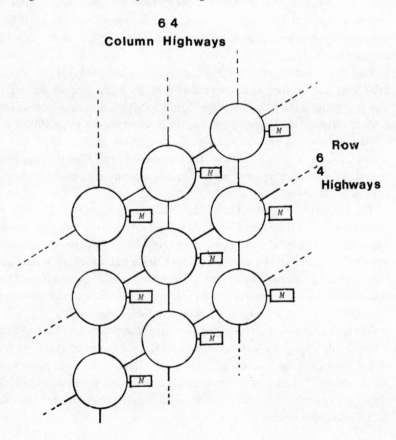

Row 6 4 Highways

on a bit-organised parallel computer let us examine two simple examples – the addition of two 16-bit integer fields, and searching through the PE set to find which processor(s) has the largest value stored in a 32-bit field.

The first example assumes that previously we have loaded three index registers ($M1$, $M2$ and $M3$) which point to the most significant bits of the two fields to be added and the result field. The programming is very simple as one only considers a single processor and the operation is automatically repeated in all other processors.

```
CF                    ! initially sets carry FALSE
                      ! in all PEs
QS        0.15(M1)    ! loads the least significant
                      ! bit of field (M1) into Q
CQPCQS    0.15(M2)    ! adds contents of C,Q, and
                      ! bit 15 (M2) together and
                      ! leaves result in C and Q
SQ        0.15(M3)    ! stores the least significant
                      ! bit
                      !
QS        0.14(M1)    ! repeat using next most
                      ! significant bit position
CQPCQS    0.14(M2)    ! and the carry
SQ        0.14(M3)    ! from the last step
```

The total operation would require another 42 instructions if we continued in this fashion. Using a looping construct it may be shortened and on the DAP there is a hardware DO construct which means that the code becomes

```
      CF
      DO        16 TIMES    ! repeat all instructions
                            ! up to and including the
                            ! next labelled instruction
                            ! 16 times
      QS        0.15 (M1−)  ! the '−' causes M1 to be
                            ! decremented
      CQPCQS    0.15(M2−)   ! by one each time the loop is
LOOP: SQ        0.15(M3−)   ! traversed
```

After the loop was finished the C register would contain any overflow which could be examined if necessary. Simple parameterisation would allow the code to be altered to deal with variable precision arithmetic provided all processing elements did arithmetic to the same total precision.

The second example is one where we begin to learn something about the fundamental difference between parallel and serial processing. The previous algorithm is an example of the trivial case where a parallel system simply performs simultaneously exactly the same work as would be done by a serial computer performing a loop. The task of finding which processor contains the largest value is at first glance not suitable for parallel implementation but provided our parallel system is based upon bit-organised computers we can adopt the following associative algorithm. A very good treatment of associative algorithms is given by Foster [2].

The algorithm is elegant and simple and is easy to describe by looking at the low level code. Later we will present a DAP-FORTRAN version of the same algorithm.

```
AT    !  sets the activity bits all
      !  to TRUE
```

This statement simply marks all PEs as candidates for having the largest element.

```
QA                !  notes the contents of A into
                  !  a temporary store
DO     32 TIMES   !  repeat for all bits in the data field
AMS    0.0(M1+)   !  logical AND of A register
                  !  and the bit pointed to by M1
```

This last instruction first produces the AND function of A and the most significant bit of the field $M1$, then later the next most significant bit and so on. Since processors with bit value 1 contain larger numbers than processors with bit value 0 the result of the last operation is to compute a reduced subset of PEs which are candidates for containing the largest element. We cannot however just close the loop at this instruction as it is possible that there are no candidate processors with a bit set in this position. We must therefore check that there are still some PEs with a value of A register TRUE.

```
RANO   M4   !  ANDs all columns of the
            !  inverse of the A registers
            !  together and places the result
            !  in index register M4
```

The last instruction uses the column highways and the individual bits of the 64-bit-register $M4$ will only be 0 if there is at least one processor with a value of 1 in the A registers of the processors in the corresponding column. Hence $M4$ will be zero if and only if there is at least one processing element with its activity bit set. We therefore test $M4$ for zero and skip if it is zero.

```
       SKIP   ALL M4 0   !
       AQ                 ! reset A if all M4 ≠ 0
LOOP:  QA                 ! remember current set
```

The algorithm is now complete. The register A in each processing element now indicates TRUE if and only if that processing element has a value equal to the largest value. If the value of the largest element is needed it may be easily extracted using the contents of the A register as a pointer.

To finish our description of the DAP it is important to describe the mechanism for input/output. The DAP at Queen Mary College (QMC) is conceptually a two-dimensional matrix of 64×64 processing elements, each associated with 4096 bits of storage. This total object may be viewed as a cuboid of store $64 \times 64 \times 4096 = 16$ megabits or 2 megabytes. The system is attached to the store highway of an ICL 2980 computer in such a fashion that the host computer may address the processing element storage as part of its own address space. Hence the DAP appears to the 2900 operating system (VME/B) as a special 2-megabyte store module embedded within the current total 6.5 megabytes attached to the QMC system. It is the task of the loading subfunction of the operating system to ensure that those tasks which need the DAP facilities load their data into the special (or intelligent) DAP store rather than into standard storage.

To summarise:
The DAP installed at QMC is a 64×64 matrix of simple bit-organised processing elements. Each processing element has a local memory of 4096 bits. The total memory space is 2 megabytes which can also be accessed for input/output by a host 2980 computer. The DAP has a single master control unit which issues a single instruction stream to all the processors. The processors, which are connected in a two-dimensional nearest neighbour mesh, have a register (the activity bit) which allows them to ignore some of the transmitted instructions.

2.3   PROPAL 2

PROPAL 2 is a parallel processing system marketed by CIMSA, a subsidiary of Thompson-CSF, the major French electronic company. PROPAL 2 was primarily designed with signal processing applications in mind but it is now being considered for a wider range of applications. The major ways the **PROPAL** design differs from **DAP** are as follows:

(*a*) more powerful processing elements,
(*b*) one-dimensional connectivity rather than two-dimensional,
(*c*) different I/O connections.

We will consider these in turn.

2.3.1 *Processing element designs*

Figure 12.4 shows the basic design of the bit-organised processing element. The single bit register *D* serves as an accumulator and a conditional register just like the activity register in the DAP design. However the 16-bit work memory *A* and the operations unit support much more complex operations than the fundamental operation of DAP.

Figure 12.4. PROPAL organisation.

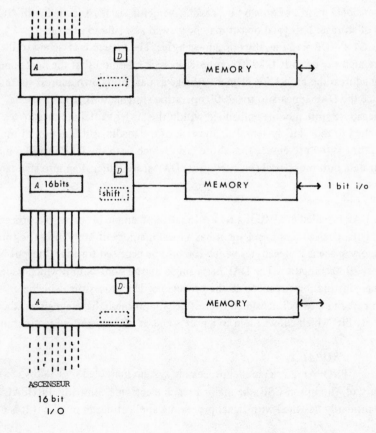

ASCENSEUR
16 bit
I/O

A prime problem for bit-organised computers is the problem of multiplication of two fields of length b bits. It is well known that the number of elementary operations for multiplication is proportional to b^2 (b addition operations each of b bits). Hence the multiplication time for a bit-organised processor will vary as the square of the precision and will be comparatively expensive compared with addition. There is therefore strong pressure to add hardware facilities to speed up multiplication. PROPAL 2 has an 8-bit shift register built into the operations unit allowing multiplication of an 8-bit field by an n-bit field to take place in a time proportional to n. Hence short precision fixed point multiplication on PROPAL is not much more expensive than addition, indeed addition of two 8-bit fields takes 1.2 microseconds whilst multiplication takes 4.6 microseconds. If one wants to multiply long fields (say 32 bits) then extra complications occur but in general the ratio of multiply time to addition time on PROPAL will be about 8 times less than the comparative ratio on the DAP.

2.3.2 Processor connectivity

A very important conclusion from ILLIAC IV experience is expressed in the concept of 'routing time'. Any attempt to program an SIMD computer rapidly finds a need to communicate data between processors. Such data movement takes time and so the execution time of most algorithms on SIMD architecture includes a component attributable directly to the time for data rearrangement – this time is called the 'routing time'. In any SIMD organisation this time is proportional to the number of intermediate processors and the bandwidth of the connection.

The PROPAL processors are connected in a ring of between 8 and 2048 processors with interprocessor communication taking place via the 16-bit A registers. In one clock cycle (150 nanoseconds) a 16-bit word can be transferred from each processor to its neighbour. Given a 1024 processor PROPAL and recognising the cyclic nature of the connectivity the maximum time for a transfer will be 512×150 nanoseconds $= 76.8$ microseconds, which is equivalent to only a few 16-bit multiplication times. In practice the shifts will usually be much less than this worst case algorithm and so there are few algorithms for which the routing time will dominate.

There are a number of obvious suggestions that can be made to reduce routing time. The most obvious is to use a higher dimensional connectivity. The most practical alternative is the two-dimensional connectivity as used in DAP, but a paper machine called Hypercube was once proposed with a four-dimensional connectivity. There are obviously technical difficulties in building increased connectivity. The number of wires leaving each processor is proportional to the product of the number of neighbours and the highway width. Hence the higher the connectivity the narrower the connection path between individual processors. The DAP has two-dimensional connectivity but data paths only one bit wide. The maximum distance apart for two processors in a two-dimensionally connected N processor system is $\sqrt{N}$ compared with $N/2$ for a one-dimensional connection. Hence the benefits of higher dimensionality are greatest for systems with very many processors.

Initial studies of parallel algorithms concentrated purely on arithmetic complexity and ignored the routing time contribution. As Gentleman [4] has shown, asymptotically the routing overhead can dominate. For example, given N^3 processors it is possible to perform matrix multiplication in one multiplication step and $\log_2 N$ addition steps, however the algorithm requires $O(N)$ data routing operations, hence asymptotically the routing will dominate. One way to prevent the effects of routing becoming important is to have very fast routing compared with arithmetic. It is not often realised that the bit-organised systems such as PROPAL achieve this by simply making the arithmetic slow!

It is very easy to propose ways of improving bit-organised parallel processors – the commonest proposal is to replace the slow PEs by more powerful ones – floating point units or 8-bit microprocessing chips being the commonest suggestions. Such suggestions are not practical unless one speeds up the data routing at the same time as one speeds up the computing. A very common modern error in evaluating computer performance is to measure only the floating point performance of the computers and to express a power in terms of a highly fictitious unit called the megaflops or MFLOPS (million floating point operations per second). Unfortunately the data organisation parts of serial computers do not vary directly as the floating point time so MFLOPS measures are misleading. Indeed, to paraphrase Henry Ford, 'megaflops are bunk'. If one were to take any of today's general purpose computers, e.g. 370 series, and reduce the floating point multiply time to zero, i.e. give them an infinite MFLOPS value it would not increase the throughput of most jobs by more than 10 per cent and it would be a highly artificial job that got much more than 50 per cent improvement. The same argument goes for SIMD computers. It is no use speeding up the arithmetic performance of the individual processing elements unless one can simultaneously speed up interprocessor data transfers.

2.3.3 Input/output facilities

PROPAL is considered by its manufacturers as an operator to be used with MITRA and SOLAR ranges of minicomputers and has two methods of input/output.

Serial I/O takes place via the 'ascenseur' which connects the PEs together and therefore is a 16-bit highway with a 150 nanosecond cycle time. A more interesting possibility is the existence of a 1-bit parallel data channel into each PE. The full potential of the parallel data channel is therefore 2048 bits wide and if the 150 nanosecond cycle time is exploited there is a theoretical data transfer possibility of 1.36×10^{10} bits per second. The potential is therefore present to handle very fast input channels provided they are very wide.

2.4   *Massively parallel processor (MPP) of Goodyear*

The MPP is a design primarily due to Fung of NASA [3] and may be crudely summarised as a 128×128 array of bit-organised processing elements with PEs of a complexity similar to that of PROPAL. The final version of MPP may well turn out to be different from current ideas, as it is still only at the design and development stage. Figure 12.5 shows the basic design of the processing element.

The 1-bit P register serves as a logical unit and also for communication to the four neighbours.

The 16-bit shaft register/binary counter allows for faster multiplication routines as in PROPAL 2.

The 1-bit G register is a mask register performing the same function as the D register in PROPAL or the A register in DAP.

The S register is an input/output register connected to row highways in contrast to the row and column highways of the DAP. The S registers allow data to be loaded or unloaded into the system along 128 row highways.

The memory of the MMP is 256 bits and the PE cycle time is planned to be 100 nanoseconds.

Figure 12.5. MPP processing element.

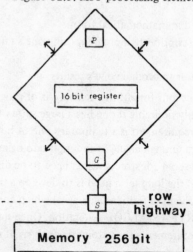

An interesting difference between the various designs of machines is the size of the store. Both MPP and PROPAL have a basic 256-bit store whilst the DAP has a 4096-bit store. For applications use it is always advantageous to have lots of store but unfortunately there is a trade-off between speed, cost and store size. Fast store chips are small capacity, expensive, and generally hotter than the slower chips. Hence if one wishes to build very fast PEs it is only practical to give them small amounts of memory. Although advances in chip technology will change the actual values there will always be a trade-off between size of memory and cycle speed. One of the as yet unanswered questions is:

Does a 128×128 PE machine cycling at 100 nanoseconds but with only 256 bits per PE have a greater throughput than a 64×64 PE machine cycling at 400 nanoseconds but with 64K bits per PE? The answer to the question is almost certainly problem dependent.

3 Programming parallel systems

The scientific user community is solidly of the opinion that 'FORTRAN was invented by God and computers came along in order to implement it'. Computer scientists are not in such complete agreement. They do believe, however, that 'FORTRAN was invented by the devil', but what language God invented is unfortunately the cause of much disagreement. There are various 'churches' which pray respectively to ALGOL 60, ALGOL 68, PASCAL, and ADA, with newer heretical sects who talk about APL or the microprocessor pet language of BASIC. A feature of nearly all current languages is their concentration on serial processing (APL is the exception which proves the rule). One programming process may be summarised as follows:

(*a*) take a task,

(*b*) express the operations needed in mathematical form,

(*c*) convert the mathematical description to a program using one's favourite language, and

(*d*) give the program to a computer to produce one's results.

There is a great urge to generate methods for automatic analysis of programs for parallelism. Such methods are highly desirable if one has a large suite of existing programs, but hopefully the requirement is a temporary one. A better long term solution is to develop programming languages and methodologies which do not require programmers to create serial constructs which need to be disentangled. It is therefore my view that the long term need is to develop a new breed of higher level languages (or problem definition languages) which contain more parallel constructs than the FORTRAN/ALGOL generation. Once such languages have been developed the requirements for automatic analysis of serial programs should almost vanish.

There are two schools of thought about the changes needed in computer languages – the evolutionists and the revolutionists. The revolutionists state that 'FORTRAN is abysmal, let's throw it away and start again'. The evolutionists state – 'FORTRAN as we have it now is not perfect; let us alter it so that it will become a better language for the future'. I am a confirmed evolutionist and the purpose of this section is to show how FORTRAN has been extended to make it an efficient and user friendly language for programming the DAP. The language that will be described is called DAP-FORTRAN [5]. DAP-FORTRAN has many features which make it specific to the DAP but the X3J3 FORTRAN standards committee is considering it as a basis for more generalised array extensions to FORTRAN.

The first facility that we must consider is the extended list of data modes. Normal FORTRAN deals only with scalar variables (or sets of them). DAP-FORTRAN knows about two new modes – vector and matrix. A DAP-FORTRAN matrix is an object with 4096 values (considered either as a long vector or as a 64 × 64 array). A vector is an object with 64 values. Variables may also have type (real, integer, logical or character) as in normal FORTRAN and we may also define sets of vectors or matrices. There is, however, a distinct logical difference between 64 vectors and a matrix, even though each have 4096 values.

The most elementary use of DAP-FORTRAN occurs when one treats a variable as a single name for a set of values and one wishes to perform identical operations on all members of a set.

$$X = Y + Z$$

adds all elements of the set Y element-by-element to the corresponding element of the set Z and stores the result in the set X. The sets X, Y and Z must have been defined to be conformal (i.e. all three are scalars, vectors or matrices). Y and Z may themselves be expressions provided the results are conformal with X. Very little, though, is needed to see how such a language construct maps easily onto SIMD architectures.

More interesting aspects of the language occur when one wishes to provide conditional operations; for example suppose one wishes only to compute the square root of Y provided it is positive. The operation, which requires an IF statement in FORTRAN, becomes

$$X(Y.GE.O) = SQRT(Y).$$

The Y.GE.O expression is a logical expression with value TRUE or FALSE for every member of the set Y. The statement only causes X to be altered if the logical expansion is TRUE.

The X3J3 committee is considering an alternative construct

$$WHERE (Y.GE.O.)X = SQRT(Y)$$

which has the advantage of being more explicit.

The logical expression in the DAP-FORTRAN construct is used in a fashion similar to an index and so the above construct is called logical or mask indexing and is an extremely powerful construct as it allows the programmer very close access to the activity which is a fundamental feature of practical SIMD systems. Practical experience has shown that a large number of apparently complex serial programming problems become trivial when one uses mask indexing methods.

The logical variable in DAP-FORTRAN is an extremely powerful object. First the reader must realise that when one implements logical variables on a bit-organised architecture they are truly implemented as logical variables rather than artificial quantities packed into a field. (IBM programmers are especially warned that LOGICAL∗1 is not a recipe for allocating a bit field!) As a logical element the individual bits in longer variables may be addressed after using an equivalence between say a set of 32 logical matrices and a matrix of 32-bit integer variables.

As an example of how one may use logical variables to perform bit manipulation algorithms directly from DAP-FORTRAN let us code in DAP-FORTRAN the maximum routine in section 2.1:

```
      LOGICAL MATRIX FUNCTION MAXP(INPUT_DATA)
      INTEGER INPUT_DATA (,)
      LOGICAL BITS_OF_INPUT(,,32)
      EQUIVALENCE (INPUT_DATA,BITS_OF_INPUT(,,1))
      MAXP = .NOT.BITS_OF_INPUT(,,1)
      DO 1 I =2, 32
      IF(ANY(MAXP.AND.BITS_OF_INPUT(,,I)),,I)
     * MAXP=MAXP.AND.BITS_OF_INPUT(,,I)
1     CONTINUE
      RETURN
      END
```

The algorithm is almost identical in principle to that discussed earlier but there are a number of interesting points to be noted:

Line 1   Note that a DAP-FORTRAN function can return scalar, vector or matrix results and so the FUNCTION statement has been expanded with a mode declaration.

Lines 2 and 3   These demonstrate how the usual declarative statements have been adapted to declare variables to be of type matrix. Vector variables are defined by declarative statements with a single blank leading subscript.

Line 5   This selects only those candidates which have sign bit zero (i.e. only positive values) as candidates for the largest value. Note that for a practical routine we ought to add some tests to deal with the case where all numbers are negative.

Line 7   This is rather self-explanatory, but it is important to note the global test function ANY which takes as argument a matrix (or vector) and returns TRUE if at least one member of the set is TRUE. Such global tests are extremely efficient to implement.

DAP-FORTRAN has a machine coded version of the above routine as a language construct and so the programmer can write statements such as:

TOURISTS (MAXP(TEMPERATURE)) =
3.0*AVERAGE_TOURIST_DENSITY.

The above MAXP algorithm is very rapid in execution taking about 32 micro-seconds on the DAP. The corresponding algorithm for finding the maximum value (MAXV) executes in about 50 microseconds independent of whether the data is fixed point or floating point.

A number of important lessons can be drawn from both the existence of these algorithms and their execution time. It is important to realise that the algorithm exploits the parallel nature of the machine and has no sensible serial equivalent. The algorithm is only valid on computers with a bit organisation and has a running time independent of the specific number of processors. The theoretical studies based on word based processors have always assumed that such operations would have a time dependence of $\log_2 N$ where N was the number of objects whose maximum value was needed.

The example is also one of the many counterexamples to the speed-up and efficiency measures. By any reasonable definition of efficiency, any algorithm which can return a largest value from a set of values in less time than a single processor would take to subtract two values must be considered as being highly efficient. If one, however, tries to define efficiency in terms of processor utilisation then on average at each substage of the algorithm half the processors are eliminated and the total processor utilisation is only some 3% giving a formal efficiency of only 3%. Experience has shown that it is not a catastrophe to continually switch processing elements off and indeed the highest performances of DAP relative to serial machines occur on problems with many logical operations rather than problems in which all the PEs are apparently fully occupied (e.g. dense matrix multiplication does not represent peak performance).

The failure of the efficiency parameter to give an indicator of good parallel algorithms is a little difficult to justify. Two possible reasons are:

(1) the lack of a true meaning of T_1 for bit-organised systems and

(2) the failure of the formula to include any component arising from the overall system organisation.

Let us consider these two points a little more. The speed-up parameter is defined by T_1/T_p. It therefore carries with it an implicit assumption that T_1 is meaningful. It is my contention that if we build a system out of bit-organised processors then T_1 is a totally fictitious quantity and its use is therefore dangerous. I also believe that the total power of the system must include some component due to the organisation, i.e. a two-dimensionally connected system is more powerful than a one-dimensionally connected system. The theoretical arguments neglect such effects.

After that digression into philosophy let us return to some more examples of DAP-FORTRAN and parallel algorithms. Many problems in partial differential equations and image processing deal with the interaction between neighbouring values in a field. A typical operation is of the type

$$Q_{ij} = \tfrac{1}{4}(P_{i,j+1} + P_{i-1,j} + P_{i+1,j} + P_{i,j-1}) \quad \text{for all } i, j.$$

In the case of image processing this would be a smoothing operation whilst a physicist would recognise it as perhaps a step in an iterative solution of Poisson's equation. In DAP-FORTRAN we can code this quite simply as:

$$Q = 0.25 * (P(,+) + P(-,) + P(+,) + P(,-))$$

This type of indexing is called shift indexing and gives a very convenient method of handling interactions between data in different processors. The alert reader will wonder about the operation at the edges. DAP-FORTRAN provides two useful options: cyclic connectivity and plane connectivity. In cyclic connectivity data, the rows (or columns) are considered to be connected in rings so that data shifted off one end arrives at the other while in plane connectivity any attempt to fetch numerical values from outside the limits produces zeros.

As a final example of DAP-FORTRAN let us consider the task of matrix multiplication. Given two N x N matrices A and B, then a normal FORTRAN program which multiplies them together would be:

```
      DO 1 I = 1, N
      DO 1 J = 1, N
      C(I,J) = 0.0
      DO 1 K = 1, N
      C(I,J) = C(I,J) + A(I,K) * B(K,J)
1     CONTINUE
```

This program is a faithful translation of the defniition of a matrix product where each element is defined by the inner product of a row and a column. At first glance the parallelism is limited but a little thought shows that the order of evaluation of the loop is irrelevant and the following code is equally valid:

```
        DO 2 I = 1, N
        DO 2 J = 1, N
        C(I,J) = 0.0
2       CONTINUE
        DO 1 K = 1, N
        DO 1 I = 1, N
        DO 1 J = 1, N
        C(I,J) = C(I,J) + A(I,K) * B(K,J)
1       CONTINUE
```

This latter code may be converted to DAP-FORTRAN as

```
        C = 0
        DO 1 K = 1, N
        C = C + MATC (A(,K)) * MATR (B(K,))
1       CONTINUE
```

Two new facilities of the language have been introduced; the first is represented by the notation A(,K) which selects the Kth column of the matrix A, the second is the function MATC(V) which takes as argument a vector and creates a matrix, all of whose columns equal that vector. MATC and MATR are therefore expansion operators which convert vectors into matrices. Expressing the DAP-FORTRAN algorithm in words one finds that simultaneously one computes the Kth component of each element of the product matrix C.

More important than understanding how the algorithm works is an understanding of the time dependence of the algorithm. The serial FORTRAN code has three nested DO loops each done N times, hence that algorithm takes a time proportional to N^3 on a serial machine. The parallel algorithm has only a single loop and so takes a time proportional to N (provided one has at least N^2 processors). The ratio of the speed of the parallel machine to any given machine is therefore a function of the size of the problem, with the parallel machine giving its best performance when the number of processors matches the size of the problem. There is therefore no magic single figure which expresses the speed of DAP relative to a given serial computer. The performance is highly application dependent and those worthy gentlemen who spend much time trying to measure performance in terms of arbitrary measures such as GAMM, POWU, MIPS, megaflops etc. are wasting their time.

Finally it must be realised that the practical programming of a real parallel system requires one to live with a number of constraints which theoretical studies are able to ignore. The simple facts of the matter are that a given parallel system has a fixed number of processors (4096 in the case of DAP at QMC). The programming task is one of matching this fixed number to real applications. An example of the type of considerations involved may be found by examining the problem of matrix multiplication in three size regimes:

(1) 64×64
(2) 128×128
(3) 3×3

In regime (1) the above algorithm is perfect whilst in regime (2) it is necessary to break the task down into a number of blocks and deal with them in a serial fashion. Regime (3) introduces totally different considerations and one should ask oneself - how do I state my problem so that I can perform many 3×3 matrix multiplications simultaneously?

References

1 Flanders, P. M., Hunt, D. J., Reddaway, S. F. and Parkinson, D., 'Efficient high speed computing with the Distributed Array Processor' in *High Speed Computer and Algorithm Organisation* (Ed Kuck, D. J., Lawrie, D. H. and Sameh, A. H.) pp. 113–28 Academic Press 1977

2 Foster, C. C., *Content Addressable Parallel Processors* Van Nostrand 1976

3 Fung, L., 'A massively parallel processing computer' in *High Speed Computer and Algorithm Organisation* (Ed Kuck, D. J., Lawrie, D. H. and Sameh, A. H.) pp. 203–4 Academic Press 1977

4 Gentleman, W. M., 'Some complexity results for matrix computations on parallel processors' *JACM* 25 112–15 (1978)

5 Gostick, R. W., 'Software and Algorithms for the Distributed Array Processor' *ICL Technical Journal* 1, 2, 116–35 May 1968

6 Kuck, D. J., 'Multioperation machine computational complexity' in *Complexity of Sequential and Parallel Numerical Algorithms* (Ed Traub, J. F.) pp. 17–47 Academic Press 1973

7 Kuck, D. J., 'ILLIAC IV software and applications programming' *IEEE Transactions on Computers*, C-17, 8, 758–70 (August 1968)

8 Richardson, L. F. *Weather Prediction by Numerical Process* Cambridge University Press 1922

PART 5

Data flow processors: design and organisation

13 The data flow approach for MIMD multiprocessor systems

J.-C. SYRE

1 Introduction

Today's need for high speed computers are becoming obvious in an increasing number of applications. Pipelined and array architectures will not reach the performance goals that scientists would like to be met by the next generation of machines, whatever the improvements in VLSI (very large scale integration) may be in the future. Computer designers must now turn to new architectures of true multiprocessors (several computing units able to work separately) and they must work with algorithm designers and language designers. Two novel approaches are at their disposal now: data driven and demand driven concepts may become the key for a departure from the sequentiality enforced by languages and machines of the last thirty years. We shall focus on data driven sequencing; further information on the other approach may be found in (BERK 75). One cannot precisely define the originators of data driven computing: Jack Dennis started data flow research in 1968, while Tesler and Enea published a report on single assignment at the same time. Dennis defined graphs allowing the expression of algorithms by explaining data dependency only; the latter are concerned with programming languages embodying syntactic and semantic features for data flow programming. Single assignment was developed by Klinkhamer (KLIN 71) and Chamberlin (CHAM 71), and data flow graphs by a larger team at MIT (David Misunas, James Rumbaugh and Paul Kosinski among others). Figure 13.1 shows how some (but not all) data flow studies have been carried out since 1968.

Section 2 introduces the concept of data driven sequencing. Section 3 defines the data flow graph approach originally studied by Dennis and briefly describes some research work on data flow. Section 4 introduces the single assignment rule and various works related to it. Section 5 gives a detailed description of the LAU system, a data driven multiprocessor system based on single assignment.

2 Data Driven Sequencing

In conventional systems the way one writes lines of code fixes the order of computations and data values only depend on this order, which must be strictly obeyed when the program runs on the machine, whatever its organization may be.

Figure 13.1.

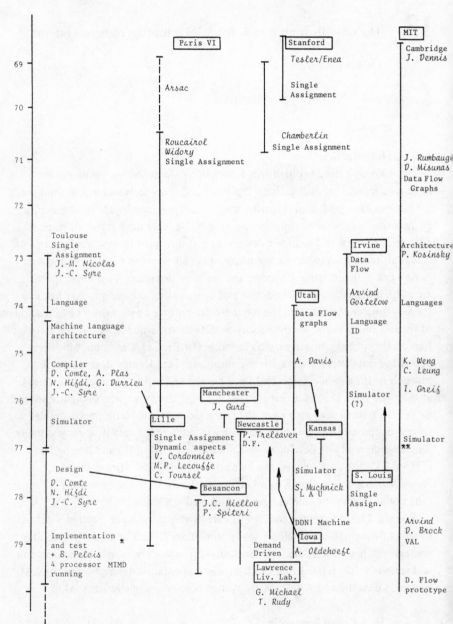

x : Workshop on Data Flow Systems, Toulouse.

xx : Workshop on Data Flow Systems, Mit.

In a data driven system, computations are sequenced by the availability of data itself. The first scheme relies on a topographic control, and data values comply with the control. The second scheme relies on the computation of data values to decide further computations of other data values. Roughly speaking, an instruction is claimed ready for execution as soon as its operands are computed. Let us take as an example the solution of $Ax^2 - Bx + C = 0$ (assuming $B^2 - 4AC > 0$).

The data flow graph (figure 13.2) shows the initial state before execution, the tokens indicating values available. Using a single assignment language, we would write

P1 $X1 = (B + SQRT (B**2 - 4 * A * C)) / (2 * A)$
      $X2 = (B - SQRT (B**2 - 4 * A * C)) / (2 * A)$

or

P2 $A1 = 2 * A$ I1
      $B1 = B ** 2$ I2
      $C1 = A * C * 4$ I3
      $D = B1 - C1$ I4
      $D1 = SQRT (D)$ I5
      $B2 = B + D1$ I6
      $B3 = B - D1$ I7
      $X1 = B2 / A1$ I8
      $X2 = B3 / A1$ I9

Nodes in the data flow graph (DFG) or statements in the single assignment program become activated only when their arguments have a value. Their activation consumes the inputs and produces output values which, added to previous

Figure 13.2.

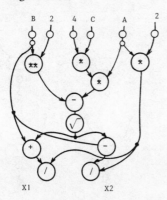

ones, generate activation of new nodes or statements. They are activated in any order; this concurrency does not affect program determinacy. For example, in program P2, I1, I2 and I3 are ready for execution at time t_0. They may produce values for A1, B1 and C1 at any later time in any order. Their computation will activate I4 and I5, then I6 and I7, and finally I8 and I9. If we had modified the relative order of I1 to I9, we would have the same results for X1 and X2.

3   The data flow graph approach

3.1   *Basic definition (DENN 73)*

A data flow graph is a bipartite directed graph with two types of nodes: links and actors. Arcs in the graph support 'tokens' carrying values from each actor to other actors by means of the links. Data links having no incident arc are input links, and some links are specified to be output links. Any link which is not an output link must have at least one emanating arc. In figure 13.2 we find six input links and two output links. Links and actors deal with two kinds of information: data and control values.

Different types of nodes and their activations are shown in figure 13.3.

Figure 13.3.

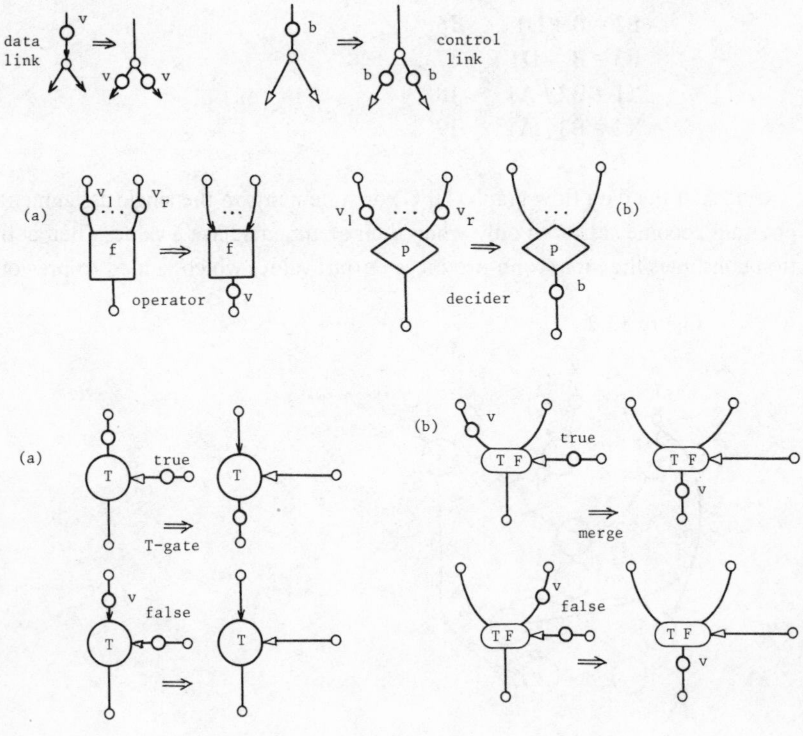

3.1.1   Execution of a DFG

Execution of a DFG is described by a sequence of snapshots. Each snapshot shows the data flow program with tokens and associated values placed on arcs of the graph of the program. Execution advances from one snapshot to the next through firing of links and actors enabled by the previous snapshot. Values carried by control arcs are boolean and those carried by data arcs may be integer, real or string. Depending on the data flow model, an arc provides storage for a single token, acts like a 'first-in first-out' queue of tokens, or may be considered as a random memory storing and delivering 'coloured' tokens. It is left to the reader to convince himself that the execution of our DFG sample is inherently parallel.

3.1.2   Extensions to complex data structures and procedures

From the preceding definitions many people have tried to extend the capabilities of DFGs. In particular, David Misunas (MISU 75) introduces data structures which could not originally be dealt with. New actors are added to create, modify a 'structure', merge two structures or extract a substructure. Procedures are also introduced with a special 'apply' operator using pointers to the text of procedures and pointers to the input and output parameters. The resulting DFGs look very different and more complex than the initial ones in that we are now faced with dynamic self-reconfiguring graphs, which do not show the parallelism as obviously as before.

3.2   Data flow languages

When problems become more complex, a graph description of them tends to be hard to make or read, so higher level languages are needed. Also, execution of data flow programs requires some form of machine language expressing the original graph, or low level mechanisms to interpret higher level programs. Since section 4 will present an in-depth description of a data driven system, we shall summarize here the principal data flow languages, almost all of them being single assignment languages.

3.2.1   ID

ID is a language defined by Arvind and Gostelow at the University of California (Irvine) about 1976. It is an expression oriented and block structured language, where a variable always represents a name of a line (as opposed to a memory cell). Some important ID constructs are blocks, conditionals, loops, procedure definitions, abstract data types and monitors (WORK 77, ARVI 77). A conditional statement takes two forms:

$$a \leftarrow (\textbf{if } b \textbf{ then } x + y \textbf{ else } x * y)$$

or

> **if** b **then** $a \leftarrow x + y$ **else** $a \leftarrow x * y$

A block is defined by statements between parentheses, one of them indicating output variables:

$$(x \leftarrow a * a, y \leftarrow b * b, z \leftarrow x + y \; ; w \leftarrow x - y, \textbf{return sqrt} \; (3/w)).$$

A loop expression is a block containing iterative operators and returning variables:

> (**initial** $x \leftarrow f(a)$; **while** $p(x,n)$ **do**
> $\qquad y \leftarrow g(x,b)$
> $\qquad x \leftarrow h(y)$
> **returns all** $y, r(x)$))

3.2.2   CAJOLE

CAJOLE is a high level non-procedural language designed at Westfield College (University of London) (OSMO 78). Its main features are listed below:

(1) There is no explicit sequencing, since a program is a list of definitions
(2) The language is a single assignment language in the sense of Chamberlin (see later)
(3) The language is functional
(4) There is a run time data dependent decision mechanism which uses guarded commands
(5) There is a mechanism for localizing names to avoid proliferation of names:

$a = b + c$ **with** $b = 16, c = b * b$ **wend**

(6) There is a bootstrapping mechanism allowing the user to define his own syntactic constructs. The general form of a bootstrap definition is [parameter list] macro name = defining expression.

A program to decrease x by steps of y until x is less than y may be written in CAJOLE as:

> **xnew, ynew** = **while** $[x,y]$ $x > y$
> $\qquad$ **do** $[x,y]$ $(x-y,y)$
> $\qquad$ **using** $(xinitial, yinitial)$
> $\qquad$ **od**

3.2.3   LAPSE

LAPSE is a single assignment language developed at Manchester University (GURD 76, GLAU 78) to support high level representation of programs to be translated in a data flow graph internal form, and executed on a data flow machine. This language allows structured data values and functional subroutines, and a disciplined use of iteration. One can also notice that in Glauert's thesis the question of introducing a qualifier OLD X to distinguish old and new values in an iteration was left open, while it is clear that the answer is yes in Gurd's report.

Finally, as in other single assignment languages for data flow programming, the power of an iterative statement is very limited in that only one block of statements belongs to its control, so we cannot easily describe an iterative process composed of several subprocesses.

3.2.4 VAL

VAL is the latest version of MIT's high level data flow language. Kosinski had defined a DF (data flow) language before, see (KOSI 73) and (WORK 77). A fully detailed description of it may be found in (ACKE 79), but we shall use the paper by James McGraw (McGR 79) to summarize its main features here. (Note that VAL is a single assignment language.) It is a functional language, since every active statement can be viewed as a function that receives some inputs and whose only effect is to produce some set of results. Both programmer and compiler can identify most concurrency without any special notation, except a DOFORALL construct similar to that encountered in Fortran extensions on array machines. VAL's run-time error handling system uses special error values as part of each data type.

As in the LAU high level language, VAL has values but no variables, in the sense that the term 'variable' refers to a modifiable data item, such as does not occur in single assignment languages. Also, VAL uses familiar algebraic notation instead of the function form for all of its expressions. Control statements include IF, TAGCASE, FORALL, and FOR ... ITER. The following expression for an iterative loop will show some of the capabilities of VAL better than a formal description.

```
FOR                    % Nth Fibonacci number
     count, fib, prefib : INTEGER
                    := 0, 0, 1 ;
DO
     IF count < =N
          THEN ITER
               prefib, fib := fib, fib + prefib,
               count := count + 1 ;
          END ITER
          ELSE
          fib
          ENDIF
ENDFOR
```

VAL's weaknesses mentioned by McGraw include lack of I/O operations (and their problems in FORALL constructs), operators in VAL clauses in a FORALL expression, and no recursion allowed. We shall add the following ambiguity, noticeable in the above expression: for VAL designers there is no doubt that count and fib, used as operands, refer to previous values. Does it mean that new values count and fib, computed at the current iteration, cannot be used as operands of other statements in this current iteration? If they cannot, most real problems will be rather hard to program in VAL.

3.2.5 DDM1

DDM1 is a project at the University of Utah, described by A. Davis (DAVI 79*a*) (see also BOCK 79, DAVI 79*b*). It is based on a graphical implementation of a data flow graph roughly similar to those of MIT. A graphical programming language has been proposed for high level programming, supporting a number of common programming constructs which can be translated into the low level programming language. The data tokens are list structures (trees, arrays). Operators include functions that concatenate, decompose and index the list structure of the data tokens.

3.2.6 Other systems

The University of Newcastle upon Tyne has been working for a while on data flow systems, and is still very much concerned with actual models of computation and their suitability for a general purpose decentralized computer. However, these seem to be little concerned with high level data flow languages. The Jumbo system (HOPK 79) is an implementation of a model combining both control flow and data flow in the sense of Treleaven et al. (TREL 80).

4 The single assignment approach

As stated before, all languages derived from research on data flow must use more or less the single assignment rule. This rule is basically a software rule for writing programs, and has nothing to do with data flow computing. In fact, we are now discussing two versions of single assignment.

4.1 First definition of single assignment

Tesler and Enea (TESL 68) define the following programming rule:

a variable may only be assigned values by one statement in a program.

So, in a single assignment language, every statement is an assignment statement which, when executed, computes a value which will be unique during the remainder of the program run. This value may be used later, at any time, by other statements. The only rule for sequencing statements is then the availability of data values. The programmer expresses the inherent parallelism of the problem (or, rather, the algorithm) and makes it explicit for a parallel asynchronous interpretation on an MIMD (multiple instruction, multiple data) type machine.

Thus, any artificial sequencing based on the way statements are written is abolished. Conventional programming rules related to the relative situations of statements in the program space are no longer constraints and are all replaced by the single assignment (SA) rule.

COMPEL was the first SA language proposal. All statements are assignment statements. New operators are introduced to deal with loops. COMPEL manipulates three types of variables: numbers, lists and functions. Block structuring exists, allowing name localization. A block header indicates input variables needed to execute it and a block terminator defines those forming the set of outputs. Special functions (EACH and LIST OF) allow list computations. EACH [a] produces all values of list a simultaneously. LIST OF [b] constructs a list of different simultaneous values of a list variable:

$$a = \text{EACH } [1,2,4]$$
$$b = a * 2$$
$$c = \text{LIST OF } [b]$$

Pure iteration (a loop-type construct) is implemented by defining a list x, and taking the last element computed, as in the following example:

$$r = \text{EACH } [vo \text{ BY } 2 \text{ FOR } n]$$
$$a = \text{LIST OF } [b * r]$$
$$x = \text{LAST } [a]$$

A special operator PRECEDING (I) allows us to extract the Ith previous element of a list as it is being computed.

4.2 Second definition of single assignment

Chamberlin (CHAM 71) takes a slightly different look at the SA rule and says:

a variable may be assigned only once in a program.

Chamberlin envisages his language as a practical solution for expressing parallelism in large number-crunching programs. His language, SAMPLE, is intentionally close to an existing programming language (ALGOL). Two types of data, numbers and tuples, are used in expressions. The IF, FOR and WHILE constructs exist, but severe constraints should be obeyed in writing them. In particular, iterative constructs use the special symbol OLD X to refer to the value of X at the previous iteration. Chamberlin's thesis includes a proposal for a data driven multiprocessor architecture, involving complex mechanisms managing dynamic generation of instruction templates, data structures and control. The program counter is replaced by files of executable instructions waiting for idle processing units.

4.3   Other works on single assignment

Besides the two important projects at Stanford (CHAM 71) and Toulouse (TEAU 73, TEAU 18) other studies have been carried out and shall only mention them here: Klinkhamer at Philips (KLIN 71), Roucairol (ROUC 73) and Urschler (URSC 73) are interested by the software and programming aspects of single assignment and its implications to parallel programming. M. P. Lecouffe at Lille (LECO 79) defines a dynamic block-level single assignment system built around a ring-structured memory. Finally, it should be pointed out that almost all data flow research teams have included a single assignment language as a high level DF language for their systems: LAPSE at Manchester (GURD 76), VAL at MIT, ID at Irvine, CAJOLE at London University, among others.

5   The LAU system: a data driven multiprocessor

5.1   Introduction

The LAU project was started in 1973 (TEAU 18) by a formal study of single assignment after the definitions given by Tesler and Enea, and Chamberlin. Initially, it was a software oriented study where the different levels of SA usage were compared and analysed in terms of parallelism exposure, programming techniques, ability to write and read programs, and algorithms. This analysis led us to adopt a low level use of SA for a definition of a high level language in 1974, and in proposals for associative multiprocessor architectures. From 1974 to 1976, a reinforced team completed the language specifications.

Machine-level control primitives to implement data driven sequencing were defined and, after some unsatisfying attempts, work was started on a machine language. First small-scale experiments of the high level language were carried out in several application fields (matrix computation, sorting, syntactic analysis, Monte Carlo methods, polynomial evaluation, payroll, and image processing), while a compiler was written. At the same time the design and implementation of a fully parametrized multiprocessor simulator allows a complete evaluation process to take place: algorithms fitting data flow principles, programming, compiling, parallel asynchronous execution by the simulator, and simulation results, giving parallelism and performance figures for a large number of machine organizations (PLAS 76). From 1977 to 1979, an MIMD machine was conceived from the simulator, built and tested. The LAU system has been operational since September 1979 with 4 processing units, and a 10-unit machine will run real problems in late 1981. In parallel with machine construction, a large effort has been made in programming finite difference and finite element methods for solving aerodynamics problems (BERG 79).

Section 5.2 gives the programming objectives of the LAU system and an informal description of the high level language. Section 5.3 introduces basic control primitives for data driven sequencing and their use in compiling high level statements. Then we give architectural considerations and implementation details on the LAU system in section 5.4. Finally, we shall show the potentialities of our system when applied to finite difference and finite element methods for solving aerodynamics problems, together with some flavour of work in progress (1980–85) at CERT in Toulouse.

5.2 Parallel programming
5.2.1 Language objectives

As stated before, current high performance computers exploit parallelism in programs rather poorly. Pipelined or array processing does not question the global sequentiality of the system and, furthermore, it has to be made consistent with it by introduction of synchronizing primitives. The greatest difficulty lies in the need of explicit parallelism performed either by the programmer himself or by the compiler. All such cases can only express a little of the parallelism inherent in the corresponding algorithms.

Our first concern was to define a tool for expressing parallel algorithms without changing their original nature by a sequentialization. Our high level language thus requires four major characteristics:

(1) It should allow implicit expression of parallelism. Obviously, single assignment does this perfectly.
(2) The programming process should be free from any hardware considerations: internal structure, memory organization, number and capabilities of processing units, and so on.
(3) It should be easy to use: in particular, no more than a one-week training period should be necessary to write, read and debug a program by any Fortran programmer.
(4) It should include powerful constructs, just like any high level language.

Though we believe that the LAU language matches its objectives, after a six-year experimental period, it is clear that some minor improvements could make it even simpler to use in some cases.

5.2.2 LAU high level language

We use Chamberlin's definition of single assignment in order to be able to design a language closer to familiar ones than those we could derive from Tesler's rule.

A variable may be assigned at most once during program execution. From now on we shall use the term 'object' instead of 'variable', since a value assigned to an object will never change. Data structures allowed are scalars or arrays (in 1, 2 or 3 dimensions); data types include integer, real, boolean and event (symbol).

All statements must be considered as assignment statements, despite a quite familiar syntax. Associated to its familiar syntax a statement will be precisely defined by its semantics. To clarify the presentation we now introduce the notion of 'data production set' (DPS) as a triple (I, S, O) consisting of:

> I: a set of input objects
> S: a set of statements
> O: a set of output objects

Also, we will make use of two interpretations of assignments: 'computation' referring to a result evaluated by an expression, and 'production' where no explicit statement exists but a special nil value forces a value into the object.

Then all statements in the language can be expressed in terms of DPSs, and rules for controlling them.

5.2.3 Simple assignment statements (computation statements)

Their syntax is identical to Fortran ones, some vector and array operators being added for programming convenience.

Let us write: $X = (A + B) * (C + D)$; this statement corresponds to the following data production set:

$$I = A, B, C, D$$
$$S = X = (A+B) * (C+D)$$
$$O = X$$

It will be executable when the I part of the DPS will indicate: all objects computed (not produced!). The execution of the DPS leads to the computation of the X value, and then the propagation of the knowledge of this computation to all other DPSs having X in their I subset. Other examples of simple statements:

$$MATR = MAT1 + MAT2 \; ; (array \; operators)$$
$$Y = VSUM \; (MAT1 \; FROM \; IMIN \; STEP \; ISTEP \; TO \; IMAX) \; ;$$

5.2.4 Expand statement

Expand is a generalized array operator. It can be compared to existing DOFORALL statements, but differs from them enormously in that the block of statements within EXPAND ... END EXPAND is still in single assignment, hence is fully parallel. The syntax of an EXPAND is illustrated by the following example (part of a finite element program solving $\Delta u = f$)

```
EXPAND /2  IB=0 TO 3 :
    LOCAL : IBLOC :
    IBLOC = IE (IB, IMA) ;
    B(IBLOC) = BB(IBLOC) + BB(IB) ;
    EXPAND /2 JB = 0 TO 3 :
        LOCAL : IBLOC, LBLOC ;
        IBLOC = IE (JB, IMA) ;
        LBLOC = JBLOC − IBLOC ;
        CASE (LBLOC > 0) : A(LBLOC, IBLOC) =
                        AA(LBLOC, IBLOC) + E(JB, IB) ;
        EC ;
    EE ;
EE ;
```

This program sequence updates a large array A given AA (the whole initial value for this array) and E, a small 4×4 array whose elements are the contributions of a P1-type tetrahedron finite element. IE is the connectivity matrix. For each contribution E(JB,IB) the corresponding element in A is computed (LBLOC, IBLOC). Also the second number B of the equation is updated (this sequence is in fact in a loop in the real program).

In this example we see that parallel programming is straightforward; here, two elements of B and four elements of A are going to be evaluated, simultaneously. The two-dimensional parallelism will be fully exploited, without any of the restrictions of existing systems. Theoretically, as there are sixteen computations, we may have four DPSs from this statement, each of them involving computation of one B(I1) and four A(I4,I3) in parallel. The '/n' postfix allows the programmer to restrict the number of DPSs (and henceforth the actual parallelism). All DPSs will run concurrently, and any piece of parallelism within each of them will be exploited too. With the EXPAND statement LOCAL objects are permitted, their scope being limited to the EXPAND body.

5.2.5 CASE statement

Though its syntax looks familiar to any programmer, the CASE statement has peculiar semantic properties which will fit our previous assumption that every statement is an assignment statement.

$$\text{CASE } (X>1) : A=Y ;$$
$$(X=1) : A=0 ; B=Y ;$$
$$(X=0) : A=0 ; B=-Y ;$$
$$(ELSE) : A=-Y ;$$
$$\text{EC} ;$$

CASE is controlled by a single object (X) which must appear in all boolean expressions. Each block controlled by an expression generates a DPS built as follows:

I = objects which are arguments outside the block
S = statements in the block
O = all objects computed in all blocks

$$\text{DPS1} : \{Y\}, \{A=Y\}, \{A,B\}$$
$$\text{DPS2} : \{Y\}, \{A=0 ; B=Y\}, \{A,B\}$$
$$\vdots$$
$$\text{DPS4} : \{Y\}, \{A=-Y\}, \{A,B\}$$

At run time, CASE will assign objects A and B whatever the value of X. In particular, if $X=1$, then A and B will be computed ($A=0$, $B=Y$), but if $X=2$, A will be computed ($A=Y$) and B will only be produced. No other statement in the program is allowed to give B a value. This may be viewed as a strong constraint, but we have not met an example where the programmer has problems with it, and it keeps the language coherent with the single assignment rule and determinacy.

5.2.6   *LOOP statement*

The LOOP statement allows expression of any type of iterative constructs: FOR, WHILE, multiple-iteration loop. Due to its generality, its syntax appears a little complicated at first sight, and it also must meet the single assignment requirement.

For each object X to be assigned by LOOP, a local environment is created and consists of three physically distinct objects:

OLD X denotes value of X at previous iteration
NEW X denotes the object computed by the current iteration
OUT X denotes that object whose value is actually computed by the
       LOOP statement.

As no ambiguity may occur, we shall use simply X to refer to NEW X and

OUT X, given that the loop termination itself will propagate final X value to other statements waiting for its computation.

The general control structure of the LOOP statement is as shown in figure 13.4.

Semantics: The LOOP control event is first set to START, and the loop header will activate the DPS corresponding to the START section of the statement. At each iteration, the loop event takes a value which is checked by the LOOP header, which in turn chooses to activate the DPS controlled by that value. One iteration, corresponding to one DPS, is performed at a time. With this property, a DPS to be executed is initialized with the results coming from the execution of the previous iteration, and produces values for the objects OUT, LOCAL and LOOP event as specified by the DPS.

A special STOP value is given to the LOOP control event by the statement STOP LOOP ⟨EVENT⟩. Its effect is to activate an implicit DPS which will assign the actual objects declared in the OUT section of the LOOP statement.

5.2.7 Procedures

Procedures exist in the language, and their declarations are the same as in current languages. A procedure is considered as a DPS, and is also an assignment statement of the actual outputs. Notice that several calls can be performed in parallel, for there may be in the program several calls with their inputs computed. So, a procedure header will take these calls into account depending on the memory requirements and space available; the header will choose between generating a copy of the procedure code that will be attached to the activated call, and updating its queue of waiting calls.

Figure 13.4.

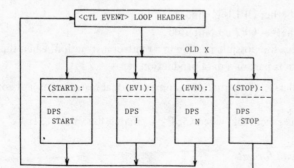

Several copies of the code can be performed in parallel, and, on the return statement, the header will allocate the now free copy to one of the waiting calls.

Recursion has been studied very little, and though there is no incompatibility, it is not yet allowed in the language.

5.2.8 Jump statements

Branching, skipping, jumping, and other related words do not occur in the language.

5.3 Control primitives for data driven sequencing

The following definitions are the result of several attempts to express data driven sequencing at lower levels. We first give instruction and data formats, then we describe four basic control primitives which will be used by the compiler and control machine instruction.

5.3.1 General instruction format

OPCODE	RES	OP1	OP2		C_0	C_1	C_2

The left part will take place in the local memory subsystem, while the right part (C_0, C_1, C_2) will be located in the control memory subsystem.

RES, OP1, OP2 are generally memory addresses (RES as result, OP1 and OP2 as operands). This three-address format does not involve any 'internal registers', which allows two important aspects of execution:

An instruction may be executed on any processing unit.
The number of processing units is extensible, hence flexibility and fault tolerance can be achieved quite easily.

C_0, C_1, C_2 denote the control tag bits of the instruction:

C_1 tells whether OP1 is computed,
C_2 tells whether OP2 is computed,
C_0 indicates the possible nesting in a control instruction, when the instruction is part of a data production set.

There are two classes of instructions: computational instructions and control instructions.

An instruction is executable when C_0, C_1, C_2 match the value '1, 1, 1'.

5.3.2 General data format

VALUE	L/R	LINK1	L/R	LINK2		C_d

Here again, the C_d tag bit is located in the control memory subsystem, and indicates whether the elementary data has a valid value field.

L/R, LINK1, and L/R LINK2 are addresses of instructions which use the data as an operand (L/R for left/right operand). More than two links may be created in additional memory words. However, experiments have shown that the average length of the 'value propagated' list is less than 2.

5.3.3 Data production set and control primitives

In the high level language we defined the concept of data production set for the semantics of the complex assignment statements. At the machine language level, the control instructions, which are close to the corresponding high level statements, will also deal with data production sets (an O set, associated with an S set). An instruction will be defined by

one or more DPS

how it operates on them.

The role of the control subsystem in the processor will be to interpret these instructions, by means of a set of basic control primitives we shall define now.

P1 SET TAG BITS (C_0,A,L)
P2 SET TAG BITS (C_1,C_2,A1, A2,L)
P3 CHECK TAG BITS (C_d,A1,A2,A3)
P4 MASK TAG BITS (C_d,A1,A2,L)

P1 and P2 deal with the S part of a DPS (instruction part), P3 and P4 deal with the O part of a DPS (data part).

We shall now briefly describe these primitives, which are the heart of the control subsystem, together with an example of the use of some of the control instructions of the machine language.

5.3.3.1 Primitive P1: SET TAG BITS (C_0,A,L)

P1 corresponds to a DPS activation. The C_0 bit is set to 1 from address A of length L in the control memory (see figure 13.5). Application to the CASE instruction (figure 13.6) follows. The CASE instruction will have to activate one of the different DPSs controlled by the corresponding boolean expression. Before execution, all DPSs are passive ($C_0 = 0$).

Figure 13.5.

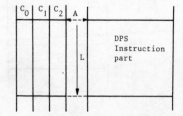

When the true expression is evaluated, the C_0 tag bit will be set for all instructions of the corresponding DPS.

5.3.3.2 *Primitive P2:* SET TAG BITS $(C_1,C_2,A1,A2,L)$

P2 corresponds to a DPS initialization or a DPS clearing operation. A mask, located at address A1 in local memory, is placed into control memory from address A2 of length L (see figure 13.7). Application to the LOOP instruction (figure 13.8): at compile time, the LOOP statement contains the images of the C_1 and C_2 bits, for each DPS (iteration), before starting the execution of a DPS. After execution, the C_1 and C_2 bits have been altered, and to execute another iteration the LOOP instruction will use a P2 primitive to restore the control memory.

Figure 13.6.

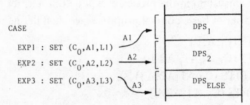

Figure 13.7.

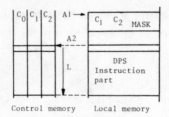

Figure 13.8.

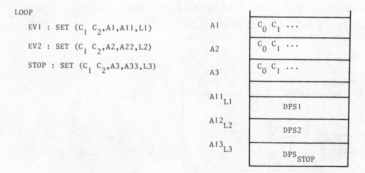

5.3.3.3 *Primitive P3:* CHECK TAG BITS $(C_d, A1, A2, A3)$

P3 corresponds to a DPS termination. A DPS is terminated when all data in its 'O' part is computed or assumed to be so (i.e. produced). When all C_d bits, from A1 to A2 are set to 1, the control subsystem will update $C_1 C_2$ at address A3, which will activate at A3 in local memory an instruction which will denote the event: 'the DPS is terminated', see figure 13.9.

Application to the EXPAND instruction (figure 13.10): several copies of the EXPAND body (DPSs) are running in parallel to perform the EXPAND. When all of them have finished the EXPAND statement is considered terminated. If there are 16 DPSs in parallel, each of them will set a data word when finished. The P3 operation on these 16 words will indicate the end of the EXPAND instruction.

5.3.3.4 *Primitive P4:* MASK TAG BITS $(C_d, A1, A2, L)$

P4 corresponds to a mask operation on the data part of a DPS. A mask, located at A1 in local memory is pushed into the C_d control memory from address A2 of length L (see figure 13.11).

Figure 13.9.

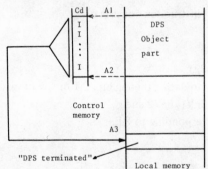

Figure 13.10.

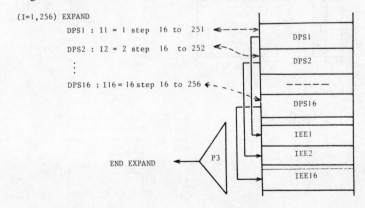

P4 is used to 'force' the production of data for a given DPS, when the DPS does not actually compute all objects in its O part.

Application to the CASE instruction: every DPS in the CASE statement need not compute all objects that may be assigned between CASE and END CASE. In the example (figure 13.12), DPS1 does not compute B, and if DPS2 is activated, then a mask '01' (0 for 'A will be computed', 1 for 'B will not be computed') will be applied to the O part of the DPS. If DPS1 is activated, a mask '00' will be applied.

5.3.4 Computational instructions in the machine language

Computational instructions are semantically defined by a simple DPS. For example, $C=A-B$ is implemented by the following instruction:

| — | C address | A address | B address | | 1 | 0 | 0 |

The DPS created is composed of

    I: this instruction
    O: C

The execution of a computational instruction consists of:

1. reading OP1, OP2
2. performing $f(OP1, OP2)$
3. writing $RES = f(OP1, OP2)$
4. propagating the result by updating the tag bits Ci1 or Ci2 of instructions using RES, by means of link1, link2 and
5. setting the tag bit C_d corresponding to RES.

Figure 13.11.

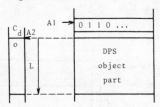

Figure 13.12.

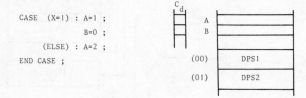

```
CASE   (X=1) : A=1 ;
             B=0 ;
       (ELSE) : A=2 ;
END CASE ;
```

5.3.5 Control instructions in the machine language

These instructions are close to the high level language.

5.3.5.1 ACT

Operates on one DPS, and controls its execution. ACT makes use of:

P4: DPS clearing (O control part initialization)
P1: DPS activation (I control part activation)
P3: DPS checking (for DPS termination).

5.3.5.2 LOOP

The general iteration process is expressed by the LOOP statement in the high level language, and by a set of machine instructions (see figure 13.13). The LOOP instruction is quite close to the LOOP statement in the high level language. It operates similarly on the different DPSs, and activates a different iteration according to the value taken by the loop control event. As far as its implementation is concerned, the LOOP statement may be represented by the following algorithm:

1. The START DPS is activated by an ACT instruction; the NEW objects receive their values.
2. A SWITCH DPS is then activated, pushing the NEW values into the OLD values.
3. The LOOP instruction is executed. Depending on the loop event value, it activates either a user-defined DPS, or the STOP DPS. An activated user-defined DPS will in turn activate the SWITCH DPS as in step 2, and the iteration process goes on.

Figure 13.13.

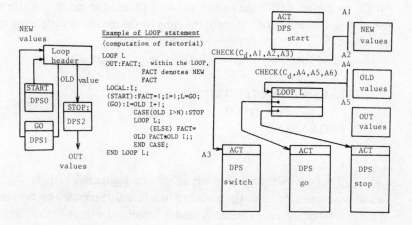

5.3.5.3 CASE

The CASE instruction, when all booleans are calculated, activates the DPS corresponding to the boolean TRUE and forces the production of objects which are not calculated. The sequence of primitives is:

1. P1
2. P4

Example of CASE programming (see figure 13.14):

```
CASE X
    (X=0):Y=2;
    (X=1):Y=3;
    (X>1):Y=4;Z=3;
    (ELSE):Z=1;
END CASE ;
```

5.3.5.4 EXPAND

The body of EXPAND forms a DPS. As each iteration is independent from the others we can execute several such DPSs concurrently. The number of copies is static, but can be fixed by the programmer, according to the level of parallelism he wishes. An ACT instruction is associated with each copy. The EXPAND mechanism splits into two instructions: STEXP (START EXPAND) and EXP (EXPAND).

There is one instruction STEXP, and n EXP instructions, according to the number of copies. The STEXP is an initialization instruction, i.e. it initializes the index of each copy, activates the corresponding EXP instruction and checks for the end of the n copies.

The EXP instruction controls its own copy: it first clears the control tag bits $Ci1$ $Ci2$ by means of (P2), increments and tests the current index, and activates the ACT instruction associated with the copy (if the index is less than the upper bound).

Example of EXPAND programming (see figure 13.15):

```
EXPAND I=A STEP B TO N :
    TAB (I)=X+I;
END EXPAND;
```

5.3.5.5 CALL

The body of the procedure is a DPS with inputs and outputs which are formal parameters. Several copies of the procedure are generated by the compiler at the request of the programmer. A header, associated with the procedure, manages the calls. When actual input parameters are calculated, the CALL instruction becomes executable and looks for an idle copy by means of the header. If there is one, formal parameters are assigned to actual parameters and the copy is activated by the corresponding ACT instruction; if there is no idle copy, the CALL instruction is put into a waiting queue. A RETURN instruction is activated when all outputs of the copy have been calculated. It tests the contents of the queue, and if there is a waiting CALL, releases it.

5.4   Architecture of the LAU system

A global diagram of a high performance data driven architecture is shown in figure 13.16. Several levels of currency are obviously taken into account by single assignment:

> Machine instruction level
> Task level
> Program level.

Each processor is itself a data driven multiprocessing unit. The actual LAU system consists of one of these units, and we shall give some details about it now.

Figure 13.14. CASE statement mechanism.

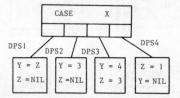

Figure 13.15. EXPAND control mechanisms.

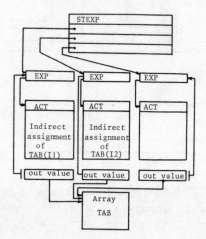

5.4.1   Global architecture

An LAU processor is composed of three main functional units (main memory, control unit and execution unit) communicating by buses as shown in figure 13.17. Basic execution takes four steps:

(1) A machine instruction is declared 'fireable' in an instruction control unit (ICU) as soon as its three tag bits (C_0, C_1, C_2) are set to '111'. The ICU stores their addresses in a file. This file continuously sends ready instruction addresses to the main memory unit.

Figure 13.16.

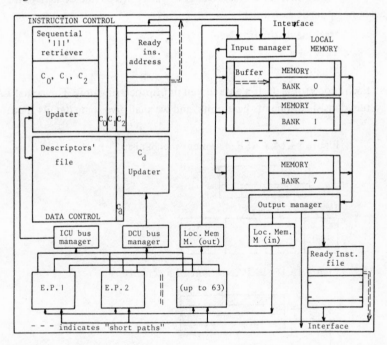

Figure 13.17.

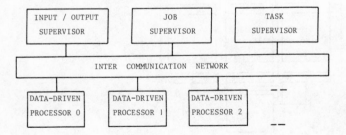

(2) The instruction is read out and sent to a file containing ready instructions waiting for execution. As soon as a processing element becomes idle, an instruction is sent to it, and its execution begins.

(3) The processing element performs the usual operations related to a three-address instruction execution: it fetches operands and computes the result. While storing the result value, the processing element will get the link addresses associated to that object.

(4) An updating sequence terminates the process: C_0, C_1 or C_2 tag bits associated to other instructions using that result as an operand will be set to 1, eventually putting them to the 'fireable' state which will be recognized by the ICU. Then the C_d bit attached to the result value is set to one.

5.4.2   Main memory

As it is a common resource for the whole system the memory unit has been designed for achieving high throughput and minimizing conflicts (see figure 13.18). An input multiplexer (cycle: 60 ns) transforms external requests into 56-bit internal requests and drives them to one of eight interleaved memory banks. Instead of global management of conflicts, we chose a two-level scheme: each bank has its own local buffer for accepting up to 32 requests (cycle: 60 ns, buffer memory cycle: 20 ns) and sends a signal to the input multiplexer when 29 requests are present. Though more expensive than in conventional memory systems, this scheme is efficient and prevents the memory from causing bottlenecks in the system.

An output multiplexer manages the eight memory bank output buffers and sends the result request to the appropriate bus (ready instruction file, processing elements, interface). Input multiplexer and output multiplexer lie on three 35 cm × 35 cm cards. Each memory bank takes one card, supporting 220 integrated circuits. TTL low power Schottky ICs, including 20 ns cycle 29705 AMD buffers and 480 ns 2114 Intel memory chips, are used.

Figure 13.18.

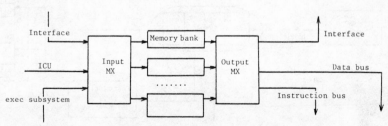

5.4.3   *Ready instruction file*

Located between the main memory and the processing elements, the ready instruction file (see figure 13.19) performs several operations:

(1) It accepts 64-bit instructions delivered by main memory and buffers them into a queue (30 ns cycle time, two independent access parts, 128 words long).

(2) It controls processing element activities, examines their global state, and sends them instructions as soon as one of them is idle. We find here the most important quality of data driven sequencing:

the instructions have no ordering at all, since they are executable, hence independent. Moreover, we can attach any number of processors, and finally a processor can take any amount of time for executing an instruction.

The ready instruction file occupies two cards and is built from about 300 ICs.

(3) It stops the activity of the instruction control unit when too many ready instructions are waiting for execution.

5.4.4   *Processing elements*

Processing elements are built with any of three types of microprocessor based technology:

(1) **AMD 2900 bit slice microprocessors**: this element needs 280 ICs, a 64-bit horizontal microinstruction in 4K micro words, and a powerful set of debugging tools. It is the most powerful unit (microcycle: 180 ns), but takes long to become operational.

(2) **Intel 8085 based processor**, with software simulating the machine language. It requires 120 ICs, and 4K of PROM. The simplest design (three weeks) was also the most quickly debugged (three weeks), but the slowest in operation. However it allowed us to produce a 4-element

Figure 13.19.

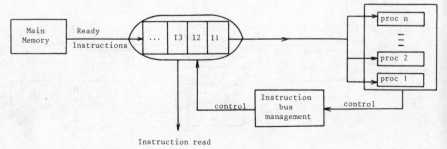

Instruction read

LAU system in late 1979, running real single assignment high level programs.

(3) Intel 8086 based processor, which cuts execution times while keeping design simplicity.

Each processing element communicates with the help of six specialized buses (see figure 13.20):

Instruction bus, used and controlled by the ready instruction file to feed the processing elements with 64-bit instructions.

Memory request bus.

Memory result bus.

Data control unit read bus.

Data control unit write bus.

Instruction control unit bus.

5.4.5 *Instruction control unit*

This unit (implemented on two boards and using 400 ICs) is the truly original part of the system, and performs three different tasks (see figure 13.21):

(1) It updates control bits in the C_0, C_1, C_2 instruction control memory, according to requests coming from processing elements.

(2) It detects ready instruction addresses whose corresponding words match the value '111'. It usually takes no time to detect such an address: when an update operation is to be performed, the corresponding word is first read out. In the case when the update leads to 111, then a 011 is written back, and the address is sent to the ready instruction address queue.

(3) It sends ready instruction addresses to the main memory subsystem.

Figure 13.20.

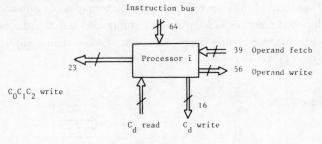

Figure 13.21.

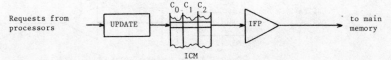

5.4.6 Data control unit

The role of the data control unit (figure 13.22) is twofold:

(1) It verifies that single assignment is respected, by examining C_d bits attached to data items in memory.

(2) It signals data production set termination by looking at slices of C_d bits in data control memory, corresponding to 'objects' part of DPSs in execution. These slices are defined by a three-address descriptor, giving start and end addresses, and the third address being sent to the instruction control unit for a C_1 updating operation when the C_2 slice is filled with ones.

The DCU is implemented on two boards of 200 ICs each.

5.4.7 Host interface

The LAU system is conceived to be a peripheral processor of a minicomputer (SEMS MITRA 15) which also supports its high level software (compiler and simulator). At present it works with a comprehensive interface simulating the host facility:

An LAU system front panel showing control and data flow, maintenance and displays.

A home-made microcomputer system including CRT, line printer and floppy disk drives. Its software system allows loading of programs into the LAU system memory, activating it and unloading results. A library manager provides the user with high level commands to run and evaluate programs.

5.4.8 Experiments

Several sample programs have been tried on the present prototype with four slow processors. Execution times are irrelevant here, but the major formal results have been successfully proved: parallelism is totally taken into account in an asynchronous machine, yielding no synchronization and exploitation of processing elements. A complete description of the LAU system is given in (SYRE 80) and (TEAU 18).

Figure 13.22.

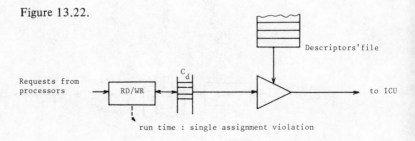

Requests from processors → RD/WR

C_d

Descriptors' file

to ICU

run time : single assignment violation

5.5 Applications to numerical problems

The computer and the simulator led us to write real world programs and test them with very accurate results, since

(1) The compiler produces exact machine code.
(2) The simulator implements the hard-wired functions of the machine, at the register-transfer level. Moreover it can dump traces of all activities in the functional units or on buses every 10 ns. Finally it measures parallelism observed by taking pictures of system activity every 100 μs.

5.5.1 A finite difference problem

$-\Delta u = 0$ within D

$u/\Gamma = y^2 x^2 + 225$ (16 × 32 grid)

approximated by a 2-order finite difference formula:

$$u(x_i, y_j) = (1/4)(u(x_{i-1}, y_j) + u(x_{i+1}, y_j) + u(x_i, y_{j-1}) + u(x_i, y_{j-1}))$$

This simple program is listed below:

```
1    PROGRAM LAPL0001
2    &
3    & CALCUL D'UN CHAMP LAPLACIEN.
4    &
5    DECLARE:
6            RESOLV: EVENT;
7            X: ARRAY (0: 511) OF REAL:
8            I, J, K, M, TR, J1, I1, TR1, TR2, TR3: INTEGER:
9            A, B, C, TEST: REAL;
10           FLOAT: ARRAY (0: 31) OF INPUT REAL;
11   &
12   DO:
13   &
14   & ROUCLE ITERATIVE DE RESOLUTION.
15   &
16       LOOP RESOLV
17               OUT: X, TEST;
18   (START):
19               &
20               & INITIALISATIONS
21               &
22               EXPAND/5 J1 = 0 TO 31:
23                   LOCAL: TR1;
24                   X(J1) = (FLOAT(J1) * FLOAT(J1)) + 225E1;
25                   TR1 = J1 + 480;
26                   X(TR1) = (FLOAT(J1) * FLOAT(J1));
27               EE;
28               EXPAND/3 I1 = 1 TO 14:
29                   LOCAL: TR2, TR3;
30                   TR2 = 32 * I1;
31                   X(TR2) = 225E1 - (FLOAT(I1) * FLOAT(I1));
32                   TR3 = TR2 + 31;
33                   X(TR3) = 1186E1 - (FLOAT(I1) * FLOAT(I1));
34               EE:
35               EXPAND/3 I = 1 TO 14:
36                   LOCAL: TR, J;
```

```
37              TR = (I * 32) + 1;
38              EXPAND/4 J = TR TO TR + 29:
39                  X(J) = 0E1;
40              EE;
41          EE;
42          TEST = 1E1;
43          RESOLV = CORPS;
44      (CORPS):
45              &
46              & TEST DE CONVERGENCE.
47              &
48          TEST = VSUM (OLD X FROM 0 STEP 1 TO 511);
49          CASE ((TEST - OLD TEST) < 0E1):
50                      STOP LOOP RESOLV:
51          EC;
52          OUTPUT 1: TEST;
53          EXPAND/4 M = 33 STEP 32 TO 449:
54              LOCAL: K;
55              EXPAND K = M TO M + 29:
56                  LOCAL: A, B, C;
57                  &
58                  & NOUVELLES VALEURS DE LA FONCTION.
59                  &
60                  A = OLD X (K - 1) + OLD X (K + 1);
61                  B = OLD X (K - 32) + OLD X (K + 32);
62                  C = (A + B)/4E0;
63                  X(K) = C;
64              EE;
65          EE;
66      END LOOP RESOLV;
67  END PROGRAM.
```

Much larger finite difference programs have been written. The interested reader may consult (TEAU 18).

5.5.2   A finite element program

This example will illustrate how data flow processing needs new algorithms. The following section of program computes matrix A and second member B of equation $Au = B$ solving $-\Delta u = f$ in a cube of side 1 divided into five P1 type tetrahedra.

```
68  PROGRAM EXELF
69  DECLARE:
70          & PROGRAMME DE TEST D ELEMENTS FINIS
71          & RESOLUTION DE DELTA U = F SUR UN CUBE DE COTE 1
72          & DIVISE EN 5 TETRAEDRES
73      &
74      & MATRICES D ENTREE
75          X: ARRAY (0: 2, 0: 7) OF INPUT REAL; & COORDONNEES DES SOMMETS
76      IE: ARRAY (0: 3, 0: 4) OF INPUT INTEGER: & CONNECTIVITE
77          F: ARRAY (0: 7) OF INPUT REAL; & VALEURS DE LA FONCTION F
78      &
79      & MATRICES DE SORTIE
80          A: ARRAY (0: 5, 0: 7) OF REAL:
81          B: ARRAY (0: 7) OF REAL:
82      &
83      & MATRICES LOCALES
84          XX, YY, ZZ, FF, BB: ARRAY (0: 3) OF REAL;
85          F: ARRAY (0: 3, 0: 3) OF REAL;
```

```
86    &
87    & INDEX
88    IMA, IST, JST, KST, J, IB, JB: INTEGER;
89    & INDEX LOCAUX
90    ILOCS, ILOC, JBLOC, LBLOC, IBLOC: INTEGER;
91    &
92    & DIVERS
93    EVMA: FVENT;
94    NP, NE, LB: INTEGER;
95    WX, X1, X2, X3, WY, Y1, Y2, Y3, WZ, Z1, Z2, Z3, R1X, B1Y, B1Z.
96    B1X1, B1Y1, B1Z1, B2Z, B2Y, B2Z, B3X, B3Y, B3Z, B4X, B4Y, B4Z,
97    D, AD, W, P, T10, T20, T30, T21, T31, T32, SF
98          : REAL;
99
100   DO:
101   NP = 7; NE = 4; LB = 5;
102   LOOP EVMA
103       OUT: A, B;
104       LOCAL: IMA, WX, X1, X2, X3, WY, Y1, Y2, Y3, WZ, Z1, Z2, Z3.
105             B1X, B1Y, B1Z, D, B1X1, B1Y1, B1Z1, B2X, B2Y, B2Z,
106             B3X, B3Y, B3Z, B4X, B4Y, B4Z, AD, W, P, T10, T20,
107             T30, T21, T31, T32, SF, E, RB, FF, XX, YY, ZZ
108             ;
109
110       (START):
111         EXPAND IST = 0 TO NP:
112             B(IST) = 0E0;
113             EXPAND/4 JST = 0 TO LB;
114                 A(JST, IST) = 0E0;
115                 EE;
116         EE;
117       EVMA = ELEM; IMA = 0;
118       EXPAND/4 KST = 0 TO 3:
119             LOCAL: ILOCS;
120             ILOCS = IE(KST, IMA);
121             XX(KST) = X(0, ILOCS);
122             YY(KST) = X(1, ILOCS);
123             ZZ(KST) = X(2, ILOCS);
124             FF(KST) = F(ILOCS);
125         EE;
126
127       (ELEM): OUTPUT 2: 0;
128         OUTPUT 3: T10;
129         WX = OLD XX(3);
130         X1 = OLD XX(0) - WX;
131         X2 = OLD XX(1) - WX;
132         X3 = OLD XX(2) - WX;
133         WY = OLD YY(3);
134         Y1 = OLD YY(0) - WY;
135         Y2 = OLD YY(1) - WY;
136         Y3 = OLD YY(2) - WY;
137         WZ = OLD ZZ(3);
138         Z1 = OLD ZZ(0) - WZ;
139         Z2 = OLD ZZ(1) - WZ;
140         Z3 = OLD ZZ(2) - WZ;
141         R1X = (Y2 * Z3) - (Y3 * Z2);
142         R1Y = (Z2 * X3) - (Z3 * X2);
143         B1Z = (X2 * Y3) - (X3 * Y2);
144         D = (B1X * X1) + (B1Y * Y1) + (B1Z * Z1);
145         B1X1 = B1X/D; B1Y1 = B1Y/D; B1Z1 = B1Z/D;
146         B2X = ((Z1 * Y3) - (Y1 * Z3))/D;
147         B2Y = ((X1 * Z3) - (Z1 * X3))/D;
148         B2Z = ((Y1 * X3) - (X1 * Y3))/D;
149         B3X = ((Y1 * Z2) - (Z1 * Y2))/D;
150         B3Y = ((Z1 * X2) - (X1 * Z2))/D;
```

```
151         B3Z = ((X1 * Y2) - (Y1 * X2))/D;
152         B4X = - (B1X1 + B2X + B3X);
153         B4Y = - (B1Y1 + B2Y + B3Y);
154         B4Z = - (B1Z1 + B2Z + B3Z);
155         CASE (D > 0): AD = D; (ELSE): AD = - D; EC;
156         W = AD/6E0; P = AD/120E0;
157         E (0, 0) = W * ((B1X1 * B1X1) + (B1Y1 * B1Y1) + (B1Z1 * B1Z1));
158         E (1, 1) = W * ((B2X * B2X) + (B2Y * B2Y) + (B2Z * B2Z));
159         E (2, 2) = W * ((B3X * B3X) + (B3Y * B3Y) + (B3Z * B3Z));
160         E (3, 3) = W * ((B4X * B4X) + (B4Y * B4Y) + (B4Z * B4Z));
161         T10 = W * ((B2X * B1X1) + (B2Y * B1Y1) + (B2Z * B1Z1));
162         T20 = W * ((B3X * B1X1) + (B3Y * B1Y1) + (B3Z * B1Z1));
163         T30 = W * ((B4X * B1X1) + (B4Y * B1Y1) + (B4Z * B1Z1));
164         T21 = W * ((B3X * B2X) + (B3Y * B2Y) + (B3Z * B2Z));
165         T31 = W * ((B4X * B2X) + (B4Y * B2Y) + (B4Z * B2Z));
166         T32 = W * ((B4X * B3X) + (B4Y * B3Y) + (B4Z * B3Z);
167         E (1, 0) = T10; E (0, 1) = T10;
168         E (2, 0) = T20; E (0, 2) = T20;
169         E (3, 0) = T30; E (0, 3) = T30;
170         E (1, 3) = T31; E (3, 1) = T31;
171         E (2, 1) = T21; E (1, 2) = T21;
172         E (3, 2) = T32; E (2, 3) = T32;
173
174         SF = VSUM (OLD FF FROM 0 STEP 1 TO 3);
175         BB(0) = (OLD FF (0) + SF) * P;
176         BB(1) = (OLD FF (1) + SF) * P;
177         BB(2) = (OLD FF (2) + SF) * P;
178         BB(3) = (OLD FF (3) + SF) * P;
179         EVMA = ASSEM;
180
181     (ASSEM): IMA = OLD IMA + 1;
182         OUTPUT 1: OLD IMA;
183         EXPAND/2 IB = 0 TO 3;
184             LOCAL: IBLOC;
185             IBLOC = IE (IB, OLD IMA);
186                 B (IBLOC) = OLD B (IBLOC) + OLD BB(IB);
187             EXPAND/2 JB = 0 TO 3;
188                 LOCAL: JBLOC, LBLOC;
189                 JBLOC = IE (JB, OLD IMA);
190                 LBLOC = JBLOC - IBLOC;
191                 CASE (LBLOC > = 0): A (LBLOC, IBLOC) =
192                         OLD A (LBLOC, IBLOC) + OLD E (JR, IB);
193                     EC;
194             EE;
195         EE;
196         CASE (OLD IMA = NE): STOP LOOP EVMA;
197         (ELSE): EVMA = ELEM;
198             EXPAND/2 J = 0 TO 3:
199             LOCAL: ILOC;
200                 ILOC = IF (J, IMA);
201                 XX (J) = X (0, ILOC);
202                 YY (J) = X (1, ILOC);
203                 ZZ (J) = X (2, ILOC);
204                 FF (J) = F (ILOC);
205             EE;
206         EC;
207     END LOOP EVMA;
208 END PROGRAM.
```

We see that inherent parallelism for computing one element is not large (the simulator gives the solution 6). As we proceed from one element to the next by iterating the loop, this code is not parallel. However, we could have computed all elements x simultaneously (this is a characteristic of almost all finite element problems). But the drawbacks would have been: (1) wasting memory space, because each element needs a 4×4 local matrix, and (2) data synchronization when accumulating these matrices into A and B. The best solution is the following: the program may process all elements in the domain simultaneously, provided that these elements have no point in common. So one can partition the set of elements in such subsets, and each iteration will perform all computations related to a given subset of elements, yielding a parallelism that may become very large (ten times the number of elements per subset).

5.5.3 Conclusion

The conclusion is clear: algorithms and numerical methods must be rethought in terms of data flow sequencing.

Research at CERT Toulouse now turns to three main topics:

(1) high speed very large computer architecture using data flow at higher levels than the LAU system does;
(2) high level data flow languages, where single assignment will not be mandatory;
(3) mathematical algorithms and numerical methods.

References

References related to the LAU system

(BERG 79) P. Berger, TEAU 21: *Programmation et évaluation du parallélisme dans le système LAU*. CERT report, Nov. 79.
(COMT 80) D. Comte, N. Hifdi, J. C. Syre: 'The LAU data driven multiprocessor system: results and perspectives' in *Proceedings of IFIP Congress, 4–17 October 1980.*
(PLAS 76) A. Plas et al. 'LAU system architecture: a parallel data driven processor based on single assignment' in *Proceedings of International Conference on Parallel Processing* IEEE 76 CH 1127.OC.
(SYRE 77) J. C. Syre, D. Comte, N. Hifdi, 'Pipelining, parallelism and asynchronism in the LAU system' in *Proceedings of 1977 International Conference on Parallel Processing*, IEEE 77 CH 1253-4C.
(SYRE 80) J. C. Syre, 'Etude et réalisation d'un système multiprocesseur MIMD en assignation unique', Thèse de Doctorat d'Etat, Université Paul Sabatier, Toulouse, June 1980.
(TEAU 18) CERT/DERI Computer Architecture Group (P. Berger, D. Comte, N. Hifdi, B. Pelois, J. C. Syre), TEAU 18: *Mise en oeuvre d'un prototype de multiprocesseur en assignation unique.* Final report, Contract SESORI 78.165, February 1980.
(TEAU 73) J. C. Syre, J.-M. Nicolas, *Techniques et exploitation de l'assignation unique.* Four reports, 1973-4, CERT.

Other references

(ACKE 79) W. B. Ackerman, *VAL, a Value Oriented Language*, Computation Structures Group, TR-218, MIT-LCS, Cambridge, Mass., June 79.
(ARVI 77) Arvind, *Semantics of loop in ID*, Note 11, March 1977, University of California, Irvine.

(BAER 68) J. L. Baer, C. Bovet, 'Compilation of arithmetic expressions for parallel computations' in *Proceedings of IFIP Congress 68*, May 68.

(BAER 73) J. L. Baer, 'A survey of some theoretical aspects on parallel processing' *Computing Surveys* 15, 1, March 73, 31–80.

(BERK 75) K. J. Berkling, 'Reduction languages for reduction machines' in *Proceedings of 2nd Symposium on Computer Architecture*, 1975, pp. 133–40.

(BERN 66) A. J. Bernstein, 'Analysis of programs for parallel processing' *IEEE Trans. Computers*, EC 15, Oct. 66, 5, 757–63.

(BOCK 79) K. Bockelheide, 'A high level graphical, data-driven language', in *Proceedings of the Workshop on Data Driven Languages and Machines*, J. C. Syre, Toulouse, Feb. 1979.

(CHAM 71) D. D. Chamberlin, 'Parallel implementation of a LAU'. Ph.D. Thesis. Technical Report 19, January 71.

(CONW 63) M. E. Conway, 'A multiprocessor system design' in *Proceedings of AFIPS FJCC 63*, pp. 139–45.

(DAVI 79a) A. Davis, 'DDN's a low level program schema of fully distributed systems' in *Proceedings of 1st European Conference on Parallel and Distributed Processing*, (J. C. Syre, ed) Feb. 1979, pp. 1–7.

(DAVI 79b) A. Davis & P. J. Drongowski, *Data Driven Computing Systems*, Computer Science Dpt, University of Utah, Sept. 1979.

(DENN 73) J. B. Dennis, *First Version of a Data Flow Procedure Language*, Computation Structures Group, TR 93, MIT, Nov. 73.

(FLAN 79) P. M. Flanders, *Fortran extensions for a highly parallel processor*, INFOTECH 'Supercomputers' report, Vol 2, 1979.

(GLAU 78) J. Glauert, 'A single assignment language for data flow computing'. M.Sc. Dissertation, Department of Computer Science, University of Manchester, Jan. 78.

(GONZ 71) H. Gonzalez & C. V. Ramamoorthy, 'Program suitability for parallel processing' *IEEE Trans. on Computers*, C20, 6, June 71, 647–54.

(GURD 76) J. Gurd, *A highly parallel computer architecture*, University of Manchester, Apr. 76.

(HIGB 78) L. Higbie, 'Applications of vector processing', *Computer Design*, Apr. 78, 139–45.

(HOPK 79) R. D. Hopkins et al. *A computer supporting data flow, control flow and updateable memory* TR 144, University of Newcastle, Sept. 1979.

(KLIN 71) J. Klinkhamer, *A definitional language*. Philips Research Lab., Eindhoven (Holland), 1971.

(KOSI 73) P. R. Kosinski, 'A data flow language for O.S. programming', *ACM Sigplan Notice*, 8, 9, Sept. 73, 89–93.

(LECO 79) M. P. Lecouffe, 'Etude et définition d'un modèle de machine parallèle dynamique dirigé par les données', Thèse de Doctorat 3ème Cycle, Université de Lille, France, July 79.

(McGR 79) J. McGraw, 'Data Flow Computing. Software development' in *Proceedings of 1st International Conference on Distributed Computing Systems*, Oct. 79, IEEE 79CH1445-66, pp. 242–51.

(MISU 75) D. Misunas, 'Structure processing in data flow computer 75' in *Proceedings of Sagamore Conference on Parallel Processing*, Aug. 75.

(OSMO 78) P. E. Osmon et al., *A data flow model of computation*, Westfield College, London.

(RAMA 69) C. V. Ramamoorthy & H. Gonzalez, 'A survey of techniques for recognizing parallel processable streams in computer programs' in *Proceedings of FJCC 1969*. pp. 1–14.

(ROUC 73) G. Roucairol, A. Widory, *Programmes séquentiels et parallélisme*, RAIRO Info. B2, Sept. 73.

(TESL 68) L. G. Tesler & H. J. Enea, 'A language design for concurrent processes' in *Proceedings of SJCC 32*, 1968, pp. 403–8.

(TREL 80) P. Treleaven et al., *Data driven and demand driven computer architecture*, Internal report, University of Newcastle, July 80.

(URSC 73) G. Urschler, 'The transformation of flow diagrams into maximally parallel form' in *Proceedings of 73 Sagamore Conference on Parallel Processing*, pp. 38–46.

(WORK 77) *Data Flow Workshop 1977*, MIT, Aug. 1977.

(WORK 79) *Workshop on data driven languages and machines*, CERT, Toulouse, France, 12–13 February 1979.

14   Parallel models of computation

PHILIP C. TRELEAVEN

1   Introduction

For parallel processing systems (whether consisting of geographically
distributed mainframe computers or composed of miniature computing elements
within a single board or chip) the most important research aspect is identifying
a 'naturally' parallel model of computation. If large numbers of computers,
possibly of different types, are to be used in parallel processing systems, then it
is necessary to have a system-wide architecture and computational model which
they all obey. Unfortunately, 'general-purpose' organisations for interconnecting
and programming these systems, based on the sequential control flow (von
Neumann) model have not been forthcoming. Recently a number of researchers
have questioned the continuing adequacy of the von Neumann architectural
model for computing in general. To quote from John Backus's 1977 ACM
Turing Lecture [2], 'Conventional programming languages are growing ever more
enormous, but not stronger. Inherent defects at the most basic level cause them
to be both fat and weak . . . '.

The question then becomes which parallel organisation (or amalgam of
features from their various models of computation) will contribute to this new
general-purpose organisation. Examination of research into data driven and
demand driven architectures reveals four principal groups of computational
models in use, namely data flow, 'multi-thread' forms of control flow, (string)
reduction and lazy evaluation – a particular form of (graph) reduction. These
groups are distinguished by the way computations manipulate their arguments
and by the way the execution of computations is initiated.

2   Models of computation

Two mechanisms which we will refer to as the control mechanism and
the data mechanism, seem fundamental to any model of computation.

The *control mechanism* defines how one computation causes the execution
of another computation, and consists of:

    (1) *by availability* – where control signals the availability of an argument
         and a computation is executed when all its arguments (e.g. input data)

are available;

(2) *by need* – where control signals the need for an argument and a computation is executed when one of the output arguments it generates is required by the invoking computation.

The *data mechanism* defines the way a particular argument is used by a group of computations and consists of:

(1) *by value* – where an argument is shared by giving a separate copy to each accessing computation, this copy being stored as a value in the computation.

(2) *by reference* – where an argument is shared by having a reference to it stored in each accessing computation.

Every model of computation has some combination of these four schemes, with data driven having a 'by availability' control mechanism and demand driven having a 'by need' control mechanism. For the various models mentioned above, figure 14.1 shows the relevant control mechanisms and data mechanisms for the different groups of computational model.

As a basis for discussing the operational semantics associated with these different computational models, simple directed graph program representations for the statement $a = (b + c) * (b - c)$ are examined. Although this statement consists of simple operators and operands, the concepts illustrated are equally applicable to more complex operations and data structures.

3   Data flow

In a data flow [1, 4, 5, 7, 10, 11] program graph, each node represents a function and each arc represents a uni-directional data path which conveys a *data token* (e.g. partial result) from the producing node to the consumer. A node performs some operation which is a function mapping inputs to outputs.

Figure 14.1. Computational models control and data mechanisms.

| | | Data Mechanisms | |
		by value	by reference
Control Mechanisms	by availability	data flow	control flow
	by need	string reduction	graph reduction

In general, a node is enabled for execution when there is a data token present on each of its input arcs. The node then executes and consumes the set of inputs removing one data token from each arc. It processes them according to the specified function and releases a set of result tokens onto the output arcs which enable further nodes. The data token provides a dual role in the data flow model supporting both the data mechanism and the control mechanism, whose flows of data and control are therefore inseparable.

Figure 14.2 illustrates the sequence of execution for the program fragment $a = (b + c) * (b - c)$ using a black dot on an arc to indicate the presence of a data token. The two black dots in figure 14.2a indicate that the data tokens corresponding to the values of b and c have been generated by some preceding computation. Since b and c are required as inputs for two subsequent nodes two copies of each data token are generated, as shown in figure 14.2b. Here the availability of the two pairs of inputs enables both the addition and subtraction nodes. Logically executing in parallel, each node consumes its input tokens, performs the specified operation and releases the result token onto the output arc. This enables the multiplication node, as shown in figure 14.2c, which executes and outputs its result corresponding to the identifier a. The execution of this program fragment clearly demonstrates the parallel and asynchronous operation of the data flow model.

4   Control flow

In the control flow [6, 7] graph notation of figure 14.3 each rectangular node specifies a function and each circular node represents an item of stored

Figure 14.2. Execution of a data flow computation $a = (b + c) * (b - c)$.

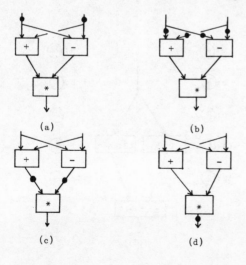

(a)   (b)

(c)   (d)

data. Each arc in the graph defines a uni-directional control path conveying a *control token* – a control token may be viewed as a NULL data token acting as a control signal – from the producing node to the node that is to be enabled. For clarity, flows of data between nodes are denoted by the references in a rectangular node, rather than by arcs. A rectangular node is enabled for execution when there is a control token present on each of its input arcs. The node then executes and consumes the set of control tokens, removing one from each arc. Next, using the embedded references, it accesses the stored data which form the inputs to the node, performs the specified function and releases the stored data results. Lastly, the rectangular node releases a set of control tokens onto its output arcs to enable subsequent nodes.

Figure 14.3 illustrates the sequence of execution for the program fragment $a = (b+c)*(b-c)$, where a blank dot on an arc indicates the presence of a control token. We also show in figure 14.3 that the control graph does not

Figure 14.3. Execution of a control flow computation $a = (b+c)*(b-c)$.

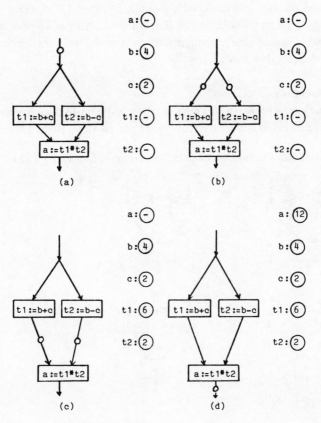

have to correspond directly to the flow of data, as it does in data flow. For example in the program fragment the addition and subtraction nodes are each activated by the availability of a single control token, whereas the multiplication requires the presence of two control tokens before it can execute.

The single blank dot in figure 14.3a indicates that the values of b and c have been generated by preceding computations and are present in their respective circular nodes. This control token is then duplicated and tokens sent to enable the addition and subtraction nodes as shown in figure 14.3b. These two nodes execute concurrently, retrieve the values corresponding to b and c, and send their partial results to the circular nodes $t1$ and $t2$ respectively. Then each node releases a control token to the multiplication, which requires the presence of two tokens before it is enabled. Finally, the multiplication executes, releasing its results to the circular node a, and a control token onto its output arc. Clearly, the asynchronous nature of this control flow model could result in a control token signalling the availability of an item of stored data before the data is actually present in its circular node. We let our definition of the model exclude this possibility as in fact it can be excluded in an implementation [7].

5   Reduction

Whereas data flow and control flow are data driven forms of computation, having a 'by availability' control mechanism, reduction computation is demand driven with in general a 'by need' control mechanism. Reduction computation is supported either by 'string manipulation' [2, 3, 9, 12] which is based on the copying of arguments – a 'by value' data mechanism, or by 'graph manipulation' [8, 13] which is based on the sharing of arguments using pointers – a 'by reference' data mechanism.

Figure 14.4 illustrates string manipulation for a reduction execution sequence involving the program definition $a = (b + c) * (b - c)$. In figure 14.4a, a computation demands the value corresponding to the definition a. This causes the node containing the identifier a to be replaced by a copy of the definition, as shown in figure 14.4b. Notice that the identifiers b and c are also replaced by copies of their respective definitions. The reducible subexpressions are then rewritten. The addition and subtraction being replaced by their corresponding values, as shown in figure 14.4c, and finally the multiplication being replaced by the constant 12 which is the value of a.

Figure 14.5 illustrates graph reduction using the same program definition $a = (b + c) * (b - c)$. In figure 14.5a a computation demands the value corresponding to a, but instead of taking a copy of the definition we merely traverse the pointer, with the aim of reducing the definition and returning with the actual value. One of the ways of identifying the original source of the demand for *a*, and thus supporting the return, is to reverse the arcs as shown in figure 14.5*b*. This traversal of the definition and the reversal of the arcs is continued until constant circular nodes are encountered. In figure 14.5*d*, reduction of the subexpressions in the definition starts with the rewriting of the addition and subtraction. This proceeds until, as shown in figure 14.5*f*, the definition of *a* is replaced by value 12, a copy of which is also returned to the computation originally demanding *a*. Any subsequent requests for the value of *a* will immediately receive the constant 12 - one of the major benefits of graph reduction over string.

6   Conclusions

The above discussions of data flow, control flow, string and graph reduction illustrate their different methods of organising computation. However

Figure 14.4. Execution of a string reduction $a = (b+c) * (b-c)$.

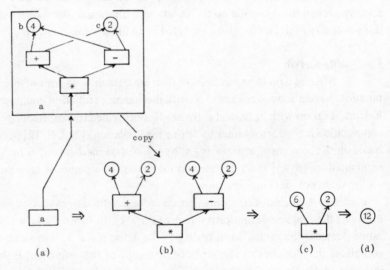

Figure 14.5. Execution of a graph reduction of $a = (b+c) * (b-c)$.

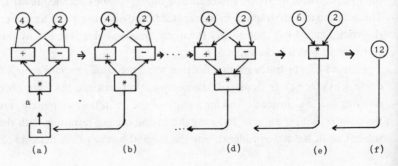

there are interesting similarities in the underlying concepts of the four groups of computational models, related to the data mechanism and control mechanisms that each group employs.

For instance, data flow and string reduction are both based on a 'by value' data mechanism. Both schemes restrict the concept of memory to the time-invariant instructions or definitions corresponding to a program. Put another way, neither data flow nor string reduction allows data to be generated and placed in a named memory cell during execution, so it may be shared and accessed an indeterminate number of times. Both schemes use a combined data and control mechanism so it is impossible, for instance, to separate flows of data from flows of control. And both schemes associate implicit operators with the references that represent arcs in the corresponding machine code: STORE in the case of data flow and LOAD in the case of reduction.

Examining all four groups of computational models, further interesting similarities are observed. First, the similarity of control signals in data flow and control flow; both are supported by tokens specifying a next instruction reference. Second, the similarity in the way instruction execution is synchronised in data flow and control flow; an instruction is enabled for execution when a complete set of tokens is available. Third, the similarity of reduction and control flow. In fact we believe control flow accessing of arguments should be viewed as a primitive form of reduction. Lastly, the similarity in the way execution is synchronised in string reduction and control flow; an expression may be evaluated when its arguments are fully reduced.

In the light of our ability to classify these forms of program representation in terms of their data mechanisms and control mechanisms, these similarities are not altogether surprising. What is more important is that the 'by value' and the 'by reference' data mechanisms and the 'by availability' and the 'by need' control mechanisms are regarded by data flow, control flow and reduction as two pairs of alternatives. Thus we may speculate that each model of computation is, although universal in the sense of a Turing machine, somewhat restricted in the classes of computation it can efficiently support. To design a model of computation which is 'naturally' parallel and general-purpose, it seems necessary to include both pairs of data and control mechanisms. This will allow a compiler writer, for example, to select the appropriate mechanisms for his particular programming language or language constructs.

We have designed such a 'kernel' computational model, which we believe represents a synthesis of the concepts underlying data flow, control flow and reduction models of computation, and hence supports these models. This kernel model is itself supported by a decentralised computer architecture, designed round a simple single-chip building block - referred to as a 'computing element'

- which may be plugged together with its duplicates (like LEGO blocks) to form a parallel computer. Unfortunately, shortage of space precludes descriptions of this kernel computational model and its computing element architecture.

References

[1] Arvind and Gostelow, K. P. 'A computer capable of exchanging processors for time' in *Proc. IFIP Congress 1977*, (August 1977), pp. 849–53

[2] Backus, J. 'Can programming be liberated from the von Neumann style? A functional style and its algebra of programs' *Comm. ACM 21*, 8 (August 1978), 613–41

[3] Berkling, K. J. 'Reduction languages for reduction machines' in *Proc. Second Int. Symp. on Computer Architecture*, (April 1975), pp. 133–40

[4] Davis, A. L. 'The architecture and system methodology of DDM1: A recursively structured data driven machine' in *Proc. Fifth Symp. Computer Architecture*, (April 1978), pp. 210–15

[5] Dennis, J. B. 'The varieties of data flow computers' in *Proc. First Inf. Conf. on Distributed Computing Systems*, (October 1979), pp. 430–9

[6] Farrell, E. P., Ghani, N. and Treleaven, P. C. 'A concurrent computer architecture and a ring based implementation' in *Proc. Sixth Symp. Computer Architecture*, (April 1979), pp. 1–11

[7] Hopkins, R. P., Rautenbach, P. W. and Treleaven, P. C. *A Computer Supporting Data Flow, Control Flow and Updateable Memory*. Tech. Report 144, Computing Laboratory, The University of Newcastle upon Tyne (September 1979)

[8] Keller, R. M., Lindstrom, G. E. and Patil, S. S. 'A loosely-coupled applicative multi-processing system' in *AFIPS Conf. Proc. Vol. 48* (1978), pp. 861–70

[9] Mago, G. A. 'A network of microprocessors to execute reduction languages' *Int. Journ. of Computer and Information Sciences*, 8, 5 and 8, 6 (1979)

[10] Syre, J. C., Comte, D. and Hifdi, H. 'Pipelining and asynchronism in the LAU system' in *Proc. 1977 Int. Conf. Parallel Processing*, (August 1977), pp. 87–92

[11] Treleaven, P. C. 'Principal components of a data flow computer' in *Proc. 1978 Euromicro Symp.*, (October 1978), pp. 366–74

[12] Treleaven, P. C. and Mole, G. F. 'A multi-processor reduction machine for user-defined reduction languages' in *Proc. Seventh Int. Symp. on Computer Architecture*, (1980) pp. 121–9

[13] Turner, D. A. 'A new implementation technique for applicative languages' *Software – Practice and Experience*, 9, (1979), 31–49

PART 6

Parallel computer algorithms

15 Parallel numerical algorithms

M. FEILMEIER

1 Introduction

One can observe two extreme positions among numerical mathematicians. Some of them consider *numerical analysis* to be the simple application of functional-analytical and other concepts of *pure mathematics*. On the other hand, some pragmatists see only their own special problems and the special computer structures necessary for their solution. They consider numerical analysis as a collection of special algorithms. It would seem necessary to develop a synthesis of both positions. The following three-step concept may be suitable:

(i) The first step attempts to develop numerical analysis axiomatically. Numerical analysis is considered to be part of mathematics and therefore possesses an axiomatic foundation. Nevertheless, this axiomatic approach is not sufficiently highly developed (see Kulisch [76]) and there is no generally accepted procedure.

(ii) The second step involves the principles of numerical analysis. These principles refer to concrete problems, but are nonetheless fairly general. As an example, it is worth mentioning the methods of applied functional analysis (see Collatz [64]).

(iii) The third step deals with algorithms for the solution of actual problems on real computers. These algorithms are fundamental to the practical implications of numerical analysis.

How can this concept be applied to the area of parallel numerical analysis? In general there is no axiomatic approach to parallel numerical analysis. The reason may be that this area is still in the early stages of development.

The principles of parallel numerical analysis are considered in sections 2 and 3. Section 2 deals with the principles for constructing parallel numerical algorithms. In section 3 the numerical stability of parallel algorithms is analysed.

Following on from this, particular classes of problems are discussed. Linear problems play a most important role – they are discussed by Evans in chapter 17. Non-linear problems are discussed in section 4. The dependence of parallel algorithms on computer architecture is discussed in section 5.

We commence with a definition: let n be the number of parameters in a problem. $T_p(n)$ denotes the number of time steps for a parallel algorithm on a parallel computer with $p > 1$ processors. $T_1(n)$ denotes the number of time steps for the 'best' serial algorithm. Then

$$S_p(n) := \frac{T_1(n)}{T_p(n)} \leqslant p$$

is termed the *speed-up ratio* and

$$E_p(n) := \frac{S_p(n)}{p} \leqslant 1$$

is termed the *efficiency* of the parallel algorithm.

These notions are of more importance in the classification of parallel algorithms. They do not reveal very much about the actual time used to perform an algorithm (see Parkinson, chapter 12).

In practice, numerical algorithms are very dependent on the type of computer for which they have been developed. It is thus, in general, possible to take the von Neumann computer as a common basis for serial algorithms. The situation is however quite different for parallel algorithms. According to Flynn [72] we can use the following classification for parallel computers:

SIMD   (single instruction multiple data computers):
       Illiac IV, Staran, ICL-DAP, Burroughs SP, STAR, Cyber 203/205, Cray-1, etc.

MIMD   (multiple instruction multiple data computers):
       DDA's, C.mmp, SMS 201, multi-mini-systems, etc.

At the moment SIMD computers are the subject of great interest. For the purposes of numerical analysis these computers can be differentiated by two characteristics:

    (i) linear memories/associative memories (see Händler, chapter 1)

    (ii) truly parallel computers/vector computers ('pipeline computers').

The second characteristic is of considerable importance for parallel algorithms: a vector computer algorithm must be *consistent*, i.e. the order of magnitude of the total number of operations should not exceed the order of magnitude of the operations in the serial algorithm.

Finally, it is worth mentioning the problem of data storage. As an example, the STAR 100 needs long vectors to work efficiently whereas the Cray-1 functions efficiently even with short ones.

2   Principles for constructing parallel numerical algorithms

The basis for constructing a parallel algorithm is either a serial algorithm or the problem itself. In trying to parallelize a serial algorithm a pragmatic approach would seem reasonable. Serial algorithms are analysed for frequently occurring basic elements which are then put into parallel form. Sections 2.1 to 2.4 deal in this context with arithmetic expressions, vectorial elements of algorithms, parallelization by permutation and recursions. It is evident that at least some of these transformations may be done by a computer (section 2.4). This is very important for the re-use of expensive serial software on parallel computers.

The above-mentioned parallelization principles rely on definite serial algorithms. This corresponds to the serial way of thinking normally encountered in numerical analysis. What is needed is a parallel way of thinking (section 2.6). (It is of note that the parallel way of thinking is the most well-known technique in analogue/hybrid computation, see section 4.2.)

Asynchronous processes require a very different approach towards parallelization as different processors have then to work on the same problem but without any synchronization (section 2.7).

2.1 Arithmetic expressions

Arithmetic expressions are fundamental to numerical algorithms. Initially, we shall confine ourselves to large arithmetic expressions and adopt the point of view of complexity theory. It is only at the end of this section that some practical consequences are discussed.

The mathematical theory developed in the following is based on a hypothetical MIMD computer characterized by five axioms:

(A) At any time any processor can perform one operation
$\in B := \{+, -, *, /\}$.

(B) Different processors can perform different operations.

(C) Before performing an operation $\in B$ a processor may perform a unary operation that incurs *no* time. (A unary operation in this context is the inverse operation to addition or to multiplication.)

(D) Operations $\notin B$, such as transfer of data, storage and rearrangement of data, incur no time.

(E) Any operation $\in B$ incurs one time-unit.

Definition 2.1.1

An arithmetic expression of the type

$$E := (\ldots (a_1 \cdot a_2 + a_3) \cdot a_4 + a_5) \cdot a_6 + \ldots) \cdot a_{2n} + a_{2n+1} \qquad \square$$

is called a *generalized Horner algorithm.*

In the following, many considerations are only relevant to the generalized Horner algorithm.

Definition 2.1.2

Two arithmetic expressions E and $\tilde{E}$ are called *equivalent*, $E \sim \tilde{E}$, if and only if a finite series of applications of the associative, commutative and distributive laws leads from E to $\tilde{E}$ and vice versa. □

All algorithms for the parallel evaluation of arithmetic expressions are based on the construction of equivalent arithmetic expressions. Incidentally, it is well known that the associative law does not hold true for the set of floating-point machine numbers. The construction of equivalent arithmetic expressions in this case *may* lead to numerical instability (see section 3.1).

We shall use the following notation:

t: number of parallel or serial time steps

p: number of processors

w: total number of operations performed by the algorithm

$|E|$: number of distinct variables in the expression E.

Example 2.1.3

The arithmetic expression

$$\tilde{E} := (a_1 \cdot a_2 \cdot a_4 \cdot a_6 + a_3 \cdot a_4 \cdot a_6) + (a_5 \cdot a_6 + a_7)$$

is equivalent to

$$E := ((a_1 \cdot a_2 + a_3) \cdot a_4 + a_5) \cdot a_6 + a_7.$$

The *directed acyclic graphs* G and $\tilde{G}$ corresponding to E and $\tilde{E}$ respectively are shown in figure 15.1. These graphs describe the serial and parallel evaluations of the given arithmetic expression. □

Table 15.1 contains a collection of well-known parallel algorithms and the corresponding t-, w- and p-values. This data refers to arithmetic expressions E

Figure 15.1.

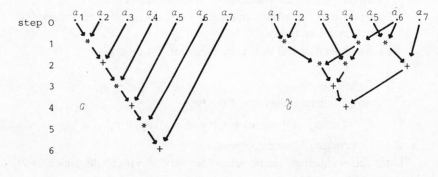

$t=6$, $p=1$ (serial) , $w=6$ $\qquad$ $t=4$, $p=3$ (parallel) , $w=8$

Table 15.1. *Survey of algorithms*

Algorithm number	Author	With division	Computing time t (in time steps)	Number of operations w	Number of processors used k
(1)	Maruyama [73]	yes	$\leqslant 6 \log_2 n + 4$	unknown	$6n$
(2)	Brent [73]	no	$\leqslant 4 \log_2 n$	$\leqslant 2(n-1)$	$\leqslant n-1$
(3)	Brent [73]	no	$\leqslant 3 \log_2 n$	$\leqslant 2.5(n-1)$	$\leqslant n-1$
(4)	Brent, Kuck & Maruyama [73]	no	$\leqslant 3 \log_2 n$	$\leqslant 3n^{1.585}$	$O(n^{1.585})$
(5)	Brent, Kuck & Maruyama [73]	no	$2.465 \log_2 n + O(1)$	$O(n^r), r>1$	$O(n^{1.712})$
(6)	Brent [74]	yes	$\leqslant 4 \log_2 n$	$\leqslant 10n - 18$	$\leqslant 3(n-1)$
(7)	Winograd [75][1]	no	$(\log_2 n)^2 + O(\log_2 n)$	$\leqslant 1.5n - 0.5 \log_2 n$	unknown
(8)	Winograd [75][1]	yes	$(\log_2 n)^2 + O(\log_2 n)$	$\leqslant 2.5n - 1.5 \log_2 n$	unknown
(9)	Vanek [75]	yes	$\leqslant 4 \log_2 n$	$\leqslant n^4$	$\leqslant 0.5n^4$
(10)	Muller & Preparata [76]	no	$\leqslant 2.081 \log_2 n$	$O(n^{1.82})$	$O(n^{1.82})$
(11)	Muller & Preparata [76]	yes	$\leqslant 2.88 \log_2 n + 1$	$O(n^{1.44})$	$O(n^{1.44})$
(12)	Snir & Barak [77][2]	no	$3n/(2p+1) + O(p^2)$	$1.5n + O(p^3)$	p
(13)	Snir & Barak [77][2]	yes	$5n/(2p+3) + O(p^2)$	$2.5n + O(p^3)$	p

[1] The parameter α used in the algorithm has the value 1.
[2] An initially fixed number of p processors is assumed.

characterized by

(∗): E contains n variables where every variable is referenced only once.

This entails no loss of generality as we can obtain (∗) by the renaming of variables.

All algorithms are based on the same principle: the directed acyclic graph describing the serial evaluation of E is a binary tree (owing to (∗)). Manipulations are performed on this tree according to the associative, distributive and commutative laws. Thus the binary tree is transformed into a directed acyclic graph $\bar{G}$ describing an expression $\tilde{E}$ equivalent to E. It is the aim of any algorithm to minimize $\tilde{t}$ ($\tilde{t}$ denotes the number of time steps necessary for the parallel evaluation of $\tilde{E}$). Algorithms (1)-(11) are based on the assumption that there are as many processors as necessary. Dependent on $|E|$, upper bounds for t, w and p are developed. If there is only a limited number p' of processors available Brent's lemma is used:

Lemma 2.1.4 (Brent [74])

If a computation can be performed in time t with w operations and sufficiently many processors then the computation can be performed in time

$$t' := t + (w - t)/p'$$

with p' such processors. □

(During the phase of restructuring an expression, algorithms (12) and (13) already take account of the limited number of processors: the corresponding graph may not contain more than p' nodes at any step.)

We shall confine ourselves to the Winograd algorithms (7) and (8). Both algorithms have a similar structure, so that one informal introduction serves for both of them.

In addition to the four arithmetic operations $\{+, -, *, /\}$ it will prove convenient to use the symbol $\div$ to denote the operation $a \div b := b/a$. The two operations $\{+, -\}$ are said to be additive and the three operations $\{*, /, \div\}$ multiplicative. We can always assume, without loss of generality, that an additive type of operation involves an addition operation. This is because any expression can be transformed into another expression which computes the same function without using the subtraction operation by replacing certain of the variables by their negations.

The *alternating expression* of n variables, denoted by $E_n(a_1, \ldots, a_n)$, is given by

$$E_n = (\ldots (a_1 \theta_1 a_2) \theta_2 a_3) \ldots a_{n-1}) \theta_{n-1} a_n),$$

where θ_i denotes one of the five operations and such that θ_i and θ_{i+1} are not of the same type ($1 \leqslant i \leqslant n - 2$). An alternating expression is called additive if θ_1 is an addition, otherwise it is called multiplicative. Any alternating expression E_n

can be decomposed as follows: there exist arithmetic expressions A, B, C with

(i) $E \sim A \cdot a_1 + B$

or

(ii) $E \sim B/(a_1 + A) + C.$

2.1.5 Winograd algorithm (8) (Winograd [75])

Let E be an arithmetic expression in which any variable occurs only once. First we calculate an alternating expression $\tilde{E}$ of additive or multiplicative type which is equivalent to E

$$\tilde{E} = (\ldots (F_1 \theta_1 F_2) \theta_2 \ldots) \theta_{k-1} F_k,$$

where F_i are subexpressions of E. A parameter α controls the choice of those variables which occur in F_1 and decomposes F_1 into two subexpressions G and H with

$$F_1 = G\theta H, \quad \theta \in \{+, *, /, \div\}.$$

Dependent on k there are two cases:

(i) $k = 1$ (i.e. $\tilde{E} = F_1 = G\theta H$): by recursive use of this procedure we obtain G and H and finally $\tilde{E} = G\theta H$

(ii) $k > 1$: we calculate $G, H, F_2, \ldots, F_k$ and use the procedure for F_2 etc. $\square$

An example is now given which serves to illustrate the difficulties which may occur during the parallel evaluation of arithmetic expressions with divisions, as the restructuring may lead to divisions by zero not present in the original expression.

Example 2.1.6

$$E := a_6 / (a_7 / (a_1 \cdot a_2 \cdot a_3 \cdot a_4 \cdot a_5) + a_8)$$

The Winograd algorithm yields ($\alpha = 1$):

$$\tilde{E} := -\frac{a_6}{a_8} \cdot \frac{a_7}{a_8} \left/ \left(a_1 \cdot a_2 \cdot a_3 \cdot a_4 \cdot a_5 + \frac{a_7}{a_8} \right) \right. + \frac{a_6}{a_8}$$

$a_i := 1$ ($i = 1, \ldots, 7$) and $a_8 := 0$ yields $E := 1$, but the evaluation of $\tilde{E}$ contains a division by zero. $\square$

Vanek's algorithm [75] (number (9) in table 15.1) avoids this difficulty!

Now we reconsider the generalized Horner algorithm in which there is a remarkable connection between t and w (t the number of time steps and w the number of operations in the algorithm):

Theorem 2.1.7 (Hyafil & Kung [77])

Let A be *any* algorithm for the evaluation of the generalized Horner algorithm:

$$E := (\ldots (a_1 \cdot a_2 + a_3) \cdot a_4 + a_5) \cdot a_6 + \ldots) \cdot a_{2n} + a_{2n+1}.$$

It can then be deduced that:

$$w \geqslant 3n - (t/2). \qquad \square$$

This statement is equivalent to

$$t < 2n \iff w > 2n.$$

Since the serial algorithm needs exactly $t = 2n$ time steps, each faster parallel algorithm needs more operations than the serial algorithm. This has certain consequences for vector computers: A vector computer algorithm should be consistent, i.e. the total number of operations must by definition not exceed the total number of operations in the serial algorithm.

At present, the actual parallelization of arithmetic expressions is carried out using more empirical methods than the above mentioned. This is not surprising because the Winograd and related algorithms refer chiefly to large arithmetic expressions. Large arithmetic expressions are, however, to be found in computer programs. A starting point would therefore be to develop computational methods of detecting and analysing large arithmetic expressions in machine-code compiler outputs.

Moreover there is probably more interest in solving another problem: that of constructing parallel algorithms which evaluate arithmetic expressions in a numerically stable manner on actually implemented computers (see section 3.3).

2.2 *Vectorial elements in algorithms*

There are many serial algorithms which contain *vectorial elements*, i.e. operations between vectors or matrices and vectors. The parallelization of these operations is straightforward. This is the reason why the terms 'vectorization' and 'parallelization' are frequently used synonymously. Nevertheless, vectorization is a special case of parallelization.

The parallelization of algorithms such as *Gaussian elimination* is fairly simple. The kernel of this problem – the computation of the inner products – can be performed satisfactorily on parallel computers (section 2.4). On the other hand, the parallel implementation of fairly simple algorithms such as a pivoting strategy gives rise to serious problems.

Many *iterative methods* – in particular iterative methods in linear algebra – are formulated in terms of matrices and vectors. But there are important iterative methods, such as successive over-relaxation (SOR), which need the application of certain tricks before parallelization becomes possible.

Many algorithms compute not just one value but a block of values. Examples are solution of equations and minimization. Other algorithms may be modified in order to calculate a block of values. One well-known example is the Worland algorithm for the initial value problem (IVP) (Worland [76]):

$$y' = f(x,y), \quad y(x_0) := y_0.$$

It is not difficult to solve a system of n differential equations on n processors but it is *not* obvious how best to solve n differential equations on $k > n$ processors!

Let us consider one single differential equation and let y_n denote the numerical approximation for $y(x_n), x_n = x_0 + n \cdot \Delta x$. Worland's proposal is then to compute $y_{n+1}, y_{n+2}, \ldots, y_{n+k}$ on k processors as shown in figure 15.2.

Example 2.2.1 $k = 2$

Algorithm:

$$y_{n+1,0} := y_n + h \cdot y_n'$$

$$y_{n+2,0} := y_n + 2h \cdot y_n'$$

for $s := 0$ **step** 1 **until** 2 **do**

$$y_{n+1,s+1} := y_n + \frac{h}{12} (5y_n' + 8y_{n+1,s}' - y_{n+2,s}')$$

$$y_{n+2,s+1} := y_n + \frac{h}{3} (y_n' + 4y_{n+1,s}' + y_{n+2,s}')$$

Speed-up ratio $S_2 = 5/3$ (measured in terms of number of function evaluations).

□

2.3 *Parallelization by permutation*

There is an obvious parallelization of the Jacobi iterative method but it is well known that this method is not the best one. However, improved methods such as successive over-relaxation seem to be serial in nature. It is therefore surprising that the *permutation* of equations and variables leads to a very satisfactory parallel algorithm.

We shall now discuss parallelization by permutation for two algorithms which refer to the same mathematical problem: the solution of a tridiagonal linear

Figure 15.2.

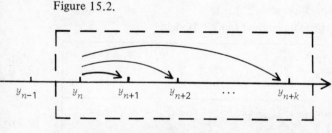

k-point block

system of equations

$$Ax = r \tag{2.3.1}$$

with

$$Ax = \begin{bmatrix} a_1 & b_1 & & & & \\ c_2 & a_2 & b_2 & & 0 & \\ & c_3 & a_3 & b_3 & & \\ & & & \cdot & \cdot & \cdot \\ 0 & & & & \cdot & \cdot \\ & & & & c_n & a_n \end{bmatrix} \begin{bmatrix} x_1 \\ x_2 \\ x_3 \\ \cdot \\ \cdot \\ x_n \end{bmatrix} = \begin{bmatrix} r_1 \\ r_2 \\ r_3 \\ \cdot \\ \cdot \\ r_n \end{bmatrix} =: r \tag{2.3.2}$$

The SOR method

$$\begin{aligned} a_1 x_1^{(k+1)} &= (1-\omega)a_1 x_1^{(k)} & & -\omega b_1 x_2^{(k)} + \omega r_1 \\ a_i x_i^{(k+1)} &= (1-\omega)a_i x_i^{(k)} - \omega c_i x_{i-1}^{(k+1)} & & -\omega b_i x_{i+1}^{(k)} + \omega r_i \\ a_n x_n^{(k+1)} &= (1-\omega)a_n x_n^{(k)} - \omega c_n x_{n-1}^{(k+1)} & & + \omega r_n \end{aligned} \tag{2.3.3}$$

with $i = 2, \ldots, n-1$ seems to have no potential for parallelization. The clue to the solution of the problem is a permutation ('red-black ordering' or 'checkerboard ordering', e.g. Young [71], Lambiotte & Voigt [75], Buzbee, Golub & Howell [77]):

$$PAP^T y := \bar{A}y = z \Leftrightarrow$$

$$\underbrace{\begin{bmatrix} a_1 & & & | & b_1 & & & \\ & a_3 & 0 & | & c_3 & b_3 & 0 & \\ & & \cdot & | & & \cdot & \cdot & \\ 0 & & \cdot a_{2k-1} & | & 0 & & c_{2k-1} & b_{2k-1} \\ \hline c_2 & b_2 & & | & a_2 & & & \\ & c_4 & b_4 & 0 & | & & a_4 & 0 \\ & & \cdot & \cdot & | & & & \cdot \\ 0 & & \cdot c_{2k} & | & 0 & & & a_{2k} \end{bmatrix}}_{\bar{A}} \cdot \underbrace{\begin{bmatrix} x_1 \\ x_3 \\ \cdot \\ x_{2k-1} \\ \hline x_2 \\ x_4 \\ \cdot \\ x_{2k} \end{bmatrix}}_{y} = \underbrace{\begin{bmatrix} r_1 \\ r_3 \\ \cdot \\ r_{2k-1} \\ \hline r_2 \\ r_4 \\ \cdot \\ r_{2k} \end{bmatrix}}_{z} \tag{2.3.4}$$

(without loss of generality: $n := 2^k$).

Application of the SOR method to (2.3.4) yields

$$\begin{aligned} a_1 y_1^{(k+1)} &= (1-\omega)a_1 \cdot y_1^{(k)} & & -\omega b_1 \cdot y_{(n/2)+1}^{(k)} + \omega z_1 \\ a_{2i-1} y_i^{(k+1)} &= (1-\omega)a_{2i-1} \cdot y_i^{(k)} - \omega c_{2i-1} \cdot y_{(n/2)+i-1}^{(k)} & & -\omega b_{2i-1} \cdot y_{(n/2)+i}^{(k)} + \omega z_i \\ & \qquad i = 2, \ldots, n/2 \end{aligned} \tag{2.3.5}$$

$$\begin{aligned} a_{2i} y_{(n/2)+i}^{(k+1)} &= (1-\omega)a_{2i} \cdot y_{(n/2)+i}^{(k)} - \omega c_{2i} \cdot y_i^{(k+1)} - \omega b_{2i} \cdot y_{i+1}^{(k+1)} + \omega z_{(n/2)+i} \\ a_n y_n^{(k+1)} &= (1-\omega)a_n \cdot y_n^{(k)} - \omega c_n \cdot y_{(n/2)}^{(k+1)} + \omega z_n \\ & \qquad i = 1, \ldots, (n/2)-1 \end{aligned} \tag{2.3.6}$$

Supposing $y_1^{(k)}, \ldots, y_n^{(k)}$ are known, $y_1^{(k+1)}, \ldots, y_{n/2}^{(k+1)}$ can be computed in parallel according to (2.3.5). (2.3.6) yields (in parallel!) $y_{(n/2)+1}^{(k+1)}, \ldots, y_n^{(k+1)}$. It is possible to formulate the SOR method in terms of vectors of length $n/2$.

Parallelization by permutation also forms the basis of the '*odd–even reduction*' ('cyclic reduction'; e.g. Lambiotte & Voigt [75], Madsen & Rodrique [77]). The idea is to eliminate certain coefficients in the equations by elementary row transformations. By permutation we obtain a tridiagonal linear system of equations of order $n/2$.

For the sake of simplicity the method is now illustrated for $n = 8$. Let $R(k)$ denote the k-th row of $Ax = r$. The elementary row transformation

$$R(2i) \to R(2i) - (c_{2i}/a_{2i-1}) \cdot R(2i-1) - (b_{2i}/a_{2i+1}) \cdot R(2i+1) \quad (2.3.7)$$

eliminates references to odd numbered variables in the even numbered equations. We get a tridiagonal system of equations for x_2, x_4, x_6, x_8:

$$-(c_{2i-1} \cdot c_{2i}/a_{2i-1})x_{2i-2} + (a_{2i} - b_{2i-1} \cdot c_{2i}/a_{2i-1} - b_{2i}c_{2i+1}/a_{2i+1})x_{2i}$$
$$- (b_{2i} \cdot b_{2i+1}/a_{2i+1})x_{2i+2} = r_{2i} - (c_{2i}/a_{2i-1})r_{2i-1} - (b_{2i}/a_{2i+1})r_{2i+1};$$
$$i = 1, 2, 3, 4 \quad (2.3.8)$$

$(c_1 := b_8 := 0)$.

The repeated application of this reduction process leads to a single equation for x_8. We obtain the other unknowns by back substitution.

The general case is discussed in the papers cited above.

2.4 Recurrence problems

Many numerical algorithms compute a series $x_1, \ldots, x_n$ $(x_i \in \mathbb{R})$ whereby x_i may depend on all x_j $(j < i)$. The equations describing this dependence are called *recurrent equations*. If there are given initial values for a certain x_k we speak of a *recurrence problem*. If one is interested only in x_n the term 'recurrence problem with scalar result' is used, otherwise the term 'recurrence problem with vector result' is employed (see Schendel [79]).

Example 2.4.1
The inner product of two vectors $x = (x_1, \ldots, x_n)^T$ and $y = (y_1, \ldots, y_n)^T$ can be written as a linear recurrence problem of order 1 with scalar result:

$$z_0 := 0$$
$$z_k := z_{k-1} + x_k \cdot y_k, \quad 1 \leqslant k \leqslant n \qquad \square$$

Example 2.4.2
The Horner algorithm for the evaluation of

$$P_n(x_0) := \sum_{i=0}^{n} a_i \cdot x_0^i$$

leads to a linear recurrence problem of order 1 with scalar result:

$$P_0 := a_n$$
$$P_k := a_{n-k} + x_0 \cdot P_{k-1}, \quad 1 \leqslant k \leqslant n \qquad \square$$

Example 2.4.3
The $L \cdot U$ decomposition of a tridiagonal matrix

$$A := \begin{bmatrix} a_1 & b_1 & & 0 \\ c_2 & a_2 & b_2 & \\ & \cdot & \cdot & \cdot \\ & & \cdot & \cdot & \cdot \\ 0 & & c_n & a_n \end{bmatrix} = L \cdot U; \quad L := \begin{bmatrix} 1 & & & 0 \\ l_2 & 1 & & \\ & \cdot & \cdot & \\ & & \cdot & \cdot \\ 0 & & l_n & 1 \end{bmatrix}; \quad U := \begin{bmatrix} u_1 & b_1 & & 0 \\ & u_2 & b_2 & \\ & & \cdot & \cdot \\ & & & \cdot & \cdot \\ 0 & & & u_n \end{bmatrix}$$

leads to a non-linear recurrence problem of order 1 with vector result:

$$u_1 := a_1$$
$$u_k := a_k - c_k \cdot b_{k-1}/u_{k-1}, \quad 2 \leqslant k \leqslant n \qquad (2.4.1)$$

Supposing the u_k are known, the l_k may be computed in parallel according to

$$l_k := c_k/u_{k-1}. \qquad \square$$

Linear recurrence problems
Definition 2.4.4
Let $m \leqslant n-1$. A linear recurrence problem $R\langle n,m\rangle$ of order m for n
equations is given by

$$R\langle n,m\rangle: \quad x_k := \begin{cases} 0 & k \leqslant 0 \\ \\ c_k + \displaystyle\sum_{j=k-m}^{k-1} a_{kj} \cdot x_j & 1 \leqslant k \leqslant n \end{cases} \qquad (2.4.2)$$

If

$$A := (a_{ik}), \quad i,k = 1, \ldots, n$$

is a strictly lower triangular matrix and

$$x := (x_1, \ldots, x_n)^T, \quad c := (c_1, \ldots, c_n)^T$$

then (2.4.2) can be written in the form

$$x = Ax + c.$$

We shall now discuss three algorithms: the column sweep algorithm applicable to
all linear recurrence problems; the log sum algorithm applicable to associative
recurrence functions and fundamental to the construction of many other
algorithms; and the recurrent product algorithm which is very economic for
linear recurrence problems $R\langle n,m\rangle$ with small m.

2.4.5 Column sweep algorithm

$$
\begin{aligned}
x_1 &:= c_1 \\
x_2 &:= c_2 + a_{2\,1}x_1 \\
x_3 &:= c_3 + a_{3\,1}x_1 + a_{3\,2}x_2 \\
&\;\vdots \\
x_{m+1} &:= c_{m+1} + a_{m+1\,1}x_1 + a_{m+1\,2}x_2 + \ldots + a_{m+1\,m}x_m \\
x_{m+2} &:= c_{m+2} + a_{m+2\,2}x_2 + \ldots + a_{m+2\,m}x_m + a_{m+2\,m+1}x_{m+1} \\
&\;\vdots \\
x_n &:= c_n + a_{n\,n-m}x_{n-m} + \ldots
\end{aligned}
$$

$$=: c^1 \qquad =: c^2$$

Step 1: x_1 is known. The expressions

$$c_i^1 := a_{i1}x_1 + c_i, \quad 2 \leqslant i \leqslant m+1$$

may be calculated in parallel. x_2 is known.

Step 2: x_1, x_2 are known. The expressions

$$c_i^2 := a_{i2}x_2 + c_i^1, \quad 3 \leqslant i \leqslant m+1$$

$$c_{m+2}^2 := a_{m+2\,2}x_2 + c_{m+2}$$

may be calculated in parallel. x_3 is known. And so on. □

Altogether we need $n-1$ steps and m processors. The speed-up ratio is

$$S_m = O(m).$$

This is not very efficient if $m \ll n$.

2.4.6 Log sum algorithm

This enables the efficient computation of associative (in general, non-linear) recurrence problems. We will illustrate this algorithm for a simple linear recurrence problem of order 1:

$$x_0 := 0$$

$$x_k := a_k + x_{k-1}, \quad 1 \leqslant k \leqslant n$$

$$\left(\text{i.e. } x_n = \sum_{k=1}^n a_k \right).$$

This algorithm exploits the associative law of addition to obtain maximal parallelization. This parallel algorithm and the well-known serial algorithm are illustrated in figure 15.3. Without loss of generality it is assumed that $n = 2^k$. This principle of *recursive doubling* holds true for any associative binary operation on a set M. Examples are addition and multiplication of real numbers, max and min operations on real numbers, addition and multiplication of matrices.

The log sum algorithm (i.e. recursive doubling) is especially suited to real SIMD computers.

2.4.7 Recurrent product algorithm

This uses the fact that the solution x of a $R\langle n, n-1 \rangle$ system

$$x = Ax + c, \tag{2.4.3}$$

where A is a strictly lower triangular matrix, allows the special representation

$$x = (I - A)^{-1} \cdot c = L^{-1} \cdot c$$

to be used with

$$L^{-1} = M_n \cdot M_{n-1} \cdot \ldots \cdot M_1$$

(see Kogge [74])

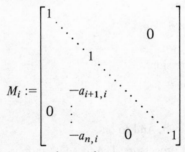

x can be computed according to

$$x = M_n \cdot M_{n-1} \cdot \ldots \cdot M_1 \cdot c$$

and this can be done by recursive doubling in $O(\log_2 n)$ time steps. The modifications for $R\langle n, m \rangle$ systems are self-explanatory.

Figure 15.3.

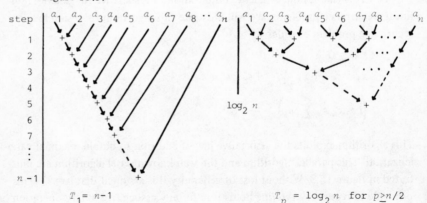

General recurrence problems
Definition 2.4.8 (Kogge [72])

A general recurrence problem $R\langle n,m\rangle$ of order m is given by

$$R\langle n,m\rangle: \quad x_k := H[\bar{a}_k; x_{k-1}, x_{k-2}, \ldots, x_{k-m}], \quad 1 \leqslant k \leqslant n$$

and m initial values $x_{-m+1}, \ldots, x_0$. ☐

H is called a recurrence function, $\bar{a}_k$ is a vector of parameters not dependent on x_i ($1 \leqslant i \leqslant n$).

Example 2.4.3 contained a fairly simple example of a non-linear recurrence problem (formula (2.4.1)):

$$u_1 := a_1$$
$$u_k := a_k - c_k \cdot b_{k-1}/u_{k-1}, \quad 2 \leqslant k \leqslant n.$$

Traub [73] suggested the transformation of (2.4.1) into a quasi-iteration:

$$u_k^{(i)} := a_k - c_k \cdot b_{k-1}/u_{k-1}^{(i-1)}, \quad i = 1, 2, \ldots. \tag{2.4.4}$$

Since $u_1 = u_1^{(i)} = a_1$ is exact, all $u_k^{(j)}$ with $k \leqslant j+1$ are exact. Under certain circumstances Traub's proposal may produce acceptable results. Nevertheless, this transformation is not advisable for the general case.

A very interesting way of solving (2.4.1) has been suggested by Stone [73]: multiplication of (2.4.1) by u_{k-1} yields

$$u_k \cdot u_{k-1} = a_k \cdot u_{k-1} - c_k \cdot b_{k-1}$$
$$q_0 := 1; \quad q_1 := a_1; \quad q_k := u_k q_{k-1}$$
$$\Rightarrow \frac{q_k}{q_{k-1}} \cdot \frac{q_{k-1}}{q_{k-2}} = a_k \cdot \frac{q_{k-1}}{q_{k-2}} - c_k \cdot b_{k-1}$$
$$\Leftrightarrow q_k = a_k \cdot q_{k-1} - c_k \cdot b_{k-1} \cdot q_{k-2}.$$

The non-linear recurrence function (2.4.1) has been transformed into a linear recurrence function of order 2. With the identity $q_{k-1} = q_{k-1}$ we obtain

$$Q_k := \begin{bmatrix} q_k \\ q_{k-1} \end{bmatrix} := \underbrace{\begin{bmatrix} a_k & -c_k \cdot b_{k-1} \\ 1 & 0 \end{bmatrix}}_{=: G_k} \cdot \begin{bmatrix} q_{k-1} \\ q_{k-2} \end{bmatrix} = G_k \cdot Q_{k-1}$$

$$\Rightarrow$$

$$Q_k = \begin{bmatrix} q_k \\ q_{k-1} \end{bmatrix} = \left(\prod_{j=2}^{k} G_j \right) \cdot Q_1 \tag{2.4.5}$$

This recurrence function may be evaluated by means of the log sum algorithm.

Definition 2.4.9 (Kogge [73])

Let H be an (in general) non-linear recurrence function of order 1:

$$x_k := H(\bar{a}_k; x_{k-1}); \quad \bar{a}_k \in \mathbb{R}^p; \quad x_0.$$

H is said to be *semi-associative* with respect to a *companion function G*, if there exists a function $G: \mathbb{R}^p \times \mathbb{R}^p \to \mathbb{R}^p$ such that

$$\forall x \in \mathbb{R}, \bar{a}, \bar{b} \in \mathbb{R}^p : [H(\bar{a}; H(\bar{b}; x)) = H(G(\bar{a}, \bar{b}); x)] \qquad \square$$

This procedure is a generalization of Stone's concept of transforming the non-linear, non-associative recurrence function (2.4.1) into an associative recurrence function.

Corollary 2.4.10

$$\forall x \in \mathbb{R}, \bar{a}, \bar{b}, \bar{c} \in \mathbb{R}^p : [H(G(\bar{a}, G(\bar{b}, \bar{c})); x) = H(G(G(\bar{a}, \bar{b}), \bar{c}); x)] \qquad \square$$

Repeated application of definition 2.4.9 yields

$$x_2 = H(\bar{a}_2; x_1) = H(\bar{a}_2; H(\bar{a}_1; x_0)) = H(G(\bar{a}_2, \bar{a}_1); x_0)$$

$$x_4 = H(\bar{a}_4; x_3) = H(\bar{a}_4; H(\bar{a}_3; x_2)) = H(G(\bar{a}_4, \bar{a}_3); x_2)$$

$$= H(G(\bar{a}_4, \bar{a}_3); H(G(\bar{a}_2, \bar{a}_1); x_0))$$

$$= H(G(G(\bar{a}_4, \bar{a}_3), G(\bar{a}_2, \bar{a}_1)); x_0)$$

$$x_8 = H(\bar{a}_8; x_7) = H(\bar{a}_8; H(\bar{a}_7; H(\bar{a}_6; H(\bar{a}_5; x_4))))$$

$$= H(G(\bar{a}_8, \bar{a}_7); H(G(\bar{a}_6, \bar{a}_5); x_4))$$

$$= H(G(\bar{a}_8, \bar{a}_7); H(G(\bar{a}_6, \bar{a}_5); H(G(G(\bar{a}_4, \bar{a}_3), G(\bar{a}_2, \bar{a}_1); x_0))))$$

$$= H(G(G(\bar{a}_8, \bar{a}_7), G(\bar{a}_6, \bar{a}_5)); H(G(G(\bar{a}_4, \bar{a}_3), G(\bar{a}_2, \bar{a}_1); x_0)))$$

$$= H(G(G(G(\bar{a}_8, \bar{a}_7), G(\bar{a}_6, \bar{a}_5)), G(G(\bar{a}_4, \bar{a}_3), G(\bar{a}_2, \bar{a}_1))); x_0)$$

The computation of x_{2^k} is shown in figure 15.4. Kogge [73] gives some examples for linear and non-linear recurrence functions for which a companion

Figure 15.4.

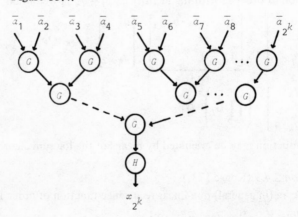

function exists. Non-linear recurrence functions of higher order may be handled by *companion sets* (see Kogge [73]).

There are some papers which discuss the maximum attainable speed-up ratio for recurrence problems. However, these papers restrict themselves in general to algebraic transformations.

> *Example 2.4.11*
>
> $\sqrt{a}$ may be computed using Newton's iterative method of approximation
>
> $$x_{n+1} := (x_n^2 + a)/2x_n; \quad n = 0, 1, \ldots \text{ and } x_0 > \sqrt{a}. \tag{2.4.6}$$
>
> There is no real speed-up for this algorithm if one restricts oneself to algebraic transformations. Application of the transcendental transformation
>
> $$y_k := \text{arc coth} (x_k/\sqrt{a}) \tag{2.4.7}$$
>
> yields
>
> $$y_{n+1} = 2y_n$$
>
> and this recurrence function may be computed very fast in parallel. (Transformation (2.4.7) and the back transformation are not feasible in practice because $\sqrt{a}$ still has to be computed!) □

2.5 Automatic translation of serial programs into parallel form

An already known serial algorithm has provided the starting point for all transformations in sections 2.1 to 2.4. It would therefore seem reasonable to look for an automatic translation of a programmed serial algorithm into a parallel one.

If one ignores the mathematical contents, parallelism in Algol and Fortran programs are hidden in DO loops. This is the reason why most compilers for parallel computers transform serial DO loops into DO loops executable in parallel (Lamport [74], 'auto-vectorizer'). This kind of automatic parallelization is fundamental to the re-use of existing (serial) numerical software on parallel computers. Compare Banerjee, Chen, Kuck & Towle [79], Evans & Williams [80] and Williams & Evans [80].

In general, transformation programs for the automatic parallelization of serial algorithms analyse the data flow of the serial algorithm. This serial data flow may be transformed into a data flow with maximal parallelism by applying certain concepts of operating systems.

A third approach results from inspection of a serial compiler's output. This output contains 'large' arithmetic expressions, at least to some extent, and these arithmetic expressions may be parallelized by the algorithms in section 2.1.

2.6   The parallel way of thinking

Most numerical algorithms are based on a serial way of thinking. This is partly due to the human way of *solving* a problem, partly to the availability of serial computers.

As an example, consider the triangulation of a matrix A

$$A = L \cdot U.$$

The computation of the elements of L and U reduces to some non-linear recurrence problems, which can only be parallelized by using certain tricks (see section 2.4). On the other hand, Evans & Hatzopoulos [79] analyse a different decomposition of A, namely

$$A = W \cdot Z$$

$$
W := \begin{bmatrix}
1 & & & & 0 \\
w_{2,1} & 1 & 0 & 0 & w_{2,n} \\
& & \cdot & & \\
w_{n-1,1} & 0 & & 1 & w_{n-1,n} \\
0 & \cdot & & & 1
\end{bmatrix}
$$

$$
Z := \begin{bmatrix}
z_{1,1} & z_{1,2} & \cdots & z_{1,n-1} & z_{1,n} \\
& z_{2,2} & \cdots & z_{2,n-1} & \\
0 & & \cdot & & 0 \\
& z_{n-1,2} & \cdots & z_{n-1,n-1} & \\
z_{n,1} & z_{n,2} & \cdots & z_{n,n-1} & z_{n,n}
\end{bmatrix}
$$

This decomposition leads in a quite natural manner to parallel algorithms. There are thus parallel algorithms if only one looks for them (see Evans, chapter 17).

A second example is the solution of tridiagonal linear systems of equations. We have discussed some methods for parallelizing well-known algorithms for the solution of this problem. But none of these parallel algorithms contains a *pivoting strategy* and there is no possibility of including one (see Lambiotte & Voigt [75]). The numerical stability of these algorithms can therefore only be guaranteed for diagonal-dominant matrices. In this context, Swarztrauber [79] constructed a parallel algorithm which is based upon Cramer's rule and needs no pivoting strategy. The numerical behaviour of this algorithm is satisfactory. There are once again parallel algorithms if only one looks for them.

Finally, it is worth mentioning those types of computer for which the parallel way of thinking is essential: analogue/hybrid computers. Analogue/hybrid algorithms are therefore a suitable starting point for the construction of digital parallel algorithms. One example will be given in section 4.2: multirate methods.

2.7   *Asynchronous numerical processes*

Asynchronous numerical processes are based on the concept of the MIMD computer. The motivation for this type of parallel algorithm stems from the fact that no parallel algorithm will load all processors equally. The synchronization of the different processors may thus lead to a considerable drop in computer performance. It would then seem reasonable to look for algorithms which work on different processors without any synchronization. Algorithms of this type are called asynchronous numerical processes (see section 4.4). Let

$$F(x) := \begin{bmatrix} f_1(x) \\ \vdots \\ f_k(x) \end{bmatrix}, \quad x := \begin{bmatrix} x_1 \\ \vdots \\ x_k \end{bmatrix}, \quad F : \mathbb{R}^k \to \mathbb{R}^k$$

Let $J := (J_j)_{j=1}^{\infty}$ be a sequence of non-empty subsets of $\{1, \ldots, k\}$ and let

$$S := \begin{bmatrix} s_{1,j} \\ \vdots \\ s_{k,j} \end{bmatrix}_{j=1}^{\infty}$$

be a sequence of elements of $\mathbb{N}^k$.

Definition 2.7.1

A sequence

$$(x_j)_{j=1}^{\infty} = \begin{bmatrix} x_{1,j} \\ \vdots \\ x_{k,j} \end{bmatrix} \in \mathbb{R}^k$$

is called an asynchronous iteration if the sequence $(x_j)_{j=1}^{\infty}$ is determined by a quadruple (F, x_0, J, S) in the following way:

(1) F, J, S as defined above, $x_0 = \begin{bmatrix} x_{1,0} \\ \vdots \\ x_{k,0} \end{bmatrix}$

(2) $x_{i,j} := \begin{cases} x_{i,j-1} & , \text{ for } i \notin J_j \\ f_i(x_{1,s_{1,j}}, \ldots, x_{k,s_{k,j}}), \text{ for } i \in J_j \end{cases}$

(3) i occurs infinitely often in the sets $J_j; j = 1, 2, \ldots$

(4) $\forall i \in \{1, \ldots, k\} \ [1 \leqslant j - s_{i,j}, j = 1, 2, \ldots \text{ and } \lim_{j \to \infty} s_{i,j} = \infty]$ □

Theorem 2.7.2 (Baudet [76])

Let F map the closed subset $D \subset \mathbb{R}^k$ into itself and let it satisfy the

Lipschitz condition:

$$\forall x, y \in D \; [\|F(x) - F(y)\| \leqslant A \cdot \|x - y\| \wedge A < 1].$$

Then every asynchronous iteration (F, x_0, J, S) with the starting point $x_0 \in D$ converges to the unique fixed point of F in D. $\qquad \Box$

3 Numerical stability of parallel algorithms

The numerical quality of an algorithm can be judged by two aspects: (i) complexity (amount of computing time) and (ii) numerical stability (insensitivity to round-off error). In the early days of parallel computing, complexity (i.e. maximum parallelization) was the prime aim. Only in the last few years has a growing interest developed for numerical stability. We shall discuss this concept of numerical stability and its application to the parallel evaluation of arithmetic expressions. Only a few brief remarks are devoted to the numerical stability of algorithms for solving tridiagonal linear systems of equations.

Numerical algorithms on real computers produce results which in general contain a certain type of round-off error. This error can be divided into two components:

(i) Inaccurate input data will produce an error in the final result, even if the computation itself is performed exactly.

(ii) Real-life computers produce round-off effors at every step.

These errors accumulate up to the end of the computation. An algorithm is called *numerically stable* if error (ii) does not exceed error (i). There are two methods of analysing the numerical stability of an algorithm: the backward analysis technique of Wilkinson [63] and forward analysis. We shall apply these methods to the Winograd algorithm of section 2.1 (see sections 3.1 and 3.2). Section 3.3 outlines the basic features of an algorithm which is:

numerically stable even for arithmetic expressions with division
well-suited for vector computers such as the Cray-1.

Section 3.4 contains some remarks on the numerical stability of tridiagonal linear systems of equations.

3.1 Backward analysis

The principle of backward analysis is as follows: the numerical evaluation of an arithmetic expression E yields a result $\bar{E}$ which contains some round-off error. $\bar{E}$ can be interpreted as the exact evaluation of E with slightly changed input data. If these deviations of the input data do not exceed the round-off error of the input data the numerical algorithm is termed numerically stable.

Mathematically, the backward analysis essentially consists of transferring the round-off errors to the input data (variables).

Example 3.1.1

$$E := a_1 \cdot a_2 \cdot a_3 \cdot a_4 \cdot (a_5 \cdot a_6) \cdot a_7 \cdot (a_8 \cdot a_{10}) + (a_9 \cdot a_{10} + a_{11})$$

We assume that the arithmetic operations satisfy the following equations (Wilkinson [63], using a single-precision accumulator):

$$fl(a \cdot b) = a \cdot b \cdot (1 + \epsilon_1),$$
$$fl(a/b) = a/b \cdot (1 + \epsilon_2),$$
$$fl(a + b) = a \cdot (1 + \epsilon_3) + b \cdot (1 + \epsilon_4),$$
$$|\epsilon_i| \leqslant 4 \cdot \bar{\epsilon},$$

where $\bar{\epsilon}$ is the machine precision.

We can move directly up the rounding errors to the variables of E and obtain (see figure 15.5)

$$fl(E) = E(a_1, a_2\rho_{13}, a_3\rho_{12}, a_4\rho_{11}, a_5, a_6\rho_9\rho_{10}, a_7\rho_1\rho_8, a_8\rho_6\rho_7,$$
$$a_9\rho_3\rho_2\rho_5, a_{10}, a_{11}\rho_2\rho_4)$$

where

$$\rho_i := 1 + \epsilon_i \qquad \qquad \square$$

It is possible to formalize this technique in order to analyse Winograd's algorithm for arithmetic expressions without the division operation. Thus Winograd's algorithm proves to be numerically stable for arithmetic expressions without division (see Feilmeier & Segerer [77]).

Example 3.1.2

$$E := a_6/(a_7/(a_1 \cdot a_2 \cdot \ldots \cdot a_5) + a_8)$$

Figure 15.5.

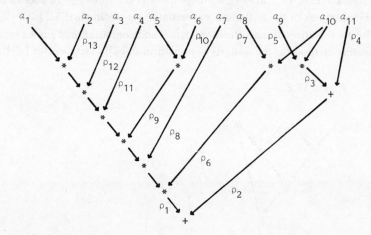

The Winograd algorithm yields

$$\tilde{E} = -\frac{a_6}{a_8} \cdot \frac{a_7}{a_8} \Bigg/ \left(a_1 \cdot a_2 \cdot \ldots \cdot a_5 + \frac{a_7}{a_8}\right) - \left(\frac{-a_6}{a_8}\right)$$

The computational graph for $\tilde{E}$ is shown in figure 15.6.

$$F_1 := a_1 \cdot a_2 \cdot a_3 \cdot a_4 \cdot a_5, \quad A := \frac{a_7}{a_8}, \quad C := \frac{-a_6}{a_8}.$$

As can be seen, it is impossible to move up all the rounding errors to the variables.   □

This example shows that backward analysis may fail for arithmetic expressions with division.

3.2   Forward analysis

This method tries to analyse the consequences of perturbations in input data:

$$x \to x(1 + \epsilon_x); \quad y \to y(1 + \epsilon_y)$$
$$x \cdot y(1 + \epsilon_{x \cdot y}) := x(1 + \epsilon_x) \cdot y(1 + \epsilon_y)$$

Linearization yields

$$\epsilon_{x \cdot y} = \epsilon_x + \epsilon_y$$

and in a similar manner we obtain

$$\epsilon_{x/y} = \epsilon_x - \epsilon_y$$
$$\epsilon_{x \pm y} = \frac{x}{x \pm y} \cdot \epsilon_x \pm \frac{y}{x \pm y} \cdot \epsilon_y \quad (x \pm y \neq 0)$$

Thus it is possible to define *magnification factors* for all types of arithmetic operations. Figure 15.7 shows the computational graph for the parallel and serial evaluations of the arithmetic expression $\tilde{E}$ (see example 3.1.2).

The combination of magnification factors and computational graphs yields an interesting method for the analysis of numerical stability (see Segerer [79]). This

Figure 15.6.

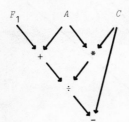

analysis can be done automatically – at least·to some extent (Larson & Sameh [78], Stummel [79]). It would thus be applicable to more complicated cases than example 3.1.2.

3.3   Rönsch's algorithm

The results of the numerical stability studies for arithmetic expressions may be summarized as follows: Winograd's algorithm (and some related algorithms) are numerically stable for arithmetic expressions without division. As far as arithmetic expressions with division are concerned, certain input data may make the algorithm numerically unstable. An interesting question arises: can input data always be found such that an arithmetic expression with division becomes numerically unstable? The answer is: no!

Theorem 3.3.1 (Rönsch [80])

Let E be an arbitrary arithmetic expression with distinct variables. Then the relative, accumulated rounding error R is bounded by the product

$$R \leqslant R_1 \cdot R_2,$$

where R_1 denotes the relative error due to inaccurate input data and R_2 denotes the number of plus and minus operations in E.   □

This means: the original expression E is always stable. Only the transformation process leading to the parallel evaluation of E may introduce numerical instability. If we succeed in controlling this transformation process in a suitable manner we can obtain a numerically stable algorithm. A careful analysis leads

Figure 15.7.

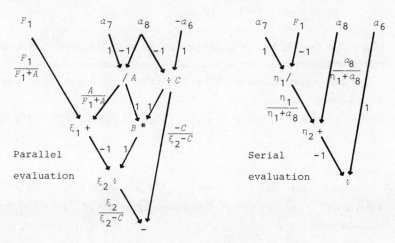

to the following restrictions in parallelizing a given arithmetic expression:

(1) The distributive law may give rise to numerical instability. It is therefore not used.

(2a) By introducing unary minus operations, binary minus operations are transformed into plus operations.

(2b) Some divisions can be transformed into multiplications.

(2a) and (2b) lead to an algorithm suitable for the evaluation of arbitrary arithmetic expressions on vector computers. The aim of this algorithm is to provide a comprehensive standardization of the separate operations in the expression. This makes it possible to use vector instructions much more effectively.

The algorithm will be introduced by an example (see 3.3.3) and is particularly suitable for vector computers with recursive pipelining features, e.g. Cray-1. This recursive feature is restricted in the Cray-1 to the ADD and MULTIPLY pipelines. It comes into operation automatically if, in an ADD or MULTIPLY vector instruction, one of the operand registers is also used as the result register. In this case, the output stream of the pipeline is fed back into the input stream. This 'short-circuiting' process provides a facility for reducing the 64 elements of a vector register to a smaller number appropriate to the particular operation.

A useful application of recursive pipelining is demonstrated in the following example.

Example 3.3.2
Consider an 8×8 matrix
$$A = (a_{ij}), \quad i, j = 1, \ldots, 8$$
If one wants to compute all row sums
$$R_i = \sum_{j=1}^{8} a_{ij} \quad i = 1, \ldots, 8$$
of A on the Cray-1, this can be done by a single vector instruction. However, the corresponding registers have to be initialized in the following manner.

The elements of the matrix A first have to be stored in a vector register $V0$ in the following form:

$$A = \begin{bmatrix} a_{11} & a_{12} & \ldots & a_{18} \\ a_{21} & a_{22} & \ldots & a_{28} \\ \cdot \\ \cdot \\ \cdot \\ a_{81} & a_{82} & \ldots & a_{88} \end{bmatrix} = \begin{bmatrix} V0(0) & V0(8) & \ldots & V0(56) \\ V0(1) & V0(9) & \ldots & V0(57) \\ \cdot \\ \cdot \\ \cdot \\ V0(7) & V0(15) & \ldots & V0(63) \end{bmatrix}$$

$V0(i)$ $(i = 0, \ldots, 63)$ denotes the i-th component of the 64 elements of the vector register $V0$.

The following three instructions are then performed:

Instructions	Comment
$VL := 64$	Vector length register is set
$V1(0) := 0.0$	Initial value for accumulation in $V1$
$V1 := V0 + V1$	$V1$ is used in recursive mode

The last eight elements of $V1$ now contain the row sums, i.e.

$$V1(56) = R_1$$
$$V1(57) = R_2$$
$$\vdots$$
$$V1(63) = R_8 \qquad\qquad\qquad\qquad\qquad \square$$

Example 3.3.3

Rönsch's algorithm will now be illustrated by an example. It transforms the binary tree representing an arbitrary arithmetic expression so as to adapt it for an effective computation making use of the recursive pipeline feature. Consider the expression represented by the tree in figure 15.8.

Using (2) (a), the binary minus operations at the nodes 3, 4 and 14 can be transformed into plus operations by introducing unary minus operations at the variables a_7, a_{10}, and a_{14}. Furthermore, three of the five division operations which appear in figure 15.8 can be transformed into multiplications, so that the tree finally has the form in figure 15.9. The change in the numbers of the different types of operation during the transformation process is shown in table 15.2.

Figure 15.8.

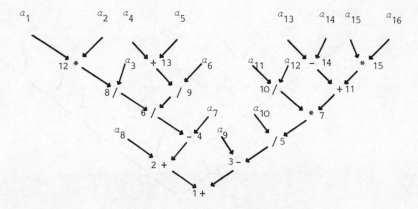

The comprehensive standardization performed by the algorithm can best be seen if the expression is represented by the so-called associative tree. In evaluating the expression according to the transformed tree (figure 15.10) vector instructions should first be used to replace the values of those variables which have been given unary minus operations by their negation.

The operations of the multiplication and addition levels can then be executed by using the recursive features of the corresponding pipelines. It is therefore necessary to organize the already computed results in the vector registers in a certain manner in order to exploit the recursive pipelining optimally.

The values of the division level have to be combined in such a way that the division can be performed in vector mode.

Finally, some remarks concerning the stability can be made:

(1) The introduction of the additional unary minus operations does not affect the stability as the negation of a machine number can be done exactly.

Table 15.2

Step	Number of operations				
	Addition	Subtraction	Division	Multiplication	Unary minus operations
① Original tree	4	3	5	3	–
② After applying (2a) to ①	7	–	5	3	3
③ After applying (2b) to ②	7	–	2	6	3
		←	sum = 15	→	

Figure 15.9.

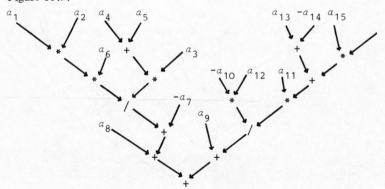

(2) According to theorem 3.3.1, the transformation of division into multiplication has no influence upon the stability. Moreover, this process has a positive effect on the time taken to evaluate the expression. Since a division requires four times longer to execute than a multiplication on the Cray-1, there is an obvious gain in speed. □

3.4 Tridiagonal linear systems of equations

There are four efficient parallel algorithms for the solution of tridiagonal linear systems of equation: $L \cdot U$ decomposition, the Givens' transformation to a bidiagonal matrix, the Gauss–Jordan algorithm and Swarztrauber's [79] method.

3.4.1 $L \cdot U$ decomposition (see section 2)

The decomposition of an $N \times N$ tridiagonal matrix needs $O(\log_2 N)$ time steps and $O(N)$ processors. Sameh & Brent [77] have noticed three serious disadvantages in this method:

(i) The decomposition may fail even if A is non-singular (see Gaussian elimination without pivoting).
(ii) Underflow or overflow can occur.
(iii) The bound for the absolute error increases exponentially with N. $(O(N^2 \cdot k^N \cdot \epsilon))$

3.4.2 Givens' transformation (Sameh & Kuck [77])

This method seems to be a very good one. $O(\log_2 N)$ time steps and $O(N)$ processors are required. The bound for the absolute error increases as $O(k \cdot N^c \cdot \epsilon)$.

3.4.3 Adaptation of Gaussian elimination

This algorithm (Madsen & Rodrigue [75]) needs $O(\log_2 N)$ time steps and $O(N)$ processors. There is no information concerning its numerical stability.

Figure 15.10.

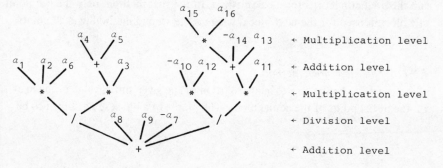

3.4.4   *Swarztrauber's [79] method* has already been mentioned in section 2.6.

4   Non-linear algorithms
A large number of non-linear parallel algorithms have already been developed. We shall consider three kinds:

(i) Numerical solution of ordinary differential equations (see sections 4.1 and 4.2).

(ii) Determination of zeros for functions of one or more variables (see sections 4.3 and 4.4).

(iii) Optimization of parameters (see sections 4.5-4.7).

These fields are not only important in practice but have also proved indispensable as a tool in many non-linear problems, e.g. partial differential equations. These algorithms provide some fundamental principles for constructing parallel methods. The efficiency of such parallel methods is limited, for example: the determination of zeros for real functions and the optimization of unimodal functions only allow a speed-up which increases logarithmically with the number of processors used.

4.1   Ordinary differential equations: block methods
Consider the equation

$$y' = f(x,y); \quad y(x_0) = y_0. \tag{4.1.1}$$

For simplicity we restrict the following description to $\mathbb{R}^1$. The generalization to a differential equation system follows clearly.

The set of all new function values which are evaluated during each application of the iteration formulae is called a block. For each k-point block k new function values are evaluated simultaneously. Block methods are thus especially suited to parallel computers.

In the following we shall consider only SIMD computers. A number of authors have shown that serial block methods can be compared with conventional integration methods as regards their consistency and stability.

Two forms of block methods are now introduced: the one-step block method and the predictor–corrector block method. In the first method, only the last point of a block is used for the next block, whereas the second method uses all points of the preceding block.

4.1.1   One-step block method
Let y_n be the approximate solution of the given initial value problem at x_n, the initial point of the actual block. The points of a block are assumed to be

equidistant:

$$x_{n+r} = x_n + rh, \quad r = 1, \ldots, k.$$

The example of a 2-point block illustrates the parallelization principle. The serial formulae for a method of order 4 are (see Rosser [67]):

$$y_{n+1,0} = y_n + hy'_n$$

$$y_{n+1,1} = y_n + \frac{h}{2}(y'_n + y'_{n+1,0})$$

$$y_{n+2,1} = y_n + 2hy'_{n+1,1} \tag{4.1.2}$$

$$y_{n+1,2} = y_n + \frac{h}{12}(5y'_n + 8y'_{n+1,1} - y'_{n+2,1})$$

$$y_{n+2,2} = y_n + \frac{h}{3}(y'_n + 4y'_{n+1,2} + y'_{n+2,1}).$$

The corresponding parallel formulae are (see Worland [76]):

$$y_{n+r,0} = y_n + rhy'_n, \quad r = 1, 2$$

$$\left.\begin{array}{l} y_{n+1,s+1} = y_n + \dfrac{h}{12}(5y'_n + 8y'_{n+1,s} - y'_{n+2,s}) \\[2mm] y_{n+2,s+1} = y_n + \dfrac{h}{3}(y'_n + 4y'_{n+1,s} + y'_{n+2,s}) \end{array}\right\} \quad s = 0, 1, 2 \tag{4.1.3}$$

On comparing the amount of time spent in function evaluations with both methods we obtain a ratio of $5:3$, if the simultaneous evaluation of $y'_{n+1,s}$ and $y'_{n+2,s}$ in the parallel case is taken into account.

By increasing the number of points in a block, it is possible to increase the order of the integration method. The principle for constructing the corresponding parallel algorithm which follows on from the above example is:

(a) Each point x_{n+r} of a block should be attached to one of the N processors (provided that $N = k$ is valid).

(b) Initially, an approximation for y_{n+r} is evaluated by the Euler method.

(c) The function values can be iteratively improved using a Newton–Cotes $(k+1)$-point formula.

As a last example, the formulae for the parallel 4-points block method of order 6 are shown:

$$y_{n+r,0} = y_n + rhy'_n, \quad r = 1\,(1)\,4$$

$$\left. \begin{aligned}
y_{n+1,s+1} &= y_n + \frac{h}{720}(251y'_n + 646y'_{n+1,s} - 264y'_{n+2,s} \\
&\quad + 106y'_{n+3,s} - 19y'_{n+4,s}) \\
y_{n+2,s+1} &= y_n + \frac{h}{90}(29y'_n + 124y'_{n+1,s} + 24y'_{n+2,s} \\
&\quad + 4y'_{n+3,s} - y'_{n+4,s}) \\
y_{n+3,s+1} &= y_n + \frac{3h}{80}(9y'_n + 34y'_{n+1,s} + 24y'_{n+2,s} \\
&\quad + 14y'_{n+3,s} - y'_{n+4,s}) \\
y_{n+4,s+1} &= y_n + \frac{2h}{45}(7y'_n + 32y'_{n+1,s} + 12y'_{n+2,s} \\
&\quad + 32y'_{n+3,s} + 7y'_{n+4,s})
\end{aligned} \right\} \quad s = 0\,(1)\,4$$

$$(4.1.4)$$

The speed-up ratio is defined as

$$S = \frac{T_s}{T_p} \left(= \frac{\text{serial time}}{\text{parallel time}} \right).$$

On considering the number of simultaneously evaluated function values divided by the number of points in one block, e.g. for the case $k = 2$, we obtain:

$$T_s = 5/2 \quad T_p = 3/2 \Rightarrow S = 5/3$$

For k-point blocks it has been shown (Worland [76]) that:

$$T_s = \frac{1}{2}(k + 3), \quad T_p = 1 + \frac{1}{k},$$

i.e. the speed-up ratio is linear in k and converges for large k to $\frac{1}{2}k$. An even better speed-up ratio is arrived at using the following predictor-corrector block methods.

4.1.2 Predictor–corrector block method

The following algorithm for a 2-point block was originally developed for a serial computer (see Shampine & Watts [69]) but is nevertheless directly suited to a parallel computer:

$$\begin{aligned}
y_{n+1,0} &= \tfrac{1}{3}(y_{n-2} + y_{n-1} + y_n) \\
&\quad + \frac{h}{6}(3y'_{n-2} - 4y'_{n-1} + 13y'_n)
\end{aligned}$$

$$(4.1.5)$$

$$y_{n+2,0} = \tfrac{1}{3}(y_{n-2} + y_{n-1} + y_n)$$
$$+ \frac{h}{12}(29y'_{n-2} - 72y'_{n-1} + 79y'_n)$$

$$\left.\begin{array}{l}
y_{n+1,s+1} = y_n + \dfrac{h}{12}(5y'_n + 8y'_{n+1,s} - y'_{n+2,s}) \\[3mm]
y_{n+2,s+1} = y_n + \dfrac{h}{3}(y'_n + 4y'_{n+1,s} + y'_{n+2,s})
\end{array}\right\} \quad s = 0, 1.$$

$$(4.1.5)$$
$$(\text{Cont.})$$

The method is of order 4 (see Worland [76]). In this case, the speed-up ratio is $S = 2$ (as before, the number of simultaneously evaluated function values divided by the number of function values in one block). In general, the k-point block method yields:

$$S = \frac{T_s}{T_p} = k.$$

4.2 Ordinary differential equations: multirate methods

The block methods of section 4.1 are implicit methods, and are used for iterative integration by applying predictor-corrector methods. In many practical problems, however, explicit methods are important for the solution of initial value problems which appear in the real-time simulation of dynamical systems. (The real-time constraints usually allow only one functional evaluation at each integration step.) The integration step size h is determined by the stability properties of the explicit method used. The step size h can become so small that the computing time of this integration step is longer than the (real-) time step h.

Example 4.2.1

Let $y' = f(y, t), y(t_0) = y_0$ be an initial value problem of an n-dimensional system of differential equations and

$$\left[\frac{\partial f_i}{\partial y_j}\right], \quad i, j = 1, \ldots, n$$

be the Jacobian matrix, where $\lambda_1(t), \ldots, \lambda_n(t)$ are its eigenvalues satisfying $\text{Re}(\lambda_i(t)) < 0$ for all $i = 1, \ldots, n$.

Without loss of generality let $\lambda_1(t)$ be the eigenvalue with the largest absolute magnitude and $\lambda_n(t)$ the absolutely smallest eigenvalue, where $|\lambda_1(t)| \gg |\lambda_n(t)|$. Assuming that an upper bound $\lambda_{\max}$ exists for the eigenvalue $\lambda_1(t): |\lambda_1(t)| \leqslant \lambda_{\max}$, then the step size h must satisfy the following inequality: $\lambda_{max} \cdot h \leqslant S_M$, where S_M is the boundary of the stability region of the integration method M employed (see Gear [71], Grigorieff [72, 77]).   □

Systems of differential equations with the properties described in the above example are called 'stiff' systems. These systems often appear in the context of practical problems.

Franklin [78] suggests a solution of stiff systems using a parallel computer of the MIMD type: each processor solves one or more equations of the stiff system. At the synchronization points (corresponding to integer multiples of the step size h) the data necessary for the functional evaluation in all processors is exchanged between them. All equations, however, are integrated with the same small step size h, determined by the absolutely largest eigenvalue $\lambda_1(t)$ of the Jacobian matrix. It is a well-known fact that those components of the solution corresponding to absolutely large eigenvalues (i.e. those eigenvalues with large negative real parts) have only a marginal influence on the total solution. However, they determine, as already described, the small step size h. The numerical solutions of the (non-stiff) components, computed with this small step size h, are often unnecessarily exact for many technical applications (e.g. if the integration error is much smaller than the input error of the data determined from the measurement of experiments). If it is possible to divide the system of differential equations into two subsystems, a 'stiff' and a 'non-stiff' subsystem:

$$y' = f(y, t) = \begin{bmatrix} s(x, z, t) \\ g(x, z, t) \end{bmatrix} = \begin{bmatrix} x' \\ z' \end{bmatrix}; \quad y_0 = \begin{bmatrix} x_0 \\ z_0 \end{bmatrix} \tag{4.2.1}$$

then the so-called 'multirate' method can be used effectively. The concept of the multirate method consists of integrating the stiff subsystem with a shorter step size than the non-stiff subsystem:

$$x_{nk+i+1} = M(x_{nk+i}, t_{nk+i}, h; \hat{s}), \quad i = 0, \ldots, k-1$$

$$z_{(n+1)k} = M(z_{nk}, t_{nk}, k \cdot h; g) \tag{4.2.2}$$

where

h is the integration step size for the stiff subsystem
$k \cdot h$ is the integration step size for the non-stiff subsystem
k is the multirate factor, $k \in \mathbb{N}$
M is a well-known integration method (e.g. Runge–Kutta, Adams methods)

and $\hat{s} := s(x, \hat{z}, t)$, where $\hat{z}$ is an approximation of z. A particular approximation $\hat{z}$ of the z-values is necessary in evaluating the stiff subsystem s at the points t_{nk+i+1}, $i = 0, \ldots, k-1$. At these points the values of z are not computed by the integration procedure of the non-stiff subsystem. The approximation $\hat{z}$ of z

is computed using extrapolation polynomials from the values z_{nk-ik} and $g(x_{nk-ik}, z_{nk-ik}, t_{nk-ik})$, $i = 0, 1, 2, \ldots$. The size of the multirate factor k is approximately equal to the quotient of the magnitudes of the absolutely largest and the absolutely smallest eigenvalues. If the multirate method is used on a serial computer to solve real-time simulation problems, then a significant problem rears its head: the numerical approximations of the stiff system $x' = s(x, z, t)$ are computed during intervals corresponding to the length h. However, the evaluation of $g(x, z, t)$ and the computation of the numerical solution of the non-stiff subsystem must be spread uniformly over k time steps, each of length h.

Chronological sequence of the multirate method (time points in the computation) is shown in figure 15.11. Under real-time constraints, this procedure requires very careful and difficult programming (see Gear [77]). With very difficult (i.e. very stiff) problems, however, it may be possible that the multirate method run on a serial computer will violate these real-time constraints.

This fact, together with economic considerations, provides a reason for the parallel evaluation of the multirate methods. Each of the different time stages (one time stage corresponds to one step size) is associated with one or more processors. This association between the time stages and the processors avoids the programming problem of the serial implementation, as each processor integrates with only one step size. On the other hand, the longer step size $k \cdot h$ can be chosen in such a way that the important non-stiff components can be computed with the desired accuracy, whereas the shorter step size h can be chosen solely to achieve stability during the integration of the stiff components.

Note that there are more than two different step sizes possible, but the larger ones should be integer multiples of the smaller. This is necessary for determining synchronization points when wishing to exchange data between the processors associated with different time stages.

A successful use of parallel multirate methods is only possible after making a complete analysis of the error and stability properties of the multirate methods. Gomm [80a] has developed a method of constructing the stability polynomial of multirate versions of linear multistep methods and has made an extensive stability

Figure 15.11.

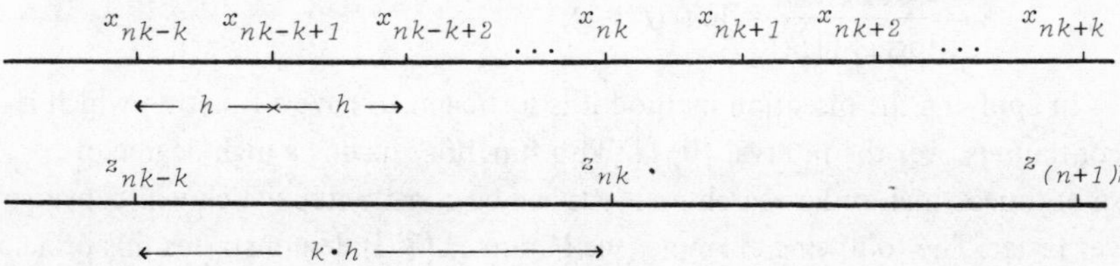

analysis of multirate Adams–Bashforth methods. Gomm's analysis shows that stiff systems with a weak coupling between the stiff and the non-stiff subsystems can be solved using multirate versions almost as well as with the normal versions, whilst taking less computing time. For a detailed discussion see Gomm [80a, b].

In the preceding sections parallel methods for the numerical solution of initial value problems have been described. For the numerical solution of boundary value problems no known parallel method exists. However, certain serial methods such as the multiple shooting method (Keller [68]) consist of several independent subproblems which can easily be performed in parallel: e.g. sequences of initial value problems, and solutions of systems of non-linear and linear equations with special block structures.

4.3 *Single non-linear equation*

First we shall consider the one-dimensional case and assume that the real function $f(x)$ has only one zero in the interval $[0, 1]$.

The methods for the determination of zeros can be subdivided into two types:

   (i) search methods

   (ii) locally iterative methods, e.g. the secant method or the Newton method.

Although methods of the first type progressively reduce the interval containing the zero, it is comparatively easy to find functions for which the local iterative methods will give no improvement at least after some iteration steps. However, the latter are important as a starting point for the construction of high order search methods.

4.3.1 *Search methods*

The simplest serial search method is the bisection method, which can clearly be performed in parallel on a computer consisting of r processors: for each iteration step the function is simultaneously evaluated at r points which thereby subdivide the actual interval into $r + 1$ equidistant subintervals. The new interval points are chosen on the basis of the signs of the function values. The bisection method needs $\log_2(1/\epsilon)$ function evaluations to enclose the zero in an interval of length ϵ, whereas the parallel method only requires $\log_{r+1}(1/\epsilon)$ evaluations. The speed-up ratio is therefore

$$S = \frac{\log_2(1/\epsilon)}{\log_{r+1}(1/\epsilon)} = \log_2(r + 1).$$

In applying the bisection method it is sufficient to have a function which is continuous over the interval $[0, 1]$. With functions having a high degree of smoothness, high order search methods can be constructed which will converge yet faster. The following example (see Miranker [77]) demonstrates this principle.

Let $f(x)$ be a function which is differentiable over $[0, 1]$ and let $f'(x) \in [m, M]$ $(m, M > 0)$ for all $x \in [0, 1]$. An algorithm is now developed for a computer able to evaluate two function values $y_i = f(x_i)$, $x_i \in [0, 1]$, $(i = 1, 2)$ in parallel.

Initially, two piecewise linear functions $\underline{S}(x), \bar{S}(x)$ are defined which enclose $f(x)$ in $[x_1, x_2]$ (see figure 15.12):

$$\underline{S}(x) \leqslant f(x) \leqslant \bar{S}(x)$$

$$\bar{S}(x) := \begin{cases} y_1 + M(x - x_1), & x \leqslant \dfrac{(M - s)x_1 + (x - m)x_2}{M - m} \\[3mm] y_2 + m(x - x_2), & x \geqslant \dfrac{(M - x)x_1 + (s - m)x_2}{M - m} \end{cases} \tag{4.3.1}$$

where $s := (y_2 - y_1)/(x_2 - x_1)$. In a similar manner we define $\underline{S}(x)$.

The zero z of f is on the right-hand side of the zero x_1^* of $\bar{S}(x)$:

$$z \geqslant x_1^* = \max\left\{x_1 - \frac{y_1}{M}, \quad x_2 - \frac{y_2}{m}\right\}$$

and

$$z \leqslant x_2^* = \min\left\{x_1 - \frac{y_1}{m}, \quad x_2 - \frac{y_2}{M}\right\}.$$

Considering each possible case, it can be shown that the inequality

$$\frac{x_2^* - x_1^*}{x_2 - x_1} \leqslant 1 - \frac{m}{M}$$

applies.

Comparing this method with the parallelized bisection method it is possible to

Figure 15.12.

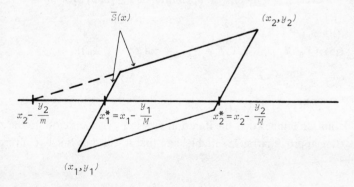

obtain a speed-up, provided that

$$\frac{m}{M} \geqslant \frac{2}{3}$$

applies.

If $f \in C^2(0, 1)$, the algorithm even has quadratic convergence, provided that the bounds m and M are improved at every iteration step:

$$m = \min_{x \in [x_1, x_2]} f'(x) \qquad\qquad M = \max_{x \in [x_1, x_2]} f'(x)$$

$$\Rightarrow x_2^* - x_1^* \leqslant (x_2 - x_1)^2 \cdot \max_{\xi \in (x_1, x_2)} |f''(\xi)| / \max_{\mu \in (x_1, x_2)} |f'(\mu)|$$

More parallel search methods of higher order are to be found in Micchelli & Miranker [75], Gal & Miranker [77] and Casulli & Trigiante [78]. On comparing these algorithms with optimal serial methods the authors however ascertained that the speed-up ratio only grew logarithmically with the number of processors working in parallel. The same results are true for the following locally iterative methods.

4.3.2 Locally iterative methods

Let $f \in C^d(0, 1)$, $f'(x) \neq 0$ for all $x \in (0, 1)$. For the following algorithm we imagine an SIMD computer with r processors. Starting with approximations $x_{0,1}; x_{0,2}; \ldots; x_{0,r}$ of z it is required to determine r improved approximations

$$x_{k+1,i} = \phi_{k,i}(x_{k,1}; x_{k-1,1}; \ldots; x_{0,r})$$

at every iteration step by evaluating function values and their derivatives up to the order d.

One locally iterative r-parallel method (see Corliss [74]) consists of a series $\{\phi_k : \mathbb{R}^{(k+1)r} \to \mathbb{R}^r, \quad k \geqslant 0\}$ of iteration functions having the following properties:

(a) $\phi_k(z, \ldots, z) = (z, \ldots, z)$

(b) For every $k \geqslant 0$ there is an open interval $I \subseteq [0, 1]$ such that

(i) $z \in I$

(ii) $\phi_k(I^{(k+1)r}) \subseteq I^r$

(iii) $(X_0, X_1, \ldots, X_k \in I^r \wedge X_{k+1} = \phi_k(X_k, \ldots, X_0))$

$$\Rightarrow \lim_{k \to \infty} x_{k,i} = z$$

where $X_j := (x_{j,1}, \ldots, x_{j,r})$.

The definition implies that the iteration series $x_{k,i}$ remains close to the zero z if the starting approximation is suitable, and that it will thus finally converge to the zero.

Let

$$\delta_k := \max_i \; |z - x_{k,i}| \; . \text{ We speak of convergence of order } \lambda, \text{ if}$$

$$\lim_{k \to \infty} \frac{\delta_{k+1}}{(\delta_k)^\lambda} = c > 0$$

applies.

Figure 15.13 gives as example the parallel secant method with $r = 3$.

$$x_{k+1,1} = x_{k,1} - \frac{x_{k,1} - x_{k,2}}{f(x_{k,1}) - f(x_{k,2})} f(x_{k,1})$$

$$x_{k+1,2} = x_{k,2} - \frac{x_{k,2} - x_{k,3}}{f(x_{k,2}) - f(x_{k,3})} f(x_{k,2}) \qquad (4.3.2)$$

$$x_{k+1,3} = x_{k,3} - \frac{x_{k,3} - x_{k,1}}{f(x_{k,3}) - f(x_{k,1})} f(x_{k,3})$$

The order of convergence is 2 compared with $1.618 \ldots$ for the serial secant method for the same time outlay provided that $f \in C^2 [0, 1]$.

The secant method is a discrete version of Newton's method: the derivative is replaced by the difference quotient. This is the reason why the serial method has not the order of convergence of Newton's method. The parallel secant method minimizes the error of discretization in such a way that the order of convergence is retained. Using more processors it is possible to approximate the derivatives of higher order, thus also leading to a higher-order convergence. There are, however, limitations to this method according to theorem 4.3.3 from Winograd [72].

Theorem 4.3.3

The order of convergence of every locally iterative method with r processors used to evaluate simultaneously function values and derivatives up to order d is bounded by $1 + (d + 1)r$. □

Figure 15.13.

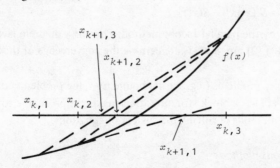

Since this theorem includes the serial case ($r = 1$), the speed-up ratio, which can be obtained directly, is:

$$S = \frac{\log_{d+2} \log (1/\epsilon)}{\log_{1+(d+1)r} \log (1/\epsilon)} = \log_{d+2} (1 + (d + 1)r),$$

i.e. the time which can be saved is proportional to $\log r$ and therefore far removed from the best case $S = r$.

4.4 Non-linear systems of equations

The parallel algorithms for finding the zero of a function of one variable are designed in almost all cases for SIMD computers. For multidimensional functions it would appear advantageous to use methods suitable for MIMD computers. We shall therefore consider not only synchronous but also asynchronous methods.

4.4.1 Synchronous methods

We have to solve the non-linear system of equations given by

$$S(x) = 0, \quad S : \mathbb{R}^k \to \mathbb{R}^k. \tag{4.4.1}$$

It is possible to regard (4.4.1) as a fixed point problem $F(x) = x$ where $F := S + I$. A parallel version of the successive approximation $x^{i+1} = F(x^i)$ can therefore be applied. Using k processors, each one is associated with a component of F. If the iteration steps are synchronized, there are certain fixed point theorems (e.g. Banach's and Schauder's fixed point theorems or the fixed point theorem for monotonic operators) which can be used to prove the convergence of the iteration sequence to a zero of $S(x)$. The time needed by each processor to do its task may vary markedly. The best solution may therefore involve using the MIMD computer in an asynchronous manner. This is discussed in the next section. A short reference has already been made to the Newton–Jacobi method, a synchronous method of higher order. Every Newton iteration results in a linear system

$$S'(x^i)x^{i+1} = S'(x^i)x^i - S(x^i),$$

which can be solved by the parallel Jacobi method. There is a theorem given by Ortega & Rheinboldt [70], pp. 320-1, concerning the convergence of the total algorithm.

Moreover, for many problems (e.g. special boundary value problems) the functional matrix $S'(x)$ has a block structure, thus making it profitable to use linear parallel block methods in solving the system of equations.

4.4.2 Asynchronous methods

Asynchronous iteration is the asynchronous version of successive approximation (see section 2.7). This iteration consists of a sequence x^j, $j = 1, 2, \ldots$ of vectors of $\mathbb{R}^k$. The sequence is defined by

$$x_i^j = \begin{cases} x_i^{j-1} & \text{for } i \notin J_j \\ f_i(x_1^{s_1(j)}, x_2^{s_2(j)}, \ldots, x_k^{s_k(j)}) & \text{for } i \in J_j, \end{cases}$$

with a starting vector $x^0 \cdot J := \{J_j / j = 1, 2, \ldots\}$ is a sequence of non-empty subsets of $\{1, 2, \ldots, k\}$ and

$$S := \{(s_1(j), s_2(j), \ldots, s_k(j)) / j = 1, 2, \ldots\}$$

a sequence of elements of $\mathbb{N}^k$.

J and S must satisfy the following conditions for all $i = 1, 2, \ldots, k$:

(i) $s_i(j) \leqslant j - 1$ for all $j = 1, 2, \ldots, k$

(ii) $s_i(j) \to \infty$ holds for $j \to \infty$

(iii) Each i occurs an infinite number of times in the sets J_j, $j = 1, 2, \ldots$.

The sequence x^j defined by the asynchronous iteration results naturally from the successive approximation if it is performed on an MIMD computer without any synchronization of the processors. A statement about the convergence is made in theorem 2.7.1 (Baudet [76]). In addition, an assertion about the speed of convergence can be made: let n_i be the number of time steps during which the i-th component of the function f_i can be evaluated (without loss of generality $n_i \in \mathbb{N}$). One iteration of a single component is called for short a 'single iteration'. The number R of such single iterations, which are necessary to reduce the error by the factor 10, can be estimated from an upper bound:

$$R \leqslant \frac{2 \sum_{i=1}^{k} \left\lceil \dfrac{n_{\max}}{n_i} \right\rceil - 1}{\log \rho(A)},$$

where $\rho(A) :=$ spectral radius of the Lipschitz matrix A. Using simulation programs we have ascertained the efficiency of asynchronous iteration.

Some results concerning search methods for root finding using asynchronous processors are to be found in Feilmeier, Gomm, Rönsch & Töpfer [80]. Further references are given in a recent paper by Miranker [79].

4.5 Linear programming

Let us now consider the general linear optimization problem

$$\left. \begin{array}{r} Ax \leqslant b \\ x \geqslant 0 \\ c^T x \to \max \end{array} \right\} ; \quad A \text{ is an } (m, n) \text{ matrix}, m \leqslant n \qquad (4.5.1)$$

Wypior [77] tackles the problem (4.5.1) for the case of weakly connected constraints. He employs the decomposition algorithm of Dantzig and Wolfe (see

Dantzig [63]) which partitions the problem into smaller subproblems. The latter are largely independent of each other and therefore offer good opportunities for parallel computation.

In approaching the general solution of the linear optimization problem we first of all refer to Gründler [79]. In his paper he describes the implementation of the well-known simplex algorithm on the SMS 201. (A detailed description of this computer is given in Kober & Kuznia [79]; see also section 5.2.)

The implementation poorly exploits the MIMD properties of the SMS 201. Each processor (i.e. module) in the SMS 201 works with essentially the same non-branched program, so that it might also be possible to implement the algorithm on an SIMD computer. The characteristic feature of the algorithm is that every row of the simplex tableau is stored in a separate module. After the determination of the pivot, each module successively evaluates the new elements of the appropriate row. The column elements are therefore calculated in parallel. The pivot is determined by the 'greatest change method' (see Müller-Merbach [73]).

The effective savings in computation time gained by using this implementation are not given. Since, however, those parts of the algorithm involving the most calculation (recalculation of the tableaux, and divisions and multiplications in pivot determination) are fully parallelized, the speed-up ratio will probably grow linearly with the number p of the processors (modules).

As the use of the greatest change method as a pivoting strategy in the serial case cannot be unreservedly recommended, the comparison of computation time for the parallel and serial algorithms proves to be somewhat problematic. The Gründler algorithm primarily utilizes the opportunities for parallelization offered by the matrix operations of the simplex method. In principle, this algorithm must be considered as being serial in nature: the progression from one extreme point to the next depends on all previous steps. Some proposals for true parallelization of the simplex, duplex and multiplex algorithms can be found in Prause [80].

4.6 *Minimization of unimodal functions without constraints*

This section deals with the minimization of a unimodal function f over an interval $[a, b]$.

Definition 4.6.1

$f : [a, b] \to \mathbb{R}$ is called unimodal if and only if:

(1) $\exists_1 \check{x} \in [a, b] \; \forall x \in [a, b], x \neq \check{x} : f(\check{x}) < f(x)$

and

(2) $\left.\begin{array}{l} x_1 < x_2 \leqslant \bar{x} \Rightarrow f(x_1) > f(x_2) \\ \bar{x} \leqslant x_1 < x_2 \Rightarrow f(x_1) < f(x_2) \end{array}\right\}$ $x_1, x_2 \in [a, b]$ $\square$

An example is shown in figure 15.14.

Theorem 4.6.2

Let $f : [a, b] \to \mathbb{R}$ be unimodal, $\bar{x}$ be the unique existing minimum and $x_1, x_2, x_3 \in [a, b]$. Then:

(1) $x_1 < x_2 \wedge f(x_1) < f(x_2) \Rightarrow \bar{x} < x_2$

(2) $x_1 < x_2 \wedge f(x_1) > f(x_2) \Rightarrow x_1 < \bar{x}$

(3) $x_1 < x_2 \wedge f(x_1) = f(x_2) \Rightarrow x_1 < \bar{x} < x_2$

(4) $x_1 < x_2 < x_3 \wedge f(x_1) > f(x_2) \wedge f(x_2) < f(x_3) \Rightarrow x_1 < \bar{x} < x_3$ $\square$

This theorem, which is easily proved, can be used to numerically isolate the minimum.

4.6.3 Serial procedure

This is the basis for the numerical minimization of the serial algorithm. Choose $x_1, x_2 \in (a, b)$ with $x_1 < x_2$ and evaluate $f(x_1)$ and $f(x_2)$. The following cases can occur:

(a) $f(x_1) < f(x_2)$

According to statement (1) in the above theorem $\bar{x} \in (a, x_2)$. $x_3 \in (a, x_2)$ is now chosen such that $x_1 \neq x_3$ and $f(x_3)$ is evaluated. Since $f(x_1)$ is already known and $x_1 \in (a, x_2)$, we can continue using x_1 and x_3. The initial interval (a, b) has now been narrowed to (a, x_2).

(b) $f(x_2) < f(x_1)$

analogous to (a).

(c) $f(x_1) = f(x_2)$

Choose two new points $x_3, x_4 \in (x_1, x_2)$ with $x_3 \neq x_4$ and evaluate $f(x_3)$ and $f(x_4)$. Then continue with x_3, x_4. The initial interval (a, b) has now been narrowed to (x_1, x_2).

Figure 15.14.

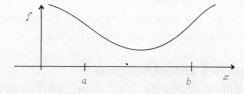

4.6.4 Parallel procedure

Given an SIMD computer with p processors it is possible to evaluate p function values in parallel. The basis for the parallel numerical minimization algorithm is as follows.

Choose p points $x_1, \ldots, x_p \in (a, b)$ such that $x_1 < x_2 < x_3 \ldots < x_p$, evaluate $f(x_1), \ldots, f(x_p)$ in parallel and determine $m := \min\{f(x_1), \ldots, f(x_p)\}$. There are two different cases:

(a) There is exactly one point x_χ where $f(x_\chi) = m$. According to statement (4) of theorem 4.6.2:

$$\bar{x} \in [x_{\chi-1}, x_{\chi+1}]$$

and we can continue with $(x_{\chi-1}, x_{\chi+1})$ as the starting interval.

(b) There are two neighbouring points $x_\chi, x_{\chi+1}$ with $f(x_\chi) = f(x_{\chi+1}) = m$. According to statement (3) of theorem 4.6.2:

$$\bar{x} \in [x_\chi, x_{\chi+1}]$$

and we can continue with $(x_\chi, x_{\chi+1})$ as the starting interval.

The serial and parallel procedures are straightforward. The most important question is the starting point for the real mathematical analysis:

How to choose points at which the function values are to be calculated, so as to achieve the desired precision whilst keeping the number of function evaluations to a minimum. (The choice of the points should be made in a systematic fashion, not at random.)

Kiefer [53] was the first to deal with this problem. He proposed a serial algorithm for bracketing the minimum of f. Avriel & Wilde [66] and Karp & Miranker [68] developed parallel algorithms. All these algorithms are optimal in the following sense: every different but systematic choice of the points leads at best to the same precision, provided that the same starting interval and the same number of function evaluations are used. Prause [80] has given fuller details of the two algorithms mentioned above than are to be found in the original papers.

The speed-up ratio S of both parallel algorithms is:

$$S \approx \log_{1.618}\left(\frac{k + \sqrt{(k^2 + 4k)}}{2}\right) \quad \text{if } p = 2k - 1$$

and

$$S \approx \log_{1.618}(k + 1) \quad \text{if } p = 2k.$$

(In the above estimations $(\sqrt{5} + 1)/2$ is approximated to 1.618.) The speed-up ratio therefore only grows logarithmically with the number of processors.

4.7 General non-linear optimization without constraints

Consider the general non-linear optimization problem without constraints:

$$f \rightarrow \min, \quad f: \mathbb{R}^n \rightarrow \mathbb{R} \tag{4.7.1}$$

Case A: It is assumed that the gradient of the objective function f is available. For this problem Straeter [73] developed a parallel algorithm which can roughly be described as follows:

Step 1: In the neighbourhood of the actual minimum point x^m (which is called the 'search centre' in the following) n points are chosen and the function values and gradients at these points evaluated in parallel.

Step 2: Using the gradients calculated in step 1 together with other values from the previous iterations, a vector $S_m \in \mathbb{R}^m$ is determined. This vector describes the search direction for a one-dimensional minimization.

Step 3: The one-dimensional minimization is performed by approximating the objective function f by a cubic polynomial. Let x^{m+1} be a point determined in this way. If with a given $\epsilon > 0$, it is found for the gradient $g(x^{m+1})$ that:

$$\|g(x^{m+1})\| \leqslant \epsilon,$$

then the iteration is terminated, otherwise we continue with x^{m+1} as the search centre.

Since the serial algorithms of Davidon [59], Fletcher & Powell [63] and of Fletcher & Reeves [64] can also be parallelized in a straightforward manner and the Straeter algorithm can also be performed serially, there is a wide range of serial and parallel algorithms.

For an unknown function f it is impossible to give a theoretical estimate for the speed-up ratio. Consider the quadratic function

$$f(x) = \tfrac{1}{2} x^T A x + b^T x + c; \quad x \in \mathbb{R}^n, \quad n \geqslant 2.$$

For this function, the computation time for $p = n + 1$ processors is such that:

in the serial case, the Straeter algorithm is the fastest

in the parallel case, the algorithm of Fletcher & Reeves is the fastest.

This leads to

$$S = \frac{T_1 \text{ (Straeter)}}{T_p \text{ (Fletcher \& Reeves)}} \approx \tfrac{5}{6} p.$$

Case B: The gradient of the objective function f is not available. For this problem an efficient parallel algorithm is given by Pierre [73]. The estimate of the speed-up ratio S shows that S grows approximately linearly with the number p of processors used, provided that n is not too large ($n \leqslant 50$):

$$S = \alpha \cdot p \quad \text{with } \alpha \in (\tfrac{1}{2}, \tfrac{4}{5}).$$

5   **The dependence of parallel algorithms upon computer architecture**

The solution of tridiagonal systems of linear equations by means of recursive doubling (see 2.4) is a simple prime example of how the structure of the parallel computer used is reflected in the construction of the algorithms. In section 2.4 this problem was only touched on in that the essential difference between vector computers and real parallel computers was mentioned. In practical problems there are great differences between the two types of machine. It is therefore worthwhile considering them in detail.

Another reason for doing this is the fact that parallel computers are used only in those cases where high or highest possible performance rates have to be achieved. In our opinion the progress of technology will not render irrelevant such considerations as:

> Despite the rapid technological progress of the last few years there still remain problems which exceed the capacity and performance of currently available computers.
>
> Analysis of the techniques of problem solving can give valuable impetus to the development of future computer architecture.

In section 5.1 the solution of linear systems with band matrices on the best-known vector machines (STAR 100, ASC and Cray-1) will be outlined. In 5.2 we describe the SMS 201, a parallel computer implementation of the (synchronous) MIMD type. Afterwards, the implementation of the Gauss–Seidel iteration method on this computer is presented.

5.1   Direct solution of a system of linear equations on vector computers

5.1.1   The mathematical problem

The subject of this section is the solution of the following system of linear equations:

$$A \cdot x = b,$$

where A is a band matrix $A = (a_{ij})$.

The bandwidth $\beta(A)$ is defined by

$$\beta(A) := \max_{a_{ij} \neq 0} |i - j|$$

that is $2 \cdot \beta(A) + 1$ diagonals of A are non-zero. Let us assume that the equation system has arisen from the discretization of a partial differential equation over an $n \times n$ grid. Thus A is an $N \times N$ $(N := n^2)$ matrix with bandwidth $\beta := \beta(A) = n + 1$.

Let A be a symmetric and positive definite matrix. In the following we consider the Cholesky decomposition $A = LL^T$, where L is lower triangular $(L = (l_{ij})$ and $l_{ij} \neq 0$ only for $j = i - \beta, \ldots, i$; i.e. L is also a band matrix).

Consider initially the general $L \cdot U$ decomposition of a full (non-sparse) matrix A by Gaussian elimination. Without pivoting it is possible to perform this according to Lambiotte [77] in the following arithmetic manner:

FOR $j=1$ (1) $N-1$

(a) $\left[\begin{array}{l} \text{FOR } i=j+1 \text{ (1) } N \qquad \text{'Evaluation of } L\text{'} \\ \qquad a_{ij} := a_{ij}/a_{jj} \end{array} \right.$

FOR $k=j+1$ (1) N

(b) $\left[\begin{array}{l} \text{FOR } i=j+1 \text{ (1) } N \qquad \text{'Modification of } A\text{'} \\ \qquad a_{ik} := a_{ik} - a_{jk} \cdot a_{ij} \end{array} \right.$

The square brackets indicate operations having vector structure. Restricting ourselves to vector operations of (b) we have linear combinations of column vectors.

For the band matrix A this core reduces to the evaluation of the linear combination (Voigt [77]):

$$(a_{j+1,j+1}, \ldots, a_{j+\beta,j+1})^T - a_{j+1,j} \cdot (a_{j+1,j}, \ldots, a_{j+\beta,j})^T \qquad (5.1.1)$$

In 5.1.1 the vector lengths vary from 1 to β. The implementation of (5.1.1) on different computers will be discussed later on.

The direct triangular decomposition is based on the following formulae:

$$a_{jj} = l_{j1}^2 + l_{j2}^2 + \ldots + l_{jj}^2$$
$$a_{ij} = l_{i1}l_{j1} + l_{i2}l_{j2} + \ldots + l_{ij}l_{jj} \qquad (j < i).$$

From these conditional equations it is possible to obtain the columns of L (Forsythe & Moler [71]):

FOR $j=1$ (1) N

$$l_{jj} = \text{sqrt}\left(a_{jj} - \sum_{k=1}^{j-1} l_{jk}^2 \right)$$

$$\left[\begin{array}{l} \text{FOR } i=j+1 \text{ (1) } N \\ \\ l_{ij} = \left(a_{ij} - \displaystyle\sum_{k=1}^{j-1} l_{ik}l_{jk} \right) / l_{jj} \end{array} \right.$$

If A is a band matrix then L is also a band matrix, and the vectorizable core of this algorithm reduces to:

$$\left[\begin{array}{l} \text{FOR } i=j+1 \text{ (1) } \min(j+\beta,N) \\ \\ l_{ij} = \left(a_{ij} - \displaystyle\sum_{k=\max(1,i-\beta)}^{j-1} l_{ik}l_{jk} \right) / l_{jj} \end{array} \right. \qquad (5.1.2)$$

The appearance of the inner product of two column vectors of L is essential to the implementation of (5.1.2). This form of the triangular decomposition seems particularly suited to those vector computers having a special inner product instruction.

On the other hand, it should be noted that the length of the column vectors used in the inner product formula varies with each execution of the loop.

5.1.2 The structure of vector computers (see Ortega & Voigt [77])

In this section the structure of the three most prominent classic vector computers is described at a depth appropriate to our purposes.

STAR 100 (upgraded version: CYBER 203/205): The central processing unit (CPU) has two multifunctional pipelines, which can be configured under microcode control. Every vector instruction initiates a stream of operands from memory to the pipelines. The result of a vector operation is then delivered to memory. By definition a vector is the contents of consecutive memory words. This relatively restricted vector conception is compensated for by a powerful instruction set for manipulating storage location contents. The timing formula for vector operations expressed in minor cycles (clock cycles or clock periods) is:

$$T = S + (l/L)$$

where

S = start-up time (that is the time it takes for the first result of the vector operation to be available)

l = vector length

L = number of pipeline results per minor cycle (pipeline rate)

The STAR 100 has the following values:

$S = 100$ nanoseconds, $L = 1$, minor cycle = 40 nanoseconds.

The word length is 64 bits. Instructions of length 32 bits are possible. Scalar operations are slower than vector operations. In the 32 bit mode the STAR 100 has a maximum execution rate 100 MFLOPS. (1 MFLOPS is a rate of 1 million floating-point operations per second.)

Texas Instruments ASC: The CPU consists of one, two or four multifunctional pipelines. A vector instruction initiates a stream of data from memory through the pipelines and back again. In the ASC any string of memory locations that might be referenced by a triply nested Fortran DO loop is defined as a vector. Moreover, the innermost loop must be incremented by 1. A loop of this kind can be performed in only one instruction at the machine language level. Thus only one start-up time is needed to execute this loop.

The performance figures are the same as for the STAR 100:

$$T = S + (l/L),$$

where $S = 100$ nanoseconds, $L = 1$, clock cycle $= 80$ nanoseconds, word length $= 32$ bits.

As with the STAR 100, the ASC has slow scalar operation compared to vector mode. Using all four pipelines the ASC is capable of executing up to 50 MFLOPS.

Cray-1: The Cray-1 architecture avoids the following essential disadvantages of the ASC and STAR 100 (Cyber 203/205):

> Even in scalar mode the Cray-1 is a very fast machine (about twice as fast as the CDC 7600).
>
> Using unifunctional pipelines the Cray-1 has such a small start-up time that even vector operations for vectors of length 2 are faster than scalar operations.
>
> The Cray-1 has 8 vector registers (V0, ..., V7) of length 64 to avoid memory conflicts arising if READ and STORE instructions have to be carried out simultaneously on the same vectors.

By definition, a vector is the contents of consecutive elements of a vector register, always beginning with the first element of the register. If a vector has more than 64 elements then it has to be divided into parts of length 64. For data transfer between vector registers and memory there are special vector READ and STORE instructions. A vector instruction uses in general three vector registers: two containing the operands of the operation and another for the result of that operation.

The unifunctional pipelines of the Cray-1 can work in parallel and even in so-called chaining mode. This mode comes into operation automatically when the result register of a vector instruction is used as the operand register for the succeeding vector operation. The execution of the succeeding instruction starts directly the first element of the result vector is available.

This situation is demonstrated by the following chaining example.

> *Example 5.1.3*
> DO 100 I=1,N
> 100 A(I) = 5.0 * B(I) + C

If $N \leqslant 64$ this loop can be replaced by the following seven statements in CAL (Cray assembler language) (let S1, S2 denote scalar registers and V0, V1, V2 vector registers):

> (1) S1 := 5.0   Transmit constant 5.0 to S1
> (2) S2 := C   Transmit contents of C to S2
> (3) VL := N   Transmit contents of N to vector
> length register (VL)

(4) V0 := B array   Transmit B array to V0
(5) V1 := S1 * V0   Product of S1 and V0 to V1   } chaining sequence
(6) V2 := S2 + V1   Sum of S2 and V1 to V2

(7) A array := V2   Transmit contents of V2 to A array.

(For the sake of clearness a Fortran-style notation has been used for CAL.)   □

The clock period of the Cray-1 amounts to 12.5 nanoseconds; the word length is 64 bits. The maximum execution rate of the Cray-1 is 160 MFLOPS.

5.1.4   Analysis of the decomposition algorithm

It is now possible to analyse the implementation of the decomposition algorithms (5.1.1) and (5.1.2) on vector computers. The inner product algorithm (5.1.2) is only of interest to those computers having a special floating-point instruction capable of executing the product.

Algorithm (5.1.1) can easily be implemented on the STAR 100 as well as on the ASC. The computing time is approximately $(N = n^2)$:

$$T(n) \approx n^4 + 200n^3 + 200n^2 + O(n)$$

For this estimate it was assumed that $S \approx 100$ and $L = 1$. There are no difficulties concerning the vector definition. The variation of the vector lengths in (5.1.1) between 1 and β presents no problems.

Assuming V1 contains $(a_{j,j}, \ldots, a_{j+\beta,j})^T$, the direct implementation of (5.1.1) on the Cray-1 would be:

          FOR l=1 (1) β
(1)   READ $(a_{j+l,j+l}, \ldots, a_{j+\beta,j+l})^T$ to V2
(2)   V3 := $a_{j+l,j}$ * V1 $(j+l, \ldots, j+\beta)$
(3)   V4 := V2 −V3
(4)   STORE V4 to memory

(V1(k) denotes the k-th component of the vector register V1.)

The Cray-1 architecture permits the chaining of the first three operations. As the instruction sequence must be executed for l ranging from 1 to β, the operation after the STORE is another READ. Since the STORE must wait until the READ is complete, the arithmetic unit will be busy for only about half the total time required by the algorithm.

Moreover, the MULTIPLY instruction is not allowed to begin with any other component of the vector register V1 except the first. However, if the vectors are stored in reverse order, the variable vector length does not entail difficulties. On top of this there are additional tricks for keeping the arithmetic unit constantly busy (see Voigt [77]).

The inner product instruction seems to be suitable for the STAR 100 as well as for the ASC because both have a special implementation of it. For vectors of length greater than 23 the inner product instruction of the STAR 100 is slower than the corresponding subtract–multiply combination which it would replace.

The situation with the ASC is much more favourable as the special inner product instruction is fast. The corresponding algorithm has a timing formula approximately given by:

$$T(n) \approx 0.5n^4 + 100n^3 + 200n^2 + 0(n).$$

The reason for the relatively large term $100n^3$ can be explained as follows.

In (5.1.2) there are inner products of different vector lengths. The ASC cannot execute a sequence of such operations with a single instruction. This large number of start-up times accumulates and results in the n^3-term.

The following procedure would help to overcome this: by filling up with zeros one can build up vectors of constant length. The resulting DO loop can be represented by a single instruction. The timing formula is then approximately:

$$T(n) \approx n^4 + 300n^2 + 0(n).$$

Exact comparisons of computing time concerning the solutions of concrete problems on the three types of vector machines outlined can be found in, for example, Gentzsch, Weiland & Müller-Wichards [80] and Hertweck, Schneider & Schwenn [79].

5.2 Iterative solution of a system of linear equations on a particular MIMD computer

We shall now discuss the iterative solution of a system of linear equations on the SMS 201 (SMS = structured multiprocessor system). The SMS 201 (figure 15.15) is a synchronous MIMD computer (see Kober & Kuznia [79]) which tries

Figure 15.15.

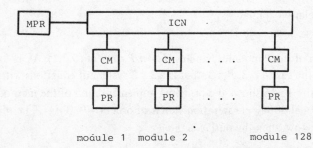

module 1   module 2   module 128

to combine the advantages of ILLIAC-type array computers and the C.mmp (see Wallach & Konrad [80]).

The SMS 201 consists (at present) of a maximum of 128 identical modules. Each of them has one processor (PR) with program and data memory plus one communication memory (CM).

The modules and the main processor (MPR) are connected by an interconnection network (ICN). There are two important system concepts:

(1) All communication between the modules and the main processor operates through the communication memories CM.

(2) The calculations are synchronized by repeated execution of the following consecutive phase cycles:

control phase cycle: the main processor selects the module programs and starts them;

autonomous calculation phase cycle: the modules perform calculations independently of each other;

communication phase cycle: the results generated in each module are exchanged between them.

5.2.1 The implementation of the Gauss-Seidel method (Nagel [78])

Let

$$A \cdot x = b$$

be a diagonal dominant system of linear equations. Without loss of generality we assume $a_{ii} = 1$. Then the Gauss-Seidel method (single step method) is described by the following formula:

$$x_i^{(k+1)} = b_i - \sum_{j>i} a_{ij} x_j^{(k)} - \sum_{j<i} a_{ij} x_j^{(k+1)}, \quad i,j \leqslant n.$$

Letting

$$t_i^{(k)} := \sum_{j>i} a_{ij} x_j^{(k)} - b_i$$

$$z_i^{(k)} := \sum_{j<i} a_{ij} x_j^{(k)}$$

the following relation applies:

$$x_i^{(k+1)} = -t_i^{(k)} - z_i^{(k+1)}. \tag{5.2.1}$$

In general, each of the P modules handles $H := n/P$ rows of (5.2.1). As an example let us consider the case $n = 3, P = 3$, that is a 3×3 system of equations with 3 modules. Figure 15.16 shows the principal implementation of the method. The computational outlay per iteration step is of order n^2/P. If $n = P$, i.e. there is one module per row, then the outlay is $O(n)$.

Figure 15.16.

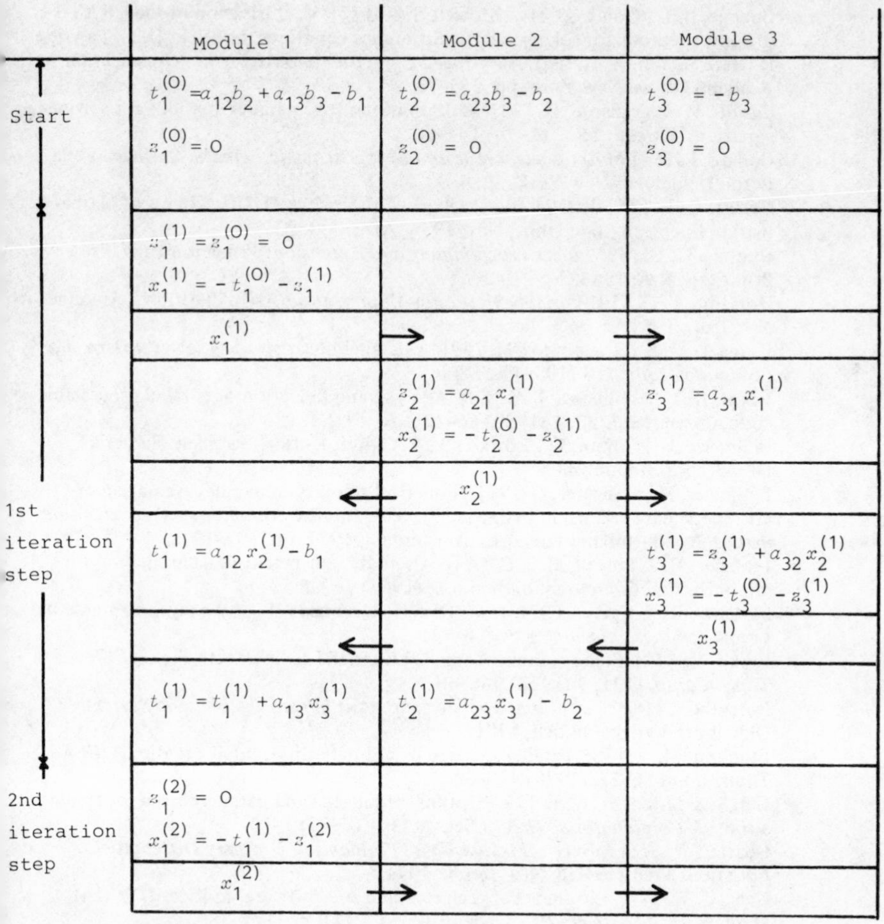

	Module 1	Module 2	Module 3
Start	$t_1^{(0)} = a_{12}b_2 + a_{13}b_3 - b_1$ $z_1^{(0)} = 0$	$t_2^{(0)} = a_{23}b_3 - b_2$ $z_2^{(0)} = 0$	$t_3^{(0)} = -b_3$ $z_3^{(0)} = 0$
	$z_1^{(1)} = z_1^{(0)} = 0$ $x_1^{(1)} = -t_1^{(0)} - z_1^{(1)}$		
	$x_1^{(1)}$ $\rightarrow$	$\rightarrow$	
		$z_2^{(1)} = a_{21}x_1^{(1)}$ $x_2^{(1)} = -t_2^{(0)} - z_2^{(1)}$	$z_3^{(1)} = a_{31}x_1^{(1)}$
	$\leftarrow$	$x_2^{(1)}$ $\rightarrow$	
1st iteration step	$t_1^{(1)} = a_{12}x_2^{(1)} - b_1$		$t_3^{(1)} = z_3^{(1)} + a_{32}x_2^{(1)}$ $x_3^{(1)} = -t_3^{(0)} - z_3^{(1)}$
	$\leftarrow$	$\leftarrow$	$x_3^{(1)}$
	$t_1^{(1)} = t_1^{(1)} + a_{13}x_3^{(1)}$	$t_2^{(1)} = a_{23}x_3^{(1)} - b_2$	
2nd iteration step	$z_1^{(2)} = 0$ $x_1^{(2)} = -t_1^{(1)} - z_1^{(2)}$		
	$x_1^{(2)}$ $\rightarrow$	$\rightarrow$	

References

Avriel, M. & Wilde, D. J. [66] 'Optimal search for a maximum with sequences of simultaneous function evaluation' *Management Science* **12**, 9 (1966) 722–31

Banerjee, U., Chen, S. C., Kuck, D. J. & Towle, R. A. [79] 'Time and parallel processor bounds for fortran-like loops' *IEEE Trans. Comp.* C-28, 9 (1979) 660–70

Baudet, G. M. [76] 'Asynchronous Iterative Methods for Multiprocessors' *J. ACM* **25**, 2 (1978) 226–44

Brent, R. P. [73] 'The parallel evaluation of arithmetic expressions in logarithmic time' in Traub, J. F. (ed), *Complexity of Sequential and Parallel Numerical Algorithms,* Academic Press, 1973, pp. 83–102

Brent, R. P. [74] 'The parallel evaluation of general arithmetic expressions' *J. ACM* **21**, 2 (1974) 201–6

Brent, R. P., Kuck, D. & Maruyama, K. [73] 'The parallel evaluation of arithmetic expressions without division' *IEEE Trans. Comp.* C-22, (1973) 533–4

Buzbee, B. L., Golub, G. H. & Howell, J. A. [77] 'Vectorization of the CRAY-1 of some methods for solving elliptic difference equations' in Kuck, D. J., Lawrie, D. H. & Sameh, A. H. (ed), *High Speed Computer and Algorithm Organization.* Academic Press, New York, pp. 255–71

Casulli, V. & Trigiante, D. [78] 'Multipoint iterative parallel methods for solving equations' *Calcolo* 15, 2 (1978) 147–60

Collatz, L. [64] *Funktionalanalysis und Numerische Mathematik* Springer-Verlag, Berlin-Heidelberg-New York, 1964

Corliss, G. F. [74] 'Parallel rootfinding algorithms' Ph.D. Diss., Dept. of Mathematics, Michigan State Univ., Nov. 1974, AD-A000573

Dantzig, G. B. [63] *Linear Programming and Extensions* Princeton Univ. Press, Princeton, N.J., 1963

Davidon, W. C. [59] *Variable Metric for Minimization* ANL-5990 Rev., Argonne Nat. Lab., 1959

Evans, D. J. & Hatzopoulos, M. [79] 'A parallel linear systems solver' *Intern. J. Computer Math.* 7, 3 (1979) 227–38

Evans, D. J. & Williams, S. A. [80] 'Analysis and detection of parallel processable code' *Computer J.* 23, 1 (1980) 66–72

Feilmeier, M., Gomm, W., Rönsch, W. & Töpfer, K. [80] 'Parallele Numerik' DFG-Report unpublished

Feilmeier, M. & Segerer, G. [77] 'Numerical stability in parallel evaluation of arithmetic expressions' in Feilmeier, M. (ed), *Parallel Computers – Parallel Mathematics,* North-Holland Publ. Co., Amsterdam, 1977, pp. 107–12

Fletcher, R. & Powell, M. J. O. [63] 'A rapidly convergent descent method for minimization' *Computer Journal,* 6, 2 (1963) 163–8

Fletcher, R. & Reeves, C. M. [64] 'Function minimization by conjugate gradients' *Computer J.*, 7, 2 (1964) 149–54

Flynn, M. [72] 'Some computer organizations and their effectiveness' *IEEE Trans. Comp.* C-21, 9 (1972) 948–60

Forsythe & Moler [71] *Computer Verfahren für lineare algebraische Systeme* Oldenburg Verlag, Munich, 1971

Franklin, M. A. [78] 'Parallel solution of ordinary differential equations' *IEEE Trans. Comp.* C-27, (1978) 413–20

Gal, S. & Miranker, W. L. [77] 'Optimal sequential and parallel search for finding a root' *J. Combinatorial Theory* Ser. A 23, 1 (1977) 1–14

Gear, C. W. [71] *Numerical Initial Value Problems in Ordinary Differential Equations* Prentice-Hall, New Jersey, 1971

Gear, C. W. [77] 'Conflicts between realtime and software' in Rice, J. R. (ed), *Mathematical Software III,* Academic Press, 1977, pp. 121–38

Gentzsch, Weiland & Müller-Wichards, D. [80] 'Möglichkeiten und Probleme bei der Anwendung von Vektorrechnern, dargestellt an der numerischen Behandlung einiger strömungsphysikalischer Fragestellungen – Erfahrungen und Testrechnungen mit den Vektorrechnern von CDC und Cray' DFVLR-Report, Göttingen, private communication

Gomm, W. [80a] 'Stabilitätsuntersuchungen von expliziten Multirate-Methoden zur numerischen Lösung von Anfangswertproblemen bei gewöhnlichen Differentialgleichungen' Dissertation, Techn. Univ. Braunschweig, 1980

Gomm, W. [80b] 'Stability analysis of explicit multirate methods' (to appear)

Grigorieff, R. D. [72, 77] *Numerik gewöhnlicher Differentialgleichungen I, II* Teubner, Stuttgart, 1972, 1977

Gründler, D. [79] 'Die Lösungsmöglichkeiten von Operations-Research-Problemen mit einer Parallelrechnerstruktur und Implementierung des Simplex-Algorithmus als Beispiel' Unpublished Diplom-Arbeit, TU München, 12.04.1979

Hertweck, F., Schneider, W. & Schwenn, U. [79] *Benchmark Tests with Cray-1* IPP-Report, Max-Planck-Institut für Plasmaphysik, Munich 1979

Hyafil, L. & Kung, H. T. [77] 'The complexity of parallel evaluation of linear recurrences' *J. ACM* **24**, 3 (1977) 513–21

Karp, R. M. & Miranker, W. L. [68] 'Parallel minimax search for a maximum' *J. Combinat. Theory* **4**, 1 (1968) 19–35

Keller, H. B. [68] *Numerical Methods for Two-Point-Boundary-Value Problems* Blaisdell, London, 1968

Kiefer, J. [53] 'Sequential minimax search for a maximum' *Proc. Amer. Math. Soc.* **4**, (1953) 502–6

Kober, R. & Kuznia, C. [79] 'SMS 201 – A powerful parallel processor with 128 microcomputers' *Euromicro J.* **5**, 1 (1979) 48–52

Kogge, P. M. [72] *Parallel Algorithms for the Efficient Solution of Recurrence Problems; The Numerical Stability of Parallel Algorithms for Solving Recurrence Problems; Minimal Parallelism in the Solution of Recurrence Problems* Stanford Univ., Ca., Stanford Electronics Labs., Sept. 1972, PB-212893, PB-212894, PB-212828

Kogge, P. M. [73] 'Maximal rate pipeline solutions to recurrence problems' in *Proc. First Annual Symp. on Comp. Architecture,* Gainesvill, Fl., 1973, pp. 71–6

Kogge, P. M. [74] 'Parallel solution of recurrence problems' *IBM J. Res. Develop.* **18**, 2 (1974) 138–48

Kulisch, U. [76] *Grundlagen des numerischen Rechnens* Bibl. Institut, Mannheim, 1976

Lambiotte, J. J. [77] *Effect of Virtual Memory on Efficient Solution of Two Model Problems* NASA Report TM X-3512, 1977

Lambiotte, J. J. & Voigt, R. G. [75] 'The solution of tridiagonal linear systems on the CDC STAR-100 computer' *ACM Trans. Math. Softw.* **1**, (1975) 308–29

Lamport, L. [74] 'The parallel execution of DO loops' *CACM* **17**, 2 (1974) 83–93

Larson, J. & Sameh, A. [78] 'Efficient calculation of the effects of rounding errors' *ACM Trans. Math. Softw.,* **4** (1978) 228–36

Madsen, N. K. & Rodrigue, G. H. [75] *A Comparison of Direct Methods for Tridiagonal Systems on the CDC STAR-100* Lawrence Livermore Lab. Report UCRL-76993, July 1975

Madsen, N. K. & Rodrigue, G. H. [77] 'Odd-even reduction of pentadiagonal matrices' in Feilmeier, M. (ed), *Parallel Computers – Parallel Mathematics,* North-Holland Publ. Co., Amsterdam, 1977, pp. 103–6

Maruyama, K. [73] *The Parallel Evaluation of Arithmetic Expressions* IBM Research Report RC-4217, New York 1973

Micchelli, C. A. & Miranker, W. L. [75] 'High order search methods for finding roots' *J. ACM* **22**, 1 (1975) 51–60

Miranker, W. L. [77] 'Parallel search methods for solving equations' in Feilmeier, M. (ed), *Parallel Computers – Parallel Mathematics,* North-Holland Publ. Co., Amsterdam 1977, pp. 9–15 and *Math. Comp. Simul.* **20**, 2 (1978) 93–101

Miranker, W. L. [79] 'Hierarchical relaxation' *Computing* **23**, 3 (1979) 267–85

Muller, D. E. & Preparata, F. P. [76] 'Restructuring of arithmetic expressions for parallel evaluation' *J. ACM* **23**, (1976) 534–43

Müller-Merbach, H. [73] *Operations Research,* 3. Auflage, Verlag Franz Vahlen Munich 1973

Nagel, K. [78] 'Lösung linearer Gleichungssyteme nach dem Gauss-Seidelverfahren auf dem Parallelrechner SMS 201' Private communication, 1978

Ortega, J. M. & Rheinboldt, W. C. [70] *Iterative Solution of Nonlinear Equations in Several Variables* Academic Press, New York, 1970

Ortega, J. M. & Voigt, R. G. [77] 'Solution of partial differential equations on vector computers' in *Proc. of 1977 Army Numerical Analysis and Computer Conference,* ARO Rep. 77-3, pp. 475–525

Pierre, D. A. [73] 'A nongradient minimization algorithm having parallel structure with implications for an array computer' *Comp. & Elec. Engng.* **1**, (1973) 3–21

Prause, D. [80] 'Parallelisierung von Optimierungsproblemen' Unpublished Diplomarbeit am Inst. f. Rechentechnik, Tech. Univ. Braunschweig, Jan. 1980

Rönsch, W. [80] 'Algorithmen zur parallelen Berechnung arithmetischer Ausdrücke mit großer Variablenanzahl' Institutsbericht des Instituts für Rechentechnik der Tech. Univ. Braunschweig, 1980, unpublished

Rosser, J. B. [67] 'A Runge-Kutta for all seasons' *SIAM Rev.* **9**, 3 (1967) 417–52

Sameh, A. H. & Brent, R. P. [77] 'Solving triangular systems on a parallel computer' *SIAM J. Num. Anal.* **14**, 6 (1977) 1101–13

Sameh, A. H. & Kuck, D. J. [77] 'Parallel direct linear system solvers – A survey' in: *Parallel Computers – Parallel Mathematics* Ed. M. Feilmeier, Munich 1977, pp. 25–30

Schendel, U. [79] 'Rekurrente Relationen' in: *Parallele Datenverarbeitung und parallele Algorithmen* Tech. Univ. Berlin, Brennpunkt Kybernetik, 1979, pp. 68–85

Segerer, G. [79] 'Numerische Qualität paralleler Algorithmen' in: *Parallele Datenverarbeitung und parallele Algorithmen* Tech. Univ. Berlin, Brennpunkt Kybernetik, 1979 pp. 51–67

Shampine, L. F. & Watts, H. A. [69] 'Block implicit one-step methods' *Math. Comp.* **23**, 108 (1969) 252–66

Snir, M. & Barak, A. B. [77] 'A direct approach to the parallel evaluation of rational expressions with a small number of processors' *IEEE Trans. Comp.* C-26 (1977), 933–7

Stone, H. S. [73] 'An efficient parallel algorithm for the solution of a tridiagonal linear system of equations' *JACM* **20**, 1 (1973), 27–38

Straeter, T. A. [73] *A Parallel Variable Metric Optimization Algorithm* NASA Langley Research Center, Technical Note D-7329 Hampton, Virginia, 1973

Stummel, F. [79] 'Perturbation theory for evaluation algorithms of arithmetic expressions' (to appear in *Math. Comp.*)

Swarztrauber, P. N. [79] 'A parallel algorithm for solving general tridiagonal equations' *Math. Comp.* **33**, 145 (1979) 185–99

Traub, J. F. [73] 'Iterative solution of tridiagonal systems on parallel or vector computers' in Traub, J. F. (ed), *Complexity of Sequential and Parallel Numerical Algorithms*, Academic Press, New York, 1973, pp. 49–82

Vanek, L. I. [75] 'The efficient optimization of arithmetic expressions for parallel execution' Ph.D. Diss., Princeton Univ., N.J., 1976, University Microfilms International, Ann Arbor, Mi., Report 76-23838

Voigt, R. G. [77] 'The influence of vector computer architecture on numerical algorithms' in Kuck, D. J., Lawrie, D. H. & Sameh, A. H. (ed), *High Speed Computer and Algorithm Organization*, Academic Press, New York, (1977) pp. 229–44

Wallach, Y. & Konrad, V. [80] 'On block-parallel methods for solving linear equations' *IEEE Trans. Comp.* C-29, 5 (1980) 354–9

Wilkinson, J. H. [63] *Rounding Errors in Algebraic Processes* Prentice-Hall, 1963

Williams, S. A. & Evans, D. J. [80] 'An implicit approach to the determination of parallelism' *Intern. J. Computer Math.* **8**, 1 (1980) 51–9

Winograd, S. [72] 'Parallel iterative methods' in Miller, R. E. & Thatcher, J. W. (ed), *Complexity of Computer Computations*, Plenum Press, New York, 1972, p. 53

Winograd, S. [75] 'On the parallel evaluation of certain arithmetic expressions' *J. ACM* **22**, 4 (1975) 477–92

Worland, P. B. [766] 'Parallel methods for the numerical solution of ordinary differential equations' *IEEE Trans. Comp.* C-25, 10 (1976) 1045–8

Wypior, P. [77] 'A parallel simplex algorithm' in Feilmeier, M. (ed), *Parallel Computers – Parallel Mathematics,* North-Holland Publ. Co., Amsterdam, (1977) pp. 235–7

Young, D. [71] *Iterative Solution of Large Linear Systems* Academic Press, New York, 1971

16 Notes on V.LSI computation

H. T. KUNG

1 Introduction

From its origins in the early 1960s, integrated circuit technology has advanced to the point where large scale integration (LSI) allows tens of thousands of components (that is, transistors, magnetic bubbles, or other information holders) to be built into a single chip (see, for example, [21]), and advance to very large scale integration (VLSI) should increase this number by another factor of 10 to 100 in the next 10 to 20 years.

VLSI technology offers the system designer a number of potential advantages. Among the factors which can be exploited are, in brief:

Decreases in cost per component.
Decreases in power consumption and physical size.
Decreases in manual fabrication effort.
Increases in reliability at the circuit level.

In section 2 we point out, however, that exploiting these opportunities offered by the technology at the *system and computation levels* is by no means trivial; a number of challenging problems have to be resolved first. As an illustration of the kind of solutions that one may use to meet these challenges, section 3 introduces a new architectural concept – the *systolic array* approach. A number of examples of systolic arrays are given in section 4. Section 5, the last section, reviews some of the recent progress in deriving complexity bounds for VLSI computation.

2 The VLSI challenge

The cycle of design and implementation of a VLSI system can be roughly broken down into steps as follows:

Task Definition
Design
    System level
    Algorithms
    Logic

Circuit level
Geometric layout
Processing
Pattern generation
Mask generation
Wafer fabrication
Chip packaging
Circuit testing

Only if all the three phases – task definition, design and processing – are successfully executed can the potential advantages of VLSI technology be fully realized. Here we concentrate on issues concerning the design phase, making the ideal assumption that processing is routine. (For issues in product definition, the reader is referred to the article by Moore [20].)

2.1   Structured VLSI designs

It is generally believed that current state-of-the-art computer aided design (CAD) technology is not adequate for the task of efficiently designing 'general' chips containing on the order of 100 000 transistors. It is estimated that the effort required to design a state-of-the-art integrated circuit may continue to double every two to three years. If this estimate is true, the effect in 'decrease in manufacturing cost per component' through the use of VLSI technology may be largely cancelled by the 'increase in design cost per component'. One could of course continue improving CAD systems, but potential improvements along this direction are expected to be rather limited because of the inherent difficulty of the problem. Orders of magnitude improvements are possible only through the use of structured, modular design techniques, in analogy to software. If a design can truly be decomposed into a small number of simple subdesigns with simple interfaces which can be used repetitively, great savings can be achieved [19]. Because of the newness of the technology and the difficulty of the problem, little experience has been obtained in structured VLSI designs. In sections 2 and 3 we offer a new approach and a few examples for the structured designs of special-purpose devices.

2.2   VLSI system and chip architectures

To use VLSI to improve system performance, new chip and system architectural concepts must be developed. To give an indication of some of the considerations, we make a naive calculation and look at the reasons for its failure.

With current technology it is possible, for example, to produce the following:

32-bit floating-point arithmetic chips which perform an operation in 1 μs,
multilayer circuit boards holding 200 chips apiece,
arithmetic units containing 10 circuit boards.

Multiplying through, we discover that our proposed machine can perform 2000
operations in 1 μs, for a rate of 2000 million floating-point operations per second
(MFLOPS).

This operation rate is far in excess of that achievable by the fastest currently
available machines, some of whose speeds on an average are indicated in figure
16.1. Since these machines are by no means obsolete, we may suspect that
something is missing from our calculation. Indeed, our architecture suffers from
two bottlenecks.

2.2.1 Bottleneck 1: Problem decomposition

In making our calculation, we assumed that all 2000 floating-point
chips could operate continuously and in parallel. In fact, any real problem has
a certain proportion of operations, such as decision points, which must be done
serially. In general, given that a problem requires that $k\%$ of its operations be
performed serially, the maximum possible speedup available through parallelism
is $100/k$. In other words, if 10% of a problem had to be done sequentially, then
a speedup factor of 10 would be the maximum possible; if only 1% of a problem
were serial, the maximum speedup would still only be a factor of 100. In general,
then, parallelism can at best be expected to produce speedups in the range of
10 to 100. Parallelism, however, is crucial to the performance of a VLSI system,
since VLSI is typically *not* faster, component-for-component, than say TTL
logic in sequential use; the potential power of VLSI has to come from the large
amount of concurrency that it may support. The challenge here is to create,
discover and express parallelism in problem formulation, algorithm design, and
program development.

Figure 16.1. Operation rates for several high speed computers.

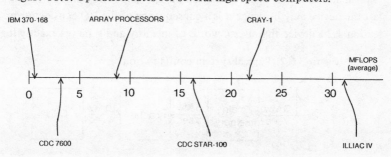

2.2.2   Bottleneck 2: Communication

Another factor which acts to limit speed is that of communication. The so-called *von Neumann bottleneck* for communications appears at all levels of the memory hierarchy of a computer system. At the system level, we are concerned with supplying data to the arithmetic unit at a rate sufficient to keep it busy. Figure 16.2 sketches a typical computer system, with storage capacities noted in megawords (Mw) and communication rates in megawords per second. Note that a typical CPU data I/O rate is 10 million words per second. At this rate, assuming that at least two operands are read from or written to the cache for each operation performed, the maximum possible operation rate is only 5 MFLOPS – a bound independent of the speed of the CPU. Similarly, the disk bandwidth provides an absolute upper bound on the operation rate. Unless on the average every item brought out from the disk is used more than one thousand times, it is impossible to achieve a computation rate of 200 MFLOPS. This reveals the fact that the effective use of VLSI is possible only after careful considerations on the communication problem have been given in the context of the whole system. We can expect a cost-effective performance improvement when applying VLSI to speed up a subsystem, only if (*a*) the subsystem represents a performance bottleneck in the present system, and (*b*) the subsystem is sped up without requiring a similar increase in the I/O bandwidth. The challenge for (*a*) is to identify bottlenecks, while for (*b*) it is to devise computation schemes capable of making multiple use of data items.

When a large computation is performed on a small device or memory, the computation must be decomposed into subcomputations. Executing subcomputations one at a time may require a substantial amount of I/O to store or retrieve intermediate results. Very often it is the I/O that dominates the speed of a computation. For example it has been shown in [9] that the I/O time for executing the n-point. Fast Fourier Transform (FFT) on a device with k words of memory is at least $\Omega(n \log n / \log k)$. Thus, an k-point hardware device can achieve a speedup ratio of at most $O(\log k)$ over the conventional $O(n \log n)$ software implementation. This upper bound on the speedup ratio holds no matter how fast the device may be, since it is a consequence of the I/O consideration. (In section 4.2 a device that uses k words of memory and achieves exactly log

Figure 16.2. Typical system configuration.

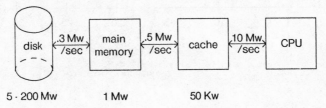

k speedup for the FFT is described.) In practice, problems are typically 'larger' than hardware. Thus, it is important to have algorithms that can be well decomposed not only for parallel executions but also for efficient executions on small devices or memories.

At the inter-chip communication level, we observe pin bandwidth limitation – the number of I/O pins that any one chip can have is limited, and each pin has a bandwidth limitation. Figure 16.3 illustrates a scenario where because of pin limitation, increasing chip density (or chip capacity) does not help reduce the number of chips needed to cover a network. In this context, networks that can be decomposed by removing only a small number of links are likely to be able to take advantage of the increase in chip capacity. The communication bottleneck due to pin bandwidth limitation is likely to be with us for the foreseeable future, because it is related to fundamental physical laws. The only solution to the problem is to design circuitry that can be partitioned among separate chips so that inter-chip communication is either completely avoided or reduced to the minimum. Inside a chip we observe that the wiring for communication can easily dominate the power, chip area and time required to perform a computation. Here we face the challenge of minimizing wiring in chip design [27].

3   The systolic array approach

We have discussed a number of challenges concerning the design of VLSI systems and computations. As a partial solution to these challenges, this section introduces the *systolic array* approach, an architectural concept first proposed for implementation of matrix operations in VLSI [13].

3.1   *Basic principle*

A systolic system consists of identical simple cells that circulate data in a regular fashion. An array structure for such a system provides simple and regular communication paths between cells. Information in a systolic array flows between the cells in a *pipeline*, resembling a factory assembly line. The

Figure 16.3. Covering a two-dimensional grid by chips with a bounded number of pins.

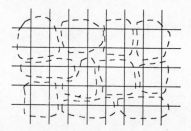

basic principle of the systolic array approach can be best illustrated using figure
16.4 - by replacing a single arithmetic logic unit (ALU) with a systolic array of
ALUs, a much higher computation throughput can be achieved without having
to increase memory bandwidth. The crux of the systolic array research is to
make sure that once a data item is brought out from the memory it will be used
effectively many times while travelling along the systolic array. The principle of
systolic arrays is applicable to all levels of a computer system which are computer-
bound. In the following we describe a simple systolic array for string pattern
matching, based on the work reported in [6].

3.2   *Systolic pattern matching array – an example*

We are given a text string $(s_1, s_2, \ldots, s_n)$ and a pattern string $(p_1, p_2, \ldots, p_m)$, with n much larger than m, and we are asked to compute positions of
all occurrences of the pattern within the text string. 'Don't care' symbols are
allowed in the pattern string. For example, if the text string is WXAYWXBY
and the pattern is WX*Y, where '*' indicates 'don't care', then the result is
10001, where each '1' indicates the beginning position of an occurrence of the
pattern inside the text string. For this problem the straightforward software
solution takes time proportional to mn, but a systolic array with m cells can
solve the problem in time n.

Let $\{r_1, r_2, \ldots, r_{n-m+1}\}$ be the resulting Boolean stream, such that $r_i = 1$ if
and only if $(s_i, s_{i+1}, \ldots, s_{i+n-1}) = (p_1, p_2, \ldots, p_m)$. Then for example, if $m = 4$,

Figure 16.4. Principle of the systolic array approach.

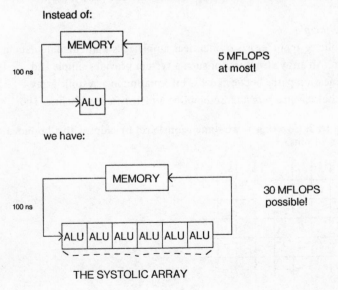

THE SYSTOLIC ARRAY

we have

$$r_1 = (p_1 = s_1) \wedge (p_2 = s_2) \wedge (p_3 = s_3) \wedge (p_4 = s_4),$$
$$r_2 = (p_1 = s_2) \wedge (p_2 = s_3) \wedge (p_3 = s_4) \wedge (p_4 = s_5),$$
$$r_3 = (p_1 = s_3) \wedge (p_2 = s_4) \wedge (p_3 = s_5) \wedge (p_4 = s_6),$$
$$\vdots$$
$$r_{n-3} = (p_1 = s_{n-3}) \wedge (p_2 = s_{n-2}) \wedge (p_3 = s_{n-1}) \wedge (p_4 = s_n).$$

One can check that the systolic array in figure 16.5, using the basic cell in figure 16.6, can compute the r_is. Each r_i is initialized to be '1'. In a synchronous manner the pattern string moves to the right and the text string moves to the left. A pattern character and a string character are compared at the cell where they meet. (Because characters in each string are separated by two time units, we see that each pattern character will meet every string character.) The value of r_i at a cell achieves its final value when the last character in the pattern string passes through the cell. One can easily modify the basic design here to allow 'don't care' characters in the pattern and to allow 'bit' rather than 'character' operations [6].

3.3 Design criteria for systolic arrays

The above pattern matching example suggests the following criteria for the design of systolic arrays:

1. The design should use a *few* types of *simple* cells.
2. Data and control flow should be *simple* and *regular*. Cells can be connected by a network with local, regular connections. Long distance or irregular communication is thus minimized.
3. There should be extensive *pipelining* and *parallelism*. Typically, several data streams move at constant velocity over fixed paths in the network,

Figure 16.5. Systolic pattern matching array.

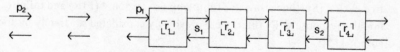

Figure 16.6. Basic cell for the systolic pattern matching array.

$$P_{out} \leftarrow P_{in}$$
$$S_{out} \leftarrow S_{in}$$
$$r \leftarrow r \wedge (P_{in} = S_{in})$$

[REGISTER r HAS VALUE "1" INITIALLY]

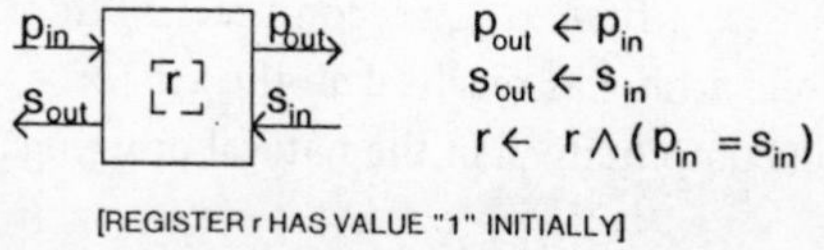

interacting at cells where they meet. In this way a large number of cells are active at one time so high computation rate can be achieved.

4. Multiple use should be made of each input data item. Thus high computation throughput can be achieved without requiring high bandwidth between the array and the memory (or the host).

We see that the pattern matching systolic array indeed satisfies these criteria. Hardware designs based on systolic arrays tend to be simple (a consequence of properties 1 and 2), modular (property 2), and yield high performance (properties 3 and 4). Further examples of systolic arrays are given in the next section.

4   Examples of systolic arrays

Many systolic arrays have been designed during the past few years for problems in areas such as matrix computations [13], database manipulation [12], and signal and image processing [6, 16]. As further illustrations of systolic arrays, in this section we present systolic arrays for filtering and discrete Fourier transforms, that were previously reported in a conference paper [16].

4.1   Systolic arrays for filtering

We here describe the basic design of a family of systolic arrays for performing filtering. Designs of systolic arrays for convolution, correlation and pattern matching can be obtained similarly [7]. Mathematically the canonical form of the filtering problem can be defined as follows:

given the weighting coefficients $\{w_0, w_1, \ldots, w_h\}$, $\{r_1, r_2, \ldots, r_k\}$, the initial values $\{y_{-k}, y_{-k+1}, \ldots, y_{-1}\}$, and the input sequence $\{x_{-h}, x_{-h+1}, \ldots, x_0, x_1, \ldots, x_n\}$,

compute the output sequence $\{y_0, y_1, \ldots, y_n\}$ defined by

$$y_i = \sum_{j=0}^{h} w_j x_{i-j} + \sum_{j=1}^{k} r_j y_{i-j}. \tag{4.1}$$

Assume that a cycle is the time to perform the function of the type I cell defined below (which in this case is essentially the time for two multiplications and two additions). Systolic arrays proposed here can compute a new y_i every two cycles. (Systolic arrays for finite impulse response (FIR) and infinite impulse response (IIR) filters were previously considered separately by the author [15]).

The weighting coefficients w_is and r_is are preloaded to a systolic array. The filtering computation starts by loading the x_is from the host to the systolic array in the natural ordering, that is, x_{-h} first, x_{-h+1} second, x_{-h+2} third, and so on. Immediately after the systolic array has received all the x_is for $-h \leqslant i \leqslant 0$, it starts outputting the computed y_is in the natural ordering at the rate of one every two cycles.

4.1.1 Description of the systolic filtering array
Basic cells
There are two types of cells, as depicted in figure 16.7. A type II cell is essentially a buffer.

The array
Let $m = \max(h + 1, k)$. The systolic array is a linear array consisting of m type I cells and one type II cell, as depicted in figure 16.8. The right-most cell is a degenerated type I cell, where input Y_{in} is always zero, and outputs y_{out} and x_{out} are ignored.

4.1.2 An illustration
Suppose $h = k = 2$. Figure 16.9 depicts the state of the array at the end of each of two consecutive cycles. Each Y_i is initialized as zero entering the array from the right-most cell; it accumulates terms marching along the array from right to left, and eventually achieves its final value y_i when reaching the left-most cell. The final computed y_i is output to the host and is also fed back to the array for use in computing y_{i+1} and y_{i+2}.

Figure 16.7. Basic cells for the systolic filtering array.

TYPE I CELL

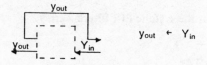

$$y_{out} \leftarrow y_{in}$$
$$Y_{out} \leftarrow w \cdot x_{in} + r \cdot y_{in} + Y_{in}$$
$$x_{out} \leftarrow x_{in}$$

[VALUES r AND w ARE PRELOADED WEIGHTING COEFFICIENTS]

TYPE II CELL:

$$y_{out} \leftarrow Y_{in}$$

Figure 16.8. Systolic filtering array.

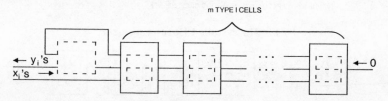

4.1.3 An efficient systolic FIR filtering array

It is seen from the illustration that only half the cells in the array are active at any given time. For FIR filtering, which corresponds to the case where $r_i = 0$ for all $1 \leqslant i \leqslant k$ in equation (4.1), another functionally equivalent design that employs data streams moving at two different speeds can make use of all the cells all the time. This more efficient design uses the basic cell illustrated in figure 16.10. Notice that each input X_{in} is delayed by one unit of time as it flows through the cell. The array is initialized by loading the w_is to the cells, one in each cell. Figure 16.11 depicts the state of the array at the end of the loading phase for the case when $h = 3$. Both the x_is and Y_is march from left to right, but the x_is travel twice as slowly as the Y_is due to the delay for the x_is in each cell. It is easy to see that each Y_i accumulates terms as travelling to the right and achieves its final value y_i as leaving from the right-most cell.

The FIR filtering problem is mathematically identical to the convolution problem. Thus designs for FIR filtering apply to convolution computations. The systolic FIR filtering array discussed here has been implemented for the convolution operator in image processing [14].

Figure 16.9. Two cycles of the systolic filtering array.

y3
Y4
Y2
Y5
X5
X4
X3
r1
W0
r2
W1
0
W2
Y6

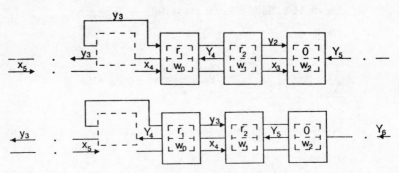

Figure 16.10. Basic cell for the systolic FIR filtering array.

Xin
Yin
x
a
Xout
Yout
Yout ← a · Xin + Yin
x ← Xin
Xout ← x
[EACH x STAYS INSIDE THE CELL FOR ONE CYCLE]
[VALUE a IS A PRELOADED WEIGHTING COEFFICIENT]

Figure 16.11. The systolic FIR filtering array.

X5
X4
X3
Y1
Y0
X2
W3
X1
X0
W2
W1
W0

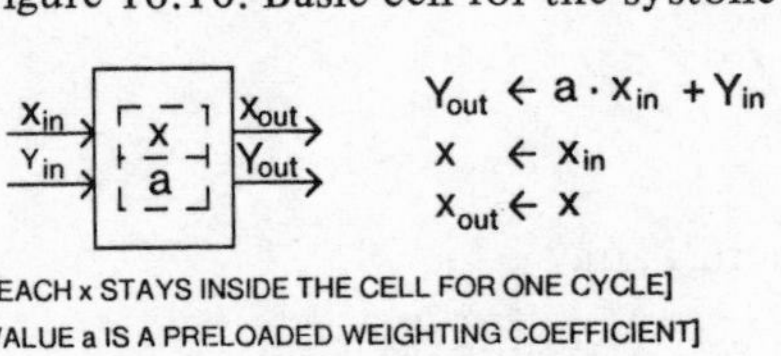

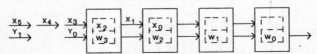

4.2   Systolic arrays for Discrete Fourier Transforms

An n-point Discrete Fourier Transform (DFT) problem is defined as follows:

given

$$\{a_0, a_1, \ldots, a_{n-1}\},$$

compute

$$\{y_0, y_1, \ldots, y_{n-1}\}$$

defined by

$$y_i = \sum_{j=0}^{n-1} a_j \omega^{ij},$$

where ω is a principal n-th root of unity.

The well-known Fast Fourier Transform (FFT) algorithm computes an n-point DFT in $O(n \log n)$ operations, while the straightforward method requires $O(n^2)$ operations. However, for parallel processing, the FFT suffers from the drawback that it requires complicated data communication (see discussions below). Here we describe a family of systolic arrays for computing DFTs in parallel that use only the simplest communication scheme, namely, the linearly connected array.

4.2.1   Description of the systolic DFT array
Basic cell
Figure 16.12 describes the basic cell:

The array
A full array consists of $n-1$ linearly connected basic cells, as depicted in figure 16.13. The input Y_{in} and x_{in} to the left-most cell are a_{n-1} and some power of ω, respectively, whereas the output x_{out} from the right-most cell is always ignored.

4.2.2   An illustration
Consider the case $n = 5$. A 5-point DFT problem can be viewed as that of evaluating the polynomial

$$a_4 x^4 + a_3 x^3 + a_2 x^2 + a_1 x + a_0$$

Figure 16.12. Basic cell for the systolic DFT array.

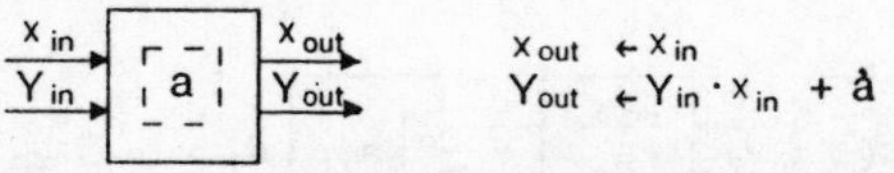

$$x_{out} \leftarrow x_{in}$$
$$Y_{out} \leftarrow Y_{in} \cdot x_{in} + a$$

[VALUE a IS A PRELOADED INPUT]

at $x = 1, \omega, \omega^2, \omega^3, \omega^4$, where ω is a fifth root of unity. Evaluating the polynomial by Horner's rule gives:

$$y_0 = (((a_4 \cdot 1 + a_3) \cdot 1 + a_2) \cdot 1 + a_1) \cdot 1 + a_0,$$
$$y_1 = (((a_4 \cdot \omega + a_3) \cdot \omega + a_2) \cdot \omega + a_1) \cdot \omega + a_0,$$
$$y_2 = (((a_4 \cdot \omega^2 + a_3) \cdot \omega^2 + a_2) \cdot \omega^2 + a_1) \cdot \omega^2 + a_0,$$
$$y_3 = (((a_4 \cdot \omega^3 + a_3) \cdot \omega^3 + a_2) \cdot \omega^3 + a_1) \cdot \omega^3 + a_0,$$
$$y_4 = (((a_4 \cdot \omega^4 + a_3) \cdot \omega^4 + a_2) \cdot \omega^4 + a_1) \cdot \omega^4 + a_0.$$

We shall see that all the y_i can be computed in a pipeline fashion by a single systolic array with four cells. The array is initialized by loading the a_is to the cells, one in each cell. Figure 16.14 depicts the state of the array at the end of the loading phase. Define, as before, a cycle to be the time to perform the function of the basic cell. The states of the array at the end of the next four cycles are depicted in figure 16.15. It is readily seen that each Y_i, initialized as a_4, gathers its terms as marching to the right, and achieves its final value y_i as leaving from the right-most cell.

Figure 16.13. The systolic DFT array.

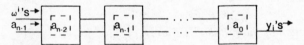

Figure 16.14. State of the systolic DFT array after the loading phase.

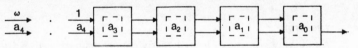

Figure 16.15. Four cycles of the systolic DFT array.

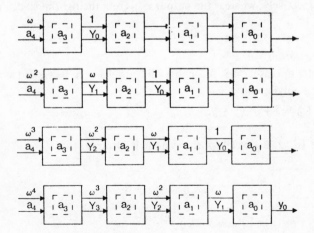

4.2.3 Discussions

A linear systolic DFT array with n basic cells can compute an n-point DFT in time of $O(n)$. Suppose that there are only k basic cells in the array, for some fixed $k < n$. Then one can compute an n-point DFT in $O(n \log n / \log k)$ time, by using the array to compute all the k-point sub-DFTs in the n-point FFT algorithm. (Figure 16.16 shows the 4-point DFTs that are in a 16-point FFT algorithm.) This represents an $O(\log k)$ speedup over the sequential FFT. The $O(n \log n / \log k)$ time is minimum in the sense that when executing an n-point FFT on a device with $O(k)$ words of local memory (as in the case of the systolic array where k words of memory are distributed among k cells), this amount of time is needed just to transfer data between the host and the device [9].

Up to this point we have been assuming implicitly that the rate that data is sent to the systolic array is not higher than the computation rate of a basic cell. If this is not the case, then to take advantage of the available bandwidth, as many independent linear systolic DFT arrays should be used as possible, so that all the arrays can input and output data in each cycle. An interesting (but maybe theoretical) comparison to the parallel FFT can be made at this point. The traditional parallel implementation of the FFT algorithm assumes that k-point DFT is performed every $\log k$ cycles, using a shuffle-exchange network of k nodes [3, 22, 26]. The parallel FFT using such a network performs an n-point DFT in $O((n \log n)/k)$ time and the best known layout of the network takes a chip area $O(k^2 / \log^{3/2} k)$ [25]. A set of $k / \log k$ linear systolic DFT arrays, each consisting of k basic cells, achieves the same performance with almost the same total chip area, but enjoys a much simpler communication structure.

The systolic approach has one more advantage in that with minor control mechanisms the same systolic array may be used for many computations such as filtering, DFT and matrix multiplication.

Figure 16.16. The 4-point DFTs that form a 16-point FFT.

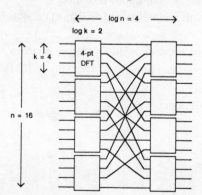

4.3   Remarks on implementation and performance

For simplicity we have so far assumed that cells in systolic arrays operate on words. In implementation each word processor can be partitioned into bit processors to achieve modularity in the bit-level [6]. A transformation of a design from word-level to bit-level is usually straightforward. It is also possible to implement cells efficiently with multistage pipeline adders and multipliers. In general, many variations on the systolic arrays suggested are possible. All these are functionally equivalent and differ only in implementation details.

Using the bit-serial implementation, it is possible to implement about ten basic cells, performing 32-bit fixed-point operations, on a single chip with present MOS technology. By using many such chips the systolic array can achieve a high computation rate, even assuming a modest bandwidth between the array and the host. This is because each word, once input from the host, is used many times in the array.

During the past year, we have designed prototypes of several special-purpose chips using the systolic approach. These include a pattern maching chip [6], an image-processing chip [14], and a tree processor for database application [24]. The pattern matching and tree processor chips have been tested and found to work. The image-processing chip will be tested when the required testing software has been developed.

5   Complexity of VLSI computation

For VLSI wires rather than logic elements dominate the cost and time required to perform a computation. To illustrate this point we consider the area and volume needed to implement a permutation network with n input ports and n output ports, as depicted in figure 16.17.

Three examples of such a network are:

the crossbar, with n^2 switches, and constant delay time.
Batcher's sorting network, with n switches and $\Theta(\log^2 n)$ delay time [2, 10][1].
the rearrangeable permutation network, with $O(n \log n)$ switches, $\Theta(\log n)$ delay, and $\Theta(n \log n)$ setup time (see, for example, [11]).

Figure 16.7. Size n permutation network.

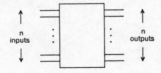

We will prove a lower bound result about the two-dimensional area A, and also about the three-dimensional volume V, required to embed an n-node permutation network with a delay of T time units. First we consider the two-dimensional case. We assume that the total chip area is a convex region, all wires have unit width, and there exists a constant upper bound on the number of wires that can cross at any one point of the region. This upper bound is equal to the number of layers in the chip. Let D be a diameter through the region, and choose a line B, perpendicular to D, such that B bisects the $2n$ I/O ports into 2 subsets of n ports each. Note that one of the subregions thus created must contain at least $n/2$ input ports, while the other must contain at least $n/2$ output ports. Now consider a permutation which maps $n/2$ input ports on one side of B onto $n/2$ output ports on the other side of B (see figure 16.18). Let d be the length of the diameter D, and let b be the length of the bisector B. Since at most a constant number of wires can cross in one unit of area, and since each wire can transmit one bit of information per unit time, at most $O(b)$ bits of information can cross the line B in one unit of time. To perform this particular permutation requires that $\Omega(n)$ bits of information cross the line B. Therefore

$$T = \Omega(n/b). \tag{5.1}$$

Since the region is convex, a well-known inequality states that $A \geqslant db/2 \geqslant 1/2(b^2)$. Hence we have $A = \Omega(b^2)$, and by (5.1) $AT^2 = \Omega(n^2)$, or

$$A = \Omega((n/T)^2). \tag{5.2}$$

This is a lower bound on the chip area A needed to embed a size n permutation network that can perform any permutation in time T; we see that the smaller the T is, the larger the A has to be. For example, if T is $O(\log n)$, then A is at least $\Omega((n/\log n)^2)$. Note that this lower bound holds even if we assume a switch takes no area at all. A consequence of the result is that Batcher's sorting network and the rearrangeable permutation network require area at least

Figure 16.18. Bisecting the set of I/O ports.

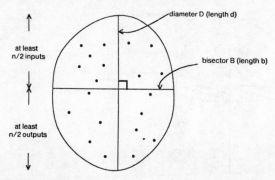

$\Omega(n^2/\log^4 n)$ and $\Omega(n^2/\log^2 n)$ for accommodating their wires, although they use only $\Theta(n)$ and $O(n \log n)$ switches, respectively.

Now we consider the three-dimensional situation. Here, B is a planar section bisecting the set of I/O ports distributed in a convex three-dimensional region (see figure 16.19). We have $T = \Omega(n/b)$, and $V = \Omega(db) = \Omega(b^{1/2} \cdot b) = \Omega(b^{3/2})$. Therefore, by (5.1) $VT^{3/2} = \Omega(n^{3/2})$, or

$$V = \Omega((n/T)^{3/2}).$$

Again we see that the smaller the T is, the larger the V has to be.

Similar lower bounds for area–time tradeoffs have been obtained for many problems, including discrete Fourier transform [28], integer multiplication [1, 4], matrix multiplication [23] and sorting [29]. All these lower bounds have actually been shown to be the best possible to within small powers of $\log n$, where n is the problem size. It has been demonstrated that some *shifting* or *transitivity* property is in fact all that is needed to derive most of these lower bounds [31]. Another emerging theory in VLSI computation is on layout complexity. Given a graph or network of n nodes, what is the minimum area required to embed it onto a two-dimensional region? Good upper bounds have been obtained on graphs such as trees and planar graphs that have good 'separator theorems' [17, 18, 30]. Surprising layout constructions have also been studied for geometrically less regular graphs such as the shuffle-exchange network [8, 25]. Lower bounds results in layout complexity are beginning to appear for simple cases such as complete trees [5].

Acknowledgements

The research was supported in part by the Office of Naval Research under Contracts N00014-76-C-0370 and N00014-80-C-0236, in part by the National Science Foundation under Grant MCS 78-236-76, and in part by the

Figure 16.19. Bisecting the set of I/O ports for the three-dimensional case.

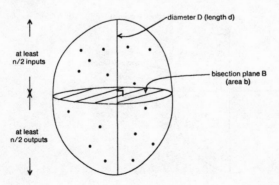

Defense Advanced Research Projects Agency under Contract F33615-78-C-1551 (monitored by the Air Force Office of Scientific Research).

Notes

[1] Asymptotic function order notation:

Let f, g be functions defined on the set of natural numbers. We use the following convention:

$f(n) = O(g(n))$, $f(n)$ is order at most $g(n)$, iff there are constants $C > 0$ and $N > 0$ such that for all $n \geqslant N$, $f(n) \leqslant C \cdot g(n)$.

$f(n) = \Omega(g(n))$, $f(n)$ is order at least $g(n)$, iff there are constant $C > 0$ and $N > 0$ such that for all $n \geqslant N$, $f(n) \geqslant C \cdot g(n)$.

$f(n) = \Theta(g(n))$, $f(n)$ is order exactly $g(n)$, iff $f(n) = O(g(n))$ and $f(n) = \Omega(g(n))$.

References

[1] Abelson, H. and Andreae, P. Information transfer and area-time tradeoffs for VLSI multiplication *Communications of the ACM* **23**:20–23, January 1980.

[2] Batcher, K. E. 'Sorting networks and their applications' in *1968 Spring Joint Computer Conf.* 32: pp. 307–14, 1968.

[3] Berglend, Glenn D. 'Fast Fourier Transform hardware implementations – an overview' *IEEE Transactions on Audio Electroacoustics* AU-17:104–8, June 1969.

[4] Brent, R. P. and Kung, H. T. 'The area-time complexity of binary multiplication' *Journal of the ACM* **28**: 521–34, July 1981.

[5] Brent, R. P. and Kung, H. T. 'On the area of binary tree layouts' *Information Processing Letters* **11**(1):46–8, August 1980.

[6] Foster, M. J. and Kung, H. T. 'The design of special-purpose VLSI chips' *Computer Magazine* **13**(1):26–40, January 1980. (An early version of the paper, entitled 'Design of special-purpose VLSI chips: example and opinions', appears in *Proceedings of the 7th International Symposium on Computer Architecture*, pp. 300–7, La Baule, France, May 1980.)

[7] Foster, M. J. and Kung, H. T. 'Toward a theory of systolic algorithms for VLSI' 1980. (Contributed paper at Conference on Advanced Research in Integrated Circuits, MIT, January 28–30).

[8] Hoey, D. and Leiserson, C. E. 'A layout for the shuffle-exchange network' in *Proc. 1980 International Conference on Parallel Processing*, pp. 329–36, IEEE, August 1980.

[9] Hong, J-W. and Kung, H. T. *I/O Complexity: The Red-Blue Pebble Game* Technical Report, Carnegie-Mellon University, Department of Computer Science, March 1981. (A preliminary version of the paper appears in *Proc. 13th Annual ACM Symposium on Theory of Computing*, pp. 326–33, May 1981.)

[10] Knuth, D. E. *The Art of Computer Programming. Volume 3: Sorting and Searching.* Addison-Wesley, Reading, Massachusetts, 1973.

[11] Kuck, D. J. *The Structure of Computers and Computations.* John Wiley & Sons, New York, 1978.

[12] Kung, H. T. and Lehman, P. L. 'Systolic (VLSI) arrays for relational database operations' in *Proc. ACM-SIGMOD 1980 International Conference on Management of Data*, pp. 105–16, ACM, May 1980. (Also available as a CMU Computer Science Department technical report, August 1979.)

[13] Kung, H. T. and Leiserson, C. E. 'Systolic arrays (for VLSI)' in Duff, I. S. and Stewart, G. W. (eds.), *Sparse Matrix Proceedings 1978*, pp. 256–82. Society for Industrial and Applied Mathematics, 1979. (A slightly different version appears in *Introduction to VLSI Systems* by C. A. Mead and L. A. Conway, Addison-Wesley, 1980, Section 8.3.)

[14] Kung. H. T. and Song, S. W. *A Systolic 2-D Convolution Chip* Technical Report, Carnegie-Mellon University, Department of Computer Science, March 1980.

[15] Kung, H. T. 'Let's design algorithms for VLSI systems' in *Proc. Conference on Very Large Scale Integration: Architecture, Design, Fabrication*, pp. 65–90. California Institute of Technology, January, 1979. (Also available as a CMU Computer Science Department technical report, September 1979.)

[16] Kung, H. T. 'Special-purpose devices for signal and image processing: an opportunity in VLSI' *Proceedings of the SPIE*, 241, Real-time Signal Processing III, 76–84, The Society of Photo-Optical Instrumentation Engineers, July 1980.

[17] Leiserson, C. E. 'Area-efficient graph layouts (for VLSI)' in *Proc. 21st Annual Symp. on Foundations of Computer Science*, pp. 270–81. October 1980.

[18] Leiserson, C. E. 'Area-efficient VLSI computation'. PhD thesis, Carnegie-Mellon University, 1981.

[19] Mead, C. A. and Conway, L. A. *Introduction to VLSI Systems.* Addison-Wesley, Reading, Massachusetts, 1980.

[20] Moore, G. E. 'Are we really ready for VLSI?' in C. L. Seitz (ed.), *Proc. Conference on Very Large Scale Integration: Architecture, Design, Fabrication*, pp. 3–14. January 1979.

[21] Robert N. Noyce. 'Hardware prospects and limitations' in Dertouzos, M. L. and Moses, J. (eds.), *The Computer Age: A Twenty-Year View*, pp. 321–37. IEEE, 1979.

[22] Pease, M. C. 'An adaptation of the Fast Fourier Transform for parallel processing' *Journal of the ACM* 15:252–64, April 1968.

[23] Savage, J. E. *Area-Time Tradeoffs for Matrix Multiplication and Related Problems in VLSI Models.* Technical Report CS-50, Brown University, Department of Computer Science, August 1979.

[24] Song, S. W. *A Database Machine with Novel Space Allocation Algorithms.* Technical Report VLSI Document V042, Carnegie-Mellon University, Department of Computer Science, 1980.

[25] Steinberg, D. and Rodeh, M. *A Layout for the Shuffle-Exchange Network with $\Theta(N^2/log^{3/2} N)$ Area.* The Weizmann Institute and IBM Israel Scientific Center, Israel.

[26] Stone, H. S. 'Parallel processing with the perfect shuffle' *IEEE Transactions on Computers* C-20:153–61, February 1971.

[27] Sutherland, I. E. and Mead, C. A. 'Microelectronics and computer science' *Scientific American* 237(3):210–28, September 1977.

[28] Thompson, C. D. 'Area-time complexity for VLSI' in *Proc. Eleventh Annual ACM Symposium on Theory of Computing*, pp. 81–8. ACM, May 1979.

[29] Thompson, C. D. 'A complexity theory for VLSI'. PhD thesis, Carnegie-Mellon University, Department of Computer Science, 1980.

[30] Valiant, L. G. 'University considerations in VLSI circuits' *IEEE Transactions on Computers*, C-30: 135–40, February 1981.

[31] Vuillemin, J. 'A combinatorial limit to the computing power of V.L.S.I. circuits' in *Proc. 21st Annual Symposium on Foundations of Computer Science*, pp. 294–300. IEEE, October 1980.

17 Parallel numerical algorithms for linear systems

D. J. EVANS

1 Introduction

The standard techniques for obtaining the numerical solution of systems of linear equations of the form $A\mathbf{x} = \mathbf{d}$ are based on either (a) a factorisation of the coefficient matrix A into easily inverted factors L and U leading to a direct method such as Gaussian elimination, Choleski, etc. or (b) a convenient splitting of the coefficient matrix leading to such iterative methods as Jacobi, Gauss–Seidel, successive over-relaxation (SOR) and others.

In this chapter new factorisation and splitting procedures more convenient for parallel computation are proposed. They are based on QIF (quadrant interlocking factorisation) and involve the factorisation and splitting of the coefficient matrix into components which are essentially interlocking matrix quadrants.

Finally, the problem of solving linear systems having a banded structured form occurs frequently in the numerical solution of partial and coupled ordinary differential equations. By using a recursive partitioning process, it is shown that new algorithms can be derived to facilitate the solution of diagonally dominant or positive definite systems. In one instance, a method is developed specifically to enable it to run on a dual computer system which permits parallel processing.

2 Quadrant interlocking methods
2.1 QIF matrix factorisation

Since an LU-type factorisation of the matrix leads essentially to a serial-type algorithm, we can ask ourselves the question: is there an alternative factorisation which is more suited for parallel computers?

Consider now a factorisation of the form

$$A = WZ, \qquad\qquad (2.1)$$

where W and Z have the matrix forms:

$$
W = \begin{bmatrix}
1 & & & & & & 0 \\
w_{2,1} & 1 & & & & & w_{2,n} \\
\cdot & & w_{3,2} & & 0 & & \cdot \\
\cdot & & \cdot & \cdot & \cdot & & \cdot \\
\cdot & & & & 1 & & \cdot \\
\cdot & & w_{n-2,2} & & & & w_{n-2,n} \\
\cdot & & & & 0 & & \cdot \\
w_{n-1,1} & & \cdot & & & & w_{n-1,n} \\
0 & & & & & & 1
\end{bmatrix}
$$

$$(2.2)$$

$$
Z = \begin{bmatrix}
z_{1,1} & z_{1,2} & \cdot & \cdot & \cdot & \cdot & \cdot & z_{1,n} \\
 & z_{2,2} & \cdot & \cdot & \cdot & \cdot & z_{2,n-1} \\
 & & \cdot & \cdot & \cdot & & \\
 & 0 & \cdot & z_{i,i} & & 0 & \\
 & & \cdot & \cdot & \cdot & & \\
 & & \cdot & & \cdot & \cdot & \\
z_{n,1} & \cdot & \cdot & \cdot & \cdot & \cdot & \cdot & z_{n,n}
\end{bmatrix}
$$

where the elements of W and Z are given by

$$
w_{i,j} = \begin{cases}
1, & i = j \\
0, & i = 1(1)\dfrac{n+1}{2}, \quad j = i+1(1)n-i+1 \\
0, & i = \dfrac{n+2}{2}(1)n, \quad j = n-i+1(1)i-1 \\
w_{i,j}, & \text{otherwise}
\end{cases}
$$

and

$$
z_{i,j} = \begin{cases}
z_{i,j}, & i = 1(1)\dfrac{n+1}{2}, \quad j = i(1)n-i+1 \\
z_{i,j}, & i = \dfrac{n+2}{2}(1)n, \quad j = n-i+1(1)i \\
0, & \text{otherwise.}
\end{cases}
$$

$$(2.3)$$

2.1.1 Computation of the matrices W and Z

By comparing corresponding terms of the matrices A and WZ, we have
(1) the elements of the first and last row of Z given immediately by

$$z_{1,i} = a_{1,i} \quad \text{and} \quad z_{n,i} = a_{n,i} \quad \text{for all } i = 1(1)n,$$

(2) then the sets of (2×2) linear systems given by

$$z_{1,1}w_{i,1} + z_{n,1}w_{i,n} = a_{i,1}$$
$$z_{1,n}w_{i,1} + z_{n,n}w_{i,n} = a_{i,n} \tag{2.4}$$

are solved to obtain the values of $w_{i,1}$ and $w_{i,n}$ for $i = 2(1)n - 1$. This then completes the *first stage* and the calculation of the outermost ring of elements of the matrices W and Z. The remaining elements of W and Z are determined in a similar manner. Thus, at least $(n-1)/2$ such stages are required to compute all the elements of the matrices W and Z.

2.1.2   Solution of the linear systems

By using the relationship $A = WZ$ the linear system

$$Au = d$$

can be reformulated as the solution of the two related linear systems

$$Zu = y \quad \text{and} \quad Wy = d, \tag{2.5}$$

where we have introduced the intermediate vector **y**.

The latter are linear systems of the form,

$$
\begin{bmatrix}
1 & & & & & & .0 \\
w_{2,1} & . & & 0 & & .. & w_{2,n} \\
& w_{3,2} & . & & & & \\
& & . & 1 & . & & \\
& & & . & . & & \\
w_{n-1,1} & & .. & 0 & & . & w_{n-1,n} \\
0 & & & & & & 1
\end{bmatrix}
\begin{bmatrix}
y_1 \\
y_2 \\
. \\
. \\
. \\
y_{n-1} \\
y_n
\end{bmatrix}
=
\begin{bmatrix}
d_1 \\
d_2 \\
. \\
. \\
. \\
d_{n-1} \\
d_n
\end{bmatrix}
\tag{2.6}
$$

We see immediately that y_1 and y_n are calculated first, then, y_2 and y_{n-1} and so on in pairs working from the top and bottom of the intermediate vector **y**.

In general, at the ith step, we have

$$y_i = d_i, \quad y_{n-i+1} = d_{n-i+1}, \tag{2.7}$$

and we reset the d_j in the following manner:

$$d_j = d_j - w_{j,i}y_i - w_{j,n-i+1}y_{n-i+1}, \quad j = i + 1(1)n - i \tag{2.8}$$

to facilitate the solution of the variables following.

Finally for the system $Zu = y$, a solution can be derived by the same process.

Full details of the solution process are given in Evans & Hatzopoulos (1979) and that of a modified method in Evans & Hadjidimos (1980) which discusses improvements for symmetric positive definite systems. The extension to banded linear systems is given in Evans, Hadjidimos & Noutsos (1981).

2.2   QI matrix splitting

The well known Jacobi and Gauss–Seidel algorithms for the iterative solution of $A\mathbf{u} = \mathbf{d}$ use the splitting of the matrix A given as $A = D - L - U$ where D, L and U are the diagonal, strictly lower and upper triangular matrix components of the coefficient matrix A respectively. In the following section we consider an alternative splitting of the matrix A into interlocking matrix quadrants in order to derive new parallel iterative methods.

We now suppose that the matrix A can be written in the form

$$A = X - W - Z, \tag{2.9}$$

where X is defined to be

$$X = \begin{bmatrix} a_{1,1} & & & & & a_{1,n} \\ & a_{2,2} & & & a_{2,n-1} & \\ & & \ddots & 0 & \ddots & \\ & & 0 & \ddots & 0 & \\ & a_{n-1,2} & & a_{n-1,n-1} & \\ & & 0 & & & \\ a_{n,1} & & & & & a_{n,n} \end{bmatrix} \tag{2.10}$$

and consisting only of the elements of the two main diagonals of A. Similarly we define W and Z by

$$-W = \begin{bmatrix} 0 & & & & & 0 \\ a_{2,1} & \ddots & & 0 & & a_{2,n} \\ \vdots & & \ddots & & & \vdots \\ \vdots & & & \ddots & & \vdots \\ a_{n-1,1} & & 0 & & \ddots & a_{n-1,n} \\ 0 & & & & & 0 \end{bmatrix}, \tag{2.11}$$

and

$$-Z = \begin{bmatrix} 0 & a_{1,2} & \cdots & \cdots & a_{1,n-1} & 0 \\ & \ddots & & & \ddots & \\ & & 0 & \cdot & 0 & \\ & & & \ddots & & \\ 0 & a_{n,2} & \cdots & \cdots & a_{n,n-1} & 0 \end{bmatrix},$$

consisting of opposite quadrants right and left, top and bottom of the original matrix A respectively.

Alternatively, the elements of the matrices X, W and Z can be given as

$$X = \begin{cases} a_{i,i} \\ a_{i,n-i+1} \end{cases}, \quad i = 1, 2, \ldots, n \tag{2.12}$$

$$-W = (a_{i,j}) = \begin{cases} 1 \leqslant j < \left\lfloor \dfrac{n-1}{2} \right\rfloor, & j < i < n-j+1 \\[3mm] \left\lfloor \dfrac{n+2}{2} \right\rfloor < j \leqslant n, & n-j+1 < i < j, \\[3mm] 0, & \text{elsewhere} \end{cases} \tag{2.13}$$

and

$$-Z = (a_{i,j}) = \begin{cases} 1 < i < \left\lfloor \dfrac{n+1}{2} \right\rfloor, & i < j < n-j+1 \\[3mm] \left\lfloor \dfrac{n+2}{2} \right\rfloor < i \leqslant n, & n-i+1 < j < i \\[3mm] 0, & \text{elsewhere.} \end{cases} \tag{2.14}$$

From this splitting of interlocking quadrants, we observe that the matrix X has an important property which is an essential ingredient for the construction of iterative methods. It is an easily soluble matrix, consisting of independent (2×2) subsystems, the solution of which can be obtained from standard procedures.

Thus, analogous to the familiar splitting $A = D - L - U$ (Varga, 1963), we can formulate the following parallel iterative methods:

$$Xu^{(m+1)} = (W + Z)u^{(m)} + d, \tag{2.15}$$

for the Jacobi QI method;

$$(X - W)u^{(m+1)} = Zu^{(m)} + d, \tag{2.16}$$

for the successive QI method; and

$$(X - \omega W)u^{(m+1)} = \{\omega Z + (1 - \omega)X\}u^{(m)} + \omega d, \tag{2.17}$$

for the successive over-relaxation QI method; where m is the usual iteration index and ω the over-relaxation parameter.

From the definition of X in (2.12) we can easily construct a permutation matrix P of the form $P = p_{i,j}$ with $p_{i,j} = 1$, corresponding to a permutation function $\sigma(i)$, defined for $i = 1, 2, \ldots, n$ by $\sigma(i) = j$. Thus, if we consider $\sigma(1) = 1$, $\sigma(2) = 3, \ldots, \sigma(n/2) = n-1, \sigma((n/2)+1) = n, \sigma((n/2)+2) = n-2, \ldots, \sigma(n) = 2$ for n even, then $\bar{A} = P^{-1}AP$ assumes the form

$$\begin{bmatrix} D_{1,n} & & & \\ & D_{2,n-1} & & \tilde{U} \\ & & \ddots & \\ & \tilde{L} & & D_{n/2,(n/2)+1} \end{bmatrix} \tag{2.18}$$

where

$$D_{i,n-i+1} = \begin{bmatrix} a_{i,i}, a_{i,n-i+1} \\ a_{n-i+1,i}, a_{n-i+1,n-i+1} \end{bmatrix}, \quad i = 1, 2, \ldots, n/2.$$

Then, we can see that the newly conceived parallel iterative methods (2.15), (2.16) and (2.17) can be regarded as (2×2) block iterative methods for which a large body of information is already known (Varga, 1963).

For instance, the following properties of these methods can be easily proved:

(1) The Jacobi QI method converges if A is irreducibly diagonally dominant.
(2) The QI matrix splitting is a regular splitting of A.
(3) The successive QI method converges if A is irreducible and possesses weak diagonal dominance.
(4) The successive QI method converges if A is real and positive definite.
(5) The successive over-relaxation QI method converges for $0 < \omega < 2$ and corresponds to a (2×2) block SOR method with $\omega = 2/[1 + \sqrt{(1 - \rho^2(J))}]$ where $\rho(J)$ is the spectral radius of the corresponding block Jacobi method.

3 Recursive partitioning (RP) methods for the solution of boundary value problems

Now we introduce the method of recursive partitioning (RP) for the solution of sparse banded matrix systems. We illustrate the method for the solution of tridiagonal linear systems but the techniques can be readily applied to more general banded systems which occur from finite difference or finite element discretisation of boundary value problems.

First we consider the general $(n \times n)$ tridiagonal matrix equation, i.e.,

$$Au = \mathbf{d}, \tag{3.1}$$

$$\begin{bmatrix} b_1 & c_1 & & & & \\ a_1 & b_2 & c_2 & & & \\ & & & & 0 & \\ & & & & & \\ & & & & c_{n-2} & \\ & 0 & a_{n-2} & b_{n-1} & c_{n-1} \\ & & & a_{n-1} & b_n \end{bmatrix} \begin{bmatrix} u_1 \\ u_2 \\ \vdots \\ \vdots \\ \vdots \\ u_n \end{bmatrix} = \begin{bmatrix} d_1 \\ d_2 \\ \vdots \\ \vdots \\ d_{n-1} \\ d_n \end{bmatrix} \tag{3.2}$$

which can be rewritten in the following block partitioned form as

$$\begin{pmatrix} \alpha_1^{(1)} & \mathbf{v}_1^T & 0 \\ \mathbf{w}_1 & \tilde{Q}_{2 \to n-1} & \mathbf{z}_1 \\ 0 & \mathbf{r}_1^T & \alpha_n^{(1)} \end{pmatrix} \begin{pmatrix} u_1 \\ \tilde{u} \\ u_n \end{pmatrix} = \begin{pmatrix} d_1^{(1)} \\ \tilde{d}^{(1)} \\ d_n^{(1)} \end{pmatrix} \tag{3.3}$$

where $\mathbf{v}_1, \mathbf{w}_1, \mathbf{z}_1, \mathbf{r}_1, \tilde{u}$ and $\tilde{d}^{(1)}$ are $(n-2)$ component vectors given by

$$\mathbf{v}_1^T = (c_1, 0, 0, \ldots, 0),$$
$$\mathbf{w}_1 = (a_1, 0, 0, \ldots, 0)^T,$$
$$\mathbf{z}_1 = (0, 0, 0, \ldots, 0, c_{n-1})^T,$$
$$\mathbf{r}_1^T = (0, 0, 0, \ldots, 0, a_{n-1}),$$
$$\tilde{u} = (u_2, u_3, \ldots, u_{n-1}),$$

and

$$\tilde{d}^{(1)} = (d_2, d_3, \ldots, d_{n-1})^T;$$

and the quantities $\alpha_1^{(1)}, \alpha_n^{(1)}, d_1^{(1)}$ and $d_n^{(1)}$ are given by

$$\alpha_1^{(1)} = b_1 \quad \text{and} \quad \alpha_n^{(1)} = b_n,$$
$$d_1^{(1)} = d_1 \quad \text{and} \quad d_n^{(1)} = d_n. \tag{3.4}$$

$\tilde{Q}_{2 \to n-1}$ is a submatrix of order $n-2$ obtained from the 2nd to $(n-1)$th rows and columns of the original matrix.

From the block form (3.3) we obtain the equations

$$\left.\begin{aligned} \alpha_1^{(1)} u_1 + \mathbf{v}_1^T \tilde{u} &= d_1^{(1)} \\ \mathbf{w}_1 u_1 + \tilde{Q}_{2 \to n-1} \tilde{u} + \mathbf{z}_1 u_n &= \tilde{d}^{(1)} \\ \mathbf{r}_1^T \tilde{u} + \alpha_n^{(1)} u_n &= d_n^{(1)} \end{aligned}\right\} \tag{3.5}$$

from which we obtain the scalar unknowns,

$$\left.\begin{aligned} u_1 &= \frac{d_1^{(1)}}{\alpha_1^{(1)}} - \frac{\mathbf{v}_1^T \tilde{u}}{\alpha_1^{(1)}}, \\ u_n &= \frac{d_n^{(1)}}{\alpha_n^{(1)}} - \frac{\mathbf{r}_1^T \tilde{u}}{\alpha_n^{(1)}}; \end{aligned}\right\} \tag{3.6}$$

and

also the reduced matrix system of order $n-2$ given by

$$\left(Q_{2 \to n-1} - \frac{\mathbf{w}_1 \mathbf{v}_1^T}{\alpha_1^{(1)}} - \frac{\mathbf{z}_1 \mathbf{r}_1^T}{\alpha_n^{(1)}}\right) \tilde{u} = \tilde{d}^{(1)} - \frac{\mathbf{w}_1 d_1^{(1)}}{\alpha_1^{(1)}} - \frac{\mathbf{z}_1 d_n^{(1)}}{\alpha_n^{(1)}}. \tag{3.7}$$

It is easy to verify by a simple substitution process that the system (3.7), when expressed in matrix notation, is configured in a similar manner to the original system (3.2) but of order 2 less and is given by

$$
\begin{bmatrix}
\alpha_2^{(2)} & c_2 & & & & & \\
a_2 & b_3 & c_3 & & & & \\
& & & & 0 & & \\
& & 0 & & & & \\
& & & a_{n-3} & b_{n-2} & c_{n-2} & \\
& & & & a_{n-2} & \alpha_{n-1}^{(2)}
\end{bmatrix}
\begin{bmatrix}
u_2 \\
u_3 \\
\vdots \\
\vdots \\
u_{n-2} \\
u_{n-1}
\end{bmatrix}
=
\begin{bmatrix}
d_2^{(2)} \\
d_3 \\
\vdots \\
\vdots \\
d_{n-2} \\
d_{n-1}^{(2)}
\end{bmatrix}
\tag{3.8}
$$

where

$$
\left.
\begin{aligned}
\alpha_2^{(2)} &= b_2 - \frac{a_1 c_1}{\alpha_1^{(1)}}, \quad d_2^{(2)} = d_2^{(1)} - \frac{a_1 d_1^{(1)}}{\alpha_1^{(1)}}, \\
\alpha_{n-1}^{(2)} &= b_{n-1} - \frac{a_{n-1} c_{n-1}}{\alpha_n^{(1)}} \quad \text{and} \quad d_{n-1}^{(2)} = d_{n-1}^{(1)} - \frac{c_{n-1} d_n^{(1)}}{\alpha_n^{(1)}}.
\end{aligned}
\right\}
\tag{3.9}
$$

Further it is easily observed that the reduced system (3.8) can be similarly partitioned and rewritten in the form,

$$
\begin{pmatrix}
\alpha_2^{(2)} & v_2^T & 0 \\
w_2 & \bar{Q}_{3 \to n-2} & z_2 \\
0 & r_2^T & \alpha_{n-1}^{(2)}
\end{pmatrix}
\begin{pmatrix}
u_2 \\
\bar{u} \\
u_{n-1}
\end{pmatrix}
=
\begin{pmatrix}
d_2^{(2)} \\
d^{(2)} \\
d_{n-1}^{(2)}
\end{pmatrix}
\tag{3.10}
$$

from which a further reduced system similar in structure to (3.7) is derived.

Thus, we can set up a recursive procedure in which the above reduction process is continued such that at the ith partitioning stage we have, identical to (3.4) and (3.9) the following recurrence relations,

$$
\left.
\begin{aligned}
\alpha_i^{(i)} &= b_i - \frac{a_{i-1} c_{i-1}}{\alpha_{i-1}^{(i-1)}}, \quad d_i^{(i)} = d_i^{(i-1)} - \frac{a_{i-1} d_{i-1}^{(i)}}{\alpha_{i-1}^{(i-1)}} \\
\text{and} \quad & \\
\alpha_{n-i+1}^{(i)} &= b_{n-i+1} - \frac{a_{n-i+1}}{\alpha_{n-i+2}^{(i-1)}} c_{n-i+1}, \quad d_{n-i+1}^{(i)} = d_{n-i+1}^{(i-1)} - \frac{c_{n-i+1}}{\alpha_{n-i+2}^{(i-1)}} d_{n-i+2}^{(i-1)}.
\end{aligned}
\right\}
\tag{3.11}
$$

The recursive procedure is then continued until the reduced system is of order 1 for n odd; and of order 2 for n even.

Case 1: n odd

For n odd the final reduced system is given, for $q = (n+1)/2$, by the system

$$\left(\tilde{Q}_{q \to n-q+1} - \frac{\mathbf{w}_{q-1}\mathbf{v}_{q-1}^T}{\alpha_{q-1}^{(q-1)}} - \frac{\mathbf{z}_{q-1}\mathbf{r}_{q-1}^T}{\alpha_{n-q+2}^{(q-1)}} \right) u_q = \alpha_q^{(q-1)} - \frac{\mathbf{w}_{q-1}d_q^{(q-1)}}{\alpha_{q-1}^{(q-1)}} - \frac{\mathbf{z}_{q-1}d_{n-q+2}^{(q-1)}}{\alpha_{n-q+2}^{(q-1)}}$$

(3.12)

which can be verified to be the single equation,

$$\alpha_q^{(q)}u_q = d_q^{(q)},$$

(3.13)

where

$$\left. \begin{array}{l} \alpha_q^{(q)} = b_q - \left(\dfrac{a_{q-1}c_{q-1}}{\alpha_{q-1}^{(q-1)}} + \dfrac{a_{q+1}c_{n-q+1}}{\alpha_{n-q+2}^{(q-1)}} \right) \\[2em] d_q^{(q)} = d_q^{(q-1)} - \left(\dfrac{d_{q-1}^{(q-1)}a_{q-1}}{\alpha_{q-1}^{(q-1)}} + \dfrac{d_{n-q+2}^{(q-1)}c_{q+1}}{\alpha_{n-q+2}^{(q-1)}} \right) \end{array} \right\}$$

(3.14)

and

Case 2: n even

For n even the final reduced system is given by (3.12) (for $q = n/2$) and can be verified to be the same as the (2×2) system,

$$\begin{pmatrix} \alpha_q^{(q)} & c_q \\ a_{n-q} & \alpha_{n-q+1}^{(q)} \end{pmatrix} \begin{pmatrix} u_q \\ u_{q+1} \end{pmatrix} = \begin{pmatrix} d_q^{(q)} \\ d_{n-q+1}^{(q)} \end{pmatrix}$$

(3.15)

which is solved to give,

$$\left. \begin{array}{l} u_q = (d_q^{(q)}\alpha_{n-q+1}^{(q)} - d_{n-q+1}^{(q)}c_q)/(\alpha_{n-q+1}^{(q)}\alpha_q^{(q)} - a_{n-q}c_q) \\[1em] u_{n-q+1} = (\alpha_q^{(q)}d_{n-q+1}^{(q)} - d_q^{(q)}a_{n-q})/(\alpha_{n-q+1}^{(q)}\alpha_q^{(q)} - a_{n-q}c_q) \end{array} \right\}$$

(3.16)

and

where $\alpha_q^{(q)}, \alpha_{n-q+1}^{(q)}, d_q^{(q)}$ and $d_{n-q+1}^{(q)}$ are as defined in (3.11).

Finally after obtaining the central values of $\mathbf{u}$ by using (3.13) for n odd, or (3.16) for n even, we proceed to obtain the remaining elements of the solution vector by a back-substitution process. By using the equations of the scalar unknown obtained at each stage of the reduction process (e.g. (3.6) for the first reduction) we derive the other elements of the solution vector as

$$\left. \begin{array}{l} u_i = (d_i^{(i)} - c_i u_{i+1})/\alpha_i^{(i)} \\[1em] u_{n-i+1} = (d_{n-i+1}^{(i)} - a_{n-i}u_{n-i})/\alpha_{n-i+1}^{(i)}, \end{array} \right\} \quad i = q-1, q-2, \ldots, 1.$$

(3.17)

and

We describe the above scheme as the tridiagonal recursive partitioning (TRP) algorithm and it is summarised as follows:

Step 1 Set up the following quantities,

$$\begin{array}{ll} \alpha_1^{(1)} = b_1, & d_1^{(1)} = d_1, \\[0.5em] \alpha_n^{(1)} = b_n, & d_n^{(1)} = d_n \end{array}$$

(3.18)

and

$$q = n/2 \ (n \text{ even}) \text{ or } (n+1)/2 \ (n \text{ odd}).$$

Step 2 Compute the following quantities in the partitioning process:

$$t_{i-1} = \frac{a_{i-1}}{\alpha_{i-1}^{(i-1)}}, \quad s_{i-1} = \frac{c_{n-i+1}}{\alpha_{n-i+2}}, \quad i = 2, 3, \ldots, q, \tag{3.19a}$$

$$\alpha_i^{(i)} = b_i - t_{i-1}c_{i-1}, \quad d_i^{(i)} = d_i^{(i-1)} - t_{i-1}d_{i-1}^{(i-1)}$$
$$i = 2, 3, \ldots, q-1 \ (n \text{ odd}) \tag{3.19b}$$

$$\alpha_{n-i+1}^{(i)} = b_{n-i+1} - s_{i-1}a_{n-i+1}, \quad d_{n-i+1}^{(i)} = d_{n-i+1}^{(i-1)} - s_{i-1}d_{n-i+2}^{(i-1)}$$
$$i = 2, 3, \ldots, q \ (n \text{ even}) \tag{3.19c}$$

and (for n odd only), compute the quantities,

$$\alpha_q^{(q)} = b_q - (t_{q-1}c_{q-1} + s_{q-1}a_{q+1}),$$

and

$$d_q^{(q)} = d_q^{(q-1)} - (t_{q-1}d_{q-1}^{(q-1)} + s_{q-1}d_{n-q+2}^{(q-1)}).$$

Step 3 Finally, compute the solution vector **u** by using the formulae,

$$u_q = d_q^{(q)}/\alpha_q^{(q)} \quad (\text{if } n \text{ is odd}) \tag{3.20a}$$

or

$$\left.\begin{array}{l}
u_q = (d_q^{(q)}\alpha_{n-q+1}^{(q)} - d_{n-q+1}^{(q)}c_q)/(\alpha_{n-q+1}^{(q)}\alpha_q^{(q)} - a_{n-q}c_q) \\[2mm]
u_{n-q+1} = (\alpha_q^{(q)}d_{n-q+1}^{(q)} - d_q^{(q)}a_{n-q})/(\alpha_{n-q+1}^{(q)}\alpha_q^{(q)} - a_{n-q}c_q)
\end{array}\right\} \begin{array}{l} \text{if } n \text{ is} \\ \text{even} \end{array}$$
$$\tag{3.20b}$$

and then

$$\left.\begin{array}{l}
u_i = (d_i^{(i)} - c_i u_{i+1})/\alpha_i^{(i)}, \\[2mm]
u_{n-i+1} = (d_{n-i+1}^{(i)} - a_{n-i}u_{n-i})/\alpha_{n-i+1}^{(i)},
\end{array}\right\} \quad i = q-1, q-2, \ldots, 1.$$
$$\tag{3.20c}$$

The TRP algorithm requires less than $3n$ multiplications, $2n$ divisions and $3n$ additions (a slight improvement over the Thomas algorithm). For repeated solutions with the coefficient matrix unchanged, only the terms $d_i^{(i)}$ and u_i need to be recalculated in $2n$ multiplications, n divisions and $2n$ additions. Furthermore, the $\alpha_i^{(i)}$ and $d_i^{(i)}$ terms can overwrite the diagonal elements, b_i and the right-hand-side elements, d_i respectively, thus giving a gain of two n-component vector storage over the Thomas algorithm.

The TRP algorithm is simply a systematic modification of the diagonal and right-hand-side vectors from both the top and the bottom of the respective vectors towards the centre where it then becomes a simple outward process to calculate the solution vector.

4   Parallel implementation of the recursive partitioning (RP) algorithm

Most conventional tridiagonal solvers (e.g. the Thomas algorithm, Varga, 1963) would not normally run faster on a parallel machine which has more than one processor because of the highly serial nature of the computation. However, it is easily observed that the recursive partitioning algorithm discussed in section 3 has a considerable measure of implicit parallelism which arises from the parallel nature of the applied recursive reduction process at both ends of the linear system. Thus, by exploiting the parallelism of the RP algorithms in a parallel program run on a parallel machine, a substantial improvement in the running time of these algorithms can be achieved.

First, we mention briefly some properties common to all parallel programs. In general, a typical segment of a parallel program has a graphical representation of the form shown in figure 17.1 where 'left before right' precedence holds, so that the completion of the execution of the segment of code S_1 must precede the start of P_i $(i = 1, 2, \ldots, k)$; and the completion of all the P_i must precede the start of S_2. The P_i themselves have no precedence relationship and so can be executed concurrently. The following points are important in the implementation of this structure:

(i)   Each code path segment $(S_1, P_1, P_2, \ldots)$ must be executed by only one processor so that when one processor takes up a path all others must be 'informed' and locked out of this path. Similarly, on completion of the path all processors must be informed so that the next set of available paths are freed to them.

(ii) Only after the preceding paths have been completed can a given path be started, i.e., $P_1, P_2, \ldots, P_k$ must be completed before starting S_2.

(iii) Variables used by $P_1, P_2, \ldots, P_k$ but defined in S_1 must be made available to all processors and all values set by $P_1, P_2, \ldots, P_n$ and used in S_2 must be made available to the processor that executes S_2. Likewise for variables used by S_2 but defined in S_1.

We now consider specifically a parallel program which is to be run on the Loughborough University INTERDATA parallel computer with two Model 70 processors sharing a 32 kb block of common core memory, with each also having a 32 kb block of private memory. Special software (Barlow et al. 1977)

Figure 17.1. Segment of a typical parallel program.

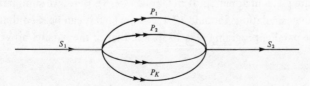

locally developed is available which enables the programmer to effect the necessary control, allocation and lock-out of resources as outlined in (i), (ii) and (iii) above during the execution of segments of the parallel program. For example, the 'FORK' and 'JOIN' constructs inserted in a standard Fortran program enable the two INTERDATA processors to 'fork', i.e., work on separate sections of code independently and in parallel; and then 'join' when only one processor is necessary to work on the program for collecting results from the section done in parallel. 'DOPAR' and 'PAREND' macros also perform a similar function. The 'GETRES(I)' subroutine offers a lock-out mechanism by permitting an exclusive use of a resource I and the 'PUTRES(I)' relinquishes ownership of the resource I.

In order to program, for example, the TRP algorithm (3.18–3.20) (for the solution of the general tridiagonal matrix system) in parallel, we arrange the order of calculation of the intermediate quantities and solution vector components in the form given in figure 17.2 in order to take advantage of the implicit parallelism of the algorithm. A similar arrangement is also applicable to the parallel solution of a symmetric quindiagonal linear system which can similarly be arranged as a recursive (2×2) tridiagonal block partitioning algorithm.

The parallel programs for the RP and block (2×2) algorithms are written in standard Fortran (except that the parallel processing constructs, FORK and JOIN, GETRES(I) and PUTRES(I), used for parallel controls are inserted) and then run on the Loughborough University INTERDATA parallel computer.

The two parallel programs were test run on matrix systems of varying order. In order to assess the performance of the parallel programs, timing results of runs on matrix systems of order 650 were taken. For example, for each program, the times for the programs to run sequentially without the parallel constructs were noted. Then, the times for each program to run in parallel mode with the insertion of parallel constructs were also noted. These and other relevant timing results taken are shown in table (A2.1) of appendix II in Okolie (1978). From these experimental results, we compute the estimates of the slow-down or efficiency losses (due to memory clashing, parallel control contentions, etc.) and the speed-up (i.e., the amount by which a program runs faster in parallel mode than it does in serial mode) of the two parallel programs. The details of the calculation of the speed-up and the various overheads for the two parallel RP programs (for the solution of the tridiagonal and quindiagonal linear systems of order 650) are given in appendix II in Okolie (1978). Here, we summarise the results of the calculations in table 17.1, from which it can be seen that the speed-up of the parallel program (1) is 175% and that of the parallel program (2) is 182%.

Figure 17.2. Order of the parallel implementation of the RP algorithm.

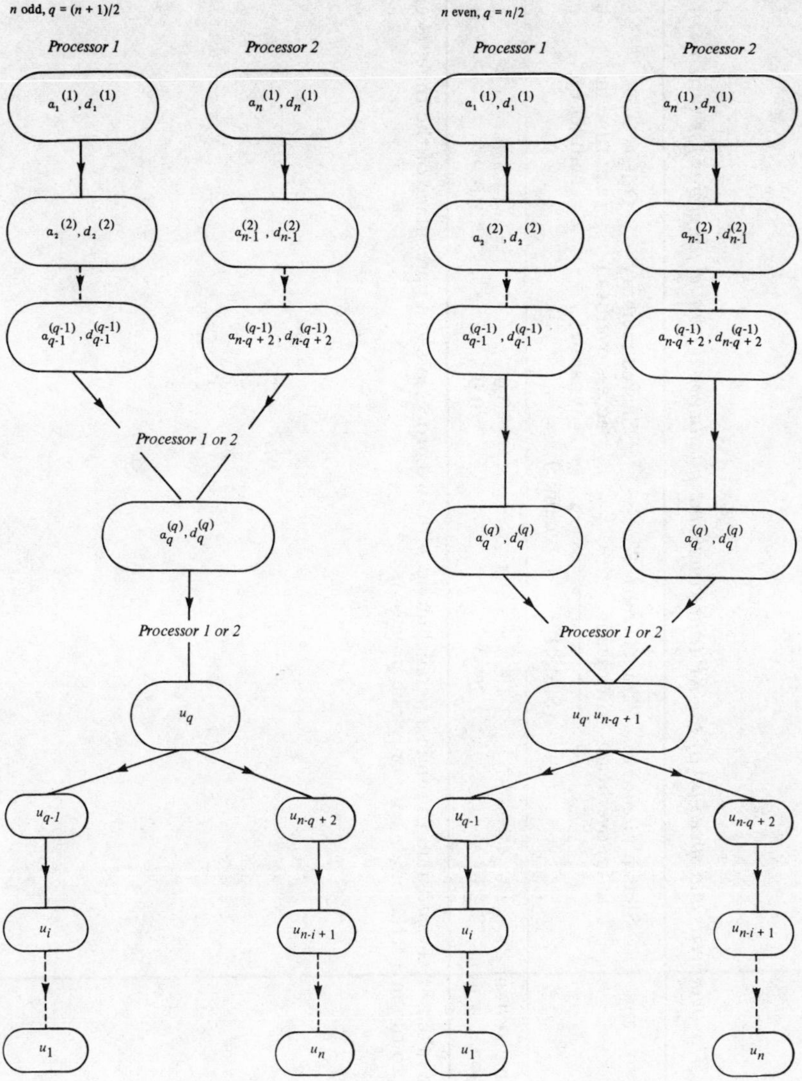

n odd, $q = (n + 1)/2$

Processor 1   *Processor 2*

$a_1^{(1)}, d_1^{(1)}$ $a_n^{(1)}, d_n^{(1)}$

$a_2^{(2)}, d_2^{(2)}$ $a_{n-1}^{(2)}, d_{n-1}^{(2)}$

$a_{q-1}^{(q-1)}, d_{q-1}^{(q-1)}$ $a_{n-q+2}^{(q-1)}, d_{n-q+2}^{(q-1)}$

Processor 1 or 2

$a_q^{(q)}, d_q^{(q)}$

Processor 1 or 2

u_q

u_{q-1} u_{n-q+2}

u_i u_{n-i+1}

u_1 u_n

n even, $q = n/2$

Processor 1   *Processor 2*

$a_1^{(1)}, d_1^{(1)}$ $a_n^{(1)}, d_n^{(1)}$

$a_2^{(2)}, d_2^{(2)}$ $a_{n-1}^{(2)}, d_{n-1}^{(2)}$

$a_{q-1}^{(q-1)}, d_{q-1}^{(q-1)}$ $a_{n-q+2}^{(q-1)}, d_{n-q+2}^{(q-1)}$

$a_q^{(q)}, d_q^{(q)}$ $a_q^{(q)}, d_q^{(q)}$

Processor 1 or 2

u_q, u_{n-q+1}

u_{q-1} u_{n-q+2}

u_i u_{n-i+1}

u_1 u_n

Table 17.1. The overheads and speed-up of the RP tridiagonal and quindiagonal parallel programs for systems of order n = 650.

Matrix systems and program	Shared memory (static) overhead	Parallel control overheads		Shared memory access overhead (dynamic)	Others (e.g. time in scheduler etc.)	Speed-up* of parallel program
		(Static)	(Dynamic)			
1. Tridiagonal system	3.1%	3.1%	1.2%	~0.0%	17.5%	175%
2. Quindiagonal system	3.2%	2.2%	1.7%	~0.0%	10.9%	182%

* The time taken by the program to run in a parallel mode with two processors as a percentage of the time taken by the program to run in a serial mode with only one processor.

5 The recursive decoupling (RD) algorithm for solving banded linear systems

In the development of the recursive partitioning algorithms of section 3 the 'one-line-at-a-time' partitioning scheme was adopted. It is possible, however, to vary the size of the block structure (by using 'two lines at a time', 'three lines at a time' etc.) in the partitioning process. The 'two-line' partitioning scheme was investigated for both the tridiagonal and quindiagonal matrix systems. It was found that the algorithmic solution derived by adopting such a partitioning strategy involves almost twice as much arithmetic work (under a sequential processing system) as does the corresponding 'one-line' partitioning method. However, there is an increased implicit parallelism of the algorithm derived compared to that of the 'one-line' method.

A similar result was also obtained on investigating the 'three-line' partitioning scheme. Thus, it was necessary to examine the extreme case in which for an nth order system, the '$(n/2)$-line' partitioning strategy is employed in the solution of the given tridiagonal matrix system. The application of this strategy for more general banded linear systems will not be discussed here.

We consider, for simplicity, the symmetric tridiagonal matrix system of order n (equal to 2^m, where m is any positive integer) given by,

$$A\mathbf{u} = \mathbf{d} \tag{5.1}$$

or in matrix notation

$$
\left[\begin{array}{ccc|ccc}
\lambda - \beta_1 & 1 & & & & \\
1 & \lambda & 1 & & 0 & \\
& 1 & \lambda & 1 & & \\
\hline
& & 1 & \lambda & 1 & \\
& 0 & & & & 1 \\
& & & 1 & & \lambda - \beta_n
\end{array}\right]
\left[\begin{array}{c}
u_1 \\
u_2 \\
u_{n/2} \\
u_{(n/2)+1} \\
u_{n-1} \\
u_n
\end{array}\right]
=
\left[\begin{array}{c}
d_1 - \phi_1 \\
d_2 \\
d_{n/2} \\
d_{(n/2)+1} \\
d_{n-1} \\
d_n - \phi_n
\end{array}\right]
\tag{5.2}
$$

where

$$\beta_1 = \beta_n = \phi_1 = \phi_n = 0$$

are introduced for convenience, and their purpose will become evident in what follows. We also assume that the matrix A is diagonally dominant.

The system (5.2) can be partitioned into two separate halves, as indicated, to give the block form

$$
\begin{pmatrix} A_1 & B_1 \\ B_2 & A_2 \end{pmatrix}
\begin{pmatrix} \tilde{\mathbf{u}}_1 \\ \tilde{\mathbf{u}}_2 \end{pmatrix}
=
\begin{pmatrix} \tilde{\mathbf{d}}_1 \\ \tilde{\mathbf{d}}_2 \end{pmatrix}
\tag{5.3}
$$

from which we obtain the following:

$$(A_1 - B_1 A_2^{-1} B_2)\bar{u}_1 = \bar{d}_1 - B_1 A_2^{-1} \bar{d}_2 \tag{5.4}$$

and

$$(A_2 - B_2 A_1^{-1} B_1)\bar{u}_2 = \bar{d}_2 - B_2 A_1^{-1} \bar{d}_1. \tag{5.5}$$

Both (5.4) and (5.5) form a decoupled matrix system of the form

$$\left(\begin{array}{c|c} A_1^{(1)} & 0 \\ \hline 0 & A_2^{(1)} \end{array} \right) \begin{pmatrix} \bar{u}_1 \\ \bar{u}_2 \end{pmatrix} = \begin{pmatrix} \bar{d}_1^{(1)} \\ \bar{d}_2^{(1)} \end{pmatrix} \tag{5.6}$$

where

$$\left. \begin{array}{l} A_1^{(1)} = A_1 - B_1 A_2^{-1} B_2, \\ A_2^{(1)} = A_2 - B_2 A_1^{-1} B_1, \\ \bar{d}_1^{(1)} = \bar{d}_1 - B_1 A_2^{-1} \bar{d}_2, \end{array} \right\} \tag{5.7}$$

and

$$\bar{d}_2^{(1)} = \bar{d}_2 - B_2 A_1^{-1} \bar{d}_1.$$

We now proceed to show that the decoupled submatrices $A_1^{(1)}$ and $A_2^{(1)}$ are tridiagonal and of the same structure as the original matrix A.

The submatrices A_1 and A_2 are tridiagonals of order $n/2$, but their inverses are full.

By definition,

$$(A_1^{-1})_{i,j} = \frac{\gamma_{j,i}}{|A_1|}, \quad i,j = 1, 2, \ldots, n/2, \tag{5.8}$$

where $\gamma_{j,i}$ denotes the (i,j) cofactor (signed minor) of A_1 and $|A_1|$ is the determinant of A_1.

Similarly

$$(A_2^{-1})_{i,j} = \frac{\alpha_{j,i}}{|A_2|}, \quad i,j = 1, 2, \ldots, n/2, \tag{5.9}$$

where $\alpha_{j,i}$ denotes the (i,j) cofactor of A_2.

It is therefore easily shown by simple multiplication that the matrices $B_1 A_2^{-1} B_2$ and $B_2 A_1^{-1} B_1$ are matrices of order $n/2$ given by

$$B_1 A_2^{-1} B_2 = \begin{bmatrix} 0 & & & & \\ & 0 & & & \\ & & \ddots & 0 & \\ & & 0 & \ddots & \\ & & & & \ddots & 0 \\ & & & & & \beta_{n/2} \end{bmatrix}$$

and

$$
B_2 A_1^{-1} B_1 = \begin{bmatrix} \beta_{(n/2)+1} & & & \\ & 0 & 0 & \\ & & \ddots & \\ & 0 & & \ddots \\ & & & & 0 \end{bmatrix}
\tag{5.10}
$$

where

$$
\beta_{n/2} = \frac{\alpha_{1,1}}{|A_2|} \quad \text{and} \quad \beta_{(n/2)+1} = \frac{\gamma_{n/2,n/2}}{|A_1|}.
\tag{5.11}
$$

It can be similarly shown that $B_1 A_2^{-1} \check{d}_2$ and $B_2 A_1^{-1} \check{d}_2$ are vectors of length $n/2$ given by

$$
B_1 A_2^{-1} \check{d}_2 = \begin{bmatrix} 0 \\ 0 \\ \vdots \\ \phi_{n/2} \end{bmatrix}, \quad \text{and} \quad B_2 A_1^{-1} \check{d}_2 = \begin{bmatrix} \phi_{(n/2)+1} \\ 0 \\ \vdots \\ 0 \\ 0 \end{bmatrix}
\tag{5.12}
$$

where

$$
\phi_{n/2} = \frac{1}{|A_2|} \sum_{i=1}^{n/2} \alpha_{i,1} d_{i+(n/2)},
\tag{5.13a}
$$

and

$$
\phi_{(n/2)+1} = \frac{1}{|A_1|} \sum_{i=1}^{n/2} \gamma_{i,n/2} d_i.
\tag{5.13b}
$$

We shall take advantage of the special form of the matrices A_1 and A_2 to derive alternative expressions for the quantities $\alpha_{i,1}$ and $\gamma_{i,n/2}$ in terms of the Sturm sequence of polynomials P_i, $(i = 0, 1, 2, \ldots)$ obtained by a simple Laplace expansion of the leading principal minors of the tridiagonal matrix of the form,

$$
C = \begin{bmatrix} \lambda & 1 & & & & \\ 1 & \lambda & 1 & & 0 & \\ & \ddots & \ddots & \ddots & & \\ & 0 & & \ddots & & \\ & & & & \ddots & 1 \\ & & & & 1 & \lambda \end{bmatrix}_{((n/2) \times (n/2))}.
$$

Thus,

$$
\left. \begin{aligned} P_0 &= 1 \\ P_1 &= \lambda \\ P_i &= \lambda P_{i-1} - P_{i-2} \quad (i = 2, 3, \ldots). \end{aligned} \right\}
\tag{5.14}
$$

By making use of the structure of A_1 and A_2 as shown in (5.2), it is now possible to express the determinants $|A_1|$, $|A_2|$ as functions of P_i $(i = 0, 1, \ldots, (n/2) - 1)$, i.e.

$$|A_1| = (\lambda - \beta_1)P_{(n/2)-1} - P_{(n/2)-2},$$

and
$$|A_2| = (\lambda - \beta_n)P_{(n/2)-1} - P_{(n/2)-2}. \tag{5.15}$$

Also, it is easily verified that the set of cofactors of A_1, i.e., $\gamma_{i,n/2}$ $(i = 1, 2, \ldots, n/2)$ is given by the relationships

$$\gamma_{1,n/2} = -1$$
$$\gamma_{2,n/2} = (-1)^2(\lambda - \beta_1)$$

and
$$\gamma_{i,n/2} = (-1)^i[(\lambda - \beta_1)P_{i-2} - P_{i-3}], \quad i = 3, 4, \ldots, n/2. \tag{5.16}$$

Similarly, the cofactors of A_2, i.e., $\alpha_{i,1}$ can be expressed as

$$\alpha_{1,1} = (\lambda - \beta_n)P_{(n/2)-2} - P_{(n/2)-3},$$
$$\alpha_{2,1} = (-1)^{2+1}[(\lambda - \beta_n)P_{(n/2)-3} - P_{(n/2)-4}],$$
$$\alpha_{i,1} = (-1)^{i+1}[(\lambda - \beta_n)P_{(n/2)-i-1} - P_{(n/2)-i-2}], \quad i = 3, 4, \ldots, (n/2) - 2$$
$$\alpha_{(n/2)-1,1} = (\lambda - \beta_n)$$

and
$$\alpha_{n/2,1} = -1. \tag{5.17}$$

Hence, the quantities $\beta_{n/2}, \beta_{(n/2)+1}, \phi_{n/2}, \phi_{(n/2)+1}$ in (5.11)-(5.13) can be expressed, on substituting for $|A_1|, |A_2|, \gamma_{n/2,n/2}$ and $\alpha_{n/2,1}$ from (5.15)-(5.17), as follows:

$$\beta_{n/2} = \frac{(\lambda - \beta_n)P_{(n/2)-2} - P_{(n/2)-3}}{(\lambda - \beta_n)P_{(n/2)-1} - P_{(n/2)-2}}$$

$$\beta_{(n/2)+1} = \frac{(\lambda - \beta_1)P_{(n/2)-2} - P_{(n/2)-3}}{(\lambda - \beta_1)P_{(n/2)-1} - P_{(n/2)-2}}$$

$$\phi_{n/2} = \frac{\displaystyle\sum_{i=1}^{n/2} \alpha_{i,1} d_{i+(n/2)}}{(\lambda - \beta_n)P_{(n/2)-1} - P_{(n/2)-2}} \tag{5.18}$$

and

$$\phi_{(n/2)+1} = \frac{\displaystyle\sum_{i=1}^{n/2} \gamma_{i,n/2} d_i}{(\lambda - \beta_1)P_{(n/2)-1} - P_{(n/2)-2}}$$

By symmetry of (5.2), if $\beta_1 = \beta_n$, then $\beta_{n/2} = \beta_{(n/2)+1}$ which agrees with the formula obtained in (5.18).

Now, by a substitution of $B_1 A_2^{-1} B_2$, $B_2 A_1^{-1} B_1$ from (5.10) and $B_1 A_2^{-1} \tilde{d}_2$, $B_2 A_1^{-1} \tilde{d}_2$ from (5.12) into (5.7) we find that the decoupled system (5.6) is the same system as $\bar{A}\bar{u} = \bar{d}$ where

$$
\bar{A} = \left[\begin{array}{cccccc|cccccc}
\lambda-\beta_1 & 1 & & & & & & & & & & \\
1 & \lambda & 1 & & & & & & & & & \\
& 1 & \lambda & 1 & & & & & & 0 & & \\
& & \ddots & \ddots & \ddots & & & & & & & \\
& & & \ddots & \ddots & 1 & & & & & & \\
& & & & 1 & \lambda-\beta_{n/2} & & & & & & \\
\hline
& & & & & & \lambda-\beta_{(n/2)+1} & 1 & & & & \\
& & & & & & 1 & \lambda & 1 & & & \\
& & 0 & & & & & \ddots & \ddots & \ddots & & \\
& & & & & & & & \ddots & \ddots & \ddots & \\
& & & & & & & & & \ddots & \ddots & 1 \\
& & & & & & & & & & 1 & \lambda-\beta_n
\end{array}\right],
$$

$$
\bar{u} = \begin{bmatrix} u_1 \\ u_2 \\ \vdots \\ \vdots \\ u_{n/2} \\ \hline u_{(n/2)+1} \\ \vdots \\ \vdots \\ \vdots \\ u_n \end{bmatrix} \quad \text{and} \quad \bar{d} = \begin{bmatrix} d_1 - \phi_1 \\ d_2 \\ \vdots \\ \vdots \\ d_{n/2} - \phi_{n/2} \\ \hline d_{(n/2)+1} - \phi_{(n/2)+1} \\ \vdots \\ \vdots \\ d_{n-1} \\ d_n - \phi_n \end{bmatrix}
$$

where each half of the decoupled system has the same form as the original system (5.2) but of order $n/2$. In computational terms the decoupling process involves only a simple modification of the two central diagonal elements and the corresponding right-hand-side vector elements at the zone of decoupling. We refer to the process of transforming the system (5.2) into the form (5.19) as level-1 decoupling. Thus, a similar transformation applied to both halves of the already decoupled subsystem in the previous equation produces a level-2 decoupling of the form $\bar{A}\bar{u} = \bar{d}$, where

$$
\bar{A} =
\begin{bmatrix}
\begin{array}{cccc|cccc|cccc}
\lambda-\beta_1 & 1 & & & & & & & & & & \\
1 & \lambda & 1 & & & & & & & & & \\
 & \ddots & \ddots & \ddots & & & 0 & & & & 0 & \\
 & & \ddots & \lambda & 1 & & & & & & & \\
 & & & 1 & \lambda-\beta_{n/4} & & & & & & & \\
\hline
 & & & & \lambda-\beta_{(n/4)+1} & 1 & & & & & & \\
 & & & & 1 & \lambda & 1 & & & & & \\
 & 0 & & & & \ddots & \ddots & \ddots & & & & \\
 & & & & & & 1 & \lambda & 1 & & & \\
 & & & & & & & 1 & \lambda-\beta_{n/2} & & & \\
\hline
 & & & & & & & & & \lambda-\beta_{(n/2)+1} & 1 & \\
 & & & & & & & & & 1 & \lambda & 1 \\
 & & & & & & & & & & \ddots & \ddots \\
\end{array}
\end{bmatrix}
$$

level 2

level 1

level 2

$\lambda-\beta_{(n/2)+1}$ 1
1 λ 1
1 1
$\lambda-\beta_{3n/4}$

$\lambda-\beta_{(3n/4)+1}$
1
1 λ 1
1

λ

$$\bar{u} = \begin{bmatrix} u_1 \\ u_2 \\ \cdot \\ \cdot \\ \cdot \\ u_{n/4} \\ \hline u_{(n/4)+1} \\ \cdot \\ \cdot \\ \cdot \\ u_{n/2} \\ \hline u_{(n/2)+1} \\ \cdot \\ \cdot \\ \cdot \\ \cdot \\ u_{3n/4} \\ \hline u_{(3n/4)+1} \\ \cdot \\ \cdot \\ \cdot \\ \cdot \\ u_n \end{bmatrix} \quad \text{and } \bar{d} = \begin{bmatrix} d_1 - \phi_1 \\ \cdot \\ \cdot \\ \cdot \\ \cdot \\ d_{n/4} - \phi_{n/4} \\ \hline d_{(n/4)+1} - \phi_{(n/4)+1} \\ \cdot \\ \cdot \\ \cdot \\ d_{n/2} - \phi_{n/2} \\ \hline d_{n/2} - \phi_{(n/2)+1} \\ \cdot \\ \cdot \\ \cdot \\ \cdot \\ d_{3n/4} - \phi_{3n/4} \\ \hline d_{(3n/4)+1} - \phi_{(3n/4)+1} \\ \cdot \\ \cdot \\ \cdot \\ \cdot \\ d_n - \phi_n \end{bmatrix}$$

where

$$\beta_{n/4} = \frac{(\lambda - \beta_{n/2})P_{(n/4)-2} - P_{(n/4)-3}}{(\lambda - \beta_{n/2})P_{(n/4)-1} - P_{(n/4)-2}},$$

$$\beta_{(n/4)+1} = \frac{(\lambda - \beta_1)P_{(n/4)-2} - P_{(n/4)-3}}{(\lambda - \beta_1)P_{(n/4)-1} - P_{(n/4)-2}},$$

$$\beta_{3n/4} = \frac{(\lambda - \beta_n)P_{(n/4)-2} - P_{(n/4)-3}}{(\lambda - \beta_n)P_{(n/4)-1} - P_{(n/4)-2}},$$

and

$$\beta_{(3n/4)+1} = \frac{(\lambda - \beta_{(n/2)+1})P_{(n/4)-2} - P_{(n/4)-3}}{(\lambda - \beta_{(n/2)+1})P_{(n/4)-1} - P_{(n/4)-2}}.$$

$$(5.21)$$

Similarly, the corresponding right-hand-side modifier quantities are given by

$$\phi_{n/4} = \frac{\displaystyle\sum_{i=1}^{n/4} \alpha_{i,1} d_{i+(n/4)}}{P_{(n/4)-1}(\lambda - \beta_{n/2}) - P_{(n/4)-2}}.$$

$$\phi_{(n/4)+1} = \frac{\displaystyle\sum_{i=1}^{n/4} \gamma_{i,n/4} d_i}{P_{(n/4)-1}(\lambda - \beta_1) - P_{9n/4)-2}},$$

$$\phi_{3n/4} = \frac{\displaystyle\sum_{i=1}^{n/4} \alpha_{i,1} d_{(3n/4)+i}}{P_{(n/4)-1}(\lambda - \beta_n) - P_{(n/4)-2}},$$

$$(5.22)$$

and

$$\phi_{(3n/4)+1} = \frac{\displaystyle\sum_{i=1}^{n/4} \gamma_{i,n/4} d_{(n/2)+i}}{P_{(n/4)-1}(\lambda - \beta_{(n/2)+1}) - P_{(n/4)-2}}.$$

In general, at the end of the tth $(t = 1, 2, \ldots, (\log_2 n) - 1)$ level of the decoupling process we are left with 2^t decoupled subsystems, each of order $n/2^t$. Hence, given a system of dimension $n = 2^m$, we require $m - 1$ $(= (\log_2 n) - 1)$ levels of decoupling to reduce the system into sub-blocks of order 2.

Example

If $n = 16 = 2^4$, then after the third level of decoupling we have the resulting decoupled subsystems each reduced to order 2 as shown diagrammatically in figure 17.3.

We shall now assume that the tth level of decoupling has been obtained and hence the process of obtaining the $(t+1)$th level of decoupling can be generalised as follows. After the tth level, the first and the last of the 2^t decoupled subsystems (each of order $n/2^t$) are of the form

$$A_1^{(t)} = \begin{bmatrix} \lambda - \beta_1 & 1 & & & & \\ 1 & \lambda & 1 & & 0 & \\ & \ddots & \ddots & \ddots & & \\ & & & \lambda & 1 & \\ & 0 & & \ddots & \ddots & \\ & & & 1 & \lambda - \beta_{n/2^t} \end{bmatrix}_{((n/2^t) \times (n/2^t))} \tag{5.23}$$

$$A_{2^t}^{(t)} = \begin{bmatrix} \lambda - \beta_{(2^t-1)(n/2^t)+1} & 1 & & & \\ 1 & \lambda & 1 & & 0 \\ & \ddots & \ddots & \ddots & \\ 0 & & 1 & \lambda & 1 \\ & & & 1 & \lambda - \beta_n \end{bmatrix}_{((n/2^t) \times (n/2^t))} \tag{5.24}$$

Figure 17.3. Recursive decoupled structure of a tridiagonal system.

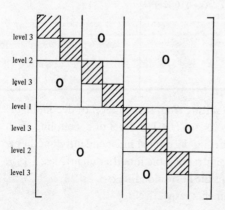

and the corresponding right-hand-side decoupled subvectors of the form,

$$\bar{\mathbf{d}}_1^{(t)} = \begin{bmatrix} d_1 - \phi_1 \\ d_2 \\ \vdots \\ d_{(n/2^t)-1} \\ d_{(n/2^t)} - \phi_{(n/2^t)} \end{bmatrix}_{((n/2^t)\times 1)}$$

and

$$\bar{\mathbf{d}}_{2^t}^{(t)} = \begin{bmatrix} d_{(2^t-1)(n/2^t)+1} - \phi_{(2^t-1)(n/2^t)+1} \\ d_{(2^t-1)(n/2^t)+2} \\ \vdots \\ d_{n-1} \\ d_n - \phi_n \end{bmatrix}_{((n/2)\times 1)} \tag{5.25}$$

The kth $(k = 2, 3, \ldots, 2^t - 1)$ other intermediate decoupled subsystems are of the form

$$A_k^{(t)} = \begin{bmatrix} \lambda - \beta_{(k-1)(n/2^t)+1} & 1 & & & \\ 1 & \lambda & 1 & & 0 \\ & \ddots & \ddots & \ddots & \\ 0 & & 1 & \ddots & 1 \\ & & & 1 & \lambda - \beta_{k(n/2^t)} \end{bmatrix}_{((n/2^t)\times(n/2^t))} \tag{5.26a}$$

with the corresponding right-hand-side decoupled subvectors of the form

$$\bar{\mathbf{d}}_k^{(t)} = \begin{bmatrix} d_{(k-1)(n/2^t)+1} - \phi_{(k-1)(n/2^t)+1} \\ d_{(k-1)(n/2^t)+2} \\ \vdots \\ d_{k(n/2^t)-1} \\ d_{k(n/2^t)} - \phi_{k(n/2^t)} \end{bmatrix} . \tag{5.26b}$$

Since all the 2^t subsystems resulting from the tth level of decoupling are independent of each other, then for the $(t+1)$th level of decoupling, each of the 2^t subsystems can now be further decoupled independently and in parallel by a process which amounts to subtracting the modifier quantities, β_{s+2sj}, $\beta_{s+2sj+1}$ and ϕ_{s+2sj}, $\phi_{s+2sj+1}$ from the corresponding $(s+2sj)$th, $(s+2sj+1)$th diagonal and right-hand-side elements respectively.

Generally, for

$$t = 0, 1, \ldots, (\log_2 n - 1) \quad s = n/2^{t+1}$$

and

$$j = 0, 1, \ldots, t$$

(5.27a)

these modifier elements, expressed in terms of the sequence P_i, are given by

$$\beta_{s+2sj} = \frac{[\lambda - \beta_{(j+1)(2s)}]P_{s-2} - P_{s-3}}{[\lambda - \beta_{(j+1)(2s)}]P_{s-1} - P_{s-2}}$$

$$\beta_{s+2sj+1} = \frac{[\lambda - \beta_{(j+1)(2s)}]P_{s-1} - P_{s-3}}{[\lambda - \beta_{2js+1}]P_{s-1} - P_{s-2}}$$

$$\phi_{s+2sj} = \frac{\sum_{i=1}^{s} \alpha_{i,1}^{(t,j+1)} d_{s+2sj+i}}{[\lambda - \beta_{(j+1)2s}]P_{s-1} - P_{s-2}}$$

(5.27b)

and

$$\phi_{s+2sj+1} = \frac{\sum_{i=1}^{s} \gamma_{i,s}^{(t,j+1)} d_{2sj+i}}{[\lambda - \beta_{2sj+1}]P_{s-1} - P_{s-2}}.$$

The quantities $\alpha_{i,1}^{(t,j+1)}$ and $\gamma_{i,s}^{(t,j+1)}$ are the $(1, i)$th and (s, i)th cofactors of the upper and lower halves of the $(j+1)$th submatrix which is obtained at the end of the tth level of decoupling, where

$$\gamma_{i,s}^{(t,j+1)} = \gamma_{i,s}^{(t,1)} + (\beta_1 - \beta_{2sj+1})P_{i-2}$$
$$\alpha_{i,1}^{(t,j+1)} = \alpha_{i,1}^{(t,1)} + [\beta_{2s} - \beta_{2s(j+1)}]P_{s-i+1}$$

(5,28)

with

$$\gamma_{1,s}^{(t,1)} = -1,$$
$$\gamma_{2,s}^{(t,1)} = \lambda - \beta_1,$$
$$\gamma_{i,s}^{(t,1)} = (-1)^i [(\gamma - \beta_1)P_{i-2} - P_{i-3}], \quad i = 3, \ldots, s,$$

(5.29)

and

$$\alpha_{s,1}^{(t,1)} = 1,$$
$$\alpha_{s-1,1}^{(t,1)} = \lambda - \beta_{2s},$$
$$\alpha_{i,1}^{(t,1)} = (-1)^{i+1} [(\lambda - \beta_s)P_{s-i+1} - P_{s-i+2}],$$
$$\quad\quad i = s-2, s-3, \ldots, 1$$

(5.30)

with the terms P_i defined as in (5.14).

The order of calculation of the modifier elements, $\beta_i, \phi_i, \quad (i = 1, 2, \ldots, n)$ can be represented in a tree-structured form as shown in figure 17.4, where all the 'tree-branching' operations at any given level can be done simultaneously and in parallel.

Finally, at the end of the $(m-1)$th level of decoupling all the 2^{m-1} sub-systems are each (2×2) matrix systems which, for $j = 2^t$, $t = 1, 2, \ldots, m-1$, are given by

$$\begin{pmatrix} \lambda - \beta_{j-1} & 1 \\ 1 & \lambda - \beta_j \end{pmatrix} \begin{pmatrix} u_{j-1} \\ u_j \end{pmatrix} = \begin{pmatrix} d_{j-1} - \phi_{j-1} \\ d_j - \phi_j \end{pmatrix} \tag{5.31}$$

The solution of the system (5.31) is given, on omitting interchanges, by

$$\left. \begin{aligned} u_j &= [(d_j - \phi_j) - (d_{j-1} - \phi_{j-1})(d_j - \phi_j)] / \\ &\quad [1 - (\lambda - \beta_j)(\lambda - \beta_{j-1})] \\ u_{j-1} &= [(d_j - \phi_j) - u_j]/(\lambda - \beta_j). \end{aligned} \right\} \tag{5.32}$$

On the introduction of interchanges the solution of (5.31) becomes

$$\left. \begin{aligned} u_j &= [(\lambda - \beta_{j-1})d_j - (d_{j-1} - \phi_{j-1})]/[(\lambda - \beta_{j-1})(\lambda - \beta_j) - 1] \\ \text{and} \quad u_{j-1} &= (d_j - \phi_j) - (\lambda - \beta_j)u_j. \end{aligned} \right\} \tag{5.33}$$

The RD algorithm given above is obviously not competitive for solving a tridiagonal system if the scheme is programmed for running on a serial machine. However, since at any level t of the decoupling process, all the intermediate sub-systems can be decoupled further in parallel, the RD algorithm has merit in its highly parallel structure. For parallel computers it is an attractive method to use since it requires only the order of $\log_2 n$ parallel operations, for a system of order n, on a parallel computer having $\log_2 n$ processors.

Figure 17.4. The order of calculation of the modifier elements in the recursive decoupling process.

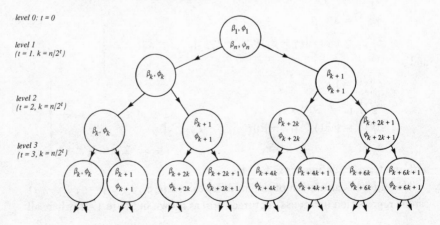

References

R. H. Barlow, D. J. Evans, I. A. Newman, A. J. Slade and M. C. Woodward, *Survey of the INTERDATA Dual Processor Computer,* Dept. Comp. Stud. Rep. 40, Loughborough University. 1977

D. J. Evans, 'On the numerical solution of sparse systems of finite element equations' in *The Mathematics of Finite Elements and Applications III, Mafelap 1978 conference proceedings.* J. R. Whiteman (edit.), Academic Press (1979), pp. 448–58

D. J. Evans and A. Hadjidimos, 'A modification of the quadrant interlocking factorisation parallel method'. *Int. Jour. Comp. Math.* 8, (1980), 149–66

D. J. Evans, A. Hadjidimos and D. Noutsos, 'The parallel solution of banded linear equations by the new quadrant interlocking factorisation (Q.I.F.) method', *Int. Jour. Comp. Math.* 9, (1981), 151–62

D. J. Evans and M. Hatzopoulos, 'A parallel linear system solver', *Int. Jour. Comp. Math.* 7, (1979), 227–38

D. J. Evans and S. O. Okolie, 'A recursive decoupling algorithm for solving banded linear systems', *Int. Jour. Comp. Math.* 10, (1981), in press

S. O. Okolie, The numerical solution of sparse matrix equations by fast methods and associated computational techniques, Ph.D. Thesis, Loughborough University of Technology (unpublished) 1978

R. S. Varga, *Matrix Iterative Analysis*, Prentice Hall, 1963

18 Parallel linear system solvers for tridiagonal systems

M. HATZOPOULOS

1 Introduction

Solving a system of linear equations is one of the most frequently encountered problems in numerical computation. In this chapter we propose two algorithms for the direct solution of tridiagonal systems of n $(n = 2^m)$ equations on parallel computers.

To facilitate the analysis and presentation of these algorithms we adopt the following model of a parallel computer (Sameh [4]):

- (*a*) an unlimited number of processors are available
- (*b*) each processor can evaluate any of the arithmetic operations in one time step and
- (*c*) no memory or data alignment time penalties are incurred.

In section 2 we discuss the *WDZ* decomposition algorithm. Recently Evans and Hatzopoulos [2] have proposed a new factorization for a matrix A in which the factors are two diametrically opposite quadrant interlocking segments of the matrix (this method was called the 'quadrant interlocking method'). The *WDZ* algorithm is a modification of the quadrant interlocking method in the case when the matrix A is tridiagonal. We show that an $n \times n$ linear system can be solved in $T_p = 4\log(n) + 5$ time steps using no more than $p = 2n$ processors.

In section 3 we introduce a Givens type reduction process. This new technique can be visualized as a Givens forward elimination process carried out from the top of the matrix and a Givens backward elimination process performed on the bottom of the matrix simultaneously. We show that this method requires $T_p = 12 + 8\log(n)$ time steps and no more than $p = 3(n-2)$ processors for the solution of a tridiagonal system. The second algorithm is more stable than the *WDZ* decomposition.

2 The *WDZ* algorithm

2.1 The WDZ factorization

Let A be an $n \times n$ $(n = 2^m)$ nonsingular tridiagonal matrix. $A = [c_i, a_i, b_i]$ where a_i $(i = 1, 2, \ldots, n)$ are the diagonal elements of the matrix and b_j, c_{j+1} $(j = 1, 2, \ldots, n-1)$ are the off diagonal elements.

Let
$$A = WDZ \tag{2.1}$$
where D $(d_i, i = 1, 2, \ldots, n)$ is a diagonal matrix,
$$W = \begin{cases} w_i & \text{for } j = i - 1, \quad i = 2, 3, \ldots, n/2 \\ 1 & \text{for } i = j \\ w_i & \text{for } j = i + 1, \quad i = (n/2) + 1, \ldots, n - 1 \\ 0 & \text{otherwise} \end{cases} \tag{2.2}$$
and
$$Z = \begin{cases} z_i & \text{for } j = i + 1, \quad i = 1, 2, \ldots, n/2 \\ 1 & \text{for } i = j \\ z_i & \text{for } j = i - 1, \quad i = (n/2) + 1, \ldots, n \\ 0 & \text{otherwise} \end{cases} \tag{2.3}$$

From (2.1), (2.2) and (2.3) we get the following recurrence relations:
$$\begin{aligned} d_1 &= a_1 \\ d_i + c_i b_{i-1}/d_{i-1} &= a_i \quad i = 2, 3, \ldots, n/2 \end{aligned} \tag{2.4}$$
and
$$\begin{aligned} d_n &= a_n \\ d_i + c_{i+1} b_i/d_{i+2} &= a_i \quad i = n - 1, \ldots, (n/2) + 1 \end{aligned} \tag{2.5}$$

Let
$$\left. \begin{aligned} \tau_i &= \prod_{k=1}^{i} d_k \\ \tau_i' &= \prod_{k=1}^{i} d_{n-k+1} \end{aligned} \right\} \quad i = 1, 2, \ldots, n/2 \tag{2.6}$$

Using (2.6) we get the following linear recurrence relations from (2.4) and (2.5):
$$\begin{aligned} \tau_0 &= 1, \tau_1 = a_1 \\ \tau_i - a_i \tau_{i-1} + b_{i-1} c_i \tau_{i-2} &= 0 \quad i = 2, 3, \ldots, (n/2) \end{aligned} \tag{2.7}$$
and
$$\begin{aligned} \tau_0' &= 1, \tau_1' = a_n \\ \tau_i' - a_{n-i+1} \tau_{i-1}' + c_{i+1} b_i \tau_{i-2} &= 0 \quad i = 2, 3, \ldots, (n/2) \end{aligned} \tag{2.8}$$

Sameh and Kuck [5] proved that each of the above linear recurrence relations can be solved in $2 \log(n) - 2$ time steps using no more than $n - 4$ processors.

Thus τ_i and τ_i' $(i = 1, 2, \ldots, n/2)$ can be computed concurrently in
$T_p = 2 \log(n) - 2$ time steps using no more than $2n - 8$ processors.

From (2.6) we get:

$$d_i = \tau_i / \tau_{i-1}$$
$$d_{n-i+1} = \tau_i' / \tau_{i-1}' \quad i = 2, 3, \ldots, n/2 \tag{2.9}$$

Thus d_i $(i = 2, 3, \ldots, n-1)$ can be computed in one time step using $n-1$
processors.

From (2.1) we obtain:

$$w_j = c_j / d_{j-1} \quad j = 2, 3, \ldots, n/2 \tag{2.10}$$
$$z_j = b_j / d_j \quad j = 1, 2, \ldots, n/2 \tag{2.11}$$
$$w_j = b_j / d_{j+1} \quad j = n-1, n-2, \ldots, (n/2)+1 \tag{2.12}$$
$$z_j = c_j / d_j \quad j = n, n-1, \ldots, (n/2)+1 \tag{2.13}$$

The factorization is completed with the computation of w_i $(i = 2, 3, \ldots, n-1)$
and z_i $(i = 1, 2, \ldots, n)$ from (2.10) - (2.13). The last computation can be done
in one time step using $2n$ processors.

Thus the *WDZ* factorization of a tridiagonal matrix can be done in
$T_p = 2 \log n$ time steps using no more than $p = 2n$ processors.

2.2   Solution of the linear system

Consider the linear system:

$$Ax = g \tag{2.14}$$

where A is an $n \times n$ nonsingular tridiagonal matrix.

Since from section 2.1:

$$A = WDZ \tag{2.15}$$

the problem (2.14) reduces to solving:

$$WDZx = g$$

Using the auxiliary vectors y and ϕ we set:

$$DZx = y \tag{2.16}$$
$$Zx = \phi \tag{2.17}$$

Then the problem becomes one of solving the three related systems:

$$Wy = g \tag{2.18}$$
$$D\phi = y \tag{2.19}$$
$$Zx = \phi \tag{2.20}$$

From the definition of matrix W the solution of (2.18) is given by the linear recurrence relations:

$$y_1 = g_1 \qquad\qquad\qquad\qquad y_n = g_n$$
$$y_2 = g_2 - y_1 w_1 \qquad\qquad\qquad y_{n-1} = g_{n-1} - w_{n-1} y_n$$
$$\vdots \qquad\qquad\qquad\qquad\qquad \vdots$$
$$y_i = g_i - y_{i-1} w_i \qquad\qquad\qquad y_i = g_i - w_i y_{i+1}$$
$$\vdots \qquad\qquad\qquad\qquad\qquad \vdots$$
$$y_{n/2} = g_{n/2} - y_{(n/2)-1} w_{n/2} \qquad y_{(n/2)+1} = g_{(n/2)+1} - w_{(n/2)+1} y_{(n/2)+2}$$

Sameh and Kuck [5] proved that each of the above relations can be computed in $2 \log(n/2)$ time steps using no more than $n-4$ processors. Thus the solution of (2.18) can be done in $T_p = 2 \log(n) - 2$ time steps using no more than $p = 2n - 8$ processors.

Matrix D is diagonal so vector ϕ can be evaluated from (2.19) in one time step using n processors.

For the solution of (2.20), $x_{n/2}$ and $x_{(n/2)+1}$ are the first computed by solving the 2×2 linear system in the middle of matrix Z. This requires at most 8 time steps. Then x is computed from the linear recurrence relations:

$$x_{n/2} = x_{n/2} \qquad\qquad\qquad\qquad x_{(n/2)+1} = x_{(n/2)+1}$$
$$x_{(n/2)-1} = \phi_{(n/2)-1} - z_{(n/2)-1} x_{n/2} \qquad x_{(n/2)+2} = \phi_{(n/2)+2} - z_{(n/2)+2} x_{(n/2)+1}$$
$$\vdots \qquad\qquad\qquad\qquad\qquad\qquad \vdots$$
$$x_1 = \phi_1 - z_1 x_2 \qquad\qquad\qquad\qquad x_n = \phi_n - z_n x_{n-1}$$

Using the same reasoning as above vector x can be computed in $T_p = 2 \log(n) + 6$ time steps using no more than $p = 2n - 8$ processors.

Thus the solution of the linear system (2.14) can be completed in $T_p = 4 \log(n) + 5$ time steps using no more than $p = 2n$ processors.

3 Orthogonal factorization

Let the linear system:

$$Ax = g \tag{3.1}$$

where matrix A is tridiagonal as defined in section 2.

The proposed method for solving (3.1) can be described as follows: we annihilate the elements $(j+1, j)$ and $(n-j, n-j+1)$ $j = 1, 2, \ldots, (n/2) - 1$ of A by applying the orthogonal transformation

$$Q = Q'_{(n/2)-1} Q_{(n/2)-1} \cdots Q'_2 Q_2 Q'_1 Q_1$$

where each Q_j is a Givens transformation such that the element in position $(j+1, j)$ is eliminated and each Q'_j is a Givens transformation such that the element in position $(n-j, n-j+1)$ is eliminated.

$$Q_j = \begin{bmatrix} 1 & & & & & & & \\ & \ddots & & & & & & \\ & & 1 & & & & & \\ & & & q_j & s_j & & & \\ & & & -s_j & q_j & & & \\ & & & & & 1 & & \\ & & & & & & \ddots & \\ & & & & & & & 1 \end{bmatrix} \quad \to j\text{th row}$$

$$Q'_j = \begin{bmatrix} 1 & & & & & & & \\ & \ddots & & & & & & \\ & & 1 & & & & & \\ & & & q_j & -s_j & & & \\ & & & s_j & q_j & & & \\ & & & & & 1 & & \\ & & & & & & \ddots & \\ & & & & & & & 1 \end{bmatrix}$$

Thus after the $(r-1)$th step $Q'_{r-1}Q_{r-1}\ldots Q'_1 Q_1 A$ is given by:

$$\begin{bmatrix} z_1 & \alpha_1 & \beta_1 & & & & & & & \\ & z_2 & \alpha_2 & \beta_2 & & & & & & \\ & & \ddots & \ddots & \ddots & & & & & \\ & & & z_{r-1} & \alpha_{r-1} & \beta_{r-1} & & & & \\ & & & p_r & q_{r-1} & b_r & & & & \\ & & & c_{r+1} & a_{r+1} & b_{r+1} & & & & \\ & & & & & \ddots & \ddots & \ddots & & \\ & & & & & & c_{n-r} & a_{n-r} & b_{n-r} & \\ & & & & & & q'_{r-1} & c_{n-r+1} & p_{n-r+1} & \\ & & & & & & & \beta_{n-r+2} & \alpha_{n-r+2} & z_{n-r+2} \\ & & & & & & & & \ddots & \ddots & \ddots \\ & & & & & & & & & \beta_{n-1} & \alpha_{n-1} & z_{n-1} \\ & & & & & & & & & & \beta_n & \alpha_n & z_n \end{bmatrix}$$

By induction it follows that

$$q_r = p_r/z_r \qquad q'_r = p_{n-r+1}/z_{n-r+1}$$
$$s_r = c_{r+1}/z_r \qquad s'_r = b_{n-r}/z_{n-r+1} \qquad r = 1, 2, \ldots, (n/2)-1 \tag{3.4}$$
$$p_r = q_{r-1}a_r - s_{r-1}q_{r-2}b_{r-1} \tag{3.5}$$

$$p_{n-r+1} = q_r' a_{n-r+1} - s_{r-1}' q_{r-1}' c_{n-r} \tag{3.6}$$

$$\alpha_r = a_{r+1} s_r + q_{r-1} q_r b_r \tag{3.7}$$

$$\alpha_{n-r+1} = a_{r+1} s_r' + q_r' q_{r-1}' c_r \tag{3.8}$$

$$\beta_r = s_r b_{r+1} \tag{3.9}$$

$$\beta_{n-r+1} = s_r' c_{n-r} \tag{3.10}$$

where $q_0 = q_0' = 1$ and $s_0 = s_0' = 0$.

From (3.4), (3.5) and (3.6) we obtain the recurrence relations:

$$z_r q_r = q_{r-1} a_r - q_{r-2} c_r b_{r-1}/z_{r-1} \tag{3.11}$$

$$z_{n-r+1} q_r' = q_{r-1}' a_r - q_{r-2}' c_{n-r} b_{n-r+1}/z_{n-r} \tag{3.12}$$

Let:

$$\tau_k = q_k \prod_{i=1}^{k} z_i \qquad k = 1, 2, \ldots, (n/2) - 1 \tag{3.13}$$

$$\tau_k' = q_k' \prod_{i=1}^{k} z_{n-i+1} \qquad k = 1, 2, \ldots, (n/2) - 1 \tag{3.14}$$

Then from (3.11), (3.12), (3.13) and (3.14) we obtain the following linear recurrence relations:

$$\tau_0 = 1$$
$$\tau_1 = a_1$$
$$\tau_2 = a_2 \tau_1 - b_1 c_2 \tau_0$$
$$\vdots$$
$$\tau_i = a_i \tau_{i-1} - c_i \tau_{i-2}$$
$$\vdots$$
$$\tau_{(n/2)-1} = a_{(n/2)-1} \tau_{(n/2)-2} - b_{(n/2)-1} c_{n/2} \tau_{(n/2)-3}$$

and

$$\tau_0' = 1$$
$$\tau_1' = a_n$$
$$\vdots$$
$$\tau_i' = a_{n-i+1} \tau_{i-1}' - c_{n-i} b_{n-i+1} \tau_{i-2}'$$
$$\vdots$$
$$\tau_{(n/2)-1}' = a_{(n/2)+2} \tau_{(n/2)-2}' - c_{(n/2)+1} b_{(n/2)+2} \tau_{(n/2)-3}'$$

Sameh and Kuck [5] proved that each of these linear recurrence relations can be computed in $2 \log(n/2)$ time steps using $n - 4$ processors. Thus τ_i and τ_i' can be computed in $T_{p_1} = 2\log(n) - 2$ steps using no more than $p_1 = 2n - 8$ processors.

Let

$$\rho_k^2 = \prod_{i=1}^{k} z_i^2 \quad \text{and} \quad \rho_i'^2 = \prod_{i=1}^{k} z_{n-i+1}^2$$

Since $q_k^2 + s_k^2 = 1$ and $q_k'^2 + s_k'^2 = 1$ we obtain the following linear recurrence relations:

$$\rho_0^2 = \tau_0^2 = 1 \qquad\qquad \rho_0'^2 = \tau_0'^2 = 1$$

$$\rho_k^2 = c_{k+1}\rho_{k-1}^2 + \tau_k^2 \qquad \rho_k'^2 = b_{n-k}\rho_{k-1}'^2 + \tau_k'^2$$

Thus $\rho_k'^2$ and $\rho_k'^2$ can be evaluated from the linear recurrence relations:

$$\rho_0^2 = 1 \qquad\qquad\qquad\qquad\qquad \rho_0'^2 = 1$$

$$\rho_1^2 = c_2^2\rho_0^2 + \tau_1^2 \qquad\qquad\qquad \rho_1'^2 = b_{n-1}^2\rho_0'^2 + \tau_1'^2$$

$$\vdots \qquad\qquad\qquad\qquad\qquad\qquad \vdots$$

$$\vdots \qquad\qquad\qquad\qquad\qquad\qquad$$

$$\rho_{(n/2)-1}^2 = c_{n/2}^2\rho_{(n/2)-2}^2 + \tau_{(n/2)-1}^2 \qquad \rho_{(n/2)-1}'^2 = b_{(n/2)+1}^2\rho_{(n/2)-2}'^2 + \tau'^2_{(n/2)-1}$$

Therefore, $\rho_1^2, \rho_2^2, \ldots, \rho_{(n/2)-1}^2$ and $\rho_1'^2, \rho_2'^2, \ldots, \rho_{(n/2)-1}'^2$ can be computed in $T_{p_2} = 1 + 2\log(n/2) = 2\log(n) - 1$ steps using $p_2 = 2(n-2)$ processors.

We also have:

$$\left.\begin{array}{ll} q_j^2 = \tau_j^2/\rho_j^2 & q_j'^2 = \tau_j'^2/\rho_j'^2 \\ z_j^2 = \rho_j^2/\rho_{j-1}^2 & z_{n-j+1}^2 = \rho_j'^2/\rho_{j-1}'^2 \\ s_j^2 = c_{j+1}^2/z_j^2 & s_j'^2 = b_{n-j}^2/z_{n-j+1}^2 \end{array}\right\} \quad j = 1, 2, \ldots, (n/2) - 1$$

So q_i, z_i, q_i', s_i' and s_i can be computed in two time steps and one square root using $3(n-2)$ processors. Using (3.7)-(3.10), $\alpha_j \ (j = 1, 2, \ldots, n)$, $\beta_j \ (j = 1, 2, \ldots, (n/2) - 1, (n/2) + 1, \ldots, n)$, and $z_{(n/2)+1} = p_{(n/2)+1}$ are obtained in three time steps using $2n$ processors.

Thus the total number of time steps required for obtaining

$$Z = Q'_{(n/2)-1}Q_{(n/2)-1} \cdots Q_1'Q_1A$$

is $T_p = 3 + 4\log n$ using no more than $3(n-2)$ processors.

Matrix Z has the form:

$$\begin{bmatrix} z_1 & & \alpha_1 & \beta_1 & & & \\ & z_2 & & \alpha_2 & \beta_2 & & \\ & & \ddots & & \ddots & & \\ & & & \ddots & & \ddots & \\ & & z_{n/2} & & \alpha_{n/2} & & \\ & & \alpha_{(n/2)+1} & & z_{(n/2)+1} & & \\ & & \beta_{(n/2)+2} & & \alpha_{(n/2)+2} & z_{(n/2)+2} & \\ & & & \ddots & & \ddots & \\ & & & \beta_n & & \alpha_n & z_n \end{bmatrix}$$

Let $Q = Q'_{(n/2)-1} Q_{(n/2)-1} \ldots Q'_1 Q_1$. It can be shown (Gill [3]) that Q has the form:

$$
\begin{bmatrix}
u_1 v_1 & w_1 \\
u_2 v_1 & u_2 v_2 & w_2 \\
\vdots & & \ddots \\
u_{n/2} v_1 & \cdots & u_{n/2} v_{n/2} \\
& & & u_{(n/2)+1} v_{(n/2)+1} & \cdots & u_{(n/2)+1} v_n \\
& & & w_{(n/2)+2} & u_{(n/2)+2} v_{(n/2)+2} \\
& & & & \ddots & \vdots \\
& & & & & w_n & u_n v_n
\end{bmatrix}
$$

where:

$$
\left.
\begin{array}{ll}
u_j = q_j \eta_{j-1} & u_{n-j+1} = q'_j \eta'_{j-1} \\
v_j = q_{j-1}/\eta_{j-1} & v_{n-j+1} = q'_{j-1}/\eta'_{j-1}
\end{array}
\right\} \quad j = 1, 2, \ldots, n/2
$$

$q_0 = q'_0 = q_{n/2} = q'_{n/2}$ and:

$$\eta_0 = 1 \qquad\qquad \eta'_0 = 1$$

$$\eta_j = (-1)^j \prod_{k=1}^{j} s_k \qquad \eta'_j = (-1)^j \prod_{k=1}^{j} s'_k \qquad j = 1, 2, \ldots, (n/2)-1$$

The vectors η and η' can be obtained in $\log(n/2)$ steps using no more than $(n-2)/2$ processors and then u_i, v_i can be obtained in one time step using $2n-6$ processors.

From (3.1) we have to solve the linear system:

$$Zx = Qg \tag{3.15}$$

Let:

$$g' = Qg$$

then

$$g' = (ULV + WP)$$

where

$$U = \text{diag}(u_i), \quad V = \text{diag}(v_i),$$

$$W = \text{diag}(w_1, w_2, \ldots, w_{(n/2)-1}, 0, 0, w_{(n/2)+2}, w_n),$$

$$P = |0, \epsilon_1, \epsilon_2, \ldots, \epsilon_{(n/2)-1}, \epsilon_{(n/2)+2}, \ldots, \epsilon_n|$$

and L is defined as:

$$
l_{i,j} =
\begin{cases}
1 & i \geqslant j, \quad i = 1, 2, \ldots, n/2 \\
1 & i < j, \quad i = (n/2)+1, \ldots, n \\
0 & \text{elsewhere}
\end{cases}
$$

Thus g' can be computed in $3 + \log n$ steps using no more than n processors.

The linear system $Zx = g'$ is like (2.20) and can be solved in $T_{p_3} = 2\log(n) + 6$ time steps using no more than $p_3 = 2n - 8$ processors.

Therefore the tridiagonal system (3.1) can be solved using this algorithm in $T_p = 12 + 8\log n$ time steps using no more than $p = 3(n-2)$ processors.

References

[1] D. J. Evans and M. Hatzopoulos: 'The solution of certain banded systems of linear equations using the folding algorithm', *Computer J.* **19**, 184–6 (1976)

[2] D. J. Evans and M. Hatzopoulos: 'A parallel linear system solver', *Int. J. Computer Math.*, **7**, 227–38, (1979)

[3] P. E. Gill et al.: 'Methods for modifying matrix factorizations', *Math. Comput.*, **28**, 505–35 (1974)

[4] A. H. Sameh: 'Numerical parallel algorithms – A survey' in *High Speed computer and algorithm organization*, D. Kuck, D. Lawrie and A. Sameh, Acad. Press (1977)

[5] A. H. Sameh and D. J. Kuck: 'A parallel QR algorithm for symmetric tridiagonal matrices' *IEEE Trans. on Comp.* **C-26** 147–53 (1977)

[6] A. H. Sameh and D. J. Kuck: 'On stable linear system solvers' *J. ACM*, **25**, 81–91 (1978)

[7] H. S. Stone: 'An efficient parallel algorithm for the solution of a tridiagonal linear system of equations' *J. ACM*, **20**, 27–38 (1973)

INDEX